Praise for

THE PRICE *of* ILLUSION

"A parade of stars and styles. . . . Think of anyone who had cachet in the world of movies, literature or fashion starting in 1970 or so, and chances are good that they pop up in this book. . . . Buck has been a fabulous Zelig in the world of memoirs."

—*The New York Times*

"If you loved *The Devil Wears Prada*, you'll adore Joan Juliet Buck's *The Price of Illusion*, her deliciously written memoir of her golden life in Hollywood and at Paris *Vogue*, which became more and more about running as fast as she could until, in one of the best blow-by-blows of being fired you'll ever read, she finally began to figure out what matters."

—*Elle*

"Buck offers sharp, candid observations. . . . [T]he author is an appealing protagonist who never takes herself too seriously, nor those around her. . . . By the end of this exquisitely written memoir, Buck emerges triumphant."

—*USA Today*

"Like a tin of caviar or a strand of heirloom pearls, Joan Juliet Buck's memoir . . . satisfies the appetite for luxury [and] poignant introspection."

—*O, The Oprah Magazine*

"Lapidary . . . elegant . . . psychedelic . . . brilliant."

—*Publishers Weekly* (starred review)

"Joan Juliet Buck had lived a more brilliant, stranger, more glamorous, sadder, happier, richer, poorer life by the age of twenty-five than most of us do in three times that long and then she went right on living it and then she wrote it down. I'm a sucker for good, smart writing and this book is nothing but good, smart writing and great stories. Terrific stuff."

—Salman Rushdie, bestselling author of *Two Years Eight Months and Twenty-Eight Nights*

"One knows from the opening paragraph that one is in the presence of a truly original, and compelling, voice; and that the scope of the book to come will be both ravishingly large and, at the same time, rife with perfect, telling details."

—Michael Cunningham, bestselling author of *A Wild Swan* and *The Hours*

"Relentlessly candid and often absorbing account of a complex life spent in and out of the fashion spotlight."

—*Kirkus Reviews*

"A dishy yet self-aware account of [Buck's] long career that stretches all the way back to her star-studded childhood, too. The book's index . . . also doubles as a veritable who's who, from Avedon to Bacall to Huston to Saint Laurent."

—*W*

"Fans of high fashion and celebrity culture will enjoy this insider account."

—*Library Journal*

"Brimming over with voluptuous details, this is delicious writing—intelligent, provocative, ironic, and so compulsively readable I simply could not put it down."

—Patricia Bosworth, *New York Times* bestselling author of *Diane Arbus*

"[A] lush, charming memoir."

—*People*

"Ms. Buck has been everywhere, done everything—the most delicious . . . pages I've read in months. . . . [S]ure to ravish the best-seller lists."

—Liz Smith, NewYorkSocialDiary.com

"*The Price of Illusion* is a spilled treasure of a book. Unexpected sudden diamonds cascade across every page. The language is dazzling, but even more overwhelming is the Proustian level of observation. Fashion is laid bare of its artifice. Celebrated giants like Peter O'Toole and John Huston show up in human form. And Miss Buck's career and family flameouts dovetail into a single, heartbreaking tragedy. If you are drawn to glamour and pain, get ready to be mesmerized."

—John Patrick Shanley, winner of the Pulitzer Prize and author of *Doubt*

"In this often hilarious yet ultimately profound memoir, Joan Juliet Buck explores life's most gorgeous surfaces and agonizing depths. She writes with brio even when she narrates times of difficulty, and achieves a remarkable mixture of modesty, exuberance, and pained confession. Buck's brilliant wit, her entirely original sense of style, her capacity to negotiate tragedy, and her gift for self-analysis make this book not only riveting but also unforgettable."

—Andrew Solomon, bestselling author of *Far from the Tree*

"A startling and memorable memoir, filled with stars and scars, matters of business and affairs of the heart, successes and failures, all seen with Buck's seemingly photographic memory in infinite detail. A must for any lover of fashion and culture, and for all those who cherish a life lived to its fullest. *The Price of Illusion* is a great record of a truly remarkable life."

—Robert Goolrick, #1 *New York Times* bestselling author of *A Reliable Wife*

"Anybody could make a riveting life story of the events and Rolodex of people in this book, but reading it, I was most reminded of James Salter's autobiography *Burning the Days,* the inquiry by a great writer into his own remarkable life. [*The Price of Illusion*] is a moving, Bildungsroman-like account of the inner workings of fame and culture, houses built of cards, aspiration and loss, and a brave search for love. At once an unputdownable romp through sixty years of a world that no one will ever know better than Joan Juliet Buck, and a great literary accomplishment."

—Peter Nichols, bestselling author of *The Rocks*

OTHER BOOKS BY JOAN JULIET BUCK

Daughter of the Swan

The Only Place to Be

THE PRICE *of* ILLUSION

A Memoir

Joan Juliet Buck

WASHINGTON SQUARE PRESS

ATRIA

New York London Toronto Sydney New Delhi

An Imprint of Simon & Schuster, Inc.
1230 Avenue of the Americas
New York, NY 10020

Some names have been changed.

First Washington Square Press/Atria Paperback edition November 2017

WASHINGTON SQUARE PRESS/**ATRIA** PAPERBACK and colophon are trademarks of Simon & Schuster, Inc.

For information about special discounts for bulk purchases, please contact Simon & Schuster Special Sales at 1-866-506-1949 or business@simonandschuster.com.

The Simon & Schuster Speakers Bureau can bring authors to your live event. For more information, or to book an event, contact the Simon & Schuster Speakers Bureau at 1-866-248-3049 or visit our website at www.simonspeakers.com.

Interior design by Dana Sloan

Manufactured in the United States of America

10 9 8 7 6 5 4 3 2

The Library of Congress has cataloged the hardcover edition as follows:

Names: Buck, Joan Juliet, author.
Title: The price of illusion : a memoir / Joan Juliet Buck.
Other titles: Memoir
Description: First Atria Books hardcover edition. | New York : Atria Books, 2017. | "Atria non fiction original hardcover"—Verso title page.
Identifiers: LCCN 2016032072| ISBN 9781476762944 (hardback) | ISBN 9781476762951 (trade paperback)
Subjects: LCSH: Buck, Joan Juliet. | Women authors, American—21st century—Biography. | Fashion editors—Biography. | Women periodical editors—Biography. | Vogue. | Americans—Europe—Biography. |Celebrities—Biography. | Rich people—Biography. | BISAC: BIOGRAPHY & AUTOBIOGRAPHY / Personal Memoirs. | BIOGRAPHY & AUTOBIOGRAPHY / Editors, Journalists, Publishers. | BIOGRAPHY & AUTOBIOGRAPHY / Rich & Famous.
Classification: LCC PS3552.U333 Z46 2017 | DDC 813/.54 [B]—dc23
LC record available at https://lccn.loc.gov/2016032072

ISBN 978-1-4767-6294-4
ISBN 978-1-4767-6295-1 (pbk)
ISBN 978-1-4767-6296-8 (ebook)

For Joyce and Jules

PROLOGUE

Shrieks of lightning hit the parking lot at Linate Airport, but the flight from Paris had been smooth. I sheltered flat against the plate-glass wall waiting for the car and wondered where this storm had come from. I told myself it wasn't personal.

The lightning and the rain created traffic jams through Milan that made me late to meet Jonathan Newhouse at Caffè Cova, where I'd been summoned for a talk before the first fashion show. When I arrived, I apologized for the weather.

He sat on a corner banquette beneath a display of porcelain, wearing new glasses that made him look like Rodchenko.

The teacups shone in the glass case behind him; the brass fittings on the mahogany glowed around us in the muted clatter of high heels and waiters' shoes and teaspoons in china cups and distant bursts of steam nozzles foaming the cappuccinos in the front room. I could feel the tight armholes of my narrow tweed coat, the tug of the pink velvet seat against the crepe of my dress, my platform shoes tight over my toes. My laptop was at my feet in a Gucci case designed for me, next to my Prada bag. New look for the new season, every label in place.

"I want you to take a sabbatical, starting today," he said.

"On the first day of the European collections? I can't do that."

"Two months, starting now," he said.

Sudden stillness. Ice water in my veins. Guillotine. It's over. What did I do?

Two thoughts collided and set off a high-pitched whine in my head. No more *Vogue*. Back to writing. I've been on show watching a show for almost seven years, and it's always the same show. I have nothing to write about.

That's the end of the salary, the end of the job, why did I think salary before I thought job? How can I take care of Jules now? He's eaten everything I earn. His apartment, Aneeta who looks after him, Johanna who relieves Aneeta, the studio for Johanna above his apartment, the taxi service, his doctors and his dentists, his meals, his clothes, his everything.

"This is between us, don't talk to anyone," said Jonathan. He pushed a piece of paper at me with one word on it, the name of the place where he wanted me to go. "It's just two months, then you'll come back. I'm doing this because I'm your friend."

"Either you're my friend, or you're setting me up," I said. "I choose to believe you are my friend."

And having demonstrated to myself how gallant I could be, I decided to proceed to the next item on the typed list my assistant had pasted in my datebook. "I'm late for Prada," I said, and before he could stop me I rose and carried my two bags through the steam and crowd of the front room, out into the rain to the waiting car, and on to the Prada show, where I stared at the shoes on the feet of the editors across the runway, and then at the shoes on the feet of the models on the runway, until it hit me that my opinion of the shoes, the dresses, the models, the hair, had entirely ceased to matter. When the show was over, the front-row editors headed backstage to congratulate Miuccia Prada, and I walked very slowly the other way, out onto the street.

Back in my hotel room, I stared at the bed, uncertain what to do next. Beautifully wrapped packages from fashion houses were piled everywhere. I knew the same gifts were in the rooms of every editor in chief in every hotel in Milan: small leather goods with logos, the new handbag, the new fragrance, the new scarf and tassel. Garment bags lay across the sofa, heavy with the fall clothes I'd ordered from Missoni and Jil Sander six months earlier. Clothes for a life I no longer had. He'd said I would come back, but I knew that wasn't true.

I looked at the name of the place where I was supposed to go. It didn't occur to me to call my lawyer.

No talking to the press, no talking to anyone, no noise, no movement. He wanted me off the planet, invisible. I couldn't stay at home; my apartment in Paris was in the center of a knot of fashion streets patrolled by *attachés de presse* and luxury-goods executives. I'd always thought that in a crisis I'd retreat to a friend's ranch in central California, but we were in one of our periodic frosts and hadn't spoken for over a year. There were others in America who'd welcome me; I could hide in their big houses by the sea as fall became winter, but there would be weekends and weekend guests and gossip, and I had been ordered to vanish.

My entire life had been one easy exile after another, but I'd lived in too many places to belong anywhere. I had nowhere to go. I looked again at the slip of paper Jonathan had given me. Cottonwood.

CHAPTER ONE

For expatriates there is no firm ground. We'd arrived in Paris from Los Angeles in May; by Christmas we were in a grand hotel in Hamburg across from a white lake full of seagulls. A Santa Claus stocking with a big red "1951" on it went up on the mantelpiece. I was four, too young to know that we were at the end of 1952. My two dolls and my hand puppet disappeared the day the stocking went up. I wondered if they'd been stolen by the waiter who brought up my dinner, or had decided they didn't like me and made a break for it. On Christmas day I tore open silver-glitter packages with red ribbons to find, nestled in layers of tissue paper, my own two dolls and my hand puppet. My friends—loyal in the end, and a promise that whatever was lost would always return.

Train stations, waiting rooms and foggy buffets, and then sunshine.

The villa above Cannes was called Coup de Vent, gust of wind. It had a Lucite grand piano in the salon, and flypapers in the kitchen. The view was splendid, the Mediterranean framed by fat fig trees on the dining terrace. When the aircraft carrier *Coral Sea* pulled into Cannes, my parents and grandparents were invited on board and photographed, composed and glowing, surrounded by dials and valves, the captain in his white uniform clearly smitten with my mother, whose Balenciaga stole set off the extreme décolleté of her gala dress.

My father was Jules. My mother was Joyce. Her parents were Morey and Esta, known to me as Poppy and Nana. They were short, but grand. Morey was dapper in his silver ties, pearl tiepin, ostrich gloves, and, until he realized that they dated him, white spats buttoned over his shoes. When he wasn't at the casino or the racetrack, he did deals; some worked out, some didn't. He moved stuff around. When the stuff was frozen, like postwar German marks, he moved himself around.

Esta wore dresses as stiff as boxes, diamond pins along the upper slope of her bosom. She bandaged the tops of her feet every day to hide a condition that split and mottled the skin. The star sapphire on her finger was turning milky from soapy water, but the sapphires on her bracelets stayed a fine dark blue. She hid her jewels at night, mostly from Morey's gambling emergencies, and mainly in shoe bags. Esta rolled her eyes when my father spoke, and when he drove us along the Grande Corniche in the convertible, she whimpered from the backseat and shrieked at each glimpse of the precipice below.

Morey sent Jules on trips around the Continent to chase schemes that never fully worked out, though they produced enough money to pay the rents on the big houses, to pay the staff, to buy the cars. So did the gambling at Longchamp, the Paris racetrack, and at the Cannes casinos. They went to the casino every night to play with money, first to the winter casino by Golfe-Juan, later to the summer casino down by the port. My mother played Poppy's numbers at roulette, "*Finale* 8"—8, 18, 28. They went to galas that ended with fireworks. Some nights I was woken by lightning, some nights by fireworks.

My mother wore espadrilles and striped dresses cut too low. I preferred her in the striped sailor sweater that covered her completely. She had a flash of white in her short black hair and didn't wear panties.

The smitten captain moved all 45,000 metric tons of the *Coral Sea* to a spot where it appeared to be perfectly centered between the two fig trees on our patio. He came up to toast his feat, but no sooner had he arrived than the aircraft carrier began to drift toward the Carlton Beach. He was hastily fetched by naval police on motorbikes, relieved of his command, and sent back to Maryland, but without disgrace. He ended his life as an admiral.

My mother played "This Little Piggy" with me, and paid special attention to the little double toe halfway up the outside of my right foot. "You were born with an eleventh toe, and they took part of it off when you were born," she explained. "When you're older, we'll have the rest of it fixed."

She helped me chase lizards and track snails, went at flies with a swatter, and bought a net to catch butterflies.

In the fall, when the swimming pool was drained, she took me by the hand down the steps into the empty rectangle. The beige sludge under our feet was so thick at the deep end that we had to turn back; we stopped halfway to watch a large green grasshopper on the silty wall.

"I think it's stuck," said my mother, and brought the butterfly net down to keep it still. Then my nanny called me to bath time, and I left my mother holding the net over the grasshopper in the empty pool.

The next day, it was as if another woman had taken her place, as beautiful as she was, with the same white flash in her short black hair, the same eyes, the same cigarettes, the same striped sailor sweater, the same laugh—but never the same smile again. This woman didn't love me at all, she only pretended. My real mother was the prisoner of an empty pool full of silt. Much later, I'd have a vision of her in the empty pool, standing bare-legged, pelted by rain and wind, shivering in her cotton shirt, alone and hungry and unseen, holding the butterfly net over the grasshopper.

After Cannes, we moved to a pink marble palace atop ceremonial steps behind a fountain in a miniature French garden in a suburb full of prodigiously ugly fretted houses forty minutes from Paris. Le Palais Rose was a 1900 copy of the Grand Trianon at Versailles, but smaller. Two eccentric, fevered aesthetes had owned it, first Robert, comte de Montesquiou, then Luisa, Marchesa Casati. One day they'd be the subjects of illustrated coffee-table books, but in the early 1950s they were remembered only as capricious and unpleasant dead aristocrats.

The Palais Rose was a fantasy about France paid for by my mother's parents, who occupied the state apartment on the main floor. The comte de Montesquiou and the marchesa Casati, both decadent loners, had never shared the Palais Rose with anyone but servants. My parents and I slept in dark rooms on the lower floor. Our windows gave onto the back garden, where an open drain sometimes released a smell that made Joyce stop and exclaim, "Clams!"

She was determined that everything in France would be wonderful, even bad smells. She loved clams, oysters, and mussels. I did not.

The furnace didn't always work, the dirt-encrusted stove had to be replaced, but the Palais Rose was huge and splendid and gorgeous and rare. There were mysterious back stairs from the master bathroom to the chauffeur's quarters, where there was a chauffeur, a chauffeur's wife who cooked, and their skinny daughter, whom the chauffeur regularly beat with a short-handled leather martinet.

There was a golden harp missing a few strings in the Grand Salon, and inlaid into the floor was a white marble sun that lit up from underneath when you clicked a brass switch in the wall. There was a winter garden where plants went to die, and many smaller salons filled with dainty chairs and unwelcoming little sofas covered with the kind of petit point embroidery that you could find in the perfume shops along the Rue de Rivoli, where my grandmother shopped for the things—evening bags, satin gloves, useless fans, and precious compacts—that her friends brought home from Paris, to reassure herself, once or twice a week, that she actually lived there. Not Massachusetts, not Chicago, not New York. "Paree," she'd say, "ooh la la."

The European toilet paper came in hard brown sheets; my father used his Army reserve status to buy Kleenex at the store on the American army base, and each tissue had many uses. Joyce and Esta removed their makeup with Pond's Cold Cream and Kleenex; each sheet was then folded over to conceal the smears of lipstick and mascara, and set in neat piles by the toilet. The smell of Pond's was lodged in my nose as the smell of *caca*; when Nana jabbed raw beef at me in her Pond's fingers with little cries of "Steak tartare!" I gagged.

At the Palais Rose, when he was home, my father became my mother. He made me breakfast before he took me to school, and at night he ran his thumbs along my eyebrows to soothe me to sleep. His healing hands were spontaneously drawn to knots in backs, cricks in necks; he'd hold his hand flat against an aching back and the hurt would go away. His touch reassured me; I didn't know he wasn't working.

Before school, we'd share a *petit pain au chocolat* from the pâtisserie at Saint-Germain-en-Laye, where, at Christmastime, and only at Christmastime, they had pyramids of chocolate-covered cherries in brandy called *griottes*, and he'd let me eat one of those as well, even before school. They were our favorites.

"Say it in French," he'd command. I'd say it in French. *Griottes.*

We'd moved to France before I'd mastered English, so French was my first full language. The adults talked baby talk to me, so my English was vague. I was a confident translator before I turned five, adept at asking for more ice, fresher bread, the meat cooked *à point, saignant,* or *bien cuit.* I had to scold the waiter if the wine was corked, "*Bouchonné.*" Nana always wanted saccharine, which didn't translate.

French was more than a party trick. The language set Frenchness inside me as a hunger for rules and form that went unmet in the margins of my family's fantasy of a beautiful French life. I envied the strict households that my school friends described, I wanted rules to rebel against, but the most Joyce and Nana ever said was speak softly in public, never grab, and never, ever, wear an ankle bracelet.

The clues I gleaned from my family were about how things looked and where they came from and how old they were and whether they went together: chairs, drapes—no, curtains—tables, luggage, radios, cameras, watches, cars, cigars; and dresses, shoes, stoles, shawls, bags, minaudières, compacts, pins, bracelets, rings. In a restaurant, Nana would say, "How pretty that ashtray is," two seconds before she popped it into her handbag, where it landed against her enamel compact with a giveaway thunk. She liked collecting pieces of Paris.

In the center of the kitchen stood a single thick pole, shiny black, that belonged in a garage, and so irritated Nana that she decided to beautify it. She'd read about marbleizing, so she bought a small can of yellow house paint with two thin brushes, and settled groaning onto a stool to get to work. She gave me one of the brushes, showed me how to drag a yellow squiggle a few centimeters before you made a zig, and changed direction. I sat on the floor to do my part. I couldn't believe I was allowed to paint a piece of where we lived, and carefully twisted my paintbrush to make my lines dawdle and jump like hers. It wasn't easy painting on a curve, the paint smelled like gasoline, but it was joy to mark the place where I lived.

"We've made it ours now," she said proudly as she heaved herself up from the stool.

Surface became everything, surface became my substance. I clung to inanimate objects and gave my allegiance to things. I made secret pacts with my toys; the tiger that served as my teddy bear would always protect me, and I would always protect him. I knew that dolls had souls.

The chauffeur's timid daughter was no fun to play with, so I wandered alone across parquet floors as wide as beaches, staring up at the gold edges of the high ceilings, rubbing my hands inside the grooves of columns, making friends with the bronze ladies who leaned on either side of the table clock. I pitied the poor caryatids who strained to hold tables on their heads and was comforted by the devotion of flattened urns that had agreed to line up as balustrades.

For my sixth birthday, I received splendid gifts: a doll's steamer trunk fitted with drawers and hangers bought at Louis Vuitton, and a toy French bulldog. His papier-mâché body was flocked like velvet, a straw ruff erupted around his neck, his paws were set on wooden wheels, and when you pulled his chain, his mouth opened with a rough scrape that could pass for a bark.

There was a party with my school friends in foil crowns throwing paper balls across the Empire table in the Directoire dining room where garlands danced in a frieze up by the ceiling. The pink streamers clung to the chandelier and remained tangled in its branches until the day we left.

"You're spoiled," declared Nana.

The new nanny warned me that if I looked at myself too long in the mirror, I'd see the devil. I kept my eyes firmly on the drain in the sink as I brushed my teeth. She also told me that I, or someone in my family, had killed Jesus Christ. I apologized, though this was the first I'd heard of it.

When I was seven, I found the rule book I'd been waiting for: *Les Malheurs de Sophie* by the comtesse de Ségur, née Rostopchine, in which undisciplined and willful little Sophie gets into scrape after scrape; she lets her wax doll melt in the sun, tears the legs off bees, steals candied fruit, puts her feet in quicklime, cuts off her eyebrows. Sophie is punished every time. Her guardian angel urges her up a stony path, but Sophie wants to play with pretty boys and girls in beautiful clothes in a garden full of glorious fruits and flowers, and breaks away from the guardian angel to join them. But the beautiful children attack her, the flowers smell foul, the fruits are poison. At last, a chastened Sophie returns to her guardian angel and sets off up the stony path.

Les Malheurs de Sophie was written in 1858 to keep little French girls in line. In it, Sophie's mother explains that the angel is God warning her that if she continues doing bad, fun things, she will find sorrow instead of joy. The deceitful garden, her mother says, is Hell, but Paradise lies up the steep stony path, which will, however, become easier as she practices being obedient, kind, and good. With that book, the guardian angel moved into my life.

It manifested itself almost at once. At a school friend's birthday party in a glittering apartment where the ice bucket was a bright red metal apple, the shining chrome table was set with pink glasses, pink paper napkins, and real place cards, and on each plate sat a gift for each guest. I'd never seen party favors before.

I walked around the table examining the different toys on each plate, a tiny bear, a tiny house, a little car, a little purse. I stopped at the little purse. It was electric blue metal, and it closed with a snap. The place card had a girl's name on it, not mine.

I went hunting for my name, and there it was, "JOHN," in very big letters. The French could never get my name right. And in the middle of my plate sat my own party favor, an ugly little yellow toy truck.

I wanted the little blue purse so badly that it made me dizzy. I palmed my ugly yellow truck, moseyed back to the purse, set down the truck, grabbed the purse, and ran to deposit it on my plate, but before I could get there, I fell and cut my chin. Instant punishment for my greed; that guardian angel had wasted no time.

My chin bled onto my new dress, adult arms picked me up with shouts for Mercurochrome and peppermint essence. I fought my way back to the plate where I'd put my yellow truck to return the stolen purse, to undo the punishment I'd just endured. But my chin kept bleeding.

That was the last time I ever stole anything.

~

My father couldn't learn French; he was too busy trying to raise money for films to take lessons. He had a louche business partner named Louis who would later turn out to have been a Soviet spy.

I overheard things I didn't understand. "What does 'financial difficulties' mean?" I asked my aunt Charlotte and uncle Don when they came to visit us. Circumstances became so precarious that my mother had to go to work as an actress to pay the bills, just as she had as a child. She played Charles Boyer's devoted secretary in a Four Star Playhouse television movie, and hated every minute.

My father's real ally was my mother's brother, Don Getz, who distributed movies, lived in Roslyn, Long Island, and traveled constantly between the States and Europe. He arrived with jars of herring that embarrassed my father, who viewed smoked fish as the mark of lower-class Jews.

Don was overweight and easygoing, with curly black hair and a profile like Marlon Brando's, and he was the only member of the family who never pretended that things were better than they were. I thought of him as a kind of outlaw who'd always speak the truth. He shuffled, sighed "Uh boy," found everything funny, and paid no attention to how he looked. My father winced at Don's khaki pants, his windbreakers, his canary yellow drip-dry shirts, but in 1954 he arranged to distribute Jacques Tati's *Jour de Fête* and *M. Hulot's Holiday* in America with him. The films had no dialogue and were very funny; they became instant hits. Tati's daffy Monsieur Hulot had all the charm that Americans impute to the French.

Jacques Tati was always at the grown-up parties at the Palais Rose, sometimes acting the part of a drunk waiter or pretending to be the chauffeur, generally causing wonderful havoc. When Federico Fellini came to dinner and played the golden harp in the Grand Salon as if its strings weren't broken, Jacques Tati posed with him and made a silly face.

It was Uncle Don who found the former O.S.S. colonel who suggested the TV series that made Jules a producer again after five lost years. The move to London was swift, a drive to the ferry in the May dawn, a bumpy Channel crossing, and a new life. The TV series, titled simply *O.S.S.*, played out on ITV in heroic half hours. Every Friday night at 7:30, a beautiful girl spy would be parachuted into occupied France to fight the Nazis; every week something would go wrong and the star of *O.S.S.*, Ron Randell, would have to parachute into France to rescue her.

Shortly after we arrived in London, Poppy had a heart attack and was taken to Saint George's Hospital, where he died a few months later. My mother was undone by her father's death and started analysis. Nana went back to New York, bought an apartment on West 54th Street and a Nash car that she drove very fast across America to visit her sister Annabelle in Los Angeles. A fat lady of fifty-eight in a black dress speeding along Route 66, diamonds and sapphires sparkling, singing along to the radio, a widow at last.

We lived in a small but elaborate mews house on Groom Place that belonged to a captain in the British Navy, whose taste in art ran to large mythological nudes; the living room had dark green wallpaper printed with snowflakes curiously shaped like Stars of David, and many books about the ballet. I found the close dimensions of the mews house comforting, and was excited that my bedroom window faced a solid wall; there could be anything, anything at all, on the other side of those bricks.

If I tried to tell my mother the things I thought I saw at night, or ask her if she believed a guardian angel could punish you, she'd scold, "That's just your imagination running away with you."

I couldn't read or write English, so I went to the Lycée Français de Londres, an alarming swirl and crash of two thousand nameless pupils. I insisted my father hold up his thumb and mouth the word "Reassured" when he dropped me off in the mornings. One day he bought me a handful of candy bars. "Make friends," he said. It worked. "Candy friends," we called them.

He explained that everything was barter, that you needed your stock of wampum to get through. The covered wagon that his grandfather Morris Buck drove west had been full of things to sell or trade, pots and pans, awls, crowbars, guns, cloth, thread. "You always need supplies," my father explained, "when you're in new territory."

He saw our family as pioneers conquering the Old World in his pale blue Sunbeam. "We're a unit," he explained. "You, your mother, and me." I preferred to think it was just he and I. He woke me up and put me to sleep, and we both had homework. He couldn't help with mine; I tried to help with his. The first things I read in English were scripts. "Why does it always say the man is thirty-five?" I asked.

"Because the scripts are for Peter," he said, "and the star is always thirty-five."

When I met him, I heard Peter's last name as Autoul, hoped he was French, and pronounced it that way for far longer than was necessary. I was homesick for Paris.

My father's real project was to film his friend John Brophy's book *The Day They Robbed the Bank of England.* While trying to cast the Irish anarchist who tunnels under the bank to steal its gold, my parents had been enthralled by Peter O'Toole in *The Long and the Short and the Tall* at the Royal Court, and had gone backstage to meet him. It turned out that Peter and his girlfriend, Siân Phillips, lived around the corner from us in the National Coal Board mews, so they came back to Groom Place, stayed up all night drinking, and by morning they'd formed their own movie company, Keep Films, named after the impregnable towers of medieval castles. A keep was strong. A keep was enduring. A keep was never conquered.

Peter was twenty-eight; he'd only been on screen as a bagpiper in a Disney movie and as a Mountie in an Eskimo film that starred Anthony Quinn, but Jules knew that Peter could be the greatest star in the world. I thought he was weird-looking, and still wished he were French. He was the son of a racetrack bookie, and Irish. Peter didn't want to play the Irish anarchist bank robber Walsh but the upper-class guards captain Monty Fitch, and so he did. In the scene where Monty understands that foul play is afoot, Peter raised his eyes to the quivering flame of a gas lamp with the electric gaze that was to become his hallmark. His hair was still curly black, his nose still bent. *The Day They Robbed the Bank of England* would change everything.

Given its title, *The Day They Robbed the Bank of England* required gold to rob; the props department manufactured innumerable gold bars, each the size of a narrow brick. Groom Place soon overflowed with props. Gold bars as paperweights, gold bars under the bar, gold bars in the dining room, gold bars as doorstops. I had four in my room.

~

Just before Christmas in 1959, when I was eleven, Jules announced we were going to Ireland to stay with my godfather. "I didn't know I had a godfather," I said.

"Yes, you do, honey. It's John."

The way he said it, the name sounded like "God."

St. Clerans was on the far side of a long ride along unpaved Irish roads, gray stone behind a round fountain in the night. I got out of the car, dazed from the airplane, nauseous from the long ride, and then I saw Ricki Huston standing next to a pillar, lit by the portico lantern.

"She looks like Garbo," my mother whispered, treading carefully on the gravel in her heels. I didn't know who Garbo was.

Ricki had wide cheekbones and hollows above her eyes. Her dark hair was parted in the middle and hung straight to her shoulders, her shoes were flat and soft and shapeless. I couldn't tell if she was thin or fat under the bumps and burls of her Irish cardigan, and the set of her mouth didn't tell me if she was smiling or wary.

Ricki had none of the careful artifice that kept my mother in tight skirts and spiky perfume, in bright, expectant smiles. She wore no makeup. She looked like what I wanted to be, a grown-up with no concession to fashion or the beauty parlor, with the straight back of a ballerina. She looked so complete that she was almost closed off. It took her a while to smile and say hello.

We climbed the steps. A little girl was twined around Ricki's legs, shy as a toddler. "This is Anjelica," said Ricki. She looked very young to me, but before we'd gone through the tall doors, she had the *Little*

Lulu comics from America that I'd persuaded Joyce to buy me at Shannon Airport.

My father carried the box with their gift in it, a massive leather ice bucket from Liberty.

My mother's heels clicked across the entry hall. "How beautiful," she said, pointing at the black marble floor.

"It's Kilkenny marble. Do you see the fossils in it?" said Ricki.

My mother made out the outlines of white shells in the black stone, and exclaimed, "Clams!"

A tall man in a long white dress to his feet stood in the second hallway, bending down toward my father. They clasped.

"Jules, good to see you. Joyce, you look beautiful. Hello, Joan." Every word John said had extra syllables in it. His face was a long scoop of new moon, the bridge of his nose flattened from boxing, his eyes hung with pouches. He looked like an orangutan when he smiled.

John Huston was their beacon: part of my father's war, part of the beginning of his career, part of my parents' meeting. They were beaming and a little apprehensive; they hadn't been to St. Clerans before, or to Ireland. Next to John, my father looked small and young, and he laughed nervously.

I'd never seen my father with anyone he worshipped.

It had been years. They didn't know Ricki, who was John's fourth wife; Evelyn Keyes, his third, was still Joyce's best friend.

A Christmas tree hung with tinsel filled the well of the staircase. My father put our box at the base of the tree with the other presents, and we went into the study. Pre-Columbian statues squatted on bookshelves against the teal blue walls. "I recognize those from Tarzana," my mother said.

"Evelyn got the rest," said John. "But you're right, it's them."

"What's Tarzana?" I asked my mother.

"It's John's old ranch, where you were conceived," she said.

I went over to touch the statues. There was a dog with a smooth red surface, a squatting man. They knew where I came from, even if I didn't.

A boy about my age strode in, nervous and energetic, his features as symmetrical as Ricki's. Tony. He was focused only on his dog, Flash, or on his father.

Gladys, John's longtime secretary, poured cut-glass tumblers of whisky and ice. I perched on the green corduroy sofa next to my father and looked at a tall wooden snake that rose above the chair where Ricki sat, then at an African statue on the table behind her, a seated woman pulling on her breasts. I'd never seen anything like it outside a museum.

I heard names: Ava, Sam. So sad about Bogie. Betty's okay now, she's doing theater again, just opened on Broadway. It's called *Goodbye Charlie.* Sydney Chaplin's in it. "Is that so, honey?" John asked, drawing out the words. My mother smiled to herself.

They had more drinks and talked about L.A. The bastards were still at it. HUAC. Dalton still in Mexico. "Julie, son of a gun, the poor fuck," my father said, tears in his eyes. He was an emotional man.

"Who's she?" I asked my mother.

"Shhh," she said. "It's a he, John Garfield."

"That was talent," said John.

"Wait till you meet Peter," said my father. "That's talent. I've never seen anything like it."

"Is that so?" said John. He was leaning over the coffee table, drawing Gladys's profile. "I'd love to meet him."

"They're in Dublin for Christmas," said my mother. "Peter and Siân, his girlfriend."

"Why don't you have them come over for a few days?" John said.

My father went to make a phone call from the kitchen.

John Huston had brought his world to Ireland, and made it bigger. He'd been my father's superior in the Signal Corps in the war, captain to his lieutenant in Alaska, major to his captain in Italy. And now he was a lord, drawing at the coffee table in a long white nightshirt, welcoming his lieutenant back to their shared past.

St. Clerans, a Georgian mansion, was a cabinet of curiosities: John's imagination made real by Ricki's hard and careful work. On one side of the marble hall was a formal living room with a large Monet of water lilies and an ibis from ancient Egypt. On the other side was a dining room with Japanese brushstroke trees on the wallpaper, and

Japanese screens on either side of a dresser where the butler laid out kedgeree. In the second hall a smell of pine and oranges, a bar full of bottles; wafts of cinnamon from the kitchen carried a promise of dessert. The stairs rose past an ancient Greek horse's head that John said had cost more than the house, to guest rooms that summoned up Napoleon or Louis XVI, Bhutan or Indonesia. John's bedroom was a green cavern where an Indian goddess held up six arms, and the posts on his bed were sculpted palms that reached the ceiling.

My parents were put in the Grey Room, across the upstairs hall from John. After dinner, I was mortified when Ricki said I'd be staying in the Little House with her and the children.

I followed Ricki, Tony, and Anjelica in the dark down the curving drive, across a bridge, past rustling hedges, through stone gateposts, and onto the thick gravel of a stable yard. The Little House had been the steward's house in the eighteenth century, and it looked like a child's drawing of a house, with a window on each side of the door, and three along the upper floor. I didn't yet know it was the real center of St. Clerans.

Anjelica's room had wide gray-striped wallpaper and two metal four-posters, Anjelica's one striped pink, the guest one, once Tony's, striped blue. A third girl arrived, Marina, the daughter of a woman who bore the unlikely name of Cherokee. She was Anjelica's age, and set out her Barbie dolls on a mattress on the floor.

Tony and his dog had the room next to Ricki's.

The next day, after fruitlessly insisting to Anjelica that her name should not be spelled with a j, I retreated downstairs to the kitchen, where I found Ricki baking soda bread. The shoes she wore were odd gray T-straps. "Years on point, my feet are distorted," she said. She'd been a real dancer, one of Balanchine's ballerinas, before she married John.

"I was put on point in Paris when I was six," I said. "My teacher was Madame Kschessinska."

Mathilde Kschessinska had been a prima ballerina in the Imperial Ballet, mistress to the tsar and two grand dukes; the Russian Revolution stranded her in Paris, Lenin took over her St. Petersburg mansion, and she lost everything. For the next fifty years she'd made it her mission to put little French girls on point before their bones were strong enough to do anything but turn into knotty little clubs.

"Kschessinska, " said Ricki. "She could do thirty-two *fouettés*. Show me your feet."

I took off my slippers.

"They'll be like mine," she said, looking at the bunions, "but what's that on your right foot?"

"That's my eleventh toe," I said.

The closet in Ricki's bedroom opened to reveal a space lined in burlap above the drawers. She called it the shrine. Tacked to the burlap were necklaces and ribbons, postcards—Egyptian vases, a Hittite head—pictures, Victorian photographs. She liked things that were discolored, fragile, rare, and strange. A reliquary hung from a necklace of filigreed gold metal rods, her party necklace. Next to it was a chain set with tiny heads—men, women, monsters—that ended in a Maltese cross made up of four rams' heads, each piece sculpted in lava from Pompeii. The reliquary was oxidized, the gold on the lava necklace dull, the lavas were the colors of earth, brown and mud and yellow, with here and there a gray blue one, a white. It took my breath away. That necklace was everything I wanted the things around me to be. Subtle and mysterious, precious but not gaudy, full of a charge I couldn't name. I went to look at it even when Ricki wasn't there.

That Christmas I saw my parents back with their own kind, in their own history. I knew the tense close quarters with Poppy and Nana, the poised diplomatic cheer as they entertained famous people in Paris or, now, in London, the welcome they put on in the living room of the mews house for actors and directors, the siphon shooting soda into whiskies for the actors in *O.S.S.*, or aged colonels who were necessary to secure the right to shoot at Horse Guards Parade, and even more whisky for Peter Autoul, the actor with the sideways nose. I'd seen my father as the man in charge. I'd seen them with my godmother Joan, with Uncle Don, with their newscaster friends from CBS, but I'd never seen them with John. After seven years in Europe, they had come home.

At St. Clerans, my mother didn't need the smiles that buffered the hotel suites and rented houses in Paris, in Germany, in Austria, in Cannes, and in London, the exclamations of delight that defined each new event as a marvelous moment. She didn't have to pretend it was wonderful. It *was* wonderful. For the first two days, she barely exclaimed at all.

On Christmas Eve we sang carols. The house was full now, with more adult guests. Tony, Anjelica, Marina, and I stood on the stairs. "Good King Wenceslas looked out," we sang. That would be John. "We three Kings of Orient are," we sang, "Bearing gifts we travel afar. O Star of wonder, star of might, star of royal beauty bright."

I sang badly, but very loud. I could feel the progress of my camel under me, slowed by the weight of all my gifts.

On Christmas morning, stockings hung at the ends of our beds. I removed tangerines and Brazil nuts wrapped in tinfoil, then a tiny silver box that I pulled open to find a Mexican fire opal, smooth and cool, orange that shaded to shards of impossible blue and green. My birthstone.

I'd been seen and recognized. I'd accept the Little House if it meant I could always have Ricki.

We gathered around the tree that filled the stairwell of the Big House. John's long wool nightshirt was red that day, for Christmas. John's secretary, Gladys Hill, and Betty O'Kelly, who looked after the estate and the horses, wore bright wool jackets. We children had new Aran Islands sweaters, and woven Aran sashes wound around our waists. Butler, cook, and maids massed around the backstairs door and darted forward as John called out their names and handed them their gifts. When that was done, the other presents were exchanged.

"Jules, Joyce, this is for you," John said, holding out a large flat parcel.

My father came forward, in his new long-sleeved polo shirt, grateful in advance. My mother followed, scarf knotted carefully about her neck, a little tremble in the hand that held her cigarette. They sat on the stairs like children, and carefully pulled the paper open to reveal a drawing by Jacob Epstein, a nude. John had given them art.

"She's called Betty Joel, she was a potter, " said John. "They may have been lovers. Some time around 1931."

The pencil nude reclined, her eyes huge, her breasts perfect, her pubis barely sketched.

"That's really, really beautiful, John," said Jules, humbled by the gift. Joyce had tears in her eyes and left for the powder room behind the stairs to compose herself.

She'd spent more than they could afford on manufactured goods of excellent quality, but their gift was not art.

Ricki unwrapped the leather-clad ice bucket from Liberty, with the crest of the lion and the unicorn, and turned it toward John, as if faintly puzzled. "For the bar, honey," John said.

Anjelica sat on a bench, examining the yellow diamond—a canary diamond it was called—her gift from John. I had an intimation that she'd always get diamonds.

"Girls," said John, " Marina, Joan, come here," and handed each of us a tin can with a picture of an oyster on its label. Ricki sent us to the kitchen, where the butler opened the tins and prized open the oysters over the sink; inside each one, lying in oyster mucus, was a real, slightly smelly pearl.

I watched John draw compulsively at the coffee table, more interested in his pencil than in what anyone said. I concluded that you put the better part of you into what you made, so that all the things that went through your head could come to life. I looked at him in his long red robe, at Ricki in her bumpy Aran sweater. You could dress up and play a part, become a bigger version of you, welcoming guests with noble condescension, ruling over your creation in a nightgown, as if you were still in bed dreaming. But you could also reject costume and artifice to be only yourself. Ricki's simplicity gave her a different advantage, power, a resonance, a distance from the game that made her, subtly, a judge. But Ricki also had a golden reliquary to wear for best, and wasn't that costume? I wanted to be bigger than life and make magic, I wanted to bake bread, I wanted to give people the best gifts they'd ever had, I wanted to be the one who saw the truth. I wanted to be the king in long red robes, I wanted to be the queen with jewels so precious they didn't have to shine.

I saw the world divided into action and audience, my mother firmly in the audience, appreciating everything, my father, even here, busy backstage, making his phone calls, making things happen. I wanted to be onstage, with the light shining on me.

Peter and Siân arrived the next day. He shambled in, black hair sticking up in curls, glasses askew, car coat dirty, green socks flashing above worn-out shoes. She was six months pregnant. They'd driven from Dublin, and were as bewildered by St. Clerans as we had been when we were new, three days ago.

My father led his discovery, his future star, to John, who waited at the foot of the stairs.

"John, this is Peter O'Toole," he said standing between them, a zoo-keeper between unicorns.

John and Peter were the same height, both thin, fonder of drink than food, elegant from being so thin, though one was in a white wool dress to his feet, and the other had slept in his clothes for days.

John inclined slightly toward Peter. He had to. This was his castle, and Peter was young.

Joyce and Ricki watched from the doorway. "John's seeing himself when he was young," said Cherokee, who'd known him a long time.

"They're all three Leos, you know," my mother said.

"Trouble," said Ricki. "'We Three Kings.' It never ends well."

~

Back in London, Joyce told everyone that St. Clerans was "a mirage in a bog." She meant the Big House. The Little House was not a mirage; it was the most real place I had ever been, and I gave it my heart.

CHAPTER TWO

I know their Hollywood through the stories they told me and stories in books. What had happened to them before Hollywood was less clear and, in the case of my father, told in such a way that I never knew what was really true and what was make-believe.

Jules was born in St. Louis in 1917, the oldest son of a sweet fragile woman called Ida and her husband, Norman Buck, a tense, precise tailor who played the piano to accompany silent films in the movie house. There's a photo of Jules at five or six, miserable and frowning in a sailor suit, posed on the back of a plaster pony. He didn't like sports, he didn't have a musical ear, but he had a perfect eye, and he hated the way he looked, which put him in a constant state of hurt and compensation. He was generous, kind, and ambitious.

His grandfather Moritz, or Morris, Buck had landed in Georgia from Hamburg around 1870; he was not the most honest of men. After some scrapes in the southern states, he set off in 1886 for the West with his Russian wife, Julia, and their small daughter, Bessie, in a covered wagon, where his son, my grandfather, was born in the middle of nowhere at Mexican Hat, in Utah Territory, and later registered in Denver, Colorado, in 1888, as Norman Buck. Morris and Julia turned east and settled in St. Louis, but Julia soon ran away to New York, found work in a sweatshop, and returned to St. Louis to kidnap her daughter, Bessie, from the schoolyard. She left Norman behind. When my grandfather told the story, he said she left him there because he was a half-breed, the son of a Comanche, a Cree, or a Sioux. No one believed him.

After a second son, Gene, was born, Norman and Ida moved to New York, where Norman's sister, the kidnapped child, Bessie, had married into a prominent real estate family called Bricken. Norman opened a cigar store in a building at 1441 Broadway that belonged to Bessie's new family. He had a carved wooden Indian outside, but so did every other cigar shop.

Norman and Ida didn't come to visit us in Europe. I saw them when my family brought *M. Hulot's Holiday* to New York, when I was five, and when *Lawrence of Arabia* opened in America, when I was thirteen. By the time I went to college in America, Ida had died and Norman had married Rose Doctorow, whose son Ed was the head of Dial Press, but wanted to quit to write novels.

Norman and Ida lived on Grand Concourse in the Bronx, where they played the piano together; Norman wrote poetry. At sixteen, Jules began to take pictures of celebrities for the newspapers, and in 1936, at eighteen, he moved to Hollywood, where he subsisted at first on peanut butter. Norman sent him encouraging letters full of injunctions to do good, do well, and to remember that he came from pioneer stock.

He was compact, willful, energetic. He knew how to compose a shot, could judge off-kilter to the millimeter, and he knew how the game worked: he photographed the studio heads at the premières, and sent them the most flattering ones. He was intuitive, guessed minor things such as someone's age or the name of their dog, and bigger things, such as outcomes. This made him, at times, very lucky.

Jules's photographs for the fan magazines caught stars at play, off guard, but glamorous. A magazine profile of him at the time describes him as a "fresh-faced youngster of nineteen." That's when he met Joan Crawford, an older woman of thirty-two. They had an affair so passionate that, decades later, he still told friends how the scratches on his back took weeks to heal. Then he fell in love with June Duprez, a British actress Alexander Korda brought over from London after she'd starred in *The Thief of Bagdad.* This was more serious; when he spoke of June Duprez, his voice grew soft and there was no mention of broken skin.

His life changed at the beginning of the war, when the Signal Corps assigned him to be John Huston's cameraman on a documentary about American Forces in Alaska. John was famous after *The Maltese Falcon*; Jules was twenty-four and had photographed movie stars. He fell under the older man's spell.

Report from the Aleutians is a dull film that documents the laying of a runway on Adak Island, and then a bombing mission. But one terrifying night, an immense Kodiak bear broke into the tent where the soldiers were sleeping, its teeth bared, its claws extended. I heard my father tell the story many times, but always as a long joke about the night a stinking giant bear raged through a tent and the panicked soldiers shit themselves with fear. He'd laugh as he told the story and say, "Oh Jesus," now and then, and laugh some more. He never admitted he'd felt any fear, but the Kodiak bear had gotten to him, and would return.

Joyce Ruth Getz was a beauty born in Chicago, where her father, Morey, did business, which meant everything and nothing, and most particularly nothing after the crash of 1929. Her mother, Esta—née Esther Miller in Lowell, Massachusetts, but she liked changing things to make them nicer—was a green-eyed beauty, a model until she grew plump at the birth of her son, Don, then fat with the birth of Joyce in 1925. But she still had beautiful green eyes.

Joyce went onstage at the age of nine to support the family through the Depression. When the family moved to New York, the name Joyce Getz was changed to Joyce Gates; prettier, and not at all Jewish. She modeled, she acted onstage, she was the little girl on the *Amos 'n Andy* radio show; she learned the professional children's smile at the Professional Children's School, where a boy named Sidney Lumet dipped the ends of her braids in the inkwell. She grew fond of Christian Science and practiced the Power of Positive Thinking.

At sixteen, she was cast by George S. Kaufman in *Franklin Street,* along with Betty Perske, a seventeen-year-old blonde. The play closed out of town, but the girls remained friends. Betty Perske was on the cover of *Harper's Bazaar,* sloe-eyed and a touch ominous. Joyce Gates was the Girl Next Door. She had a brighter smile, a cheery and expectant look that posed no threat. Black hair, black eyes, a short, high-bridged nose, apple cheeks. She was on the cover of *Official Detective Stories* and *Charm,* on war bond posters, ads for Coke, and ads for ration books. She posed heavy-lidded in satin for languorous glamour shots, lugged her model book from appointment to appointment, modeled coats in department stores in New York, sometimes in New Jersey. She lived with her parents and brother on the far east end of 52nd Street, a good address across from the elegant River House.

Joyce and Betty went out to Hollywood in 1943 with their mothers. Betty was discovered by Howard Hawks, renamed Lauren Bacall, and cast in *To Have and Have Not.* She met Humphrey Bogart and they fell in love. He was married.

Joyce, already renamed Gates, refused to go as far as becoming "Rusty Gates," and was discovered by no one. The only parts she got were minor, mostly Gypsy maidens in costume romances.

I don't know who her boyfriends were before my father and I'm not clear who introduced them. It was in Los Angeles, in 1943; she was eighteen, Jules was twenty-six, in uniform, just back from the Aleutians. He fell in love at once and asked if she was free the next night and the night after that and the night after that.

"He was the first decent man I met," she told me.

He went off on the Italian campaign; his friends took her out. She wrote him to apologize for having squirted a siphon's worth of soda on his friend the producer S. P. Eagle at El Morocco. A professional beauty, she knew how to fend off advances.

He kept all of her letters—long missives on pale blue airmail paper; his are nowhere to be found.

Jules and John filmed the war department documentary that would be *The Battle of San Pietro* in the Liri Valley; with them was Eric Ambler, the British spy novelist, who recorded their time there in great detail in his memoir, *Here Lies Eric Ambler.* James Agee wrote how John wandered into danger, and Jules saved him. They were strafed by German planes, fired on by snipers, and abandoned the Eyemo camera in the middle of a piazza as they ran for shelter in a cave. Jules filmed the women of San Pietro carrying bundles on their heads, their children in rags, dead American soldiers heaved into mattress covers; body bags did not yet exist. He lay on a machine gun as it shot into the night, and to set the stage for the action, he filmed soldiers walking into shot, walking out of shot. Decades later, the two of them would be unjustly accused of having faked the battle footage.

The Battle of San Pietro was briefly released and reviewed but instantly withdrawn by the War Department, and held back for twenty years. John's grandiose narration and my father's stark images made the destruction too real for the film to be effective propaganda.

Jules and Joyce married in January of 1945 in the big house of rich friends on Sunset Boulevard; he was still in uniform, as was his best man, Major John Huston. The maid of honor was Joan Harrison, a crisp British blonde in a top hat, who wrote scripts for Alfred Hitchcock and was the original model for every one of Hitchcock's crisp, mysterious blondes. Lauren Bacall looked at Joyce's ring with envy; Humphrey Bogart had not yet left his wife.

Morey and Esta wished Joyce had found a richer, handsomer, more famous man, but they were at the wedding. Ida and Norman had been gently discouraged from making the expensive journey across the country; they sent a family self-portrait posed in a mirror, dressed in fine clothes, flanked by a photo of Jules in uniform, and a photo of Joyce in model pose. Ida and Norman smile; Gene wears the sneer that younger siblings reserve for the brother who won't share his glamorous new life.

Jules and Joyce checked into the La Valencia Hotel in La Jolla for their honeymoon. Captain Buck was in uniform, Mrs. Buck wore her white going-away suit. They sat by the picture window over the ocean in the empty bar and ordered drinks. The maître d' said, "I think you'd be more comfortable somewhere else."

They didn't move.

"I have to ask you to leave," said the maître d'. "This hotel is restricted."

Jules looked too Jewish to be allowed in. His bride had changed her name from Getz to Gates and knew the score. They went to San Diego instead.

They bought their furniture that April, when William Randolph Hearst emptied his vast storerooms of imported antique treasures. The Renaissance sideboard, the chest, the Flemish pew chair, a praying figure, and a wooden priest they named Saint Darryl, after Darryl Zanuck, the head of 20th Century-Fox, Jules's boss. Joyce cut down a pair of Dutch consoles and glued them together to make a low round coffee table. They both had taste, and when it came to style, she had no fear.

At Fox, Jules became associate producer to Mark Hellinger. The script for the first feature he worked on, *The Killers*, was written by John Huston. It was directed by Robert Siodmak in uncompromising black and electric white, the first of what the French called films noirs, in appreciation of the density of contrasts as much as the story lines. It was Burt Lancaster's first movie, Ava Gardner's seventeenth. She was twenty-four and just divorced from the bandleader Artie Shaw.

One night after *The Killers* wrapped, my parents took Ava with them to see John, who was lonely at his ranch out in Tarzana. After drinks, dinner, more drinks, John tried his new skill as a hypnotist on my father. In her autobiography, Ava Gardner wrote that Jules was an easy subject. She saw him fall into a trance, then into a state close to hysteria as he relived events from the Aleutians that she judged to have been agonizing moments in battle. She didn't know that it was the Kodiak bear. "It was then I realized that John had a bit of a cruel streak in him," she wrote, "for he seemed to enjoy his mastery over Jules."

My parents went to bed to recover, and John chased Ava around the house until she woke them up to drive her back to Los Angeles.

Two days later, John married another actress, Evelyn Keyes.

Evelyn Keyes became my mother's best friend. She was a thin, sharp Southerner who knew a great deal about men, sex, and Freud, and had become famous as Scarlett O'Hara's whiny younger sister in

Gone with the Wind. Ten years later, after her lover Mike Todd left her to marry Elizabeth Taylor, she would take Artie Shaw as her fourth husband and become his eighth wife, Ava Gardner having been his fifth.

The atmosphere in Hollywood turned sour as the postwar Red Scare bred the House Un-American Activities Committee. Jules was not a Communist; he had the American mistrust of socialism, but he knew every American had the right to his beliefs. His friend Philip Dunne founded the Committee for the First Amendment to protest the first witch hunt. Jules joined at once.

In October of 1947, the Committee for the First Amendment—made up of movie stars, writers, and directors—marched on Washington to assert the right to freedom of speech on the first day of the congressional hearings against Hollywood's presumed Communists. Howard Hughes loaned them a plane.

Jules appears on the edge of newsreels from that day, an anxious sheepdog keeping the marchers in line, taking care of Gene Kelly and Lucille Ball, Danny Kaye, Katharine Hepburn, Myrna Loy, Burt Lancaster, Edward G. Robinson, Margaret Sullavan, Fredric March, William Wyler, Evelyn with John, Bogart with Bacall. Joyce had stayed at home.

That day, the first "friendly" witnesses gave up their right to freedom of speech and testified. Howard Hughes withdrew his plane. The Committee for the First Amendment returned by their own means to Hollywood, where they were called dupes and patsies. To avoid being blacklisted, Humphrey Bogart publicly recanted his belief in the First Amendment in a ghostwritten fan magazine article entitled "I'm No Communist."

Studio heads issued warnings to their directors, actors, and writers. Walt Disney, creator of Mickey Mouse and inventor of American happiness, denounced his own animators. The town was divided. Trust vanished, and with it went the gambling élan, the fire that carried a motion picture to completion.

I was born in the middle of the witch hunt, aptly with eleven toes, and named Joan. My godparents were Joan Harrison and John Huston. We had a housekeeper named Josephine and a black standard poodle named Jacques. This quintet of Js lived in a house on Beverly Crest Drive surrounded by eucalyptus trees. I have a memory of women sitting on the floor, their skirts fanned out around them like lily pads, charms tinkling on bracelets, ice cubes knocking against the inside walls of glasses. I remember grapefruits in Palm Springs, as big as beach balls.

My father produced more dark thrillers with Mark Hellinger at 20th Century-Fox: *The Naked City* and *Brute Force,* and then *We Were Strangers,* directed by John on location in Cuba, and starring John Garfield, whose Hollywood career ended when he refused to name names before HUAC; he died at thirty-nine, broken by the witch hunt.

There was little for my father and his friends to do but make increasingly silly motion pictures that would offend no one. My father produced *Love Nest,* a comedy for which he paid a new actress named Marilyn Monroe $250 a week, and then *Treasure of the Golden Condor,* an adventure starring Cornel Wilde.

Joyce opened a decorating shop with her friend Lorraine, where they sold lamps made of wicker-clad French soda siphons and Italian church candlesticks left over from the Hearst sale. Joyce despised overhead lighting, space-age shapes, and, most of all, Art Deco.

As the HUAC began its second round of hearings in the spring of 1951, Joyce took off to Europe with Esta and Joan Harrison. I stayed at home in my crib, watched over by Jules, Josephine, and Jacques the dog.

They went to Paris and Rome, to the Hotel du Cap, and to Venice, my grandmother looking for casinos, my mother looking for beauty and glamour. She saw antique furniture in situ, examined every detail of hotels and museums, learned about flattering light from the pink table lamps in restaurants. She bought evening dresses in model size at the couture sales, and when she returned with satin stoles from Pierre Balmain, two Schiaparelli dresses, and a fake Dior, Joyce told Jules, "There's a wonderful world out there. We don't have to stay in Los Angeles one minute longer."

In May of 1952, the house was rented, the furniture put in storage, and Jacques the dog given away. Morey and Esta picked us up at the airport in Paris in a long car driven by a uniformed chauffeur who sat in front of a glass partition, and our European adventure began.

CHAPTER THREE

After the first Christmas at St. Clerans, all wishes came true. A sudden effervescence sent the atoms into a faster spin, each atom found its golden mate, and glory rained down. The dark green living room of the little mews house became a blazing foundry of success.

The place burst with superlatives. When the Greatest Actor in the World Peter O'Toole wasn't collapsed around a glass of scotch in the armchair under the painting where nude Psyche shone a lamp on nude infant Eros, it was the Greatest Composer-Lyricist in the World Lionel Bart, twirling a houndstooth-checked cap, talking about his musical *Oliver!*

According to who was coming to drinks, photos of Peter O'Toole and photos of Lionel Bart alternated on the mantelpiece, the only constants being family pictures from Cannes, my godmother Joan Harrison and Eric Ambler on their wedding day, Uncle Don and his family, Nana and Poppy during the first weeks in Paris.

Jules sat at the desk under the nude Saint Sebastian shot full of arrows, always on the phone. Joyce operated the soda siphon at the bar by the door, stardust fell on the center of our lives and glittered out to the periphery.

My parents' friend Nicole Milinaire, a French television producer, told a casting director to give me a screen test and I was cast as a Scots waif in a movie about a dog called *Greyfriars Bobby.* My wish for the spotlight granted, I was fitted for costumes, given lines to learn and a tutor to help me master the contractions of an Edinburgh accent.

Jules was not happy about it. It wasn't his idea, he didn't want me to become an actress, and it was a Walt Disney movie. Walt Disney, the enemy of the First Amendment and the embodiment of every right-wing Southern California lunacy he'd fled.

He and Joyce had come all this way, and now he was going to let their only child—who, incidentally, spoke perfect French—work for Walt Disney?

"You're not falling behind in school over this!" he said.

"It's shooting in the summer holidays, Daddy!"

"Well, keep quiet about it," he warned, "you're not yet the legal age to act," and negotiated my contract without reading the script.

He had more important things to do than read a Walt Disney script for his daughter. While Peter was at Stratford-upon-Avon playing both Shylock in *The Merchant of Venice* and Petruchio in *The Taming of the Shrew,* Jules was making him into a star. His old friend and sometime associate Sam Spiegel, the S. P. Eagle on whom my mother had squirted soda water at El Morocco, was setting up *Lawrence of Arabia,* an epic that David Lean would direct. Jules knew that Peter had to be T. E. Lawrence. Sam Spiegel and David Lean had doubts that the roistering six-foot-two black-haired Irishman could play the composed five-foot-five blond homosexual colonel. Jules showed them Peter as Monty Fitch, ramrod straight in his guardsman's uniform, flinching at the flickering gaslight, and all competition was eliminated.

Peter drove down from Stratford in the middle of the night in a brand-new green Jaguar and stood, arms open in the middle of Groom Place, bellowing, "Where's my darling little Yid?" at our windows. Peter was cast, and Keep Films was on its way.

There was some housekeeping to attend to first.

My father took me to see Peter in hospital; he had a bandage over his face and swollen eyes. When the bandage came off, his nose was no longer bent. Now he could be not only the best but also the most beautiful actor in the world.

Siân's baby was placed on my bed in a basket. "This is Kate," Joyce said.

I could hear the living room hubbub rise up the narrow stairs, the siphon shooting soda at the bar by the door, the click of lighters, and imagined I could distinguish the different kinds of smoke, Peter's Gauloises, Joyce's Rothmans, Siân's Du Mauriers, Jules's Romeo y Julietas.

I thought constantly about St. Clerans. I wished I could see Ricki.

"Who's Garbo?" I asked Siân.

"Oh darling!" she said, and she and Peter took me to see *Anna Karenina* at the Chelsea Classic on King's Road. Garbo's eyes were set like Ricki's, her cheekbones as wide, but there was a pose and a nervous contempt to her that Ricki didn't have. I didn't like Anna Karenina's frizzy hair and knew that Ricki would never wear those ruffles. Or throw herself under a train because of a man.

Ricki came to London in July and took me to see *The Visit.* Friedrich Dürrenmatt's play wasn't for children, so it was flattering that she was taking me, and that it was just the two of us. Ricki wore a dress for the city, and red lipstick; she was polished but still singular, and her new shoes were another pair of low T-straps. By a chrome column in the theater foyer, she showed me the program and explained that Lynn Fontanne and Alfred Lunt were the great couple of the American theater, and that the director was a genius named Peter Brook.

The play began. A woman in a coat comes back to the town where she was seduced and betrayed years before; she's rich now, and she tells the townspeople that she will give them all her money if they kill the man who wronged her. I had trouble assimilating the fury of her revenge, but one scene struck me deeply. Two men in blocky suits, walking like robots, repeated in unison: "We sold our souls for a bottle of schnapps."

"Do people do that?" I asked Ricki afterward.

"People sell their souls for less," she said.

She took me back to St. Clerans to spend a fortnight with Anjelica and Tony before I began filming. It was only my second time there, but it felt like coming home. The Irish grass was yellow green under a blue sky. The car rumbled over the cattle grid and turned onto the gravel in front of the Little House. By the statue of Punch in the middle of the yard, Anjelica a little taller than at Christmas, was waiting for me.

She showed me her playhouse, an old dairy set near the Big House kitchen. I told her, “You know, I used to live in a palace, too, but mine was pink marble.”

I had the perfect alibi to dodge any enticement to get on one of the ponies: “The insurance won’t allow it. I start shooting in two weeks.”

I had fifty-two sentences to say and a dog to carry. While Betty O’Kelly put Anjelica through her paces on her pony out in the paddock, I followed Ricki wherever she went, on her rounds at the Big House to check on lightbulbs and plumbing, into the flower garden to fill flat baskets with sweet peas, and back into the flower room in the Big House to put them in vases.

Ricki had grown up in her father’s restaurant in New York, and was as confident in her kitchen as she was in her body, kneading dough, pouring olive oil from a bottle that she covered with tinfoil to shield it from the light, rubbing a roasting pan with the inside of the butter wrapper, cutting meat, separating stalks from leaves. She taught Anjelica and me how to make dinner with vegetables that we picked in the garden, how to roast lamb or a chicken—killed well out of sight on the far side of the stable yard, though Tony watched and swore that it ran around without its head.

Anjelica shared the costumes that Ricki collected for her, Victorian dresses and crinolines, children’s coats. We raided the trunks in the red sitting room upstairs in the Big House for kimonos from Japan, saris from India, headdresses from the Caucasus, silks to wind and drape and pin into costumes.

John was away making a film, but we didn’t need John to get into costume. Ricki produced hats, feathers, veils, and nets to teach us the beauty of disguise. The only trick to transformation was believing you were what you wanted to be.

Anjelica and I sat facing the cow pasture, on the steps at the foot of the pillars in front of the Big House; she wore a billowing taffeta skirt from 1860, I wore a voile dress from 1812. We screwed up our eyes and tried to wish the past into being.

That summer we began to share another world, rooted in make-believe. It endures to this day as the ability to walk into each other's imaginations and find there the romantic, the uncanny, the hilarious. The other world usually overrides the things that separate us, our different ways of being, hers through emotion, mine through rumination. It overrides her love of horses, my pedantry; her physical endurance, my weaker constitution; and even, most of the time, the fact that I tried to make her mother my own. When we lose our access to that other world, forget to play, we stop talking, sometimes for years at a time.

Ricki took us on expeditions to the ruins of great houses, driving the blue Opel, a hamper in the back full of jars of mashed sardines to make sandwiches on the brown bread we'd baked.

We came through a rusted gate in a light rain and walked around the once-great Dunsandle House. It was as ruined as the keep in the St. Clerans stable yard, the great roofless house was dissolved into fallen masonry. I was moved by the plaster garlands that clung to rain-wet walls, Anjelica by the sad sheep with toothpick legs watching us from hillocks in the limestone plain.

We played Essences on every car trip, Ricki, Anjelica, Tony, sometimes Betty O'Kelly, sometimes Anjelica's friend Lizzie Spender, sometimes Tony's friends. "I'm a person, guess who?" you'd say, and then be asked questions, such as: What kind of a day would you be? What kind of tree? What kind of sardine—fresh? Tinned? Too old to eat? What kind of shoe, what animal, what invertebrate, what noise in the night—thunder? Footsteps? Banshee? Dripping tap? What god, what curse, what star, what candy bar?

~

Greyfriars Bobby was shot at Shepperton, where a plaster version of 1855 Edinburgh spilled down the length of the largest sound stage. In the graveyard where the Skye terrier Bobby sat on his master's grave, fake flowers were stuck into the fake grass. Toothless washerwomen scrubbed plaster steps, elderly men in kilts heaved to and fro, gaunt policemen marched in pairs.

At five every morning for six weeks, a car came for me and a bleary, irritated Joyce, who wore a suit and carried one of the good handbags. Sometimes we collected other urchins from houses with gladioli in the front gardens, true Scots with red hair and baffling accents. I held my hands under the hot-water tap in my cold dressing room before I went into Hair, where they combed fuller's earth into my scalp, and Makeup, where they smeared me with Pan-Cake. My part consisted of running up and down the plaster street with a dog in my arms as Ailie, while Vincent Winter, the boy I thought of as my costar, hopped behind me on his crutches as Tammy. When we stopped running, we spoke in a choppy burr, mainly about pennies.

I was barefoot and wore rags until halfway through the story, when Ailie the child waif became Ailie the child tavern waitress and graduated to a tweed dress, an apron, and shoes. The true stars of the film were a pair of Skye terriers, Bobby One and Bobby Two, who shared the part of Greyfriars Bobby. Bobby Two was meeker; he knew he was number two.

Everyone knew their place. Bobby's enemy, the graveyard keeper, was played by Donald Crisp, who'd been in D. W. Griffith's *Birth of a Nation* and *Lassie Come Home*, and was so old that, when called for a scene, he'd take ten minutes to set down his newspaper, fold his glasses, and rise from his chair. Lawrence Naismith, who played the tavern owner, was decades younger, but he timed his movements to those of the older star.

It was six weeks of pure happiness, pretending with other people who were pretending the same thing. I accepted the camera's attention with gravity and care, knew my lines and hit my marks, and felt pity for my stand-in. I loved to hear the assistant call "Settle down" before the "And" that preceded, with a beat that made my heart leap, the life-giving injunction "Action!" I loved how the director Don Chaffey brought his palm down like a karate chop to yell "Cut!" I loved doing multiple takes, loved that if something wasn't right—and given the amount of children, the dog, and the prickly temper of Donald Crisp, it rarely was—you tried again.

If I was in bliss, my mother was not. She'd hated being a child actress, and now here she was, a chaperone among a gaggle of Scottish stage mothers. She sat apart from the other mothers, smoking and writing limericks for the next day's call sheet while fending off the advances of an assistant director she called "Charm Boy" under her breath.

Walt Disney arrived to inspect the shooting. Joyce stayed in her chair and refused to meet him.

He had a gray suit, gray hair, a gray mustache a bit like Poppy's, and a big empty smile. We posed with Bobby One, all three of us alert and delighted.

At the end of filming, I wanted to take the studio home with me, and all the children, and both dogs and the old men and the crew and the boxes and the cables and the brutes and the clapperboards and the scrims and the measuring tape that was brought to the tip of my nose before my close-ups.

"Back to real life," said Joyce. "You're starting Latin this year."

I thought I was the center of the universe, but it turned out that the center of the universe was Peter O'Toole.

Peter, his hair now short, straight, and gold, went off to Jordan to be Lawrence, and then to Spain. Filming took two years. My father stayed home, biding his time.

"Why aren't you on the set with Peter?" I asked.

"They don't let Jews into Jordan. Even Sam has to stay on his yacht off of Aqaba. And it's not my movie."

My father was building the future of Keep Films. He'd maneuvered Peter's contract with Columbia Pictures so that it did not contain the regular clause that bound an untested actor in a starring role to a lifetime of Columbia movies. Jules and Peter were free to make whatever pictures they wanted once success hit, and Jules was lining it all up.

We moved to a bigger house. There were no stars on the wallpaper in the living room this time; I wondered if we were leaving all this wonderful luck behind.

Greyfriars Bobby came out a year later. "It's a shock the first time you see yourself on screen," said Siân, who mostly acted onstage. I'd seen my face on the small screen in the post-synch studio at Shepperton while I dubbed my lines, and thought I was prepared.

Disney movies opened without fanfare. Jules and Joyce took me and a group of school friends to see *Greyfriars Bobby* at a cinema with a gigantic screen. I sat, impatient, in the first row of the balcony waiting for my hour as the preliminary story unfolded without me. At last Bobby was in Edinburgh, and here were the waifs, and there I was, and there was my face, my immense unformed face as big as a city block. I couldn't see Ailie; I could only see Joan, waiting for cues.

I blushed for months at having been revealed to be so lacking. My father wouldn't entertain the idea of my doing any other movies. I knew how much he worshipped talent and what contempt he had for schleppers. If he didn't want me to act, I probably had no talent. I'd sit on the staircase to eavesdrop on calls about the daughter in *El Cid* or the little girl in *The Innocents*, but Jules waved away all offers. "Get on with your studies," he said.

I took on the bitter mien of a has-been star, a disappointed twelve-year-old Gloria Swanson.

Our third Christmas at St. Clerans, John had a new Polaroid camera. Anjelica, Tony, Betty O'Kelly, and I clustered around him to see the first picture develop in front of our eyes, and then wailed, "I look awful!" "I look silly!" "I look fat."

John took a long breath. "Do you realize that each of you only looked at yourself? Not one of you looked at the whole picture."

I did, I wanted to say. I'm better than vanity, I try to see the big picture, I'll stop looking for myself.

But I still longed to act, and read books about actors and theater people. Siân gave me biographies of grandes dames of the London stage, Edith Evans and Flora Robson. I read the autobiography of Harpo Marx, and *Act One* by Moss Hart, and when I ran out of adult books about theater, I read children's books about theater.

Peter was home on a short break from *Lawrence of Arabia* when we all went to lunch at a country restaurant; he grabbed the book I was reading and looked at the title.

"*The Swish of the Curtain*?" he asked. "The Swish? Of the Curtain?" He was laughing.

"It's a very good book," I said. "It's about children who start a theater company."

"Does that mean you want to be an actress?" He said it: "act-ress."

"Oh no," I assured him. "I want to be an assistant stage manager."

I knew my place.

Anjelica and her toy poodle, Mindy, came to live with us, while Ricki slowly moved to London. I, too, had a dog now, a black standard poodle like Jacques, the dog we'd left behind in Beverly Hills ten years earlier. An hour after Joyce bought him for me, the vet sadly declared him to be monorchid. "That means he only has one testicle," Joyce explained, "we should take him back." But I was already in love, and named him after Vladimir in *Waiting for Godot.* He was unruly and a little peculiar.

I insisted Anjelica walk the dogs with me in Hyde Park every Sunday morning at seven. The disappointed movie star wanted some discipline around her.

"But you don't even get up at seven on schooldays!" Anjelica protested.

"It's not us, it's the dogs, we have to think of the dogs," I said. "I thought you cared about animals."

Anjelica and I wore velvet skirts to the première of *Lawrence of Arabia,* Ricki loaned Siân the magnificent gold reliquary necklace, Peter, still blond, looked like a god, Joyce smiled the smile of all triumph, and Jules beamed at Sam Spiegel, who hadn't yet realized that he didn't own Peter. I wondered why there were no women at all in the film, and decided that some of the young Arab boys in kaffiyehs had to be girls in drag.

The adults went to celebrate after the première, while Anjelica and I went home. The dogs had celebrated *Lawrence of Arabia* by shitting all over the central hall. While I made the discovery that toothpaste efficiently masked the smell of dog shit, Peter O'Toole became the biggest star in the world.

Everyone became rich and important overnight. And we all became one tribe. My parents bought a house on Chester Street that they shared with Peter's sister, Pat Coombs, and her husband, Derek, an heir to department stores in the Midlands.

Jules was proud that the house was Georgian, like St. Clerans, and three windows wide. In Georgian architecture, he said, three windows wide was vastly superior to two windows wide, which was so modest as to almost be workers' housing. The house of the earl and countess next door, he pointed out, was only two windows wide. Which explained the countess's habitual bad humor. The countess did not care for Vladimir.

Not many people did, besides me. He bit, he shat, he growled. One day, not long after he'd had a dog fight with my father over a cooked chicken, I came home from school to find Vladimir gone.

"Peter's driver is taking care of him now," said my mother. "He has a garden."

My father liked the house neat.

Our house expressed everything Jules believed about the importance of good tailoring: The front door was painted midnight blue, the same color as the Duke of Windsor's dinner jackets. The carpet on the stairs was Pat Coombs's choice, ochre yellow, just like the carpet at Christian Dior in Paris. The walls were Dior gray. Piranesi prints depicting antique dungeons and viaducts were framed with papal pomp all the way up the stairs, past the winter garden, past the grand drawing room where the Coombses and my parents would give a party every June.

Pat and Derek Coombs occupied the basement, ground, and first floor. The entrance to our part of the house was through a gilded iron gate beyond which were our living rooms and, above, my parents' bedroom; the house narrowed as it rose, and in my room on the top floor, I felt as if I were swaying in the top branches of a brick tree.

Jules greeted guests with: "Most expensive walk-up in town!" while Joyce worked the soda siphon, and at cocktail time, visitors congratulated me on grades that I hadn't earned.

Our carpet was beige, deep, and everywhere. Everything was fully finished, upholstered, seamed, and beveled, perfectly maintained. The house was like a quilted batten to shut out the world.

My room was papered in a turquoise toile de Jouy that I'd chosen in a weak moment of wanting to be a pretty *jeune fille* in a pretty room.

As a reminder of the source of all this bounty, a pair of photos hung in a single frame on the wall. I awoke every morning to Peter in costume as T. E. Lawrence next to T. E. Lawrence himself, posed identically in the same flowing Arab robes and headdress. All good fortune stemmed from Peter, our house god.

It was the first house my parents had owned since they'd left Hollywood. When their real furniture arrived from storage in Los Angeles, it looked as if a museum had disgorged treasures into the living room. Hulking great pieces of Renaissance wood, saints, church candlesticks, the low table made of two Flemish consoles, an octagonal church seat. Grander than anything at St. Clerans, except maybe John's four-poster bed.

Ricki rented a house near us in London, and now two streets away I had the freedom to sculpt clay on the kitchen table, to play with Anjelica, to ask Ricki endless questions.

John was shooting *Freud* in Munich. In the fall of 1961, the student who lived in Ricki's basement overheard people in a coffee bar talking about someone who was pregnant by John Huston, and came home to tell Mrs. Huston. The baby, a boy, was born the next spring in Rome, and named Danny. His mother was a young actress, Zoë Sallis.

Ricki never mentioned it; Anjelica took it hard. "Your parents aren't like other people," I told her, "that's why these things happen."

After *Becket* (Peter as King Henry II betrays Richard Burton as Thomas à Becket) and *Lord Jim* (Peter racked with guilt among Cambodian temples) came *What's New Pussycat?*, from a script by a young comedian named Woody Allen.

Peter, an Englishman-about-Paris, had too many girlfriends. They were played by Ursula Andress, famous as the first Bond Girl; Romy Schneider, Europe's sweetheart; Paula Prentiss, a temperamental American; and Capucine, an ex-model as thin and nervous as a greyhound. Peter Sellers, in a long black wig, played Peter's analyst, a madman married to a termagant in a Valkyrie helmet. The film was designed in high style by Richard Sylbert, who tracked down the last

Hector Guimard–tiled Art Nouveau house in Paris to serve as the analyst's home.

What's New Pussycat? was shot in Paris. Jules billeted the movie stars to the Hotel George V, but set up his own headquarters, and Peter's, at the smaller Hotel de La Trémoille, where he secured the undying loyalty of the concierge, telephone operator, waiters, and chambermaids with constant and generous tips.

They shot everything in Paris. After *What's New Pussycat?* came *How to Steal a Million*, an even more stylish comedy, this one about an art heist, directed by William Wyler. Peter was opposite Audrey Hepburn, who played a forger's daughter improbably clad in natty little Givenchy coats, jersey helmets, and a lace cocktail mask.

Joyce and I would take the 9:00 p.m. Friday plane to Orly to join Dad at La Trémoille. I recovered my Paris in the streets around La Trémoille; the bookshop on the Rue François 1er, the pen shop on the Rue Marbeuf, the *cahier* shop on the Rue Pierre Charron. My mother bought me new clothes from the Left Bank; I read *Elle* every week as news from home, and I wanted only what I'd seen in its pages.

We'd have late dinners with Peter, Siân, and actors from the picture, and then go dancing at Castel's, where models, pop stars, and *Paris Match* journalists outdid one another to catch Peter's attention. Everyone drank too much, my parents included. I'd end the evenings hunched in the phone booth, prim and sober in my little dress, dialing for taxicabs to convey the mess of adults home to La Trémoille.

~

In London, Jules had a car and driver now, a discreet midnight blue Rover with a license plate that read "JB 46," not a Rolls-Royce—a Rolls was vulgar. The driver was called Bert. My father had the leather seats slipcovered in military Melton cloth, so that his suits would not shine. Peter, the star, had a Daimler Princess, with seats upholstered in Connemara tweed, which shed, to the dismay of his driver Lionel.

Jules's dressing room at home was the same color as his office, a dark olive he called Napoleon green, and in his closet hung some forty identical gray suits, custom-made at Brioni in Rome, all single-breasted, because double-breasted suits only looked good on tall skinny men with waistlines. Hundreds of shirts from Turnbull & Asser revolved through the Mayfair Laundry to return in cellophane envelopes that he stacked and dated, so as to wear them in strict rotation and never fray a cuff.

Joyce wore good suits and antique gold chains. Her handbags were as solid as the Rover, worn in rotation, like my father's shirts. Each of her Hermès Kelly bags remained as impeccable as the day it was bought.

Nothing would ever wear out.

At the premières of the Keep Films movies, she wore her new diamonds and the smile of a queen. On those première nights, our job was to be the audience that dazzles the audience. At the premières of other people's movies, she wore the antique jewelry. She knew not to upstage.

A little pep pill before the car to the theater, a glass of champagne in the car for each, a smile to win, a smile to keep the luck coming. My father knew that the key to success was the perception of success.

Those were the champagne years.

When *Lord Jim* opened, Siân was in a play, so I was Peter's date. I was sixteen, still too short, my face still too round, my dress too demure, and my bangs too carefully combed to make an impression as anything but a daughter. Before we exited the Daimler, Peter said, "Shut your mouth and look surprised," but gave no clue as to how to raise the inner edges of his eyebrows to create the expression of amused disdain that made him look like a prince.

While Keep Films prospered, Uncle Don made himself at home in London, and even more in Cannes; he rented a house in the hills above, where he went to play golf and see his friends. He was never happier than at the Cannes Film Festival, and later was my key to how it worked.

Don had a way of getting around the normal order of things through bonhomie, economy, and a sense of adventure. His stories had fewer famous people in them than my parents' did, and were much funnier. He made spectacular mistakes.

One Easter, he'd bought a fine smoked salmon to share with his friends above Cannes; he wrapped it carefully in foil and plastic, packed it in his suitcase, and boarded the plane to Nice. His suitcase did not appear on the luggage carousel at the Nice airport, but proceeded on to Dakar, then Cairo, and landed for weeks at Addis Ababa. By the time the suitcase returned to Nice, Don was in London, and when he arrived at last to claim the suitcase, he was told it was in quarantine.

"Uh boy, it smelled like nothing I've ever smelled," he said. "The smoked salmon had melted in the African heat, there was stinking smoked-salmon slime on everything inside the suitcase. I lost all the new clothes I had in there, I even had to throw away the suitcase."

"For God's sake, Don," said my father. "Tell me that's the last time you pack a smoked salmon in your suitcase."

"That's the last time I pack a smoked salmon in my suitcase," Don said.

My parents would never pack food in a suitcase. Their suitcases were from Gucci in Rome, heavy, expensive black leather banded with green and red webbing, tightly packed and locked for each journey, the locks secured with knotted leather thongs.

I rooted around in their things to find out if they'd ever made mistakes. The tiny chest of drawers on my father's dresser held rubber bands, plastic stays for his shirt collars, his shiny brass L.A. police photographer's badge, and a Purple Heart medal that was never explained.

The cubbyholes of my mother's desk were jammed with letters and bills she'd get to one day, but in the *semainier* I found a short story with her name below the title, "The Blue Hour," written with the cool precision of Katherine Mansfield. "The blue hour" is what the French call those forty minutes late in a Paris afternoon when the sky turns bright blue black, opaque. There were few details and little action; the suggestion of a love affair in the sharp, pained prose astounded me and made me cry.

It took some maneuvering to get her to tell me that she had written a story, and then ask to see it, and to read it again in front of her, so that at last I could tell her how good it was. "You're brilliant," I said.

"I only tried it once," she said. There was no question of publishing it.

~

With success came art. Peter and Siân, Pat and Derek, Jules and Joyce bought from the same dealer, Ricki's friend Leslie Waddington. At least one pink and blue Milton Avery seaside scene per household, a Paul Klee of a crying face and many Jack Yeats landscapes for the O'Tooles, a small Renoir of a fat child for the Coombses, and for my parents, a remarkable Cubist Fernand Léger. It went up in the living room on a wall between two windows, as if it needed to be shielded from the gray London light.

My father took me by the shoulders, an unlit Montecristo "A" cigar in his hand, stood me in front of the Fernand Léger, and solemnly announced:

"One day, you're going to be a very rich woman, and this is going to be yours. So don't go falling for the first fortune hunter that comes along."

I stared at the undulating landscape, the trees shaped like thumbs, the circles, the red lines, the checkerboard foreground, to officially take in the wealth he was bestowing on me. It was the most beautiful painting in the world.

I was entirely protected by him, and completely asphyxiated. He knew too much about me. It was he who'd urged a jar of Arrid on me, who told me how to deal with blackheads, explained how to shave my legs: "Make a paste with the soap, honey."

I was fifteen when he took me out of school for the day and off to Paris to translate for him at the Cambodian embassy, to explain to the officials why they should let him shoot *Lord Jim* on location among the temples of Angkor Wat. I felt odd through the day, and after we'd landed back in London—two planes in one day, I'd never done that—my period arrived. I'd been waiting for it for so long that I feared I was going to be a child forever. My father understood what had happened without being told, and handed me a glass of gin for cramps.

I called Joyce, who was skiing in Klosters with Pat Coombs. "Oh darling," she said with an emotion that surprised me.

The remnant of the eleventh toe was removed in the hospital. Now I could wear low-cut shoes like all the other girls, but I still looked like a child. To pass for sixteen to go with Joyce to see *I Am Curious (Yellow)*, an X-rated Swedish film, I put on a new red suit from Paris with a tight skirt and tied a chiffon scarf over my back-combed hair.

"How do I look?" I asked, hoping I could join her tribe of beauties.

"You look like an interesting kook," she said.

The tribe of beauties consisted of Joyce, Siân, and Ricki. They were known as such around town, the wife of the producer, the wife of the star, the wife of the director, noticed by all when they went to have their hair cut in the whine of dryers and the sweet fug of lacquer at Vidal Sassoon's. Joyce's black and white hair was now brown, Siân's brown hair was now red, Ricki's remained brown, but they all had the same sharp cut, executed by Vidal or Ricci Burns. Siân and Ricki had the cheekbones of Italian Madonnas, Joyce had velvet eyes, and her perfect nose was untouched by surgery.

The Joyce I wanted to look like wasn't the one I saw every day; it was the way she looked in a photograph my father had taken when we lived at Coup de Vent above Cannes, when I was five. In it, she wore the striped sailor sweater and no makeup at all, and the white flash in her black hair was like a lightning bolt above her huge, wide-open eyes. I never saw the photograph enough; one day my father had opened a box of his pictures on the round coffee table, and it was on top of the pile. I sat down next to him to look at it again. There was such intensity in her eyes, such a startled beauty to her face, and not a trace of the fake model smile she smiled so well.

I reached for it and asked, "Can I have that?"

"No," he said, "that's not for you." And, for once, he took back a photograph of his and closed the lid on the box.

"But that's exactly what I want to look like, that's who I want to be," I said.

"No, you don't, honey. You want to be you," he said. "Now bug off."

I wasn't turning out to look like her. When I was eighteen, she wrote to Evelyn Keyes: "She's bright and curious, attractive though not a beauty—she has what is called a contemporary face—does that convey anything?"

It was the nose. The nose was a curse, the nose was destiny; I had mapped out enough invisible architecture of cause and effect to believe that one should not go against destiny. Of course, Peter had had a nose job to become a movie star, and so had Siân. Even Ricki had allowed the bump on her nose to be scraped down long ago, before she met John, so it was possible that fame and love were waiting at the other end of hospital and bandages and two black eyes, but I didn't want the shame of knowing I'd pretended to be someone other than me. If I'd been surer of who I was, I might have dared.

My mother's nose had always been short, high bridged, symmetrical. I bolted from the office of the Harley Street plastic surgeon she took me to see before he'd finished the examination. "For God's sake, make up your mind!" she said on the way home. I said I'd take what nature had given me. Anything else would be cowardice.

Jules reassured me about my face.

"The empress Farah Diba," he'd say. "Stand up straight."

"Audrey Hepburn?" I'd ask, hopefully. There was a beauty, a star with a nose.

"Maria Callas," he'd reply.

He didn't want me to compete with the real beauties. I belonged with the exotics. And just as he'd assigned roles to everyone—Joyce, paragon of loyalty; Peter, volcanic genius; Siân, theater actress only—I was to be a brain, a worker.

"You can do anything," he said, "anything you set your mind to. And you can do it in French."

I had to do well in school; that was my role, my talent. I knew I wasn't that brilliant. But, thanks to Joe McCarthy and my mother's longing for the Riviera in 1951, I was in a position to receive the kind of education under which even lesser minds could flourish.

"I didn't get all As at A levels, Dad. I did really badly in Spanish," I protested.

"It's all a game, honey," he said. "When will you learn that?"

He'd barely finished high school, but when his future in-laws, Esta and Morey, announced his marriage to Joyce Gates in a New York newspaper, he'd become a graduate of both Columbia and the University of Southern California.

"I wish you'd been a Communist," I said.

He didn't like any mention of Communists. "You're too romantic," he said, "I don't want you with some lefty student eating baked beans out of a can next to a gas heater that you have to feed with shillings in a bedsit on the Finchley Road."

To dissipate my urge for bohemian squalor, he included me in the dinners at the White Elephant with him and Joyce and Peter and Siân, the Coombses, and whatever exciting famous person was in town. Hence late bedtimes, hence inattention in morning classes, hence bad grades. I never said no to outings with stars.

I graduated to my first black dress, my first earrings; the mirrored walls of the White Elephant reflected a young woman who was almost the empress Farah Diba, almost Maria Callas, and I listened to the CBS reporter Charles Collingwood talk about the thousand-year war in Vietnam with an approximation of poise, if not beauty.

But when I was sixteen, my body became an insubstantial envelope that could barely contain new tides raging inside me; my heart ran away, my blood pounded and took my breath with it, I lost my balance, and sometimes I blacked out. The sight of one particular boy at the lycée so undid me that I could barely walk. The glimpse of a pink worm on a rainy sidewalk turned my stomach and made me faint.

Dr. Woodcock suggested I carry smelling salts. "The vapors," Mom said, rolling her eyes. "Knock it off," said Dad.

I never fainted at the White Elephant; there was nothing there to set me off. What set me off was the feeling of a presence, a volume and fleshy texture to the air, an awareness of sex as a separate, foreign, invisible entity, the Great God Pan that I'd read about in one of Ricki's books in the Little House. It was not the kind of sex I'd been entertaining myself with in the *Kama Sutra* I sneaked down from a high shelf in the hallway bookcase, nor the unsatisfying doings in *Last Exit to Brooklyn*. I had an abstract and baroque view of what sex might be.

The lycée boy had curly hair above a high forehead, wore a dark old-fashioned overcoat to his ankles, and stood on the steps of the lycée defiantly puffing on the end of a cigar, a romantic hero, King of the Road.

He was two years older, a math whiz who reveled in saying he was poor. I didn't know that his father had founded a London acting school, that his uncle was Alec Guinness. He struck me as purity itself, which was confirmed when we sat knee to knee in my bedroom, where he was supposed to be tutoring me in math. He wrote out the injunction "Existence before Appearance" in capital letters on my autograph animal, a toy cow previously signed by Peter, Siân, Lionel Bart, and Jack Lemmon. I read those words and knew he'd gauged the measure of my futility. What happened next was brief and inconclusive, but it shattered me.

Self-consciousness immobilized me. What was I supposed to do? What was I supposed to touch? Was I supposed to talk? Was this the *Kama Sutra,* and if so, was I a cow or a gazelle? Was that a lingam? That had to be a lingam but should I even be looking at it?

He was as paralyzed as I was, for different reasons, panicked by the signs of wealth so carefully put in place at Chester Street.

Two weeks and one more fumble later, he called me to say that nothing had happened between us, or would ever happen again. I took in that I was not going to be welcomed by any man. It was not a happy beginning to a love life. The emotions the clumsy eighteen-year-old mathematician had set off in me gave me a flu that lasted for weeks. I pined for him, I languished, and for years I looked so sad when I went out dancing that I eventually invented a fiancé who'd died, to explain my expression.

Dinners resumed at the White Elephant, where I was a well-dressed, bilingual, witty, fundamentally inert public daughter sitting up straight among names any fool would recognize. Good clothes, famous people, everything for show: this is what was normal. I longed to find the real and the true, but the boy I'd thought was real had rejected me. I was ready to be absorbed by fashion.

CHAPTER FOUR

Ricki bought a tall house on Maida Avenue, facing the Regent's Canal, and started a new life, with the children's Irish nanny, known to all as Nurse, to help her. On Sundays, she hauled a leg of lamb out of the oven; Anjelica and I set the table for lunch in the basement kitchen for ten, twelve, fourteen people. Sometimes after lunch, a soft, agreeable man named John Julius Norwich prompted us to talk in blank verse, while he played the piano. In Ricki's bathroom was a small antique porcelain box with "A Trifle from Norwich" written on it, as allusive and reticent as he was.

The house was unfinished, reckless, and magical, the living room a patchy sky blue, the hall walls daubed with sample squares of dark orange; none of the doors really closed. The sofa was a Venetian bed with animal feet, a chaise longue was supported by the spread wings of an eagle, a framed photo of people on a beach by someone named Diane Arbus rested against a nail-head trunk, flowers stood in test tubes, gourds were displayed in an open cabinet with peeling paint, and you could dance to Motown on splintered floorboards. It was the opposite of being battened into wall-to-wall and upholstered fine, fine taste at home, where nothing was unfinished and there was no mess, not one spill, no room to breathe.

Sometimes I knew things I shouldn't. For the Easter holidays, I was at St. Clerans. I was fifteen. While Anjelica and her friend Lizzie were out on their ponies, Ricki took me to County Clare to look at an octagonal house near Lisdoornvarna. I wondered if she was looking for a place to live, and if so, why. I thought the house was eccentric and enchanting.

Ricki said, "There's too much work to do here, too much to change."

"It's easier to live with other people's mistakes than your own," I said.

"How did you know that?" asked Ricki.

I could hear respect for me in the question, and suddenly had to tell her something else, but I didn't know what it was until I opened my mouth.

"I'm not coming back this summer . . ." I waited for the rest to come into my head and found myself saying, ". . . because I'm pregnant."

Ricki froze and turned away. Why had I said that? I'd never even been kissed.

I didn't go back to St. Clerans that summer. Joyce and I joined my father at the Grand Hotel in Rome, where John Huston was directing *The Bible*, in which Peter played "the Three Angels," envoys from God. John introduced us to his new girlfriend, a tall countess named Valeria. I wondered what had become of his girlfriend Zoë, the mother of Danny, who would by now be two years old.

Women in lace veils gathered in the hotel's lobby on their way to meet the pope. Under the crushing Roman heat in the dining room, Peter and Siân gave me and my parents the salt pills they'd learned about in the desert in Jordan. There was hushed adult talk.

"What? What?" I asked, until Joyce, in the soothing voice she used for unsettling news, said, "Ricki's had a baby."

"You can't tell anyone," said Jules.

"She's called Allegra," added Siân. "Lovely name."

In London, Anjelica whispered that the father was John Julius with the soft face who talked in verse and played the piano after lunch on Sundays, but not to tell. John Julius? He had none of the reckless vigor I expected from a progenitor. Had he been there more often than those Sundays? He wasn't there now. If it hadn't been for the little box in her bathroom that said "A Trifle from Norwich" I could not have imagined he was Ricki's lover. I thought of him as a gray cloud, but John Julius lived with his wife and two children just across the Regent's Canal, in a house angled out of sight from Ricki's house on Maida Avenue.

The baby, Allegra, was beautiful. Motherhood seemed such a strange thing, milkiness and privacy, all movements slower, and then the baby's first steps, her first words, and all around it the big secret word you didn't say—Father—and sometimes a glimpse of him in the sky blue living room, not often, not for long.

She was doing it alone.

One morning at Chester Street, as my father waited for the espresso pot to release its coffee fug into the kitchen, he announced, "I'm with Ricki in anything she wants to do. I think it's terrific. And the baby is wonderful."

I heard support for me in any wild thing I'd ever do, any adventure, any love affair, even with married men.

But this was not about me. He was beginning to pull away from John. He'd applied to become a British subject. It was an acceptance he craved so much that it didn't occur to him to share it with his wife or his daughter. "I'm the first white heterosexual who's applied to become a British subject since T. S. Eliot, and we're both from St. Louis," he said. The Home Office vetted him for two years before they granted him the hardback blue British passport, the mark of achievement, the mark of class. No more St. Louis. No more cigar store. No more Hollywood. He went to the American embassy, presented his British passport to a consul, and then proceeded to ceremonially tear his American passport into little pieces. The thick paper resisted, but his will was strong.

"Oh Julesie," said Joyce when he told her, not impressed.

He was a platinum producer now, producing big movies with the best independent company in England. Peter was a huge star, Keep Films was a force to be reckoned with, the movies had legs, they were laughing all the way to the bank, there was no looking back.

The lucky pictures had a theme to their titles. *The Day They Robbed the Bank of England* had brought gold bars into the mews house in Groom Place. *How to Steal a Million* gave my mother the budget to decorate the Keep Films office on Eaton Place as the most solid movie company on the face of the earth. Napoleon green walls, ormolu lamps, an armillary sphere, a globe of the world and a globe of the sky, all eighteenth century, a partner's desk for Jules and Peter, where Peter never sat.

The Christmas gift list covered five typed pages and included everyone from airport officials, maître d's, concierges, and barmen to dentists, chiropractors, lawyers, and the few agents Jules respected. He handed out £5 and £10 tips everywhere, £5 cab fare home to any school friend who came to see me, and if they had ambitions to act, they got a screen test. Those who wanted to direct asked for film stock and received it at once; he optioned three plays by my friends. When a girl from school confessed that she needed an abortion and didn't know where to turn, I told her to call Dad; he set it up, paid for it, and told her to keep it a secret from me.

He took care of everyone. He was British. I didn't know what to be.

"I'm staying American," said Joyce, and went to work for the Democrats Abroad. I knew nothing about America except that we had the bomb, Republicans were bad, Democrats were good, and something vague about Quemoy and Matsu that Kennedy and Nixon had argued about on television. I felt stateless. The inside of my head was French, but a French education didn't get you a passport. My heart was whatever Ricki was, but that was Italian American and ballet and Irish countryside and the baby Allegra, that wasn't a country. If I was British, it wasn't good-suit-and-success British like my father, it wasn't Melton-wool-seats-of-the-Rover and the-head-of-immigration-meeting-you-when-you-landed; it was Portobello Road and shopping-for-clothes British, Dolly Bird British. French was for the mind; I'd find French men who loved books as much as I did, and try to get into the École Normale Supérieure, where Simone de Beauvoir had met Jean-Paul Sartre. To be safe, I also took the English exams.

I had one English friend at the lycée, and one French one. Emily Boothby lived alone at the top of a big house because her parents were in Iceland, where her father was the British ambassador. She was a logical blond beauty who was studying ancient Greek at twelve, and introduced me to the novels of Evelyn Waugh. Lydie Dattas was the music teacher's daughter, a tall skinny girl with chalk-white skin, poetic and skittish. We both excelled at recitation and essays, but she stubbornly insisted that when she grew up she'd live in Paris and own lions. My third friend, Luceen Kachadourian, was part of a huge family firmly embedded in the Armenian community. I wasn't like any of them.

~

My father had long wanted to bring Peter and John together on a film and now he set Dalton Trumbo to writing a script about Will Adams, "the first white man in Japan," a sixteenth-century British seaman who became a samurai.

"John and Gladys are coming to stay at with us to discuss Will Adams, and John is bringing Valeria," said my mother, "so we'll need your room for a few days." I was happy to go sleep at Ricki's house, but Joyce summoned me home early; John, Gladys, and Valeria had suddenly left.

I found my parents sitting shell-shocked in the living room. There had been a monumental fight about Will Adams, right there around the coffee table, and the friendship was over forever. "No more John?" I asked. My father shook his head.

No one who wasn't there that night really knew what happened. Outraged letters flew between John and my father; Jules tried to draw people to his side, John pulled them back to his. My mother said the fight was about money.

She wrote to Evelyn Keyes:

> What we had for years believed to be affection and trust were really patronizing exploitation—tinged with contempt. I'm not being melodramatic—as you know better than most, John lives and thrives on an atmosphere of drama and unreality and I would have thought there was no facet of his personality that could have surprised or shocked us—how can there be disillusion when there are no illusions?

Jules had broken free of the spell. They never spoke again.

I wasn't sure if I still had a godfather. Anjelica and I hugged and swore that no matter what our fathers did, nothing would alter our friendship. There was no St. Clerans that summer; instead, Anjelica stayed with us in a rented villa at Cap Ferrat, where we had thirteen balconies and a jetty into the Mediterranean.

By the time Allegra was in her own chair at Sunday lunch, wearing a mobcap and examining books, Ricki was flamboyant again, and magnificent. She wore new Cossack boots with slanted heels from Anello and Davide, purveyors to the Royal Ballet, and carried an Hermès bag so battered that the dye had peeled off the leather and left it looking like a river rock.

Nana came to stay.

"Your friend Ricki, it's a crime what she's done to that Hermès," she said, clucking. "No self-respect."

I chose to ignore Nana's real message—that no married woman had a child with someone else's husband—and took her at her word, which allowed me to judge her shallow. If Nana was shocked by Ricki's handbag, I could let my clothes take the blame for whatever I chose to do in future.

To hell with Existence before Appearance. Appearance before Existence was within my grasp, and so much more fun.

We all bopped along to the Beatles, fashion came to the lycée, and I became a mod, devoted above all to style. A girl named Jane Gozzett arrived at the lycée fresh from a year in Paris, where she'd had an actual lover. She knew people in fashion. Her face was white, her teeth were brown, but in the right light her cheekbones were like Marlene Dietrich's. Jane taught me how to shop for old clothes at Portobello Road, explained that matchy-matchy was a no-no, and that rust was a perfect color. Our references were Art Deco, Art Nouveau, the long necks of prewar shop-window dummies, the embroidered dressing gowns on prostitutes in Icart drawings, and most of all, Josef von Sternberg's *Shanghai Express*—Jane was Dietrich, I'd be Anna May Wong. Style was sex and drama.

I stood at the number 14 bus stop near the lycée with Jane, Lydie, and Emily watching Roman Polanski film *Repulsion*, all four of us mesmerized by Catherine Deneuve crossing the street in a manicurist's uniform. Everything was happening in London.

Jane imported the crinkled crepon Cacharel shirts that everyone was wearing in Paris, and soon we London lycée girls looked as if we, too, were everyone in Paris, and not O-level students in South Kensington.

The one I bought had a checkerboard pattern of pale pink and apple green. I stared at my pink-and-green sleeve during class, entranced by the happy colors. They were so clean that they looked almost helpless—innocent, that was the word, the opposite of the orange-and-mauve checkerboard on the shirt of the girl sitting next to me. Orange and mauve were happening colors, today colors, but marred by a knowing smokiness.

And while my friends were drinking in pubs and discovering marijuana, I got high on color, ecstatic with color. Color hit almost every one of my senses: colors were flavors; they were salty, sweet, sour, bitter—black tasted like licorice—colors were sounds with pitches and frequencies all the way from warm-bath bass—dark brown—to the terrible high piercing wail of ice blue. And when you placed two colors together, they became textures: grainy, smooth, rough—blue with brown was definitely rough. It challenged you to take in two opposing forces. Maroon with yellow was always rubbery, not just because of the erasers on pencils; yellow brought out the dull paste thickness of maroon, and poor maroon had no decent relationship to any other color, and sounded like a fart.

I could taste, feel, and hear what I saw; the only sense that color didn't touch was smell, but for that I had perfume, and perfume itself gave off colors, sounds, textures, and even had another dimension, like a tunnel going back through time. Perfume had the power to convey actual feelings. My mother's Calèche smelled like indecision; Ricki's Shalimar sounded like a temple bell muffled by smoke and velvet curtains; and my own teenage Vetiver spray smelled like the stamping of a small foot.

At lunchtime I'd go to the little haberdasher near the lycée to riffle through their bins of plain rayon scarves looking for a further rush of color, and I'd lay scarves next to each other to see what the colors set off. Fabric was easier to play with than paint; you didn't have to let it dry, you saw the effect at once. I laid a dark purple scarf on the counter next to a bright red one, and the contrast between the purple and the red was so intense that it was a completion, a perfect union, an answer that filled me with a breathless joy and a dizzying sense of peace.

I bought the purple scarf, and the red one. I had to. Apart, they were no more than scarves, not even silk, machine hemmed, but together, they created a reverberation that felt like power.

My father understood talent and had a perfect eye for composition and symmetry. I had a perfect eye for color and the symbolism of costume. I couldn't read humans as easily as I could read the meaning of their clothes.

At fifteen I wore a skinny French coat with gigantic floppy lapels, a short shift from Mary Quant in a color she called curry, and a miniskirt in a color she called plum. Mary Quant understood that colors were flavors. In Portobello Road I found a silky knitted sweater with orange crochet borders; orange, almost rust. "That looks like shit," my father said. He didn't understand. Ricki did.

We all went to Biba on a Kensington side street to get the tiny dresses with tight armpits that made us into dolly birds for twenty-one shillings. Jane sold Biba the cloche hats and chenille berets that she crocheted in class, and the hats sold so well that Jane hired old-age pensioners across London to fill her orders. Jane took me to meet Barbara Hulanicki, who was Biba herself, and soon I was making brooches for her out of giant coat buttons painted with Art Nouveau patterns, copied from a French book about Art Nouveau and executed in slow-drying model-car enamel. Instead of the yellows and browns of Art Nouveau, I used dark blue (soft, warm, bitter), aquamarine (hard, cold, sweet), and silver (liquid, cool, sour).

By the time I was sixteen, I was not just a mod, I was a purveyor of mod. I got my name in the papers. "You're a pro," my father said proudly, though he shouted at me whenever I spilled the model-car enamel on the leather top of my antique desk.

On Saturday afternoons we paraded along King's Road where Jaguar XK-Es unfurled ribbons of Moody Blues past the open doors of boutiques blasting the Stones. The Beatles and the Rolling Stones were always just out of sight. The entire town was an endless party. American journalists were dispatched to watch us be beautiful and come back with interesting words about our mores and sexy pictures of long-haired blondes in miniskirts and see-through chiffon tops.

Anjelica was photographed for British *Vogue.* Logic saved me from being too jealous: her legs were longer than mine, and her father more famous. But the tide of Voguery rising all around us was missing me so narrowly that it was only a matter of time before I, too, was noticed, and transformed.

I was wearing a dress in a pale mauve (borderline too sugary), almond boots (gray beige, not yellow beige), white lipstick, and my ironed black hair hung straight down my back the day Tom Wolfe turned up at a Sunday afternoon party in a white suit, a flap of blond hair over one eye. His *Kandy-Kolored Tangerine-Flake Streamline Baby* had been out a year and he'd come to London to write about us. I pointed out a girl who was "starved to near-perfection"; he wrote it down. I told him about Jane and her lover the harelipped Turk; he wrote it down. He asked if I'd heard about a place where people went dancing in daytime.

"How do I look?" I asked my mother before I went to lunch with him the following Saturday. "Very contemporary," she said. I thought he might appreciate that my jeans jacket was made of suede, just like my miniskirt. It was so short that for decency I wore two pairs of underpants. At lunch, he took notes on what I said—Tom Wolfe writing down my words, there at Alvaro on a Saturday—and asked if I would show him where to buy clothes. While he tried on King's Road trousers, I sat on a chair, blushing. Behind the curtain of a changing booth, Tom Wolfe was in his underwear. I was the only seventeen-year-old virgin in London.

Standing on the yellow carpet of the landing by our winter garden, I asked him, "What is the most important thing in the world?"

"Status," he said, and added that he'd marry me if I wrote a book.

He went back to New York. I was in love. My father said, "Cut it out," but every word out of my mouth was Wolfe, and if the conversation refused to cohere around Tom Wolfe, I brought up every manner of wolf: Siberian wolf, timber wolf, wolf man, Steppenwolf, Howlin' Wolf.

"You should forget the Wolfe and find yourself a cub," said Ricki.

We were at Sunday lunch in her kitchen. Allegra, though not yet three, was reading aloud from a book about hootie owls. Ricki had gathered young blond actors—Michael York, Peter Eyre, James Fox—an American playwright called Adrienne Kennedy, and the art dealer Leslie Waddington, and now they all knew that I needed a cub, not a Wolfe. I was about to say I'd take James Fox, but James Fox was looking with longing at Anjelica, who was twice my height and all angles.

To cover my embarrassment, I said, "Let's make a landscape out of people's names!" Paper was found, and we all set to drawing a map made of people's names. Lloyd Bridges rose over Larry Rivers, Jean Shrimpton was caught in Oliver Reed, Helen Twelvetrees was a forest, Rock Hudson an escarpment, Admiral Byrd flew through a sky where Ringo Starr twinkled next to Keith Moon, Claude Rains fell on John Houseman, Tab Hunter followed James Fox and Tom Wolfe through Jayne Meadows, and the family doctor, Patrick Woodcock, perched on Marietta Tree.

A few weeks later the first letter arrived from Tom Wolfe, a single page of Canson paper folded in two and closed with a gold seal, my name and address rendered with calligraphic flourishes. I deciphered the curls inside to read: "Come to Rotten Gotham."

"Where's Gotham?" I asked my mother.

"That's New York!" she said.

"Why is it rotten?" I asked.

His piece came out in the *Telegraph* magazine in November, titled "The Life and Hard Times of a Teenage London Society Girl." Jane's lover, the harelipped Turk, had become a clubfooted Kurd. Tom Wolfe had met a few other young women, combined me with a blonde or two, and named the collective creature "Little Sue," but I knew Little Sue was me. "Starved to near-perfection" was all over the article.

Rotten Gotham. I didn't have to cry about the boy at the lycée anymore, I didn't have to be French, I could be an American with a new life in New York. Why continue studying philosophy at the lycée to prepare my entry into the École Normale Supérieure? I wasn't Simone de Beauvoir, and Sartre was not pretty. I'd go to Sarah Lawrence to study anthropology under Joseph Campbell, find out everything about pre-Columbian cultures, and discover the central reason for human existence. I'd move to New York, write a book, and marry Tom Wolfe. That was my destiny.

One weekend in Paris in my father's suite at the Trémoille, I found a copy of French *Vogue* open to a portrait of Peter as the psychotic Nazi in *The Night of the Generals.* A little too much eyeliner, as usual. But further on in the magazine, I had a revelation: pages and pages shot in Greece of a woman who didn't look like a model—slight, a little rounded, with a sad face and no makeup except charcoal around the eyes. The model laughed and sulked and cried. The pictures told stories that seemed to be about me. She sat at a taverna table, anxious in bulky clothes and silver bracelets, the scene so real I could taste the retsina and hear the soundtrack to *Zorba the Greek.* She lay back on a rock as a naked man rose from the sea, his ass to the camera, facing her, and, for once, she was smiling.

The photographs were by someone called Bob Richardson. I placed the Paris *Vogue* under my first volume of the *Diary of Anaïs Nin.* Together they told my future. Maybe not just New York. Adventure, writing, tears, and a knowing smile when I looked at a naked man. I applied to Sarah Lawrence. Tom Wolfe was waiting.

~

The next Keep Films picture was *Great Catherine,* an eighteenth-century romp based on a obscure one-act play by George Bernard Shaw. Jeanne Moreau was the empress Catherine the Great, Peter a bemused prude of a British diplomat at her court, Zero Mostel her counselor Potemkin. The director was the kind Peter liked best, an unsure man who was to make only one more film before vanishing.

On screen in black and white, Jeanne Moreau was a bewitching condensation of female energy; in color in our living room at Chester Street, she was a short lady in a thick tubular dress smoking Benson & Hedges Golds, but with the same tired eyes, the same beautiful cracked voice. My father made a deal with her manager that I'd be her press attachée, at £10 a week, paid by him.

And now I rose with him at five to be at my studio, Shepperton, by seven. There was much fuss about real antique diamond jewelry for the empress borrowed from S. J. Phillips in Bond Street, eighteenth-century-platform mules custom-made by Roger Vivier, and a whip with a fake diamond pommel. In Potemkin's study, Zero Mostel repeatedly mangled a wide silk curtain on which the art director had carefully painted hundreds of Russian saints. I inherited a facsimile crown, the diamond-pommeled whip, and, much later, the curtain.

"What's the film about?" I asked Peter one day at Shepperton. "Read the bloody script," he said; that wasn't an answer. The film was about nothing, a romp without a heist. As Jeanne's *attachée de presse* I shepherded journalists around the studio, marked up contact sheets, and flew to Paris to distribute photographs to newspapers and magazines that printed them immediately. I flirted with the second assistant director and a photographer, but not so overtly that they'd notice.

I waited for Jeanne to give me advice about being a woman; instead, she gave me dresses and coats designed for her by Pierre Cardin, who, although homosexual, was her lover. She gave me a furiously modern gold brooch given to her by her next lover, the director Tony Richardson, who was also homosexual, although married to Vanessa Redgrave. The tangle of gold shavings looked a little like shredded wheat and a lot like pubic hair, which gave a sinister meaning to the diamonds caught in it.

"You're returning that," my father said. "It's much too expensive to accept."

I went to see Jeanne in Paris, where François Truffaut was directing her in *The Bride Wore Black*, stayed at La Trémoille, went dancing at Castel's, and, in a valiant but incomplete attempt to be dissolute, spent a night kissing a man on his bed in a hotel room. The next day on the set, Jeanne's boyfriend Cyril said, "I hear you were wild at Castel's last night." Jeanne took my chin in her hand and said the words I'd been waiting for: "*Ma chérie,* it's better to have a bad reputation than none at all."

Sarah Lawrence accepted me. I spent two weeks with Jeanne in her house near Saint-Tropez, where she made me read George Groddeck's alarming *The Book of the It.* I prepared for college in America: cut off all my hair, bought a red plush fedora from Herbert Johnson and a yard of dark green William Morris cotton from Liberty printed with thistles and spiky leaves. I packed a mannish camel-hair coat for protection, the plush fedora, a green velvet suit from the debutante boutique Annacat, bronze leather boots from Anello & Davide that buttoned all the way to the knee with real buttons, and a Victorian buttonhook to fasten them. Joyce had given me an Edwardian glove case with ivory glove stretchers set into its lid. I was not ready for New York in 1967.

My friend Emily had just married Piers Paul Read, Jay to us, a novelist who had a Harkness fellowship, and they were going to New York by ship. I'd travel with them.

My parents saw me off on the *Queen Elizabeth*, wiping their eyes in the tiny cabin, and then there were five days walking pale green corridors holding sticky wooden handrails, locked in the smell of linoleum and fuel, wild rice at every meal, with Jay's fellow Harkness fellows who spoke of inner space and tensile steel. I couldn't read through the constant jolts of ocean against steel hull, so I drank gin and white wine in various bars on the *Queen Elizabeth*. Nothing outside or around us but immutable gray, cold spray, a bright white wake that beckoned if I stared at it too long. One tipsy night at dinner, I declared that my mission in America was to learn from Joseph Campbell the secret of the religious origins of theater, and also the meaning of life. Emily said, "You can't be serious."

As a tug pulled us up the Hudson to the West Side docks, the cars driving along the rim of the city looked too big to be real. From the gangplank I saw Nana marooned among a tide of porters, her diamond brooch flashing like an alarm.

At Nana's apartment, I called the number Tom Wolfe had given me, but when a woman answered, I quickly hung up. A girlfriend, a wife?

Sarah Lawrence was fake Tudor houses separated by walkways. My room had an atmosphere of utter gloom, compounded by a sulky roommate from New Jersey. Joseph Campbell wasn't going to teach me anything because he was not there. Word was he'd been run off campus for racism by a great-niece of Chiang Kai-shek. But my father had said there was nothing I couldn't do, so I took anthropology as a science subject. Instead of discovering the key to the perennial fire of the human spirit, I'd investigate gene transmission among fruit flies.

Nonetheless, I signed up for theater under Wilford Leach, who had a southern accent and a flap of hair over one eye like Tom Wolfe. To make sure I was accepted as an acting student, I gave Will Leach my full family credentials—Jules Buck's movies, my past as a child actress, Peter O'Toole.

Will Leach wasted no time. "There are two very talented graduate students who are going to make a movie. Maybe you'd like to meet them?"

That was the problem with boasting about Keep Films. The next words were always "financing," "free film stock," "lights and equipment," or a polite inquiry about how to get a script to Peter O'Toole.

"What are their names?" I asked. I had to keep an open mind.

Their names were something "de Niro" and something "de Palma." They might be fellow Europeans, allies in this strange new world.

"Are they Italian?" I asked.

"Italian American," said Wilford Leach.

No, I said, I didn't want to meet them. Why ask Dad for film stock for boys who weren't real Italians?

I didn't understand the Sarah Lawrence girls. A blonde with a short beaked nose sounded English, but announced, "I'm from Connecticut, you know what that means." I didn't. The American debutantes with hairless nostrils were nothing like my lycée friends. I missed Emily's logical mind, Jane's devotion to style, Luceen and her wild Armenian family, the mad poetic purity of Lydie Dattas, my sexy friend Joce and her advice about which part of the body to present first, which I had not yet tried out.

The taller Sarah Lawrence girls had lovers, the shorter ones had fiancés. I had fruit flies. Sometimes I called Tom Wolfe's number from the pay phone, but it was always a woman who answered—the same one or another, I wasn't sure—so I hung up each time.

I spent weekends on a foldout couch at Nana's on West 54th Street, across from the garden of the Museum of Modern Art. Her apartment smelled like Ivory soap and paper napkins. The perfume bottles that my father had given her were arranged unopened on a tray in her bedroom, waiting for an important occasion. I called Tom Wolfe, but now a man answered, so I hung up. Could he have a boyfriend? I was afraid to call him anymore.

After the list of classes I'd chosen was sent to my parents, a telegram arrived from London. "You are not in college to be an actress. Learn something real. Dad."

I obeyed without a second thought. If I couldn't act, I'd write. That was just as easy, if less fun. The school paper was called the *Emanon*—No Name spelled backward, a little too close to "enema." My first movie review was an impassioned defense of Polanski's *Fearless Vampire Killers* that I titled "Take That, Bosley Crowther." On the day the *Emanon* was published, I was sitting alone in Bates dining hall, dipping a clove-flavored Constant Comment tea bag in and out of my mug, when a girl came over to ask if I was Joan. She liked what I'd written. Then another girl, and another. I'd found a place in this new world.

A fashion editor at *Glamour* wanted to meet me; a friend at British *Vogue* had tipped her off about me. I didn't know if it was about my background or my style, which, no matter how individual, couldn't make up for the shortness of my legs or the volume of my nose. I went to the *Glamour* offices in my green velvet evening suit. Frances Stein had almond eyes, sharp cheekbones, and sat with that day's *New York Times* open to Peter, bearded, and Katharine Hepburn, wimpled, in a double-page ad for the première of *The Lion in Winter*, which was to take place in exactly one year's time.

"That's my father's movie!" came out of my mouth.

Her eyes went back to the ad, scanning for a name.

"It'll say Keep Films. That's his company with Peter O'Toole."

She examined me across her desk—my London haircut growing out, my round face filled out by Sara Lee, a college mess stuffed into a green-velvet suit and knee-high bronze-leather buttoned boots. I hoped she could tell they were real buttons.

Apparently she could. She took me under her wing and kept me safely there for the entire year that led up to the première of *The Lion in Winter.*

In the spring, Grandpa Norman died in Florida and was buried in New York. My father flew in from London, alone, and I joined him at the funeral.

After a short gathering at Great-aunt Bessie's, he took me back to the Lombardy, a hotel as anonymous as La Trémoille. "The Burtons stay here," he said in the elevator, to make me appreciate where we were. He went straight to the phone at the desk, back to work, back to business. I hadn't tried to phone Tom Wolfe in months, but now I picked up the second line and dialed the number. I almost screamed when he answered. It was the first time I'd heard his voice in two years.

Yes, he'd been in Virginia working on his book, but now he was back. And when could we see each other? "Now?" I asked.

He came to pick me up at the Lombardy. In a white suit. I wished I'd put on more makeup.

Dad grunted at Tom from behind the phone.

"You look like Simone Simon in that black beret," Tom Wolfe said. I liked the French allusion. Would he find out my hair was dirty under the beret?

As we left for dinner, Jules put his hand over the receiver, asked, "Where are you planning to sleep tonight?" caught himself, continued: "What I mean is, are you going back up to Sarah Lawrence tonight, or are you staying at Don's, or Esta's, or do you want to stay here on the sofa? Do you have cab money? Do you have the train fare?"

"I'll make sure she gets wherever she has to go," said Tom.

He took me to a restaurant in the Indian part of Lexington Avenue. Conversation was choppy. I couldn't tell him I'd applied to Sarah Lawrence because of his letters, that I'd come to New York to see him. To write a book and marry him. I transferred all my disappointment onto Sarah Lawrence and diverted him with tales about the endless tubs of Baskin-Robbins and the missing Joseph Campbell.

He took me to see his apartment on Beekman Place. A doorman, moldings, bookshelves, and, on a bookshelf, a photo of a dark-haired woman.

"I think I know her voice," I said. "She answers the phone."

"That must have been the answering service," he said.

So that was it. We didn't have those in London.

He took me to see where he worked, a walk-up studio in the east sixties, a room with bare floors, a typewriter on a round table away from the window, a student lamp.

"This is the book," he said. Reams of triple-spaced typing, channels of white between each line. He read me some pages. I asked for more. He handed me a sheaf of paper and went into the kitchen while I read. I couldn't make much sense of the pages, which started and ended in the middle of the book. I was honored and moved. I looked up to see his blond hair flapping on his forehead.

"It's called *The Electric Kool-Aid Acid Test*," he said.

And then we kissed, an innocent little kiss, and he took me downstairs and put me in a cab.

I went back to the Lombardy to keep my father company on the day of his father's funeral. And to prove that I could be trusted not to have sex with Tom Wolfe.

CHAPTER FIVE

I gave a Marxist reading to my sexual inhibition, which came down to the problem of ownership. I belonged to my father until I could earn my way, and only then could I share my body with a man.

All I needed was a salary. I'd have an erotic future and twice as many lovers as any of the tall Sarah Lawrence girls, and I would live outside the rules.

In the spring of 1968, the anthropology professor announced to the class: "You are no more than your genetic potential." I decided at that instant that I would never reproduce.

A week later, while explaining caste and kinship in America, the professor singled me out: "You, Joan, for instance, can never marry a Rockefeller."

I called my mother in London, crying.

"That's all right, darling," Joyce said. "You can always marry a Rothschild."

Her letters to me were brief, dashed off under the hair dryer at Vidal Sassoon's, mainly about dinners at the White Elephant. Ricki's letters were long, full of jokes and advice:

> The only way to attract the cool is to be cool—hard to achieve at any age, particularly if your shading, like certain stars, is on the

red range. But it can be done. So shine on, Harvest Moon. Give my love to the trolls when you see them. They are as they are and enjoy them as they are. They are there for your entertainment, if not for your solace.

Solace arrived when *Glamour* asked me to replace the book critic during her maternity leave, and Frances Stein hired me as her assistant for the summer. I'd have a salary.

John had cast Anjelica as a fair maiden in *A Walk with Love and Death.* I had two jobs at *Glamour.* Our careers had begun and so had our lives. And I wasn't working for my father; this job was real. I had a desk, and above my desk I pinned fashion drawings from *Elle* by someone named Antonio Lopez.

I earned $50 a week as a fashion assistant and a $350 for each book review, which meant that I didn't have to be a virgin anymore.

Edward was an English hairdresser, not really the man I'd been waiting for, but in the summer of 1968, he crossed the Atlantic to join me in New York. That proved it was me he wanted, not some generalized pussy.

I was living on East 47th Street in the bachelor apartment Uncle Don had rented after his divorce, before he moved to London. And there I was, for a few weeks, a girl with a live-in boyfriend. So this is sex, I thought. And not long after, Is this all there is to sex?

Edward the hairdresser took me to meet Antonio Lopez in his studio behind Carnegie Hall. Here was the man who drew better than Alphonse Mucha, better than Aubrey Beardsley, and he was friendly and funny, a handsome Puerto Rican with a mustache who wore a scarf as a belt and an antique panama over his curly hair, and here was his boyfriend, Juan, and here were two girls, Donna and Jane, who knew Andy Warhol and posed for Antonio, and here was shy Bill Cunningham, who photographed their neighbor Editta Sherman as she danced the Dying Swan in full tutu in the corridor of the Carnegie Hall Studios, though she had to be at least sixty.

I didn't tell my parents about Edward; the hairdresser part would not have pleased them, and he didn't yet have a job in New York. Frances, the volatile editor who'd hired me, was gone within weeks, but continued to hold me close when she went to work for Halston. Julie Britt, a gentler soul, became my boss.

I called in the galleys of *The Electric Kool-Aid Acid Test.* I tried to temper my rave with the measured prose found in men's magazines, but it was still a rave.

The day it was published, my father's friend—and, more important, Tom Wolfe's friend—Gay Talese called to say, "Congratulations, Joanie, you're in print!"

"Do you think Tom will like it?" I asked.

"Why would he see it?" asked Gay.

"Because it's a review of his book," I said.

"No, it's not," said Gay. "It's the piece about kitty litter in *New York* magazine."

I bought the latest *New York* magazine. There it was. Double page. Kitty litter. Shopping. Byline: Joan Buck.

I called 411 and asked for Joan Buck. They gave me a phone number.

"Is that Joan Buck?" I asked.

"And who is calling?" replied Joan Buck, in a slight southern accent.

"I'm Joan Buck, too."

Joan Buck was silent.

"We both have bylines this week, so we have to do something about it."

"If that's the case, we do," Joan Buck said. "What magazine are you in?"

"*Glamour,*" I said, "but it's a book review."

New York trumped *Glamour.*

"I used to work at *Glamour,*" said Joan Buck. "That's where I started."

I felt I was in an alternate universe.

"What year were you born?" I asked, in desperation.

Joan Buck was six years older. Trumped again.

"We could use our middle names," said Joan Buck. "Mine's Hamilton."

"Mine's Juliet," I said, plucking Norman's mother's name out of the air. Ricki had given me a tin hatbox with "JJB" stenciled on it. It was predestined.

"I'll be Joan Juliet Buck," I said. It sounded like John Julius. I liked that.

Edward the hairdresser moved on to a girl at William Morris who represented singers from *Hair*, and I was alone again. At boutique openings, I watched older fashion editors cast about for men, and hoped I'd never be that pathetic. On weekends I lived on sesame breadsticks and pineapple-chunk cottage cheese; at *Glamour* I played dress-ups on my living dolls, the models; at night I read galleys for review between chapters of *War and Peace.*

I returned to Sarah Lawrence in the fall, but Joseph Campbell did not. Anthropology now centered on the Igbo and the Cubeo. The writing teacher told me to walk across the Brooklyn Bridge at dawn, and in the dorm, the girl in the next room vomited in our shared bathroom after every meal.

My parents called before my birthday to ask what I'd be doing. "Nothing," I wailed.

"If nothing's coming to you, do something for someone else," said my father. "That usually works. Call your grandmother."

Nana didn't suggest anything for my birthday, so I invited her to dinner at an almost French place off Park Avenue called the Brasserie. Nana fussed into the bright restaurant, lipstick smeared on her cheeks as rouge, her immense black bosom stuck with sapphires, her hand tight around her bag, new bandages on the tops of her feet; she hauled herself into the little booth with two grunts. To approximate Paris, I ordered onion soup and white wine for both of us. My twentieth birthday, and I was taking my grandmother out on a date. I deserved a medal.

The crust on the onion soup was thick and salty. Nana asked about my life, as grandmothers do. I hated college, I said, hated New York, didn't have a boyfriend. I missed London, I missed Paris.

She touched the napkin to the lipstick on her mouth and sighed. "If your mother had married a handsome man, you'd have been beautiful, and you wouldn't have these emotional difficulties."

Enemy camp. Wrong side. Of course she'd blame him. It's not my father's fault, I thought. It's my mother's fault. She's the one who doesn't hear me, doesn't see me. I launched Ricki at Nana, a rain of Ricki, Ricki whose beaten-up handbag appalled her, Ricki, Ricki, so she'd know I didn't love my mother, her daughter, so I didn't have to say I didn't love her.

After Nana went off in her cab, I walked to Grand Central, and cried all the way back to Sarah Lawrence. Nana and I had the same green eyes, didn't that make me beautiful? In my dorm room the next morning I told myself she had no understanding of my arsenal; she didn't get wit, élan, panache, style. The only currency she understood was beauty.

But even if I didn't have beauty, I could see beauty, I could understand beauty, I could make beauty. I had talent for what they did at the magazine, where I could play with words and pictures, where I felt strong and capable, excited and happy. Where what I suggested usually happened, where the monthly reader ratings proved that my pages were well liked.

I dropped my midweek classes, signed up for anything on a Monday or a Friday, and on the following Tuesday I was back at my desk at *Glamour*—still empty; who could ever fill my place?—where I carried on as if I still had my summer job. I did the same thing on Wednesday and on Thursday, and the same thing every week after that. When it came to work, my confidence was golden. Julie was delighted and no one questioned my presence. Nothing was official, I wasn't getting paid, but it was perfect.

The double life functioned for two months. Uncle Don had moved to London, the apartment on 47th Street was empty, and that's where I slept. I worked during the day, studied at night, and had no dates to distract me. But then my parents and the O'Tooles arrived for *The Lion in Winter*, and there were parties every night, and late tables afterward at Elaine's. Frances Stein and her husband were my guests at the première, and Halston was my date.

I couldn't be at Sarah Lawrence, at *Glamour*, and at parties every night. I knew which one had to go.

"You're paying Sarah Lawrence a fortune for them to tell me I'm bright," I told my father, "but *Glamour* pays me to *be* bright."

It was easy to convince him that my byline on two book reviews meant more than any future degree. "Okay," he said, "you can drop out, but don't write only for the magazine, write for yourself as well." I could live at Don's, but had to be responsible for the rent. I'd have to find a roommate.

With perfect timing, the personnel department at Condé Nast called me in to say that I'd been working there for two months without pay, which was no good for insurance or for Social Security, so they would have to hire me back.

I found a roommate, Sally, a responsible older woman of twenty-eight from Chicago who wanted to model in New York to be near her fiancé, an intern at Roosevelt Hospital. She cleaned up Uncle Don's second bedroom and her fiancé, Steve, came to put together her spindle bed.

Sally was a midwestern adult, composed and regular; she kept to a schedule and made her bed every morning. When she went out for modeling jobs, she removed her glasses and wore a fall. One evening, she cooked an elaborate dinner for Steve and set the table with candles, but he never arrived. The next morning, she found out he'd killed himself. She went into shock. I didn't know what to do, so I persuaded her to go back to Chicago for a while to be with her family.

While Sally was gone, Ricki came to stay with me. I gave her my bed and slept on the couch. I was the hostess now, awed to see Ricki move among my uncle's teak furniture, to hear her brush her teeth in my bathroom, to watch her eat the English muffins I toasted for breakfast, to watch her drink the coffee I made.

"I owe your father my new car," Ricki said. "I gave him a picture, that charcoal self-portrait by Bernard Buffet, and he gave me the money for the car. It's beautiful."

I brought her to *Glamour* to meet my boss Julie and Miki Denhof, the art director I revered; she took me down to Washington, DC, to see her friend James Earl Jones in *The Great White Hope* at the Arena Theater. We rode back to New York City on a train full of troops returning from Vietnam.

Ricki lay in my bed while I crouched on the covers. I wanted her to fall in love with someone new, someone who wasn't delicate and shadowy like John Julius.

"I want you to be happy," I said.

"I'm happiest in homosexual company," she said. I wasn't sure what she meant.

Ricki packed her bag and left for London, Sally returned, as shocked and sad as when she had left. She was determined to stay in New York.

I went back to London for Christmas. Anjelica gave Ricki a Cartier watch bought with the money she'd earned acting in *A Walk with Love and Death.* She was about to play a lady-in-waiting in *Hamlet* and understudy Marianne Faithfull as Ophelia.

At my parents' New Year's Eve party, Ricki wore a silk beauty mark on her décolletage, but left early and alone; she had her car.

Back in New York, I opened a letter from Ricki asking for turquoise tights. It was easy to grab them from the *Glamour* accessory cupboard—no one but Ricki wanted turquoise tights—but instead of posting them, I shoved them in my desk drawer.

On the morning of January 31, I awoke and thought I heard a voice saying I was going to hear bad news. I couldn't move my limbs, I couldn't eat. I bought a blueberry yogurt on the way to the office, and had just set it down on my desk when the phone rang.

International crackle, London, Joyce, scared voice.

"Is Dad all right?"

"Your father's fine," she said, a breath, and then—"Ricki was killed in a car accident."

On January 29, in eastern France, a small truck collided with Ricki's new car. She was not driving; she was not alone. The young man who was driving was in hospital in France with a broken arm.

The person I loved most in the world was dead. I don't think my mother ever forgave my scream.

And then I was standing in line at the bank downstairs to deposit a check, which seemed important to do. The dark green marble walls rose to infinity above me. I was alone among strangers.

And now it was Sally's turn to tell me I had to go home to my family.

In London I went straight to Maida Avenue, and slept in a little room on the top floor of Ricki's house. I remember Anjelica torn open, Tony entirely silent or talking too loud, Allegra uncomprehending, watching Nurse, who moved about as if deaf. Without Ricki's proud mystery, the air in the house was thick and cold. I bought ready-to-cook chickens on Sloane Street, bread and salami and tomatoes, desserts. Grief needs food.

I answered phone calls, opened telegrams that weren't for me, let people in, saw people out. Ricki had left no will. Gladys Hill swooped up to the bedroom and left with Ricki's jewelry, the reliquary, and the necklace of lava stones from Pompeii. It rarely snows in London, but that week it did, and left a white quilt on the metal bed in the garden.

The French authorities would not let Ricki's body return to England until they had seen the purchase papers for the gold Cartier watch; it was a matter of customs duty. And so our treasures betray us.

Ricki would have been forty in three months. I was twenty, Anjelica was seventeen, Tony was eighteen, Allegra was four. Who would take Allegra? My parents could do nothing after the rift with John. Leslie Waddington offered to take Allegra, then Gladys announced that John had decided Allegra and Nurse would go live at St. Clerans.

Back home at Chester Street, my mother was napping. My father stood behind the little desk in his study, fiddling with rubber bands, his cigar case, a penknife. He couldn't look at me.

"Ricki's car . . ." he began.

"I know, she told me in New York, you gave her the money for it," I said. "But it's not your fault. It's not."

He put his arms around me. We hugged, then he stood back and said, "Okay, now, pull yourself together, you're coming to dinner with us and Gore Vidal."

Without a body there could still be a memorial service, and someone decided that a Quaker meeting would best convey the inclusive nature of Ricki's beliefs. It was held at the Friends Meeting House on Saint Martin's Lane.

The congregation included everyone we knew, and Quaker strangers, the only people who didn't care where Jules Buck was standing, who didn't care whether John Huston had arrived, who didn't dread being caught between the two.

John Julius stood by a column.

John walked in. Jules went to shake his hand, and John turned away.

John Julius went to John. John took his hand.

It's all the same two names, I thought, round and round, John and Jules and John Julius.

Ricki's funeral, no Ricki, not even a body, just an idea of Ricki.

I tried to see Ireland from the window of the plane on the way back to New York. Richard Avedon reached me at the office. He'd so loved Ricki, he said, he'd just photographed her for *Vogue*, but now the pictures would never run. When I went to see him in his studio, Avedon was in tears. "Here," he said, and showed me two neat piles of prints, assemblages of pictures taken in Ricki's house. Ricki's hand hovering over the test tubes she used as vases, Ricki in the background as Nurse fed Allegra, Ricki as a blur by the Venetian bed in the living room, Anjelica and Allegra and Tony lying on it like royals. Everything I wanted to remember and hold about her, just out of focus, out of reach.

"You should have one of these," said Avedon, his hand over the thick pile of 12-by-24-inch prints on the right. "These were the first ones, they're not so good," he said, and then, pointing at the left-hand pile, "These are the new ones. See how the color's much, much better?"

"Yes, it is," I said. I could tell. Much better.

Avedon's hand swooped over to the right-hand pile of imperfect prints, the ones with bad colors, plucked off one inscribed "To Tony," took a pen, changed the "Tony" to a "Joan," and handed it to me in a thin envelope.

A gust of February wind in the street snapped the envelope in two with a loud crack. At home, I saw the color had chipped in radiating lines, like broken glass.

I told my father the story on the phone. "He didn't put cardboard in the envelope for a twelve-by-twenty-four-inch?" he said. "That's just crappy. Fuck Richard Avedon."

But I had the things she'd given me. A red chiffon William Morris scarf from Liberty, enamel belt buckles, a red Mexican belt with silver nail heads, the tin hatbox with my foreshadowed initials on it, "JJB."

I tried to tame New York by cooking dinner, by going out on dates. I found a temporary French boyfriend, an heir. Despite Nana's efforts, I avoided the son of her neighbor Mrs. Lapidus. I went to bed with a social Italian American businessman, a French photographer, and the French art director of *Esquire,* Jean-Paul Goude, whom I liked best. Unfortunately, he only liked black girls. Sex felt dangerous, and was not the fun I'd expected. I had trouble calibrating the correct proportions of cool and desire, indifference and emotion.

I cried when I was home; Sally was always home, and cried all the time. She didn't dare try to be a model anymore, she didn't have a job, and in the spring, she moved to the East Village.

Bob Richardson came loping into *Glamour,* tall, skinny, and sublimely tragic. Here was the genius of fashion photography. He was forty-one, dressed like a Bob Dylan song come to life, dressed, in fact, like Bob Dylan on the cover of *Nashville Skyline,* an old leather vest over a tired chambray shirt, a flat-topped hat over his gray curls. Cheekbones sharp as triangles, lower lip in a full pout, he paused before each word, like a psychic, an analyst. I didn't know he was stoned, on speed, and schizophrenic. I only knew that he was the one who'd taken the Greek photos I'd loved so much in Paris *Vogue.*

He shot a fashion story for us on Staten Island, and raged that the model was not finding the essence of the Gypsy student prince he'd asked her to be. Anjelica could do that, she would adore this man, I thought. In my eagerness to make the photos more dramatic, I accidentally set fire to a field of dry grass.

That night I dreamed I was in an antiques shop with Ricki. She pressed a small gold heart into my palm and said, "This is mine, but I'm giving it to you for a little while; please take care of it."

In the morning, Anjelica called to ask if she could she live with me. *Hamlet* was coming to New York for three months.

We were together again. There was always that place of play, that other world waiting for us; we played so as not to cry. If we got silly enough we wouldn't have to know that Ricki was dead.

We made Uncle Don's apartment into a mystical fun house. I painted Uncle Don's bedroom a blue that I thought was the same as the study in St. Clerans, but it came out too dark, so I nailed the William Morris cotton with its thistles and burrs to the wall and taped up Indian scarves around it. Anjelica painted the second bedroom a glossy mauve pink, to make it a toy, to make it her own. We bought rubber snakes from a joke shop and draped them on bamboo poles, took down the glass globe from the dining room ceiling so Anjelica could paint a moon face on it, and set it on the table as art.

We went out with the French photographers and art directors whom I'd gathered around me, ate surf and turf at Max's Kansas City, and if no one had invited us there, we perched in booths with acquaintances to make meals of the free chickpeas. One minute Anjelica and I were feral children unleashed on the city, the next giddy divas dressed for conquest. She was tall and even thinner than before; I was chubby.

When *Harper's Bazaar* wanted to photograph her, I took the call and insisted that they could use only Bob Richardson. They fell in love, as I knew they would, and lived together for four years. If I'd known then that he was schizophrenic, I wouldn't have sent Anjelica into four years of purgatory.

My boss at *Glamour* sent me to a diet doctor who put me on pink, mauve, and blue amphetamines. 138 pounds, 135, 131, 128, 126, 128 (shit), 125, 124, 123, 121. I ate a nightly steak the size of the palm of my hand, and cooked it in Mazola. 118 pounds, 117, 116, 114.

Anjelica left for Ireland, and a young Austrian model named Eva Gschopf took over the second bedroom. The French photographer Guy Bourdin was in love with her; her boyfriend was Guy's young Vietnamese assistant, Duc. Eva was enchanting, solemn and light. Her limbs were so tapered and her fingers so fine that she seemed like a drawing. She talked about the woods around Vienna, the woods full of tall trees. We went to the top of the Empire State Building so she could see the sunset. She thought modeling was stupid, and loved to dance with the hippies at Bethesda Fountain in Central Park on Sundays, where she would launch herself into the densest knot of strangers and take off, eyes closed, borne by the music, in rapture.

I didn't like it among the hippies: too much dope, a smell of crushed bananas, sinister boys with blue prism glasses. I couldn't tell the difference between one kind of music and another, I preferred to dance with people I knew, and I hated the clueless hippie style. A print of brown and purple leaves, in midsummer? That leather hat plunked on your head? Black shoes with a lace granny dress?

I'd taken to wrapping my head with scarves and wearing only Silk Road treasures from Sam Hilu's Odyssey warehouse, caftans and Tibetan robes, an embroidered coat that smelled of goat, peasant blouses, belts hung with bells. I'd wear each thing once, Eva would admire it, I'd sell it to her and then buy something else with the money. "Now I look like I have really traveled," Eva said. "My suitcases will be full!"

One night as I ate my diet dinner and Eva ate a plate of beans, I had a vision of a tree. A dark, tall tree that scared me. I'd read my Jung. The life force, I thought, nature: I needed to become more grounded.

The pills were working. 113, 112, 110, 109. I spoke very fast. My parents were coming to Washington, DC, for the première of a musical remake of *Goodbye, Mr. Chips*, starring Peter and Petula Clark. It didn't sound like a very good idea to me; Petula Clark was so five years ago, and could Peter even sing?

Eva was in bed with her boyfriend, Duc, when I pushed open the door to the second bedroom to say I'd be in DC until Sunday morning.

At the hotel in DC, my father said, "You really have lost weight, but what's the schmatta on your head?"

He liked the Palestinian wedding caftan I wore to the première no better. I didn't like the film, which was directed by Herbert Ross, a choreographer. Another first-timer, to please Peter.

We flew back to New York the next morning. I wanted them to approve of my new life. To see where Anjelica had stayed, and how I'd painted Don's old bedroom. They wanted to check up on me. "We want to meet Eva," my father said, "get a measure of who she is." I hoped they'd like her. I'd have to hide the thing about the hippies in the park. They wouldn't like my gang of French photographers, or Antonio and Juan. I didn't tell them I was in love with an art director who didn't like white girls.

My apartment was empty. No Eva, no Duc. Eva's bed was made. *The Magical Mystery Tour* was on the record player turntable, the needle on the record, in the middle of "The Fool on the Hill."

"Take us to meet her in the park if that's where she is," said my father. "Today's the day. We're busy with the picture the rest of the week." I had to risk it.

My mother donned a safari suit for the expedition to Central Park.

"She's not a hippie, she's a famous model," I said, doing the full PR spin on Eva. "But you know how foreigners like to look at everything new that's happening in America."

We could hear the music as I coaxed them across the grass, and when we got to Bethesda Fountain, my father's eyes went from the Jamaican steel bands to the white boys in blue glasses to the girls in nightgowns and farmer hats to the mixed-race men wearing dresses, and over to the men playing African drums. I caught the hippie smell of pot and rotting cream cheese and squashed bananas, I saw it all through his eyes, a jangle of freaks bathed in criminal clouds of pot smoke.

Joyce was looking around with her model face, mouth half open, eyes wide, prepared to appreciate.

"Let's get out, now," said Dad. "Cut, finish, over."

Then he said, "Get her out of the apartment. I'll pay the other half of the rent."

"You can't buy my friends away from me," I shouted, and I ran out of the park in a fury. I couldn't let him go on controlling me. I'd be twenty-one in a few weeks. I had a job. My friends would see me through.

The apartment was still empty when I got home.

That night I left a birthday party and went down to Max's Kansas

City, where I sat on a ledge with my heart pounding until one of the French gang told me to go inside to see Mickey, who hung up the phone behind the bar and told me, "Go home, right now."

Something terrible had happened. I took a cab to the Lombardy to get my father. Joyce answered the door of the suite. "It's about Eva, I have to go home, and I'm scared."

"Your father's already taken his pill," she said. "He's out for the count." She picked up her bag and came with me to Don's apartment.

I sprinted toward the phone, which was ringing in my bedroom. It was a German model I didn't know, Margrit Ramme.

"Prepare yourself," she said. "Eva is dead."

"How can she be dead?"

"I don't know," said Margrit.

I hung up. My mother lit a cigarette. "Not again," she said.

I put her in my bed and took the couch, where I lay sleepless, frozen with dread, another chunk of the world broken off. This couldn't be happening again, the third time in ten months.

In the morning, Eva's modeling agent, Eileen Ford, called to tell me that Eva had died during what she called "a sex and drugs orgy" in a hippie commune.

"That's not Eva," I said. "She's not like that."

Joyce said, "Don't shout at Eileen Ford."

I did as I was told and packed Eva's bags with the clothes I'd sold her, and gave them to two messengers who arrived too soon. I asked Al Aronowitz, a journalist at the *New York Post,* to investigate for me, and he found out the full story. She'd gone with another model to look for a friend in Woodstock and they'd ended up at a commune in Hurley, where she climbed trees with a boy named George. On Sunday evening, Eva climbed around the rotted branches on the north side of a tall pine to get a better view of the sunset; a branch broke and she fell fifty feet. The commune had no phone, so the hippies put her in a station wagon and drove her down the mountain to a hospital, where she died of a punctured lung.

She'd fallen from a tree. Was that the tree I'd seen?

The story in the *New York Post* was headlined, "The Girl of the Sunsets, Dead in a Fall from a Tree." I thought Al's story would clear her name, would make people see it wasn't drugs, but her friends preferred to think she'd wanted to fly.

I told my parents I wanted to come home to London. I weighed a hundred pounds.

My twenty-first birthday party at Annabel's had only my parents' friends in attendance. I held up a narrow champagne flute and made a toast: "To my best friends, in urns."

CHAPTER SIX

Marooned in the shallows of Belgravia, still in shock, I perched in my bedroom while my parents went on location in Venezuela for *Murphy's War*, their very own *African Queen* set on a tramp steamer at the mouth of the Orinoco River, with Peter as Bogart and Siân in the Katharine Hepburn role.

I didn't want to try for a British university, and I was forbidden to work by our family doctor, Patrick Woodcock, until I'd gained back some of the weight lost to the diet pills. I had a generous allowance and use of Bert the driver. All I wanted was to find out why three people had died around me in less than a year. The roommate's fiancé was a distant incident; Ricki's death was a loss that I'd never get over; Eva's fall from the tree was incomprehensible. Had someone willed all this to happen? Had my unconscious, my "It," caused the chain of events? My parents looked at me with concern, my mother inquired if the relationship with Eva was more than friendship, but no one mentioned a therapist, not even Dr. Woodcock.

I concentrated on lunching with girlfriends at Aretusa and shopping for old clothes at the antiques markets with the money that my father's secretary, Maggie, handed me.

Derek Coombs came up from downstairs to give me my first assignment since I'd left *Glamour*. He was going to stand for Parliament to represent a district of Birmingham near his family's stores. Eighteen-year-olds would be voting for the first time, and he wanted me to draft his letter to them. I was an American Democrat, Derek was a British Conservative, but he was family, and it was just one page.

The propaganda letter I wrote to move eighteen-year-old British boys and girls to vote for Derek Coombs was printed in blue ink, with Derek's picture on the upper left. Pat Coombs, her friends, and I canvassed around Birmingham wearing blue horse-show rosettes, smiling over clipboards. People who'd lived in the same prefabricated government housing since the war spat at us. We drove around in a van painted Conservative blue and delivered our messages through a loudspeaker. "Look at the pound in your pockit!" I declaimed in a Midlands accent. "A vowte for the Conservatives is a vowte for freedom and democracy in our country!"

My parents returned from Venezuela before the election, Joyce wearing pre-Columbian jadeite beads, Jules full of sudden plans to buy a copper mine.

The Conservatives won in a landslide on June 18. Derek Coombs gave my "Letter to the Eighteen-Year-Old Voter" full credit for the Tory victory, though he'd won his seat by a mere 120 votes. My fame spread among my friends. The grandson of the late press baron Lord Beaverbrook wanted to go into politics and thought I should write his speeches. Tim was blond, blue-eyed, impatient, and rude, which I took as a mark of integrity. Only phonies pretended to be nice.

Lunch, dinner, bed, dinner, bed.

Tim worked for an Australian named Rupert Murdoch, owner of *News of the World* and the *Sun*, overseeing the launch of twenty-one magazines on the British market. He had a modern townhouse by the Thames in a development with an Olde English name, and already, at twenty-seven, an ex-wife. Tim made me the editor of one of Murdoch's new publications, a direct-mail heat-set web-offset magazine wrapped around classified advertising for temporary employment agencies. The job got me the National Union of Journalists card that I needed to work in England.

I had a staff of five, none happy to answer to a twenty-one-year-old. The magazine was for, and about, temporary secretaries, which seemed a sad, old-fashioned job. I wasn't going to name it *Secretary.* Or *Assistant.* Or *Temp,* or *Tempo,* or *Temporary,* or *Part-Time.* This was a magazine for young women who worked. *Working Woman* sounded too dreary. I blithely called it *Working Girl,* unaware that "working girl" was a euphemism for "hooker."

My parents were so delighted with this man in my life, the first one they'd actually seen in the flesh, that they rented an apartment for me in Roebuck House, a modern building on Stag Place, ugly but close enough to the Houses of Parliament that, should I marry Tim, should he be elected to Parliament, should he live with me rather than in the development on the river, he would be within the division bell area and able to cast his vote in Parliament at a moment's notice.

"You can keep both places," Joyce daydreamed aloud. Beyond any speculation as to romantic or political destinies, Roebuck House, Stag Place, London SW1, was a good address for someone named Buck, and it had twenty-four-hour doormen. Jules wanted me to be under surveillance, married or not.

Long before the spring launches, Rupert Murdoch aborted all his new magazines and put his money into radio instead. I broke up with the future politician and called my friends in Paris. Guy Bourdin arranged for me to see Francine Crescent, the editor in chief of Paris *Vogue.*

It was 1970; London fashion had moved beyond the sharp-edged innocence of Happy Dolly Bird to the bulky handmade rags of Distressed Peasant, and skirts were long. I was happy to have found a look that combined my great-grandparents' frontier spirit with my earlier Jewish heritage, while giving a nod to the possible Comanche ancestor, and also subtly evoking the pain of the Third World. I wore a heavily distressed suede outfit to my ankles, its laced bodice complemented by laced platform boots, my head wrapped to suggest Ottoman harems over a base note of shtetl. Jules called the look "Downtown Warsaw" when he wasn't saying "You look like a bag lady."

I arrived at the *Vogue* mansion on the Place du Palais-Bourbon in my buckskin costume, lugging a portfolio full of tear sheets. The mansion's immense doors were painted the same midnight blue as our front door on Chester Street, and I knew this was where I belonged.

Francine Crescent was a woman around forty in a canary yellow suit. The neckband of her sheer white sweater had the texture of a gauze bandage, the "ac" of the André Courrèges logo like a Band-Aid floating askew over her collarbone. The look was so far from Distressed Peasant that I wondered if she knew what year it was. Her office looked out over the Place du Palais-Bourbon and was separated by a glass wall from a large room full of dour fashion editors in V-neck sweaters and kilts, with dachshunds and cocker spaniels napping in baskets under their desks.

Francine Crescent turned the plastic pages of my portfolio. I listened to the click of her nails, studied the clashing yellows of her suit and her hair. Can't she see that canary and lemon don't mix?

When she looked up, she saw a sneering turbaned Levantine in torn suede.

The pages slid along. My book reviews, a piece about a hip East Village hairdresser, fashion sittings where I'd been the assistant. The dummy issue of *Working Girl.*

"You do fashion, but you edit and you write also?"

I nodded. "*Oui.*"

"But, in French also?"

"Yes," I said patiently, "but these are American and English publications, so they asked me to write in English."

With a frown, she exclaimed, "Ah! But—you are a professional!"

I modestly lowered my eyes.

The editor in chief closed the book, shook her head sadly, and said, "We have no room for professionals at *Vogue.* And anyway, I've already hired a young woman for the job. She's an ambassador's daughter, so she has good taste."

I marched out of her glass enclosure and past the thin-lipped editors in kilts, making as much noise as possible with my platform boots. I'll be back, I thought, you'll see.

The young woman she hired was Winston Churchill's granddaughter.

Guy Bourdin was sorry about *Vogue*, and asked me to work for him. "You can be my gag lady," he said.

"Bag lady?" I asked. Not him, too.

"Gag lady," he said. "You can invent the gags."

We both mourned Eva. He was now living with her best friend, Sibylle. It would make a kind of family. He'd been the star of Paris *Vogue* since his first accessories photographs had launched him fifteen years earlier, when he was still a painter; he'd posed models in hats with a butcher's shop display of calves' heads. His Charles Jourdan shoe ads, much copied, appeared to show young girls who had just been murdered. He preferred his models to look like dolls, sleeping dolls, dead dolls.

The apartment at Roebuck House was rented to an American journalist, and I moved across the Channel to work for Guy in Paris, the center of the world. Andy Warhol was there making a film called *L'Amour,* starring Karl Lagerfeld. Yves Saint Laurent was the king of fashion, Guy Bourdin was a genius, and I was his gag lady.

"You can do makeup, can't you?" Guy asked.

The only makeup I knew how to do was the masklike Peking Opera style I'd learned in theater at Sarah Lawrence, which was fine with Guy. He bought me a full set of Leichner greasepaint that included endless shades of red, to create lips like those on dolls.

I used the greasepaint on myself to make a white face, with red around my eyes. In China, I felt, there was a great, focused purity. I'd read a book about Mao's Long March, and begun another about the Cultural Revolution. The fact that Mao had eliminated the Peking Opera and sent all artists and intellectuals to practice self-criticism while doing hard labor in rehabilitation camps was immaterial. I decided to dress as simply as a Chinese peasant, with a workman's jacket over a long denim skirt, complemented by high-heeled green boots two sizes too big, a gift from a fashion editor at *20 Ans.* My hair still hidden under a tightly wrapped turban of printed nylon, I looked dignified yet authentic. No one said, "Downtown Warsaw."

Guy's studio was in the Marais, a ground-floor room without running water, entirely occupied by a papier-mâché moon seven feet in diameter perched on a wooden scaffold, made for an ad campaign. Guy's assistant Jean-Claude spent most of his time repainting the moon. Too brown, Guy would say, too gray, too dark, too blue, too yellow, and at last a "*Oui*" to a passable version of lunar white. The moon took up so much space that *Vogue* had to rent a second studio for Guy to work in.

Guy was a squat man with the face, body, and hair of a Breughel peasant, the one with the pitchfork. He was superstitious, strange, and difficult. He spoke in a whine. I wasn't sure what would amuse him; he didn't laugh a lot, and the pressure to come up with gag ideas emptied my mind. I did most of my shopping for props at the taxidermist Deyrolle and sewed the heads, wings, and claws of birds onto hats. I was shamed by my incapacity to create anything more startling than hats with bits of dead bird on them.

My ankle-length denim ensemble wasn't Communist China enough, so I went to the BHV, a department store dedicated to the tools of the workingman, where I rooted through the jewelers' smocks and welders' helmets to find garage-men's overalls, in bright blue cotton as thick as tenting, that zipped from crotch to collar. They made me look like a revolutionary engineer, which gave some thematic support to the full Chinese makeup, while the wrapped head added the suggestion of Rosie the Riveter toiling away in a wartime Allied factory.

Guy, delighted by my new costume, announced that I had to come with him to *Vogue* to approve the clothes they wanted him to shoot.

"If they are too bourgeois, too conventional, you must say so, right there in front of them, out loud. Speak frankly," he ordered.

We marched through the midnight blue doors and up the staircase, Guy in his dun brown Breughel peasant smock, me in an effusive combination of Peking Opera, factory worker, and Hattie McDaniel.

Hanging racks had been pulled into the center of the room, where the dachshunds wriggled under desks. Francine Crescent sat behind her glass window in the back, wearing another banal turtleneck.

The editors were the same dour lot I'd seen two months before. They wore pleated skirts, navy blue shoes, and had not been to the hairdresser's. They glared at me above little smiles. The ambassador's daughter was absent, presumably out combing the boutiques for more banal fashion with which to bore the Paris *Vogue* reader.

An editor presented the clothes; she held up one limp printed dress after another, then a flock of navy blue suits. Guy squinted at me.

"Alors, Jo-An?" he murmured. *"Vous aimez?"*

I shook my head.

"Qu'est ce que vous pensez?" he asked in an unfamiliar tone of respect.

I shook my head harder and crossed my arms. I had to remain impenetrable. We were there to jostle the minor nobility of *Vogue* with our secret language of peasant and factory worker.

"Alors?" he asked.

I took a deep breath and said, *"Non."*

"Non?" asked Guy.

"Non, non, non." The same word De Gaulle had used to keep England out of the Common Market, now turned against the French. "*Non,*" I added, to make my point.

Francine Crescent came out of her glass cage to confer with Guy, while I stood as immobile as a blue canvas statue. Did she recognize me under the makeup?

One of the editors, a woman with a very long last name, promised she'd have more clothes, new clothes, different clothes to show him in two days, but what clothes did he want?

Guy looked at me. "What do we want, Jo-An?" he asked.

"We want *really* beautiful clothes," I said. The editors looked at me in my Peking Opera factory getup. I looked at the editors in their navy blue shoes. Guy took me away.

My friends hated *Vogue.* They lost photographs, they chose clothes with tin eyes, they put the wrong girls on the cover. The magazine was overdressed and out of date, dedicated to a world of privilege and exclusion. It should have been the summit of all that was beautiful, and instead, it belonged to brilliantined executives with Saint-Tropez tans who were always grabbing half the free airplane tickets for their own holidays, leaving the photographer and the model to soldier on with only a suitcase of clothes and a curling iron in the wrong voltage.

Jane Gozzett took me foraging in the shabbiest of all flea markets at the Porte de Montreuil, where I proudly paid 70 francs, which translated to £7 or $12, for an Art Deco chaise longue covered in equally Art Deco cut velvet.

Antonio and Juan now lived in an Art Deco apartment that belonged to their friend Karl Lagerfeld, a plump German of exquisite taste who designed for Chloé and other ready-to-wear houses. We all sat at the Café de Flore, watched by an old beatnik painter named Shirley Goldfarb, who wore a pair of sunglasses with windshield wipers on them. We actively ignored her, gossiped about the sex life of Marlene Dietrich—Karl knew everything—dined in a huge group at La Coupole, and went to old films at the Cinémathèque. Karl bought us magazines at the Drugstore Saint-Germain just before it closed at 2:00 a.m., along with manicure kits and lighters and whatever else caught our eyes. Karl paid for everyone and everything, like my father did, but I felt free.

Anjelica and Bob Richardson came to Paris, looking magnificently tragic. Anjelica was modeling, mostly in Milan, and Bob was trying to get work in Paris. He said he'd work with me. I told the editor of *20 Ans* that the great Bob Richardson would do a story for them, but only with me, and only my dream of China. Isabelle Weingarten, a model who'd starred in a Robert Bresson movie, posed for us in the Chinese clothes I owned, with one Mao suit from the Chinese shop in Saint-Germain to show the reader that she, too, could be Chinese. I put Isabelle in the satin Shanghai pajamas from a London antiques market, with a stuffed monkey on her shoulder. Bob's dream and mine coincided: I wanted Isabelle to be Anna May Wong, he wanted her to be an opium addict.

Guy found out about the Chinese pages before they came out, and confronted me at the top of the stairs outside his apartment door, and that was the end of the gag lady. I styled sittings for *20 Ans* and supplemented the freelance money by doing makeup on brides who hired me because they didn't know any better.

"You should be writing," said my father. But I was living. I knew men who had been arrested in May 1968, who had been beaten by the police, and was actually sleeping with one of them. I knew Jim Haynes, a father of the counterculture and the proud founder of *Suck*, the European sex paper. Jim said that radical pornography was the weapon of the revolution. I liked the theory, avoided Jim's orgies, but loved waving around a magazine called *Suck*.

On one of those February days when Paris families have left for the ski slopes and the weather perversely turns warm, I was helping Jim sell *Suck* outside the Café de Flore. Business was brisk. A man and a young woman crossed the Boulevard Saint-Germain; he was Michael White, a theater producer Jim knew from London.

"This is Anna," said Michael White.

She wore a gigantic skunk fur coat, her hair was in a bob, her eyes hidden behind sunglasses. I wore Chinese makeup, a blue silk pinafore, and matching clogs. Anna Wintour was an assistant fashion editor at *Harper's & Queen*. She seemed terribly shy.

The magazine *20 Ans* photographed me as their girl of the month, which enhanced my aura for a few weeks and attracted Maurice, a beautiful man, half Indonesian and half Dutch, who mysteriously lived in a chic converted maid's room above Yves Saint Laurent's apartment on the Rue de Babylone. Maurice was always just out of reach, even in bed; he liked boys as well as girls. He wore a mint-green suit from Yves Saint Laurent and a bracelet by Claude Lalanne that was a bronze cast of his lips, a gift from someone who wanted him, as did we all.

Six weeks later, Jane Gozzett confessed that she'd spent the night with Maurice, and then my friend Manuella, Anouk Aimée's daughter, fell in love with him. Every person I knew in Paris, London, and New York, with the exception of Anjelica, was in bed with Maurice.

I wasn't used to having that much competition, and from both sexes. After some nights of sleepless rage, I packed my bags, sent the Art Deco chaise longue to London, and finally moved into the apartment at Roebuck House.

"I did better in Paris once I moved to London, and so will you," said Jules.

His cigars had reached epic proportions. Despite the rift, he'd kept the humidor from John Huston topped with a silver plaque that read, "To The Only Buck Worth a Million." Among the compact Uppmans and Romeo y Julietas, the new long Montecristo As had to lie sideways, nine and a quarter inches of blue brown tobacco as smoothly finished as his suits.

He carried the giant cigar in his left hand, unlit.

"Don't wave that thing around," my mother would say. But it was his scepter. He handed out cigars to every man around him, even the ones who didn't smoke. He was generous, and there was always something to celebrate.

In Jules's Napoleon green office at Keep Films, Peter's awards were aligned on the mantelpiece; the Golden Globes that looked as if they'd been dipped in syrup, the perfect miniatures of Donatello's *David* that the Taormina Festival gave if the star guaranteed his presence. Oscar nomination plaques on the wall. No Oscars.

None of the statuettes were for Jules. He made everything happen, he didn't need to take anything as crass as credit, he said. Discretion. Low-key is the key to class. He worked hard putting together the pictures, but he worked even harder at taking care of Peter, his stellar prize, his unruly partner, half of Keep Films. At first, Peter called him "my business partner." By the end, he was calling him "my manager." But that was at the end, when the admiration and the loyalty had died.

Jules and Joyce moved from half a house on Chester Street to half a mansion on Upper Belgrave Street. The Fernand Léger and a fine pink Milton Avery bird were joined by an impressive Ben Nicholson, each painting set off by its own picture light under a discreet brass shade. The reception rooms were as imposing as those of an embassy; in the library, my father's eighteenth-century globes—one of the Earth, one of the sky—were aligned on top of the bookcases, along with his armillary sphere showing the progress of the planets.

His enthusiasm grew boundless, as did his generosity. After Jack Hawkins lost his voice to throat cancer and could no longer act, Jules brought him into Keep Films and gave him half his desk. To supervise the flurry of new projects, he hired a serious young producer named David Korda, a nephew of his idol Sir Alexander Korda; David's arrival imparted the heft of history to Keep Films.

I went back to Paris for couture week, met Andy Warhol and Paul Morrissey, became a slightly plump It Girl. At Fred Hughes's birthday party at Club 7 on the Rue Saint-Anne, I sat between Shirley Goldfarb the beatnik painter from the Café Flore, and René Ricard, an angry young poet from the Factory who wore kohl around his eyes. They hated each other on sight and traded insults while Andy took Polaroids. I knew I had to remember everything everyone said; I pushed away my wine and asked for Perrier. Later, I wrote about that dinner, sent the story into a *Daily Telegraph* competition, and won a prize for it.

I was twenty-two and finally having fun. Fred, Andy, and Paul asked me to be the London correspondent for their magazine *Interview.* I'd never kneel to pin a model's hem for a fashion sitting again. The only job I wanted was features editor of British *Vogue,* but it belonged to the brilliant and beautiful Oxford graduate Marina Warner.

Karl Lagerfeld took me and Pat Cleveland, a young model Antonio had brought to Paris, to see some boys who sold old couture near the Place de la République. Pat and I took turns trying on clothes; Karl decided which of us looked best in what. I bagged a Marcel Rochas suit and then held my breath at the sight of a small black crepe jacket, edged with curlicues of gold leather, cut like the Duchess of Windsor's Mainbochers. Pat Cleveland grabbed it; to my relief, on her it looked like a costume. She handed it over to me. It fit perfectly. The shape hugged my waist, the arms were the right length, and I looked exactly the way I had always wanted to look.

"It's yours," said Karl. "It could be Schiaparelli."

And I could be the Duchess of Windsor.

My father was right; all I'd had to do to become prized in Paris was move back to London.

Soon, Karl showed his shoe collection for Mario Valentino in Antonio's new apartment on the Boulevard Saint-Germain. I sat on the floor with Anna Piaggi from Italian *Vogue,* who wore a pink hussar uniform and a lacquered pillbox hat shooting out black feather antennae. The living room was crowded: fashion editors, Paloma Picasso and her Argentineans, Jane Gozzett, models, hangers-on. A raised runway ran from the mantelpiece to the center of the room.

Pat Cleveland walked down the runway toward us, naked, a mauve feather nestled like a falling petal in her pubic hair. "Don't look at me, look at the shoes!" she sang. Our heads snapped down to her feet.

More models came out, in leotards, wearing suede shoes with patent heels as viciously high as a sado-masochistic Allen Jones sculpture. The models hopped as if they were on hot coals.

The music changed, and a tiny round person with long black hair staggered onto the runway in equally high heels. She wore a black leotard and laddered black tights and, after two faltering steps, eased herself up onto the mantelpiece. It was Shirley Goldfarb, our stalker from the Café Flore.

Warmed by the spotlight, she began to sing "Over the Rainbow" in a state of pure joy that I recognized as the way I'd felt on the set of *Greyfriars Bobby.*

The fashion audience burst into titters that turned to laughter. Shirley Goldfarb soldiered on to the end of the song, refusing to acknowledge that she was the joke. "*C'est grotesque,*" I heard from my left.

After the show, Shirley was nowhere to be seen.

"Did you think that was too degenerate?" Karl asked me.

"Yes," I said. I didn't want to be her friend, but I didn't like to see her humiliated.

His assistant said, "It's like the dwarves at the Spanish court—"

Karl interrupted him. "In the eighteenth century, noblewomen at court wore monkeys on their shoulder to make themselves look more beautiful in contrast."

I hadn't realized the fashion world was that cruel.

~

That summer of 1971, *The Ruling Class* was shooting at Twickenham Studios with locations at a stately home up north. A young Hungarian director, Peter Medak, had taken Jules and Peter O'Toole to a matinee of Peter Barnes's play, and O'Toole fell in love with the fourteenth Earl of Gurney. Peter had twice played King Henry II; he'd played officers in prey to various delusions, elegant playboys, adventurers, even three angels of God, all at once, but here—at last—was a part that used every shade of his repertoire from light comedy to Gothic horror. It was perfect material for Keep Films. Jules missed the second act while he bought the film rights on the phone, and before the curtain came down, *The Ruling Class* was theirs.

United Artists financed the film on the condition that Peter play Don Quixote in their musical *Man of La Mancha.* Jules agreed.

The Ruling Class was a surreal critique of the British aristocracy interrupted by vaudeville routines and a spot of Verdi. The story begins as the thirteenth Earl of Gurney dons a tutu from a hatbox for a spot of autoerotic asphyxiation that kills him when he accidentally kicks away a fine set of library steps, which leads to the release of his son Jack from the insane asylum where he's been living quietly as Jesus Christ; enter Peter in a white suit and flowing blond Christ locks. Once cured of his holy delusion, Jack embraces evil and becomes Jack the Ripper. They were making the film they'd always dreamed of.

I inherited the props from the accidental suicide scene, the library steps, and the tutu hatbox, which was an antique Louis Vuitton. The curtain from Potemkin's study in *Great Catherine* ran along the living room window at Roebuck House, the sofa was my old bamboo bed painted black, the coffee table had once been Nana's. Between the movie-prop swag and the repurposed family furniture, only the little twelve-dollar Art Deco chaise longue proclaimed my personal taste. I wore my hair like Ricki, tried to cook like Ricki, made dinner for Manolo Blahnik, who was beginning to make shoes, Eric Boman, who took photographs, Peter Schlesinger, who painted, and Grace Coddington, who wore good hats and was a fashion editor at British *Vogue.* I was *Interview*'s London girl, I wrote little texts for *Harpers & Queen*, I reported from the House of Lords for underground newspapers. When I had nothing to do, I went to the Keep Films office to help the secretaries sign photos of Peter for the fans. We could all do Peter's signature.

This wasn't quite a life. I didn't have a job, I didn't have a boyfriend, I dreamed that Ricki was alive, of Eva falling from a tree. A friend gave me Marie Louise von Franz's *Problem of the Puer Aeternus*, in which she explains that people who refuse the demands of earthbound life can be violently called back to earth, in falls from mountains or from trees. The book sent me to a Jungian therapist, who paid close attention to what I said about Ricki and Eva.

"You are going to put up photographs of Ricki and Eva by your bed so you see them before you go to sleep and first thing when you wake up. If you live with them consciously, they won't be ghosts anymore. And you are going to bed with paper and a pencil, so you can write down your dreams."

I taped Ricki and Eva onto the wallpaper. Eva sleeping in the back of the car on the way to a sitting in Connecticut, Ricki in photos that Dad had taken, none of them posed: Ricki in profile, Ricki with John, Ricki in the same shot as me, but not with me. From morning to morning they stopped being ghosts.

As I began to make peace with my dead, Maurice, the elusive seducer whom everyone in Paris had desired, died in Brazil after falling from a cliff.

In the spring of 1972, *The Ruling Class* was invited into competition at the Cannes Film Festival, and Jules announced it was time for me to start playing the game. "No more downtown Warsaw for you," he said, and took me to the Saint Laurent boutique on Bond Street. It was run by the fearsome, impeccably cool Lady Rendlesham, who recognized him and greeted him with what was, for her, warmth. He asked if he could make a quick phone call; she produced a telephone and set it on a counter. I came out of the dressing room to hear my father shouting into the receiver, "Wire them the ten thousand pounds today!" while waving an unlit Montecristo A in his hand. Lady Rendlesham went to fetch him a match and an ashtray. He covered the receiver and said, "You don't have to, honey."

I winced. *Honey?*

"No, no, it's fine, please do smoke," Lady Rendlesham said. "We love the smell of cigars here."

He outfitted me in style, but like a man: a checked tweed jacket, a navy blue blazer, two silk shirts, two pairs of gabardine trousers with pleats in the front. I insisted on wedge-heeled sandals, to bring some feminine levity to the new wardrobe.

It worked faster than I could have imagined. I went about London in my gray flannel Saint Laurent oxford bags and wedgies, a white silk shirt and a double strand of fake pearls, and, above the ensemble, a smile outlined in dark red lipstick left from Guy Bourdin days. The art director of British *Vogue*, Barney Wan, took me to lunch at Mr. Chow and said nice things. Soon, Marit Allen called from *Vogue* to ask if she could photograph me for her pages featuring girls-about-town. The moment had come.

I leaned back on my twelve-dollar chaise longue from the Montreuil flea market next to a vase of tulips, and basked in my new persona for Marit's camera.

Peter came to Cannes from Rome with his Don Quixote *Man of La Mancha* beard. My parents set up at the Hotel Majestic. Uncle Don let me sleep in the bedroom of the suite where he presold movies at the Hotel Martinez. While Jules waved his Montecristos through meetings at the Majestic, while Joyce was at the hairdresser, Don showed me the real festival. He introduced me to filmmakers with reels under their arms and shoulder bags full of scripts and flyers; some were screening documentaries in the tiny rooms at the back of the Palais des Festivals, others showing porn in little cinemas on the Rue d'Antibes.

The Croisette was sunny, with a light breeze that smelled of mimosa, and at every table on the Carlton terrace people were talking about *The Ruling Class*. Peter thought it was a masterpiece. Jules said it was a masterpiece. It had to be a masterpiece. Jules was tensely coiled around what needed to be done for the masterpiece, and he was worried: the president of the jury that year was Joseph Losey, not a friend, something to do with the HUAC days in Hollywood.

I paid no heed to any tensions about the film; I was photographed exiting and entering parties in my new Saint Laurent wardrobe, and ran about with a notebook and a tape recorder, pretending I was in Cannes on assignment. Robert Redford granted me a short interview on the Carlton terrace. I met Barbet Schroeder, an anthropologist turned filmmaker, whose films fascinated me. My new friends Andy Warhol, Fred Hughes, and Paul Morrissey were there presenting their film *Heat*, which starred my old friend Patti D'Arbanville. They melded with the cast of the Merchant Ivory film *Savages*. I wanted to welcome this bohemian glamour into my world, and organized a huge lunch party on the terrace of Uncle Don's suite at the Martinez.

Don returned from his own lunch to find forty strangers eating shrimp and drinking champagne on his office terrace, and striking poses on the ledge. "Who's going to pay for all this?" he asked.

"Dad, of course," I said.

Don ran his hand through his hair and said, "Don't ever do this again."

The Ruling Class was acclaimed at Cannes, but won no prizes.

The June *Vogue* came out before the London première of *The Ruling Class,* and there I was in the back pages, on my Art Deco cut-velvet chaise longue. I was in *Vogue.* I was real at last.

Then came the call. British *Vogue*'s editor in chief, Beatrix Miller, heard I'd interviewed Robert Redford and wanted to meet me. She found the interview "a bit thin," but, lighting a cigarette from a gold box, told me that Marina Warner was leaving for Vietnam, and *Vogue* needed a features editor. The pay was only £10 a week, but did I really need the money? Wasn't my father . . . ?

"Of course," I said, with the grace of a tycoon's daughter.

My father toasted me that night. "You're a pro now," he said, proud.

I was the features editor of British *Vogue* at twenty-three and everyone was talking about my father's film. The year 1972 felt as good as 1960, the first year of Ricki, the year of *Greyfriars Bobby,* the year Peter was cast as Lawrence of Arabia. This kind of luck must come every twelve years.

But *The Ruling Class* was an unstable talisman. United Artists wanted twenty minutes cut before they'd distribute it in the States. O'Toole was outraged. He was back in Italy tilting at windmills while singing "The Impossible Dream" at Sophia Loren, fulfilling his part of the bargain with United Artists, who now wanted to mutilate his masterpiece. The film, Peter said, must never be cut.

Keep Films had become about keeping Peter happy. Jules thought *The Ruling Class* was too long, but said only that Peter Medak had overused the zoom lens. Caught between United Artists and Peter, he took out his frustration on outsiders and spent the days screaming

"Cocksucker!" on the phone, mostly at United Artists and their London representative, Dan Rissner. One night, at Mr. Chow, he lunged across the table and tried to throttle Dan Rissner until Peter Medak intervened.

"Your father punched Dan Rissner in the face," Michael Chow assured me the next day, "at the table at the top of the stairs under the green kite."

"Your father never punched Dan Rissner!" said Joyce.

To save *The Ruling Class,* Jules and Peter kidnapped the negative from Humphries Laboratories in Peter's Daimler, with Lionel the driver at the wheel. The president of United Artists delivered an ultimatum: Keep Films must return the negative or buy back the film.

Jules borrowed the money for Keep Films to buy back the picture. "Nobody buys back their film, ever," Don told me. "Why did your father have to do that?"

The Ruling Class opened at the Odeon Haymarket, and would play there for a whole year, but that was only one cinema in one city in one country. Don came in to try to sell the movie in various territories, but its length was a problem for everyone, not just UA.

It was now urgent for my father to recoup the borrowed money. He had to edit *The Ruling Class* down to a reasonable length, and hope that Peter wouldn't find out. Peter found out, and was enraged.

Jules gave *The Ruling Class* to Avco Embassy to distribute, but something went very wrong. The masterpiece brought in no money. *The Ruling Class* was the beginning of the end of Keep Films.

Peter lost confidence in Jules, Jules lost confidence in himself. He'd put together pictures he believed in, constructed fine deals that always made Keep Films the winner; he'd relied on instinct, he'd trusted his hunches, he'd believed in the luck of the unpredictable choice. He had no strategies left, only bluster. His hunches went awry, and, unsure, unable to trust himself anymore, he began to reach for what he thought other people wanted, to grab at trends, to try to please. To please Peter, I think, he annexed a noxiously hip personage whom Peter had met at Tramp's nightclub, a man from advertising who wore sideburns and pastel cashmere sweaters and said he had access to money. My father made him coproducer on the next picture, *Man Friday*, a version of Robinson Crusoe shot in Mexico.

In the office, Jules would still hold court, wave his cigar, tell more old Hollywood stories, but the moment O'Toole wandered in, and now Peter came often, he'd lose his thread, remove his glasses, and retreat to make calls in an outer office. Andy Birmingham the accountant and David Korda sensed the discord, but no one wanted to believe things were bad.

I saw nothing, I knew nothing. I no longer popped by the office to help the secretaries sign photographs of Peter for the fans. I existed in the world now. I had a job, and from the day *Vogue* hired me, I had a boyfriend.

Harald Baumgartner had been a weight lifter as a teenager in Austria, but the steroids they'd fed him had given him rheumatic fever, which had weakened his heart; he'd studied art in Rome and now he designed printed fabric. The Viennese accent and the set of his eyes made me think of Eva, the blond pageboy made me think of a saint on the curtain from *Great Catherine.* I found him handsome and poetic, yet fragile, even if his muscles were a little large for my taste. His Bulgarian mother had met his Austrian father by the Black Sea in Varna, her family home, just before the Second World War. She didn't know he was a Nazi soldier until she joined him in Vienna, and though she gave their son a Norse name and soon got a divorce, it was a story I should have kept from my parents.

My father called Harald "the Nazi" behind his back, and "you Commie" to his face.

"Get on the first plane back to Moscow!" he shouted one night at dinner.

"I hate the Communists more than you do," Harald answered. "They took away everything my family had."

"Perhaps he could get that peasant shirt dry-cleaned once in a while," Joyce whispered.

"But it's been in his family for generations," I said.

"Have you talked to him about deodorant?" Joyce asked.

Harald and I held hands in the park, we listened to music, we went to the country to look at Romanesque churches. I hoped this was love. He was with me; wasn't that enough? It wasn't. Having a boyfriend gave me a strange license to sleep with other men. I thought of it as making up for lost time.

A rustle of taffeta kept summoning me to Paris, which was as compelling as the garden full of beautiful children in beautiful clothes playing among beautiful flower beds in Sophie's dream in *Les Malheurs de Sophie.* Because I was now at British *Vogue,* I was invited to Paris parties and fashion shows, and I went. The death of Maurice had brought together all the people who'd fought over him. Clara Saint, who ran the press for Yves Saint Laurent and picked the members of his circle, seemed to have a list of Maurice's conquests.

Clara loved gay boys and gay boys loved her. When Rudolf Nureyev had made his dash to freedom at Orly airport in 1962, it was Clara who collected him from the police and took him home with her. Her straight boyfriend was Thadée Klossowski, the son of Balthus the painter, a dreamy young man with the profile of an eagle. He wrote, a bit. Clara brought Loulou de la Falaise to Yves as his bird-of-paradise assistant without portfolio. She liked bringing the bright ones in.

She invited me to a glamorous dinner at the house of Charlotte Aillaud, an architect's wife and the central hostess in the world of Saint Laurent. I was dazzled by the other guests and ended up in bed with the most lighthearted of the unmarried Rothschilds, Eric, a Prince Charming banker given to giggles and bad puns. I knew our night was part of his playboy rounds, but when I saw that his house was a cottage tucked away on a cobblestoned street in a run-down part of Paris, I decided there was some substance to his style, and hoped that Harald wouldn't find out.

Harald went on his annual trip to New York in October to sell his designs; I went to see a play about Queen Victoria, and in the bar at intermission, found myself standing next to the man whose voice had been the voice of my emotions since I was fifteen. Leonard Cohen asked for my number, I wrote it on a postcard imagining that he'd never call, but he did. Across the table from him in a Chinese restaurant, I apologized for my fancy clothes, but he reassured me, "I like girls of the bourgeoisie." He was on his way to Scotland to build a wall for a Zen monastery, a humble project that awed me even more than the voice. He had a house on the Greek island of Hydra.

"Come to Greece with me," he said.

Harald was about to return from New York, I had to be at *Vogue* every day, and I couldn't imagine myself alone with Leonard Cohen on a Greek island. It would be the greatest dream come true; it would look like the Bob Richardson photos from Paris *Vogue*: him, me, him naked in the sea, me—crying? He knew too much in every realm. He was older; his skin might drag against mine. At what age did men's bodies wrinkle? I didn't love Harald, but his skin was as smooth as water.

I said I wanted to, and later, I said, "I can't." Harald returned from New York.

Leonard sent me dark brown chrysanthemums in a box five feet long, with a poem. A photo booth strip of Leonard was stapled to one side, my phone number was stapled in the center, and the poem ended with the line, "Never lie to a great poet, or even a minor one."

CHAPTER SEVEN

I feared the luck of 1972 would wither in 1973. The year began with Harald, in Vienna. I stayed in Pension Nossek on the Graben; there was no room for me in Harald's mother's apartment, which was no more than a kitchen with a table flanked by two beds, hers and Harald's. She was a short, stout woman, a cashier in a magazine store behind the cathedral; her boyfriend was a bloodless man who wore a broken fedora over knowing eyes and sold vegetables from a cart. He'd done much better, Harald said, when there was still a black market. I was transfixed by the idea that I was seeing the other side, the raw sad lives of those who'd caused the war, and lost it. I wanted to see Eva's family, but they were away.

Nana died in New York in February; I joined my mother and father at the Lombardy. There was no funeral. "I'm going to go with Don to bury Esta's ashes in Cannes," Joyce said, "or maybe we'll hire a boat and scatter her ashes on the Mediterranean, outside the Casino, where she was always so happy."

I tried to see Anjelica, who was living at the Chelsea Hotel with Bob Richardson, but he kept her so close that she was, in effect, his prisoner. I was in New York to meet *Women's Wear Daily*; they offered me ten times my British *Vogue* salary to be their London correspondent.

I'd be able to pay my rent without my father, and I'd be in print every day. I took the job.

The London office of Fairchild Publications was around the corner from Roebuck House; along with *WWD*, there was a daily publication devoted to shoes, another to men's fashion, and one to metal. A telex spewed forth never-ending rolls of directives, and a secretary retyped our stories onto the same telex to send them to New York. It was so gratifying to be in instant written communication with my bosses that I'd go by on the weekend to see what new assignments they'd thought up. I duly covered Royal Ascot, Wimbledon, Henley, charity balls, and fashion shows. I stood outside parties with our photographer to capture aristocrats, stars, drag artists, and playboy property developers as they arrived, and when I couldn't identify a face on a contact sheet, I'd make up a name.

The work was dreary, but I loved being in print every day, and the London correspondent of *WWD* had more clout than the features editor of British *Vogue*. Clara Saint gave me a better seat at Saint Laurent, and placed me with Pierre Bergé at lunch after the show. He glared—men whose life it is to organize a scattered genius rarely access the softer register—then took my hand and said, "I hope you will always remember who your real friends are, and put us ahead of your professional interests."

I knew the right answer. "Oh my God, Pierre," I said, "I love you and Yves so much, of course."

After six months, the balls and the grandees began to pall; I'd put everyone I knew in the pages of *WWD*, I'd contributed to some vicious In and Out lists, what was I going to do next? Harald took me to Italy that summer, showed me the pink dawn over Umbria, took me to the Etruscan necropolis at Cerveteri, gave me my first taste of tortellini, of arugula, of balsamic vinegar, and walked me through the Forum. He said he wanted to move back to Rome, and if I loved him, I'd go with him. I wasn't sure I loved him, but I wanted him to think I did, so when John Fairchild asked if I knew a replacement for the Rome correspondent, I lied that my Italian was as good as my French and proposed myself. Harald bought me a ring, a moonstone etched with a face.

We moved to Rome right after the Yom Kippur War, and straight into the oil crisis. My parents rented Roebuck House to the man from advertising whom Peter had met at Tramp's.

Our Rome apartment had three terraces joined by metal spiral staircases, which rose to a rooftop pavilion. The square below had a fountain surrounded by statues of boys on tortoises, but the mass of stone under us obscured the street. Harald and I shared a workroom by the trellised terrace where we ate our meals. Our part of Rome was palazzo upon palazzo in gray herds, cobbled piazzas, feral cats, the stutter and buzz of motorbikes. Down a narrow street was the ghetto, with restaurants for deep-fried artichokes, a church built into a Roman temple, and a synagogue I never went into.

The first person I interviewed was Federico Fellini. "People only want to see what they've already seen, be told what they already know," he said. Not me, I thought.

The Italian postal service had been on strike for several years, so the only mail we received was brought by visitors from London. I learned the language from television, newspapers, and comic books: the Italian version of *Astérix*, and pornographic comics I bought in Piazza Venezia. I supplemented that vocabulary with the Italian words for satin (*raso*), makeup (*trucco*), and the all-purpose exclamation "Bravo!," sometimes in its female form, "Brava!," which covered any fashionable Roman eventuality.

The Italians called that time the Years of Lead. The Left rioted, the Right held rallies, anarchists blew things up. There were assassinations, kidnapping, bombs. As I walked home, carrying a plastic bag with three *etti* of ham and a hunk of Parmesan, I would find a cloud of tear gas rolling down the street as metal shutters slammed over storefronts. Fashionable men in Gucci hardware hedged their bets with gold hammer-and-sickle charms on chains around their necks; armed bodyguards rode next to the driver in the front of tiny Fiat 500s to protect the dignitary crammed in the back; Gulf State weddings kept Rome couture afloat, and Colonel Gadhafi launched a competition for Italian designers to create a national uniform for Libya.

People who lived in Milan were more reasonable; Tai and Rosita

Missoni made stripes into wonderful clothes, lived in the country next to their factory, swam every morning, and were grounded and kind. I adopted them as my Italian family.

I reported on fashion, and carried my typed pages through ancient Rome to telex my copy from the general press office in Piazza San Silvestro, twenty minutes away. Harald drew his patterns, inked in the colors, and cut out his mistakes with a scalpel at the table by the window, and went to the gym, which he called the palaestra, to begin what he called his summer program. At night he drank too much slivovitz with his friend Jan, a stateless Pole who'd been stuck in Rome since the war and stank of neglect.

I hated the Pole, hated the slivovitz, but I'd claimed this life. Harald turned mean when he drank slivovitz; he got into fistfights with strangers, and sometimes threatened our friends.

Then Jack Nicholson was on the cover of *Time* magazine, and inside was a photo of Anjelica, his girlfriend now, laughing in a bikini in his living room, carefree, loved, spotlit, with a star of her own, back home where she'd been born, where I'd been born. I'd driven myself into a cave of Mitteleuropean drunks in a mountain range of musty palaces above streets full of tear gas. For solace I would walk through the Forum up to the Palatine Hill, stop at the hidden Roman fountain along the way, and hide in the ruins of the empress Livia's house. I'd sit under a parasol pine on a little knoll, and wonder what I was doing in this life with Harald.

When my parents asked me to join them in Cannes for a few days, without Harald, I accepted with relief and left without delay. Keep Films had no movie there that year, but Anjelica was in Cannes with Jack. I liked that he enjoyed success more than Peter did, though Anjelica was alarmed by the frenzy he set off. We spent half an evening dressing up for Jack's big night, and swept into the Majestic bar in long white dresses, as if making an entrance at the Big House at St. Clerans. Josephine Baker swiveled toward us from the banquette where she was holding court, held out her arms, and declared to the room that we were angels.

Back in Rome, I dropped names to everyone—Cannes stories,

movie stars, Jack, Anjelica—but at home I barely talked. One morning, Harald slammed my coffee cup from the table, knocked me out of my chair, held me down on the terrace tiles, and closed his hands around my throat. His muscles, pumped up from the palaestra, were intractable under my slapping hands.

I couldn't breathe, I couldn't make a sound. My saliva turned foamy in my throat. I fought until his hands released my neck, pushed him back, scrambled to my feet, ran down the corridor, out of the apartment, and hammered on the door of the painter across the landing. When he let me in, I fell into a heap. I crouched by the door for an hour or more, wiping the foam from my mouth onto my bathrobe. The painter brought me a glass of water and asked if he should call the police. I shook my head. When the painter's apartment filled with the smell of lunch, I went back to our apartment. Harald was out, probably at the palaestra. He'd cleaned up the terrace; the broken coffee cup was in the garbage.

I'd asked for the job. The entire *Women's Wear Daily* Roman office was the workroom I shared with Harald, and his paints, and his inks, and his paper, and the scalpel he used to cut out his mistakes, and might at any moment use on me. I needed John Fairchild's permission to run away. I couldn't let my father know he'd been right.

I tiptoed around Harald for the next two months until he went to Bulgaria to see his family. Now would be time to run away, but John Fairchild brought me to Paris to help cover the July haute couture, which was the social and professional climax of his year as publisher of *WWD*. This was not the moment to bring up my weight lifter boyfriend. I devised the term "Naïve Chemise" to describe Yves Saint Laurent's shirred smocks, and bought myself a black oilskin raincoat shaped like a tent. Pretty things would take the danger out of my life.

Pierre Bergé gave a dinner at Maxim's; Yves wasn't there, but all his friends were. I wore a white dress cut as low as the ones my mother wore in the old days in Paris, and exchanged glances with Eric Rothschild. Our night together had been two years earlier, but the revealing white dress sharpened his focus. He remembered everything and invited me out the next night.

When Eric drove me back to my hotel, I wore a red turtleneck of his against the morning chill. "Keep it," he said. "It looks good on you." He sent an immense bouquet of white roses to the hotel; I felt like Cinderella. I tore up his note to make sure Harald would never find it.

I didn't tell John Fairchild anything. In Rome, I hid the red sweater and the new black raincoat inside a carrier bag in the back of the closet, and, as I'd promised, joined Harald in Bulgaria. He wouldn't hurt me in front of his family and this was my chance to go behind the real Iron Curtain, instead of the imaginary one around me in Rome.

A postcard from Eric made it through the Italian postal service in September. He'd spelled out his home address and added "Fall Fashions of Paris" across the top of the card. The message read: "The clothes you tried on in the summer are ready for a new fitting."

I didn't want to tear up this card; it was time to run away. Harald went on his yearly selling trip to New York, but my escape was delayed by the ready-to-wear shows that I had to cover in Florence and Milan.

The editor in chief of *Women's Wear Daily,* Michael Coady, was in Milan. "This is where all the fashion is, all the energy, the Missonis, everything," I said. "I should move here."

"When?" he asked.

"Now?" Harald was returning to Rome any day.

After Michael Coady said yes, I told him about the morning on the terrace when Harald tried to strangle me. His mouth fell open.

"No more men," I promised. "I won't ever get into that kind of trouble again."

Back in Rome I called Harald's New York hotel. He'd checked out, which meant he'd be on the night plane, and in Rome by morning. I packed my new clothes, put the moonstone ring on Harald's work-table with a note saying I was in London, and went to the airport at dawn to take the first plane. I wore the coat he'd never seen and a new fedora so he wouldn't recognize me in case his plane landed before I boarded mine.

I didn't call my parents until I landed. At Upper Belgrave Street,

Joyce listened to the Harald story stunned and dismayed, but was cheered that I'd seen Eric Rothschild again. As we sat in the living room, Harald called; he'd arrived home, found the ring on his desk, and gone back to the airport. He'd just landed.

"I'm not coming back to you," I said, "and you know why."

"My heart," he said, "you're killing me." The rheumatic fever.

He came to see me at Upper Belgrave Street, my parents' fortress. My mother was upstairs on the phone to my father across the street while David Korda listened from behind the dining room door to make sure Harald didn't attack me. Everything I'd wanted to leave now kept me safe from Harald. After a brief, tense talk, he went back to Rome. I never saw him again. Three years later, at thirty-two, he died of endocarditis. His damaged heart.

~

My mother went with me to Rome to help me pack up the apartment, and drove us north to Milan in a rented station wagon on November 1, the Day of the Dead, surrounded by cars full of families and flowers headed to cemeteries with bouquets.

Northern Italy was covered with thick, unrelenting fog that autumn. In the *residenza* next door to the Fairchild Publications Milan bureau, the rooms were orange tweed, white Formica, dark wood slabs. My bed was a single. No more dangerous terraces, no more violent Harald, no more drunken Pole, no more men. Joyce was in another room, happy to be in Milan for a few weeks, to meet my friends the Missonis, and, though I didn't know it, to get away from the misery of Keep Films. "Your father's fine," she said. He was setting up some Western.

Bernardo Bertolucci's *Last Tango in Paris* had taught me things about sex and mourning and now he was filming a political epic titled *1900*, in Parma, where he'd been born. I told *WWD* that, for my first story, I'd visit his set.

In *1900*, Bertolucci set out to tell the story of the twentieth century as the conflict between peasants and owners, Communism and Fascism. The peasant was played by Gérard Depardieu and the landowner was the Robert De Niro I'd refused to meet at Sarah Lawrence, who'd become a star in *Bang the Drum Slowly* and *Mean Streets.*

I stood in the village of Guastalla to watch a funeral scene. I'd stood on the edge of sets all my life, I'd been part of the action when I was eleven, but I'd never felt such intensity on a film before. Mourners followed a cart carrying the bodies of four old men; each mourner wore a bit of red, a muffler, a kerchief, a rose. They plodded to the playback of a tune I didn't know, which someone explained was "The Internationale." The reds were like fresh blood in the white fog, sharp as sobs. The scene was set in 1920, I was told; the old men had been killed in a fire set by Fascists. "The Internationale" was the Communist anthem. Everything expressed Bertolucci's idea about power struggles. I'd never imagined politics rendered as emotion, and I embraced the glorious intensity. I wanted to melt into the scene.

I'd sworn to devote myself to my job. Instead, I fell in love.

He was in movement the first time I saw him, a copy of the *Herald Tribune* folded in a pocket of his long dark overcoat, as long and dark as the one the boy wore on the steps of the Lycée. Tall, big hands. He was playing Attila in the film, the Fascist foreman who is the embodiment of evil.

Donald Sutherland had the face of a newborn baby, elongated, a newborn's pale blue eyes. An undefended face, without the practiced expressions of a movie star, no special set to the eyebrows or glint or stare or smirk, but an open face where awe, surprise, delight, doubt seemed to change the substance of the skin and the bones, but not the shape. A face that was all-registering. If I can see through him to what he's feeling, I thought, he can see through me as well. Later that evening, after a conversation in the bar that was supposed to be an interview, but was not, because I had no questions, he took me to look at the baptistery in the fog. The baptistery was twelfth century, eight flat sides knobbled with saints. He loomed over me, huge in his dark overcoat, our breath fog on fog. Later still, we played chess, and soon, he came to Milan to take me to dinner.

"That's nice he's taking you out, " said Joyce, who was still in Milan. "I saw him in *Johnny Got His Gun,* Dalton's movie; he's good."

We ate in a hushed, elegant restaurant by La Scala. He was thirty-nine; he lived in Paris with a woman and their baby, who was nine months old. I said I'd just run away from a Bulgarian who'd tried to kill me in Rome, which was true, and had a boyfriend in Paris, which was almost true. He touched the place where my blouse fell open on my collarbone, and I felt naked.

His driver was waiting to take him back to Parma.

"I'll come to tea tomorrow," he said, and he did.

It was after nine when he left. I stumbled down to Joyce's room, and sat on her bed.

"How was your tea?" she asked.

"I'm in love," I said, and burst into tears.

"Oh darling," Joyce said, "it's one of those things." She lit a cigarette. "Years from now you'll be at a party and your eyes will meet across a crowded room, and you'll both know you had something special. It's a moment."

"But this is real," I said. "I know it's real. What can I do?"

"No, it isn't, darling," she said with a pretty laugh. "He's an actor. It's make-believe. It can be wonderful, but it won't be real." She took my hand. "What about Eric Rothschild? Shouldn't you be concentrating on him?"

"I don't want Eric," I said. I wanted this absolute flash that had left the tea untouched in the new cups.

Joyce went back to London. I wrote a long, passionate piece for *W* about Bertolucci and the importance of *1900.*

Donald brought me violets, and drove the eighty miles from Parma to spend a few hours with me almost every night. He left a can of shaving foam, a razor, a tired pale blue shirt. The messages he left with the switchboard were from "Attila."

The violets represented him, us. The flowers so much smaller than the leaves, meek, hidden, purple. We didn't say "we." We said "it." It went beyond anything I knew. The hard surfaces in my hotel room vanished, but the air around us became as warm and solid as flesh. It was as if I'd found a way into the heart of impulse, feeling, and sensation, where nothing else existed.

Soon after it began, he took out some weed and rolling papers, to extend the magic. The weed was unnecessary, but I came to expect the rolling of the joint, the flash as the paper ignited, the moist crackle burning green.

I skittered to Parma to interview everyone who was in *1900*, everyone except Donald. I raced up and down the back staircase from my room to his, my knitted cape flapping like wings. I was electric with desire, alive only when I was with him, and everything I did was to please him, no matter how far away he was. He liked me thin; I lived on cappuccinos and exotic fruit from the shop next door. A month before, I hadn't known Cape gooseberries existed; now they were my main sustenance. I wore the colors of Parma: violets, mauves, and purples. I tried to be as magic and insubstantial as Parma itself.

"Don't write about me," said Donald, when he saw I had a diary.

"I'll never write about you," I said.

It wasn't a lie. My awe was so full of biblical fear that I didn't dare spell out his name in the diary. He was just dashes, like the name of G-d. Joyce had said it wouldn't last.

I knew enough about movie sets to know that once the lights and cables were packed up and everyone went home, everything vanished, and the first things to go were love affairs. Still, Anjelica was with Jack Nicholson; why shouldn't I be with Donald? But I wasn't Anjelica, and she hadn't met Jack on location; they'd met at his house in the middle of his real life. Milan wasn't Donald's real life, nor mine, only my temporary rescue perch. We'd met in a fog. He had a baby, a woman who loved him; I guessed he loved her. The only safe place to put myself was on the side of the guardian angel. I'd have to protect him from me. I began to split in two.

I led two lives. I didn't sleep.

On weekends, he went back to Paris to be with his family. Prompted by my father, I went to Paris to see Eric, to even out the balance, to have someone else. I wore a bare Missoni dress without a bra to go with him to Maxim's. The bandleader asked if we had a request. I did. The tune that played constantly on the set of *1900* was the theme song to my secret, so I asked for "The Internationale." Eric laughed; he liked the prank of playing the Communist anthem to the patrons of Maxim's.

I joined my parents in Los Angeles for Christmas. Donald was going to be in Laguna Beach, as far from me in California as he was in Italy. It was the first time I'd been back to California as an adult. There were bushes with pink flowers around Bungalow 8 at the Beverly Hills Hotel, where my closet was bigger than my room in Milan.

"If you left *Women's Wear,*" Joyce said, "we'd get you a little house here in the flats, and Skip Hathaway wants to sell her little pale blue Mercedes. You could have that, if you learned to drive." I'd live in Los Angeles and write a novel about mystery and passion. I'd never again have to write about shoes or fashion shows.

I went to visit Anjelica at Jack's house high on Mulholland Drive. The house was simple, with sliding doors. I was draped in my Missoni cashmere cape as gray as Milan, and looked alien to Anjelica, who was in jeans. I watched Jack for signs he was like Donald, found none, and casually asked if he knew him. He did not.

Donald sent me a hundred mauve roses, the color of Parma, and drove up the coast to see me. A friend loaned me his empty house on Beachwood Drive for the afternoon, without asking questions.

When I returned to Milan, my narrow room was full of presents, tributes from those I'd praised in *Women's Wear Daily.* I stalked through the January fog in sunglasses.

"How Hollywood," said Anna Piaggi.

"It's where I'm from," I said.

I dreaded the day *1900* would end. Five weeks left. Four. I had barely eaten or slept in months. I asked Donald for nothing, a proud Jane Eyre approach that robbed me of the power of speech. When we were clothed, I stammered, I sulked.

Fellini cast Donald as Casanova, and now he wasn't my secret anymore; he was going to be a star. I saw myself as the heroine of an overheated romance novel: six months before, I'd been on a Roman rooftop fighting off a deranged Bulgarian weight lifter; now my secret lover was a movie star, and he was playing Casanova. Had he been practicing on me? I worked myself into a frenzy, weeping in the mirror to the swell of Bach's "Sleepers Awake" on the tape deck.

The next day, I told Donald I couldn't go on, and two hours later rose from his bed to say it really couldn't go on. I went to Paris to spend the weekend with Eric in his cottage on the cobbled street.

I wished Eric had some grass. I didn't know what I was doing there and he didn't know how to fill two days with me.

"Don't you have any clothes that aren't velvet?" Eric asked. "You know, jeans?"

"No," I apologized. I pretended to be lighthearted and tried to be fun, but I didn't know my lines for the part.

On Monday morning, Eric read the *Herald Tribune* at breakfast while I examined the fine Chinese porcelain cup that held my tea to give myself something to do. Eric sat forward and said, "There's been a robbery at the Bank of America in Berkeley Square. They got into the vault."

The Day They Robbed the Bank of America. I gave a great hoot of laughter. Eric looked puzzled. "Do your parents bank there?" he asked.

I called London. Yes, my father said, they had things in the vault. They didn't know yet what was gone. Scotland Yard would call them in as soon as they knew. He gave the words "Scotland Yard" all the dignity he gave to "Buckingham Palace."

"Give my best to Eric," he added. "It's very thoughtful of him to have you call."

"Have you lost a lot?" I asked.

"It's going to be fine," said my father. "Reassured."

~

My editor Michael Coady heard that Donald had been cast as Casanova, and called, shouting, "You buried the lede! Isn't he also in *1900*? Go interview him."

"I'll have to approve all my quotes," said Donald.

"Of course," I said. I'd already given him everything; why shouldn't I give him that?

We sat down with the tape recorder in his Parma hotel room. I presented public questions, he presented public answers. He spoke to me as if to a stranger, for the benefit of strangers, forgot me, talked about his baby, about its mother, the woman he loved. That was the public Donald. That was the real Donald. Who had that been for four months of nights?

I transcribed in my room in Milan. His voice on the tape talking not to me but to the public, rewind, every sentence proof that his life was nothing to do with mine. It's an interview, I told myself, it's the fake dance for the newspaper. It's not us. I know the difference. Play the game. You know what you're doing. This isn't the truth, this is publicity. You asked for it. You could have said no. Why do you always do what you're told?

As promised, I brought the transcript back to him in Parma, where he read it with a felt-tip pen in his hand. I heard his pen go through one line, another line, another, another. He didn't look at me. He was only protecting himself from the press. Protecting himself from me. The dark overcoat lay across a chair. He handed over the transcript, now all black lines except some words about Bertolucci, some about Fellini. I took the train back to Milan; I didn't want him to drive me.

I'd betrayed myself, and felt a vengeful malice grow toward the skinny girl who'd fallen in love. I downed three gingerbread cakes in a row at the *caffè* next to the office, bought cookies on the way to the hotel, went out alone for pizza, stuffed down more starch, drank more cappuccinos, ate more, so much that my stomach hurt, and then hurt so much that I could barely walk. I made myself too ill to write the profile, and asked *Women's Wear Daily* for sick leave.

I left Milan on a Saturday, the day Donald always went to Paris. He came to see me, and afterward he stretched out in the deep water of my bathtub as I sat on the edge in my robe. I wanted to gather in the months he'd been with me here, and, without taking off the robe, slipped into the safe warm water with him.

Linate Airport rumbled and shook with each plane that landed. His flight to Paris was at 4:00, my flight to London at 3:55. We parted at the metal detector, but Gérard Depardieu arrived, put his arm around me, waited for me, and bought me Perugina kisses in a heart-shaped silver plastic box left over from Valentine's Day.

Joyce met me at Heathrow. I showed her the silver plastic box of Perugina kisses and said it was from Donald. She was not impressed.

Dr. Woodcock said it was my appendix, and an ulcer. "No more champagne, darling," he said, "and if you've been smoking pot or snorting cocaine, you have to stop. No more of that, ever. Your body can't take it."

"I'll never do another drug," I promised.

The night before I went into the hospital, Michael and Tina Chow gave a dinner at their new house, where Michael had installed a small swimming pool. At the end of dinner, David Bailey stripped down to his jockeys and jumped in the pool; I pulled off my boots and followed him into the pool with all my clothes on.

"What are you doing?" shouted Tina.

I wanted to feel the way I had in the bathtub with Donald, but the weight of my clothes sank me. Tina loaned me dry clothes; nonetheless, I caught a cold that complicated the operation.

When I came to after surgery I saw the sweet faces of my parents. Jules looked exhausted and sheepish. His first words were, "Boopah came through."

"Who's Boopah?" I asked.

"The private health insurance, BUPA." He beamed. "They're paying for everything."

"Peter's going to come see you soon," said Joyce. "He's been sick, too, much sicker than you."

"But it's a real secret," Jules warned. "The papers keep calling. Don't tell anyone."

"And don't ask him what he had," said Joyce.

Flowers arrived from Donald, but it was a pot of frilly pink azaleas, not mauve roses, not even violets. He wasn't paying attention. He was already Casanova.

When Peter came to see me, he was gray and his long hair was pewter brown. He collapsed in the chair in his usual way, knees up and elbows on the armrests, but the elastic was gone.

"Our stomachs, right?" he said. He ran his hand down his torso.

"No," I wanted to say, "my heart."

We compared hospitals. He'd been in the Royal Free, I was in the Harley Street Clinic.

"London looks like Jordan now," Peter said.

"There are women here in black veils and face masks," I said.

"They'd be the slaves," he said. "You can tell by the leather masks. The sheiks are all in the Wellington; you've got the servants getting their bits fixed here at the Harley Street. I saw a man in robes roasting a goat by the lift. Take a close look at your dinner."

We tried not to laugh too hard—our stitches. He was going to Ireland to convalesce.

Jules set out to make his first film without Peter in thirteen years. He'd fastened on a comedy Western called *The Great Scout & Cathouse Thursday*. He said he could get Steve McQueen and Paul Newman. His new partner, the man from Tramp's with the pastel cashmere sweaters, said he had a commitment for half the budget from the merchant bank Guinness Mahon. Uncle Don tried to raise the rest of the budget through presales, but Jules couldn't get Paul Newman and he couldn't get Steve McQueen. He lost the first director he wanted, and then another. Uncle Don and David Korda tried to talk him out of the project, but he would not give up. Persistence, perseverance, his virtues. He hit the office at daybreak, drank his morning coffee with slugs of brandy, handed out sherry midmorning. Soon, he stopped eating. He didn't sleep.

My mother smiled gamely through it all. She smiled all the time, no matter what was happening; she smiled to make things good, to make things better, she smiled as if everything depended on her smile. Around the time of *The Ruling Class*, she'd developed trigeminal neuralgia, a pain in her cheekbones so severe that only careful doses of a strong drug called Tegretol could control it. I wondered if it came from all the smiling.

I went back to Milan, still slow from the operation; my shoulders hurt and I could hardly walk. Donald was in Rome for fittings for Casanova. When he called, he told me he was going to rent a villa on the Appia Antica, a good place for a family.

I would go mad if I didn't stop thinking about Donald. I tried to find another man who'd set off the same things in me. I went off with a French writer who was staying on Lake Como, and on a Sunday morning awoke in his bed in a stranger's house paralyzed by what was diagnosed as rheumatic fever. I was trapped in that bed for weeks, unable to move except in the middle of the night when I made my way to the only telephone, which was in the kitchen, to call the *residenza* for messages. The receptionist so mangled Donald's new pseudonym that I wasn't sure he was the one who'd called. Finally, a doctor gave me cortisone that blew me up like a parade balloon, and I returned to Milan.

Bloated and wretched on my single bed, I knew I had to quit, leave Italy, write a novel. In fiction, I'd be able to say what I couldn't express as a reporter for *Women's Wear Daily*. I'd be able to describe the mystery that was driving me mad. I told Michael Coady I couldn't interview one more designer, and gave him my notice. "But I wanted you to interview the chef at Savigni about his risotto," said Michael.

"Come west, rest," Anjelica wrote. Before I went to Los Angeles, I stopped at a British health farm to recover. I ate my meals with a television actress named Hazel Court.

"I must thank Hazel for being so nice to you," Jules said.

You don't have to thank everyone who's nice to me, I thought. He still didn't have a director for the Western.

"Why are you making a Western?" I asked. "Bertolucci's *1900* is the entire history of the first half of the twentieth century. That's a film worth making."

"Don't be a snotnose," he said.

~

I arrived in Los Angeles in a July sunset and unpacked silky Milanese presents at Jack's house on Mulholland Drive. He was in Montana making *The Missouri Breaks*. Anjelica showed me how to be Californian. I watched her water the plants in the evenings, learned how to turn off the electric coffeemaker and how to close sliding doors, how to say, "Let's blow this joint," and "We're clean outta smokes." Allegra was living with John Huston's fifth wife, Cici; we went to see her the day that John walked out. Allegra came with us to stay with Jack in

Montana. Every morning Anjelica and I debated whether this was the day to tell her about her real father. It never was.

I pined for Donald and hoped Eric would somehow turn up. I took driving lessons. I was almost twenty-seven. Skip Hathaway's Mercedes was waiting for me, and so was the little house in the flats of Beverly Hills.

I thought my father was still rich.

When Jules came to Los Angeles, he said, "I hired your friend Hazel Court's husband to direct *The Great Scout & Cathouse Thursday.*"

"You didn't have to do that," I said.

He was anxious, irascible, and, for once, thin. Maybe this wasn't the time to ask about a house.

"I've got Lee Marvin, Robert Culp, and David Cassidy's girlfriend Kay Lenz," he said. "Oliver Reed's playing the half-breed, and your friend Sylvia Miles is going to be the madam. She's absolutely thrilled."

Another thank-you for being nice to me. As he drove us down to Beverly Hills, he said, "I've told the costume designer to make Robert Culp's costume out of polyester."

"Polyester?"

"It's a white suit, it'll be easier to clean, and no one will know the fucking goddam difference!" he shouted.

"Is Skip Hathaway's Mercedes still for sale?" I asked.

The rage came out in a battering of "Fucks" and "Fuck yous," but it wasn't the words, it was their speed, it was his face. He parked, shouted at me in the middle of the street, but when we reached the curb he stopped to hug me, and pulled me into Beverly Stationers, where he bought me an electric typewriter and a ream of white paper.

Write your way to your own car. Get to work.

He left town without handing over the cash I expected. The typewriter was American voltage, so I assumed he approved of my choice to stay in Los Angeles. This was simply what Joyce called "a bump." There hadn't been any of those in a very long time.

I pined for Donald, but managed a fling with a TV actor who'd once been a child evangelist, which didn't count as an affair as much as anthropology. I joined him in New Mexico on the set of *Bobbie Jo and the Outlaw,* a title that sounded so much like *The Great Scout & Cathouse Thursday* that I wondered if Dad had stumbled onto a trend. I spent the money I'd saved from *Women's Wear Daily* on pawn silver and small Navajo rugs. There was another fling, with an alcoholic stand-up comic who liked to pass out in Jack's living room, until I gave up on the flings and went back to pining, a slow, bloated houseguest who didn't smoke dope, haunting Jack Nicholson's kitchen.

In late summer, my money ran out. I couldn't ask for a loan. I had the electric typewriter, but a novel would take years. I'd have to make this temporary difficulty fun.

My solution was to take up a position in one of the wood-paneled phone booths next to the Polo Lounge at the Beverly Hills Hotel, dressed in a perfect Italian outfit—Valentino was best—on the alert for anyone from London who knew me as Jules and Joyce's daughter, anyone who knew me as British *Vogue*'s features editor, as *Women's Wear Daily*'s Italian correspondent. Status would save me.

"I didn't know you were in L.A!" said Joan Collins; "Joanie!" said the studio head; "Darling, is that you?" asked the producer; I'd laugh and explain that my purse had been stolen, and each person offered to help. It was usually a $100 bill. Sue Mengers invited me to dinner.

Maybe this was how life worked. I didn't have to prove my loyalty or flatter anyone with my prose; all I had to do was sustain an aura of importance with good clothes and a cheerful attitude. The assumptions of others would provide. I wasn't panhandling at the Beverly Hills Hotel, I was using the system. It wasn't humiliating but empowering, a wonderful game to counter life's bad surprises. I didn't tell Anjelica. I told Helena instead.

Helena Kallianiotes was the belly-dancer and actress who lived next door to Jack and ran his house; her hair was dyed jet-black and she spent most of the day in a white satin nightgown. She was writing a script about a prostitute and a rich woman, and after I told her my Beverly Hills Hotel ruse, she said she'd pay me $100 a week to help her. "You can put in how rich people talk," she said.

For my twenty-seventh birthday, Anjelica gave me a large crystal ball. Jack said, "It's to see what you're going to do next." I'd overstayed my welcome. Anjelica's hug was a little uncertain; we didn't speak for the next two years.

The next day, I paid $25 cash up front for a room at the Sunset Marquis and started the novel at a card table on the new electric typewriter. Tom Wolfe was said to be working in another room; Jean-Paul Goude was on another floor. My entire life, past and present, was here in this crappy music hotel. I typed out a title: *The Midnight Baron and the Sunset Marquis.* It pleased me so much that I stopped right there.

I had to get assignments. I went to New York, and wore my Milanese mauves and violets to meet Leo Lerman and Alex Liberman at *Vogue.* Leo had a body like Humpty Dumpty, a beard, thick glasses, and a photo of Maria Callas openmouthed in midaria on the wall behind him. He wore a violet scarf, showed me his purple socks, complimented me on my choice of mauves, and took me to lunch at the Rose Room in the Algonquin. Of course he knew Evelyn Keyes and Betty Bacall and Otto Preminger, he knew everyone and loved everything I loved, mauve and purple and Proust and Rilke and Gustav Klimt and Erich von Stroheim. He knew Marlene Dietrich. He'd read everything I'd read, and so much more. He wanted to know about Bertolucci's film, about Italy, about Los Angeles. He wanted to know about *Casanova.* He knew everything.

"You are the other woman," he said.

Alex Liberman seemed to know it as well; he wanted to send me on the set of *Casanova* in Rome. I said I wouldn't interview Donald Sutherland, but I would speak to Fellini. In London, on the way, I spent a night at my parents' house. The Ben Nicholson was gone from above the sofa, and the lonely cord of a picture light trailed down the wall where the Fernand Léger belonged. I believed Joyce when she said, "The paintings are out on loan."

Bert the driver was gone. There was only one secretary left at Keep Films.

I spent one night with Donald at the villa on the Appia. On a mirror in the upstairs bathroom was a declaration of love written in red lipstick, but I didn't know whether it was from his legitimate companion or another girl like me. I pretended I hadn't seen it. Through the dining room window the next morning, I watched him pick a blue flower in the garden, not quite a violet, but close. I waited for him to bring it to me, but he put it in his buttonhole.

He'd become a movie star. Instead of a flower, he gave me a silver medallion engraved with his profile as Casanova on a key chain, a crew present for the wrap party. I accepted it as if it were a violet, and clipped it to the handle of my bag.

I went back to Los Angeles. Leo Lerman gave me enough assignments to get by. I could survive without much money. I drove an apple green Mustang with one red door from Rent-A-Wreck, found a $200-a-month apartment on Fountain Avenue, and borrowed a dinette set from the building's super. The only living room furniture was a large piece of foam rubber upholstered in mattress ticking that John Schlesinger and Michael Childers had removed from their new house.

I wrote every day, but it was hard to set down the feelings I'd had in Milan, so the novel became a movie script that I called *The Interview.*

I dressed up in my Italian clothes for dinners at Sue Mengers's house in Bel-Air. At a charity lunch, I took the table centerpiece to give the parking attendant instead of a tip. I was proud to be so resourceful; when I found a pair of heavy French cast-iron sphinxes in a junk store, I pawned my watch to buy them. Through Henry Jaglom, I met Anaïs Nin, who wore mauve and lived in a house paneled with wood almost the same color. I learned that the free life she'd lived in Louveciennes had included a banker husband who paid the bills. I wished she'd put that in her diary.

Sometimes Donald came to Los Angeles. The moments alone were unchanged, but briefer. The light was harsher.

My father's Western started shooting in Mexico before the money came through. The merchant bank defaulted, or had never really committed the money to the man from Tramp's. To keep the camera rolling, Jules met the payroll out of his own pocket and took Andy, the Keep Films accountant, on desperate trips to find financing from studios in Los Angeles, lawyers in New York, business syndicates, and men in porn. He didn't sleep at night, nodded off in meetings, and when Andy kicked him awake, he rambled on about the Second World War. He wasn't eating at all.

American International Pictures finally put up the money, but only enough to cover costs and payroll; there was no producer's fee.

It was spring—not that you could tell—when my father came to Los Angeles to show the Western to AIP. He opened the door to his room at the Hilton, and went back to lie on his single bed.

"You're very thin, Dad," I said. "Are you eating?"

"You're fat," he countered. I drove him to the screening; he didn't comment on the Rent-A-Wreck Mustang.

The Great Scout & Cathouse Thursday was a mess. I told him I loved it. He could tell I was lying, so we fought.

Leo Lerman and Alex Liberman sent me to the Cannes Film Festival for *Vogue,* to write about Bertolucci and *1900,* on which I was now an expert. I stopped in London on the way.

The paintings had not returned. Joyce had to tell me the truth: "Your father had to meet the payroll for the Western himself. We got a good price for the Nicholson, and a very good price for the Léger."

"So we're rich again!" I said.

"No," she said, "they went to pay for the Western."

~

In Cannes, Uncle Don found me a secret room at the Martinez, three floors down from his business suite, behind an unmarked door with neither a lock nor a key.

"Just don't leave anything valuable lying around," said Don. "No one notices this door."

"Where's the phone?" I asked.

"Tip the switchboard operator, and if there's a call for you, the maids will come knock. You can use their phone in the linen closet," said Don. "You'll be alone until tomorrow, and then the Penthouse Pet gets in from L.A. and she'll be in the second room."

"The Penthouse Pet?"

"We're in bed with Bob Guccione," he said, with a shrug.

He was preselling a film called *Caligula,* which promised to be even worse than the Western. The posters bore a cracked Roman coin and announced a script by Gore Vidal, Malcolm McDowell as Caligula, Peter O'Toole as Tiberius, John Gielgud as Nerva, and Helen Mirren as Caesonia, whoever that was. Bob Guccione, as producer, had chosen a director named Tinto Brass.

A knot of Asian buyers came in, sat down, and asked questions.

Uncle Don answered, "Yes, there is sex in it."

"Will it be an X?" asked one.

"Maybe," said Uncle Don. "Well, probably."

The buyers rose in a body and walked out.

"Is this going to be a porno?" I asked Don.

"Koreans," said Don, "humorless. Listen, I'm worried about your father. He isn't making any sense."

You're preselling a porno and you're worried about my father? I thought.

~

"Peter wants to see you," said Joyce when I stopped in London on my way back to Los Angeles. The man from Tramp's no longer rented my apartment in Roebuck House, so I stayed there. He'd given it thick new carpets and a nightclub paint job. I set a pot of Parma violets on the table by the window to make it mine.

Peter's hair was long and still that odd shade of pewter. I set out the big ashtray and two cups of tea, and noticed how insubstantial Peter was. Compared to him, Donald was as dense as earth.

"It's Jules," said Peter.

"What about him?"

"He's making all the wrong decisions," he said. "It's a disaster."

I waited for details. Peter waved toward his lower belly, which had nothing to do with my father. He said, "Keep Films is a bloody mess," then added, "I just need a little bit of femininity."

His eyes touched mine. My heartbeat altered. I'd known Peter since I was nine years old.

He took a joint from his pocket. "This is all I can do since the operation," he said. "No more alcohol." He struck a match.

"It'll eliminate the subclauses," I said.

"Did I understand you right?" he asked. "You mean the subordinate clauses? It increases mine."

No! I meant subtext. Subtext. That was the word, but it was too late to correct myself. Subtext. I took a hit on the joint, my first in over a year. I was twenty-seven now, he was forty-three, a few years older than Donald.

"I've been learning the sonnets," he said, "all of them."

"Shakespeare?" I asked.

"Of course, Shakespeare," he said. "Who else?"

"More tea?" I asked. It could have been Donne. Keats.

"I think he's mad," said Peter. "Jules, I think he's going mad."

That's impossible, I thought. You are all perfect. Keep Films is a beautiful machine that you built together to turn out formal films where you play madmen. Or kings. More madmen than kings. How many madmen, how many kings?

"Dad looks a little thin," I said. "He's not a thin person."

"Your mother's on those pills, she can't do anything, she wouldn't do anything, she's the loyal wife. Jules won't listen to your uncle, and he doesn't listen to me." His eyes were blue like Donald's, but not as pale.

"Please, Joanie. Do something."

"What am I supposed to do?" I asked.

"Come home and keep an eye on him."

He relit the joint, moved his chair closer to the table. His eyes on mine, he caressed the violet's velvet leaves. I felt an abyss open up below me, ready to change perception to sensation. That sensation would be incest.

"'Where the bee sucks, there suck I,'" he began, very slowly. "'In a cowslip's bell I lie; there I couch when owls do cry.'"

Ariel's song from *The Tempest*. My heart beat as fast as it did when I was with Donald.

"'On the bat's back I do fly'"—the blue eyes on me, too tight—"'after summer merrily. Merrily, merrily shall I live now . . .'"

I had to stop the words coming at me. "That is *so* beautiful!" I exclaimed, too loud, as if I were in his dressing room after a performance, and added, "Bravo! Bravo! Bravo!"

He stopped. The moment was over, I'd killed it. He stood up. "Come back to London and sort Jules out," he said. "You're the only one who can." Then he left. I didn't see him again for thirty-three years.

Beatrix Miller took me to lunch. Did I have a beautiful house in Los Angeles? No. A nice car? Well, no. A boyfriend? Um, no. I had a script. "I need you for the Diamond Jubilee issue," she announced, and offered me my old job, but this time at a decent salary. I had nothing to keep me in Los Angeles, and two reasons to move back to London. Before I left, I attempted to give the foam rubber octagon in my living room to someone who'd appreciate its peculiar charm. A costume designer with a Louise Brooks haircut came to see it, glanced at my mess of books, coffee mugs, and ashtrays and said, "You'd love my ex-husband." He was called John Heilpern, wrote for the *Observer,* and was the dramaturge at the National Theatre. I packed my books and clothes, and arrived on my father's birthday.

Nothing was the same in London. Siân had left Peter for a young actor. My parents had sold Upper Belgrave Street and moved to Eaton Square. Jules no longer smoked cigars. Joyce was selling her diamonds. My father looked beaten, but smiled when he told me he'd bought the rights to all eleven volumes of Upton Sinclair's Lanny Budd series.

"This is a project you'll like, Joanie," he said. "It covers the history of the first part of the twentieth century. It's like what Bertolucci tried to do in *1900,* but longer."

Now that all was lost, he was trying to please me.

CHAPTER EIGHT

I tried to keep an eye on my father, as promised. I dined with him and Joyce in the new Italian restaurant they'd found on Sloane Square, but I couldn't talk to him. He was not yet sixty, but he'd stopped listening, his attention entirely consumed by fighting off any evidence of failure. He couldn't afford to host large tables anymore, but he did anyway; he still tipped as if every day were Christmas, spending money he didn't have to prove that he had money. When I asked him what he was going to do, he shouted at me; I shouted back. One night, as Joyce and I stood on the pavement, we watched him go into a rage and gun his car down the center of Eaton Square as if to drive a bloody gash into the very heart of London.

Meals with my parents wouldn't make things better. Sometime during those first weeks back in London I resolved that I would help them by becoming a success. I'd do very well at *Vogue,* write scripts that sold, finish my novel, and make it a bestseller. My brave diligence would save the day.

Working with Beatrix at British *Vogue* was like being back at school under a benevolent headmistress, but after seven weeks in the cork-floored halls at Hanover Square, I started doubting I'd done the right thing. Then the phone rang at the office. It was John Heilpern with an invitation to go to the opening of a revival of Tom Stoppard's *Jumpers* the following night.

I met him backstage at the National; he was bearded, confident, a Northerner. Ready to be amused.

"How come you invited me yesterday?" I asked. "Did your girlfriend crap out on you?"

"Yes," he said.

He'd studied law at Oxford, and he didn't lie. I went to bed with him that same night. I'd tiptoed around playing at passion for two years, and I was in a hurry for things to be real. We'd known each other two weeks when I read in the *Daily Mail* that Donald was carrying on in his trailer with a young actress. I turned to John in bed and asked him when we were getting married. "Before Christmas," he said, but it took longer.

John knew why I had a key chain with a Casanova medallion clipped to my shoulder bag. One morning I heard the sound of something metallic dropping into the tin wastebasket, and after he'd gone to the theater, I saw it was Casanova. I left it there.

The night I introduced John to my parents, they were holding court at the White Elephant on the River, ten people around the table. Joyce could see I took this man seriously—my bangs were sticking to my sweating forehead, my hands were trembling. She was cordial and intrigued. John was tall, good-looking, single; she loved what he wrote, and he was at the National Theatre. He told her his father had been a bookie in Manchester; "Peter's father was a bookie in Leeds!" she said. He was practically family.

I wanted John and my father to talk about theater and films, but Jules glared at John with the eyes of an enraged chicken and by dessert he was humming "The working class can kiss my ass, I've got the foreman's job at last," to the tune of "The Red Flag."

"Your father's distinctly odd," John said as we walked along the Thames after dinner.

I sat on the sofa reading John's *Observer* profiles: Graham Greene, Rudolf Nureyev, John Osborne. Serious black-and-white articles about towering figures, on the front page of the culture section, written with a tenderness that made me see each one in full. John could access the truth inside people. Ever since the interview with Donald, I'd felt the form was nothing but flattery and betrayal. John's pieces were the opposite of flattery, but his words were never a betrayal. He described his subjects with a coherence and an empathy that made them want to keep him close. Rudolf Nureyev, John Osborne, Arthur Koestler, and Peter Brook were his friends. I was happy to think that they'd come to him for who he was.

I didn't like writing profiles. I was too permeable to remain myself around others, and my only gift was a form of channeling, taking in everything around my subjects. I'd transcribe the drone of the exchange, alert to a change of tone, of temperature, and if the subject had talent, their voice pulled me inside them, and I'd learn something. I preferred to write about places, moments; a close reading of inanimate objects could give me the meaning of a time.

Faber and Faber were about to publish John's book, *Conference of the Birds,* the story of his journey through Africa on a theatrical safari with Peter Brook. I took John's author photo, draped him in the unmistakable patterns of a Missoni scarf, and gave him one of my cast-iron sphinxes to hold, to stamp him as mine. Arthur Koestler gave the book an ecstatic blurb. The reviews were excellent and our party for the book even better.

I happily cooked for thirty, then forty people, roasted meats, sautéed vegetables, and made a dessert with black currants in syrup. Bacall came, and somehow Laurence Olivier, and actors from the National Theatre, and my old friends and John's, though Jules and Joyce couldn't make it.

My *Vogue* and John's *Observer* created a force field around us.

I'd been with John a year when Karl Lagerfeld said, "I'll make your dress if you get married," so it was time to send out invitations. Karl flew me to Paris to be fitted for a ruffled mauve taffeta dress under a mauve ottoman silk riding habit, both made of antique fabrics.

We exchanged our vows at Caxton Hall registry office. John's eight-year-old daughter, Rachel, came from Los Angeles, and so did Sue Mengers; Karl brought Jacques de Bascher, Anna Piaggi, and Paloma Picasso. Uncle Don and his youngest daughter, Janis, came from New York, and so did Bacall, and Joyce's old friend Lorraine. My matron of honor was Manolo Blahnik.

We had a blast of a party at Mr. Chow; Michael put black currants in the champagne to make it as mauve as my dress. I didn't know that my father had to take out one more loan to pay for it.

We moved to a top-floor flat one grimy block west of the fumes of Earl's Court Road. I tacked Alexander Pope's line "Luxurious lobster-nights farewell, For sober, studious days" to the wall by my desk, and tried to work on my novel, but there were parties all the time, always in Paris. When Loulou married Clara's boyfriend Thadée, there was a ball on an island in the Bois de Boulogne. When Paloma married an Argentinean playwright, there was a ball at Le Palace; I wore my mauve wedding outfit. Karl refused to join us for New Year's Eve at the Lido with Rudolf—"Nureyev, too vulgar! The Lido, worse!"—but invited Rudolf to his Venetian Ball at Le Palace; I wore the mauve wedding outfit again, topped with a white wig. Karl said, "I really have to make you something else."

Anjelica arrived in London to join Jack, who was shooting *The Shining*. She brought Allegra, who already had Ricki's composure, her appetite for books, wordplay, words. John Huston's last wife, Cici, had finally told her that her real father was John Julius Norwich. She saw him in London and met her grandmother, Lady Diana Cooper. I happily took her with me to screenings and to lunches, a blond, thirteen-year-old version of Ricki with whom to resume the interrupted conversation.

I left *Vogue* to become associate editor of *Observer* magazine, but it was brief. The machinists on the presses in the basement regularly went on strike, and so did we journalists. I had an agent now, so I quit the *Observer* to write scripts, but then the firemen went on strike, the garbage men, pilots, nurses, food truckers, hospital auxiliary services. Miners' strikes caused brownouts that stopped the country cold. More sheiks arrived to shop for mansions, liquor, decorative items executed in semiprecious stones, and Playboy Bunnies; the well-bred became their middlemen. The chancellor of the exchequer vowed to "squeeze the rich till the pips squeak," and film production dried up. Music was punk, punk was fashion. Pasty teenagers gathered at World's End with safety pins through their noses, their hair in spiked ridges, their faces made up like ghouls. The IRA set off bombs. I lived in fear of bombs, asteroids, and nuclear war. My parents talked about moving to the States. John and I talked about moving to New York. I felt the old world breaking around us.

I had to get to work on my novel, but there were more parties in Paris, so I put aside the script that was delaying the novel to put on the mauve wedding costume for yet another ball among the night-crawlers at Le Palace. Finally, a glamorous art dealer named Martin Summers and his wife, Nona, loaned me their chalet in Gstaad, out of season, in spring. I camped among their things, lived on two eggs and one slice of ham a day, walked the alpine meadows every afternoon, washed my T-shirts in shampoo and dried them in the sun. In two months, I wrote the first hundred pages of my novel.

~

It was the 1979 British invasion of New York. John and I arrived at the same time as Tina and Michael Chow, just after Eric Boman and Peter Schlesinger, a year or so after David Shaffer the child psychiatrist and his wife, Serena, who gathered us all for Sunday lunches in their house in the Village. Anna Wintour had been there since 1976 and couldn't understand why anyone would waste their time in Europe.

It was August. Dazed by the heat and clangor of New York, Tina Chow and I sat with immense plates of tuna salad at the Dover delicatessen, wondering what would happen to us in New York and why the streets were full of rats.

John was the *Observer*'s cultural correspondent. I wrote pieces for Leo Lerman at *Vogue* and tried to finish the novel.

A young editor at Random House, Jonathan Galassi, gave me a small advance for the novel. John stacked copies of the *New York Times* in his study to stay on top of the endless cultural events, and covered as many of them as the *Observer* could take.

We were living on the small profit from selling the Earl's Court Square apartment at the wrong time, on John's salary from the *Observer*, which was on the brink of closing, and the little that *Vogue* paid for articles. The rent on the rambling apartment on upper Madison Avenue was so high that we mostly ate at home. We were together all day long. John could hear if I was typing in the room next door, I could hear if John was typing in the room next door. Or not typing in the room next door. To break the constant panic, we gave dinners for new friends who rehearsed avant-garde theater pieces for decades, and new half-French friends, Alain and Nora Coblence, and Leo Lerman and his companion, Gray Foy. Mary Ellen Mark, who'd been in Africa on the famous safari, brought Candice Bergen, who developed a crush on John. I cooked fish or lamb for fourteen or twenty as I had in London, and before dinner, John carefully poured a few drops of the same Guerlain "Extrait de Pot-Pourri aux Algues Marines" that Ricki had used, and that we couldn't afford, into round brass holders on the lightbulbs.

Michael Chow opened his New York Mr. Chow on East 57th Street. John and I ate there for free, though Tina explained that we were to tip the waiters generously. On other nights we went to Elio's, where Elio and his partner, Ann, kept our bills low.

One day, a breathy female voice on the phone claimed to be Jackie Onassis. "Good joke," I said, and hung up. The voice called back. "It's really Jackie," she said. "Valentino wants you to do a book with him."

She was an editor at Doubleday. I knew that. I was already writing a book. She knew that. She wanted to have lunch, and asked me to pick the place.

"My friends just opened a restaurant called Mr. Chow on 57th Street," I said. She'd never been. I called Tina with the news, and asked if she would put us a little apart from the other guests, so Jackie Onassis could feel private.

Jackie Onassis arrived at twelve thirty, wearing trousers and an old beaver coat that struck me as the confident expression of classy thrift. Tina put us at the corner table in the big room.

Jackie Onassis spoke in breaths of marvel, and made it clear that the subject was me, not her. At the end of lunch, she lit a cigarette and looked around the room. The restaurant was completely empty.

"The food is delicious," she said, "but I'm worried for your friends. Is it always like this?"

"What did you do?" I asked Tina after Jackie Onassis had left.

"I canceled the other reservations," said Tina. "Did she like it?"

I didn't want to do the Valentino book, which was going to consist mostly of photographs. Jackie Onassis lunched with John, read his book, flirted with him, and flattered him. Nothing came of it but more lunches. Women adored him, and it was nice that in our precarious situation, the most famous woman in the world was paying close attention to John.

~

My parents moved back to Los Angeles after almost thirty years in Europe. Jules waved his British passport when he landed, absurdly proud to be returning home as an alien without a green card.

Los Angeles was sunny and simple, but it was the end of the line.

They found an apartment on Carmelita, where Doheny Drive meets Santa Monica Boulevard. Their refrigerator held little besides domestic champagne, but they still had a few middling-good paintings, the furniture from San Simeon, the giant round coffee table made from the two Renaissance consoles, the marquetry chairs bought from Mark Twain's daughter. A table draped with a leftover length of tapestry fabric held Jules's eighteenth-century globes, the armillary sphere, and a statue of the goddess Kwan Yin.

They sold things off to get by. The toy bulldog on wheels, my sixth-birthday present, was displayed in the living room, now so gray it looked like an antique. They couldn't believe how much money it brought in when they sold it.

The pain in Joyce's cheekbones came more often now, but she sounded cheery on the phone, if slow, through her Tegretol haze. "Your father's going through the contents of his filing cabinets," she said, "most of which are on the living room floor, and he's a little low."

I went to the MacDowell Colony to finish my novel, but I fell under the spell of a poet there, and returned jangled and guilty. John and I almost broke up; I rented a small office on East 60th Street in which to finish the book, hoping that if we were apart during the day, I wouldn't go looking to other men for inspiration.

The Only Place to Be was about people who wanted to be famous. It was too long and didn't really have a plot, though it had some amusing character descriptions and, inevitably, an affair with an actor whom I named Kid Crane, after the words "Crane's Kid Finish" on a box of stationery. Jason Epstein, the head of Random House, decided it, or I, was "The Intellectual Judith Krantz." In a hurry to promote the book, he hired a young publicist named Peggy Siegal who pulled together four hundred people, mostly young actors I didn't know, for a party at Elio's. Elio chipped in with ice sculptures for the buffet, a truck with movie première searchlights, and replaced the restaurant's awning with one that read "The Only Place to Be." Joyce flew in, Anjelica flew in, Jules stayed at home.

The book was well reviewed in the *Times*, *People*, and *Newsweek*, but not a bestseller. I sulked that I wasn't being taken seriously, that the publicist's efforts had made me look like a socialite who'd dashed off a book between manicures. I went to Los Angeles for more interviews, more signings, more parties. John stayed at home, worn out by all the fuss, worn out by me.

The *Los Angeles Herald Examiner* quoted me saying that the lust for fame was the single motivation for human behavior on the day that Sue Mengers was giving a dinner for me. When Jerry Brown, the governor of California—black-haired, handsome, with furious dark eyes—arrived late at Sue's dinner, he stuck out his index finger to count my nine pearl necklaces one by one from my collarbone down. Without taking his finger off my solar plexus, he declared, "I don't agree with what you said in the paper today. You really think people only do things to become famous?"

"Isn't that why you became governor?" I countered.

Sue's living room whirled around us, Anjelica and Joan Collins and Billy Wilder and Sue and Jean-Claude and twenty others mere backdrop as we discussed the spell of image, the Jewish ancestry of Saint Teresa of Ávila, and the central theory of Ernst Schumacher. He was ready for anything that was in my head, I was primed for anything that was in his. Finally, a real playmate.

After the dinner, Anjelica and I wound ourselves into a frenzy of speculation over the governor. In our St. Clerans world, the knights were poets or movie stars, why not a governor? He'd broken up with Linda Ronstadt, he was single, I was not.

Sue screamed "Mrs. Brown!" on the phone. He'd asked for my number. Sue was thrilled.

Soon, at his house in Laurel Canyon, we talked through the night. He thought aloud; I caught what he thought and lobbed it back. I wanted this ball game, this exchange. This was the intensity I craved. Wherever it led and whatever it meant. It wasn't only talk, but it wasn't yet sex.

If I'm like this, I thought, as I drove down Laurel Canyon back to my parents' flat on Carmelita, I can't be John's wife. I can't be anyone's wife. I am not steady, I am not consistent, I can't keep the promises of a wife.

I confessed to my mother. Nothing had happened, but I knew it would.

"When I went to Paris with your grandmother and Joan Harrison," she said, "I had an affair with Claude Terrail, the man who owns La Tour d'Argent. I was very young; it was my secret. Your father never knew."

It was the first break in her perfection; I wished she had told me when I was twenty-six and sitting on her bed in the *residenza* in Milan, when I needed so badly to know.

John and I separated. I'd tried to have a normal life, and failed.

Our little English group fell apart; separation was contagious. David and Serena Shaffer divorced. David Shaffer fell in love with Anna Wintour. The cards reshuffled into a new deck.

~

I was alone in New York, the new minor boldface celebrity socialite novelist. I started smoking again and lost twenty-six pounds. I dashed about in new clothes and heels and landed on the Best-Dressed List. My mother was delighted by the pictures of me in the papers. I owed allegiance to no one but Leo Lerman at *Vogue*.

Jerry and I talked about Ivan Ilyich and he introduced me to the chants of Hildegarde von Bingen. Because he'd been a Jesuit, I read

Saint Ignatius Loyola; because of our first conversation, I read Saint Teresa of Ávila, and I read Rumi in bed, eating rice crackers and the occasional chocolate-covered cherry in brandy. *Griotte.*

I saw him rarely, but long-distance was familiar, and less obtrusive than marriage. Longing is love without responsibility.

Leo and Alex constantly sent me to Paris on assignment for *Vogue,* where they put me up at the Ritz, always in the same princess room facing the column of the Place Vendôme. The bathroom light switch set off Baroque music. I'd invite Helmut Newton, his wife, June, and my school friend Jane Gozzett for pastry and tea-sandwich picnics on my bed, with drinks from room service.

I was in Paris at the Ritz the Sunday it happened.

My father answered a ring at the doorbell of the apartment on Carmelita, and four young men burst in and threw him to the floor. The tallest one had a gun.

They held him down with their feet and said, "Give us your money."

"I don't have any," he said.

The tall one pistol-whipped him, another reached into the pocket of the jacket hanging on a chair, found the British passport, tossed it aside, and took Dad's silver Tiffany money clip that held two twenty-dollar bills.

"Get your wife," said the tall one, holding the gun to my father's head.

Dad called out, "Joycie!"

The tall man with the gun went loping down the hall as my delicate mother emerged from the bedroom, half-asleep in her negligée. She stared him down, reached for the panic button, and pressed it as she said, very loud, "Get the fuck out of my house, you motherfucker."

He turned and fled with the three others. When the police arrived, my parents, in shock, were afraid to open the door.

Joyce had been heroic; Jules never recovered. Within a week, he had taken to barking at young men on the street, barking like a dog.

"Can't you get him to stop?" I asked when my mother told me.

"He hasn't done it too much," she backtracked. "Just twice. He seems to be in better shape."

They came to New York that Christmas. Jules was cheerful, despite the ordeal. It looked like his long depression was over, but they both had problems with their eyes. He'd just been operated on for a detached retina. She was going to have a cataract operation in January, and Evelyn Keyes was going to stay with them. I bought him a gold money clip from Tiffany to replace the silver one, booked a table at Elio's for New Year's Eve, my treat, and invited Gay and Nan Talese to join us.

Dad was happy to talk about the old days with Gay and Nan, happy to be at Elio's, happy to be in New York, so happy that he kept ordering more champagne. The money clip had been a mad $400, and I'd figured on two, maybe three bottles of champagne, but now it was five, now it was six, and then a seventh arrived. I held his hand tight. For the first time in nine years, he wasn't depressed. I was happy to pay the bill.

I went to Los Angeles for my parents' thirty-ninth wedding anniversary. Joyce met me at the airport, alone. She'd had the cataract operation, and took off her sunglasses to show me her eye.

"I can't drive," she said, "but I found an Israeli who drives for me."

"Where's Dad?" I asked.

"Evelyn's left," she said. "You know how she goes on about Freud, and how your father hates anything to do with analysis . . ."

"She went all Oedipus on you?" I asked.

"Well, it's not true! Not everything is Oedipus and incest! It may have been true for her, but it's not true for everyone, and it's certainly not true for us," she said, and quickly added, "That suitcase has seen better days. Don't you have any Vuittons left?"

In the car, she lit a cigarette and began in French, "*Votre père a un problème . . .*"

"Why are you speaking French?"

She pointed to the back of the driver's seat. Not in front of the servants.

She continued in French. Jules had decided that Evelyn was "*mal.*" "*Elle a dit terrible choses.*"

"What kind of terrible things?" I asked.

"Il a dit de partir, il a jeté Evelyn dehors. Il a scrubbed *le* guest room *avec ammoniaque."*

So he'd asked Evelyn to leave, then scrubbed the guest room with ammonia. He was neat; he'd always emptied wastebaskets and rubbed down kitchen counters.

She nodded, took a deep breath, and went on—*"Et après, il était un ours."*

"And after, he was a bear?"

"Oui," she said, *"pas en anglais"*—her finger pointing at the driver's seat again.

He had become *possédé* with the *esprit* of a Kodiak bear, she said. Possessed with the spirit of a Kodiak bear.

I shook my head. She switched to English, "You know, that bear, when he was in the Aleutians during the war with John, the bear that went raging into the tent one night and attacked everyone. He says it's that same bear," she whispered. "That bear took hold of him."

I took one of her cigarettes.

"How is he now?" I asked.

"You'll see," she said.

The apartment on Carmelita was silent. Joyce dropped her keys on the dining table with a clang that brought my father into the main room.

He was naked, running at a slow lope in a wide circle, not looking at us, his hands held up, their palms striped with red.

"Get dressed, Jules," my mother ordered. Docile as a dog, he went back to the bedroom.

"His hands . . ."

"The ammonia burned through his skin, but he's not injured."

He returned dressed in unfamiliar clothes, a short-sleeved shirt over his trousers, white loafers. He didn't wear short-sleeved shirts, he didn't wear white loafers.

His hands were bleached white, the lines on his palms outlined in blood. He hugged me.

"Oh Joanie, I'm so . . ." He sobbed, and then looked up at me. "You're taller than me in those heels."

"I've been—" he began, interrupted himself—"Joycie, open some champagne!" He stood by the coffee table, moved to a chair, then to the sofa; he told me to sit on the far side of my mother, and when the champagne was poured, he said we should all stand up to toast.

"Toast me, toast me," he said, "for God's sake, I can't toast myself."

"To the best father in the world," I said.

"We need an audience," he said, and held out his glass to the empty sofa.

"I have to rent a car," I said.

"Your father will drive you," said Joyce with a smile.

In the elevator, he wiped his palms with a wet Kleenex and said, "I really was a bear. I took the shirt I was wearing that day to the laundry. They're Koreans, they recognized the smell of Asian bear, they burned it. Ask your mother."

Erratic and slow, he got us to Budget Rent A Car, where he took three Styrofoam cups from a pile by the coffee machine, filled them from the candy jars on the counter, and came over to show me seven Tootsie Rolls in one cup, three Hershey Kisses in the second, three lollipops in a third.

"Three with seven and three, three, that's good," he said, and placed the cups in a Budget Rent A Car shopping bag.

Outside, I found him staring at the sidewalk.

"I dropped them, and only one stayed in. That's a bad omen, isn't it?"

"It's a good omen, Dad!"

He put his hands on my arms and said, "You know, I was never sexual with you."

"I know that," I said.

"Why are people so interested in incest?" he asked. And then he began talking about Einstein.

I told him I'd stay at Anjelica's.

"He thought he was a bear," I sobbed at her kitchen table, "an actual bear."

"He needs a doctor," she said, "a psychiatrist."

He hated psychiatrists; he saw analysis as proof of weakness. I knew Jungians, but Jungians only dealt with symbolic bears, and it was Freud who'd set this off. I could imagine the scene, Evelyn tipsy, talking about Freud, Oedipus, incest. She must have meant emotional incest. It must be that. Of course it was that. His spirit was all over me like glue.

"There's this thing called emotional incest," I told Anjelica.

"I'm sure there is," she said.

I called David Shaffer, who did not believe in the unconscious but was the head of child psychiatry at Columbia Presbyterian. He'd know the perfect person for Dad.

While I explained the bear, Anjelica took a call on the other line, twisting the phone cord, crying. A producer was pressuring her to give a script to Jack, some Mafia comedy that she'd be in and John Huston would direct.

It was always about our fathers.

I found a doctor I could afford. He quizzed me after he'd seen Jules.

"You father says you lived in a pink marble palace where Federico Fellini played the golden harp and someone moved an aircraft carrier to please your mother?"

"That's true," I said.

"Are you sure?" asked the doctor. "It doesn't sound real."

"It's my life, too," I said. "I was there."

The doctor went on to practical matters. "Is he proud that he doesn't need to sleep?"

"Very," I said.

"Does he eat three meals a day?"

"He says he doesn't have to eat."

The doctor explained that the apparent rise out of depression had been my father's passage from a depressed state to a manic one. "Your father's cycles are very long," he said. Nine years down, I calculated, 1975 to 1984. Yes, bad years. Nine years up before that, 1966 to 1975, the champagne years, the British passport and the fight with John Huston, all the way through the Western he wouldn't abandon. "Your father is a classic manic-depressive and has to go on lithium," said the doctor.

I had new bills to pay, and new clothes to cancel.

~

Alex Liberman understood the situation. I went from eight big articles a year to eighteen, twenty-two. I was still going out in my Best-Dressed clothes, but came home as sober as when I'd left, and got back to work until dawn. The weekends were ideal, forty-eight uninterrupted hours. I didn't cook for anyone, I didn't have dates.

I wrote as fast as I could, titanic amounts of copy for *Vogue* and *Vanity Fair*—Chanel, Dior, actresses, Tom Stoppard, Jeremy Irons, Azzedine Alaïa—to make enough money to pay for the doctor and cover the damage, because, despite the lithium, there was damage. A rented red Mercedes he crashed and abandoned on a freeway; a hotel where he ran out of cash; six fake suede coats bought from a man sitting next to him on a plane.

He didn't have credit cards. Because of the British passport, he wasn't in the United States legally. He didn't technically exist.

Each phone call from Joyce about a new crazed mishap was prefaced with: "You mustn't tell anyone about this." She hated asking for money, but there was no one else to ask. I was typing as fast as I could, but now I called my parents' old friends in London to say that Dad was out of control, manic, yes, but not really crazy, and could they help? The property magnate who financed psychic research sent $5,000; Uncle Don, grumbling, came up with almost as much. I couldn't call Peter. I went to the ballet with a hypochondriac millionaire because I hoped he'd bid generously on Dad's armillary sphere and his eighteenth-century globes when they came up at Christie's. He didn't bid at all.

I took out a $20,000 loan from the bank, clawed back a thousand to buy myself a string of baroque pearls from a Chinese store on Third Avenue, used an intaglio of Plato for the clasp, and told everyone that these were my pearls of wisdom.

Billy Rayner, the kind comptroller at Condé Nast who knew everything, sent me to a lawyer friend on Wall Street, who suggested I take over my parents' affairs and become their guardian. But they weren't old and they weren't sick. Jules was sixty-seven, Joyce was fifty-nine. I came out of his office furious, but I had to give my mother the chance to turn down my offer.

"Oh darling, that would be so wonderful," she said.

"Couldn't you get a job?" I asked, and hung up.

I went to Europe to do three more stories for *Vogue*, and stayed out of touch for weeks, until I called on her birthday.

"Happy birthday, Mom," I said. "I've been very busy working . . ."

"So have I," she said, "I got a job at Pratesi."

She was selling sheets on Rodeo Drive, unrolling luxury Italian bedspreads, laying out imported boudoir pillowcases across the glass tops of the display cases for people she hoped she didn't know. The Tegretol probably helped her keep smiling.

Alone during the day for the first time, Jules went through his papers and the boxes of photographs, those he'd taken in the 1930s, those he'd taken during the war.

The Kodiak bear never returned, but Jules still had tantrums. Joyce said nothing; only when I visited and noticed dents, broken lamps, missing leather-bound scripts, did I understand the depth of his rage.

I used my father's state as an excuse to go to Los Angeles often, though it was really to see Jerry. When Jerry did come over, my parents would disappear into their room to leave us alone on the couch. He wasn't governor anymore; he was re-forming himself as a human being and thinking hard about what America was, what America should be, and he quizzed me. What did I want? Fame? Power? Money? Well, I wanted to finish this second novel I'd started, I said. That wasn't an answer. What were my larger ambitions? I shrugged. Happiness, most likely. Fulfillment. A sense of belonging. "That's what everyone wants," he said. Where in America had I gone to school? I'd gone to school in Paris and London. College? Sarah Lawrence, but I'd dropped out. My college was Condé Nast.

"You're trying to fit me into your grid," I complained.

"I don't know anyone else like you," he said. "You're part of this vague elite, you don't come from anywhere, you don't represent anything."

As a true Californian, he went to forage in the kitchen. "There's nothing in the icebox!" he said, holding the door open on six splits of California champagne and two rectangles of Philadelphia Cream Cheese.

The next day I took a stand with my father.

"You have to eat real meals," I said. "Every day, three times. It's very important for your condition."

"Okay, honey," he said.

I went to Gelson's to buy green vegetables and red meat, real cheese, good fruit, and made dinner. "I'll open a nice bottle of white wine," my father said.

"It's the food that counts," I said, "not the wine. Never mind the wine."

"You have no sense of pleasure," he said.

One evening, I bought a roast chicken, bean shoots and sesame oil, lettuce and tomatoes. Jules stood watching as I pulled the white meat off the chicken and set it in the bowl with the bean shoots. The smell of the sesame oil drew him to the table.

"I remember that," he said, "that's what the cooks made at the camp in Cambodia when we were shooting *Lord Jim.* We ate chicken and bean shoots outside under the moon by the temples at Angkor Wat. I remember how they cut the chicken, here—" he held out his hand "—give me the knife, there's a special way they cut it, they didn't do what you're doing, let me show you."

I handed him the big kitchen knife; he sat down and hacked the chicken into neat squares I recognized from Chinese restaurants.

He was looking down at the meat as he cut it, and he was smiling.

He was making food. He was doing something with his hands, something simple, something real, and he was smiling.

CHAPTER NINE

Leo Lerman edited *Vanity Fair* for a year until Si Newhouse replaced him with Tina Brown on New Year's Day 1984. She tripled the fees for her writers and called each one of us "my star"; I believed her. Leo was installed in an office near Si on the executive floor, a house god dispensing wisdom to editors as WQXR played in the background. His assistant Stephen booked the same theater seats and the same restaurant tables as before. Leo's glasses grew thicker. At parties, Gray Foy kept by his side to murmur hints—"Amy, blue dress, new hair"—so that Leo could exclaim, "Amy! What a glorious blue dress, and I like your hair." He was going blind.

Anna Wintour was creative director of American *Vogue* for a year. When Beatrix Miller retired, Si Newhouse sent her to London to edit British *Vogue.* I knew she wouldn't stay long in London.

Without Leo, *Vogue* no longer wanted essays about the "Pursuit of Happiness," only paeans to the exquisite. That meant Rothschilds, mainly, and every Paris-based ex-model who dabbled in antiques. At *Vanity Fair,* Tina Brown was hungry for movie stars, and assigned me the French ones. The interviews kept my parents going, kept me on TWA Flight 800 to Paris, kept me returning to the princess room at the Ritz. Condé Nast was as lavish as Jules in the Keep Films days. I didn't know how spoiled I was.

I had close friends in Paris: Nicole Wisniak, the creator of the magazine *Egoïste*, and Helmut Newton, who asked me to dirty up the text for his book *World Without Men*, and paid me with two photographs: a kiss and a handshake that he'd titled "Rich Girl, Poor Girl" and inscribed, "To my favorite pornographer."

In the summer of 1984, Jerry Brown gave me a paperback of Henry James's *Beast in the Jungle* and told me our relationship couldn't go on. I read it lying on my bed, and when I tried to get up, my back had locked; the pain was such that I had to sleep on the floor for weeks. When the pain passed, I turned to Philippe Collin, a Parisian film critic of matchless wit, taste, and modesty, whose ambition was to make just one film, about Immanuel Kant, "because nothing ever happened to him." If the man who would be president didn't want me, I'd trade quips with a master of literary games and gather a new reading list. Philippe was twenty years older, but looked my age. His wife had left him for a German theater director named Klaus Michael Gruber, who was famous for motionless productions that thrilled audiences who considered boredom the mark of great theater.

The summer started with Philippe in a borrowed tower in Tuscany, and continued, after a bumpy parting at the Florence train station, in a house on France's Atlantic coast that Nicole Wisniak had rented and filled with her friends, women with broken hearts who dissected their pain at all hours of the day in all corners of the house, to the alarm of Nicole's husband, another Philippe. He'd walk into a room, catch our anxious whispers, and back out in horror.

They were the most elegant heartbreaks in the world.

Nicole had a newborn baby and went about looking like a Rossetti portrait in lace négligées with satin ribbons to the ground, her long red hair tumbling to her elbows. She was capable of exalted enthusiasms that gave wings to her friends, but also subject to dark moods that could last for months. She produced *Egoïste* single-handedly from her bed, and devised most of the ads inside it, each one a triumph of conceptual wit. She'd begun *Egoïste* in 1977; by 1985, there had been all of five issues. She was brilliant, competitive, and discriminating, but in no hurry. Her husband ran *Le Figaro*, but no one in France ran anything during the month of August. Philippe would glance at the headlines, then retire to the terrace to read a thriller.

The house was sprawling, all beams and tiles. Nicole's guests were her most intimate friends who incidentally embodied French fashion: Hélène Rochas and Inès de la Fressange. Inès, as thin and tall as a fashion drawing, had a cartoon way of thrusting her head forward to ask "*Oui?*" and then throwing it back for full-throated laughs. Her currency was cheerful enthusiasm, word games, and puns; she was congenitally helpful, and casual about being the embodiment of the house of Chanel, as reborn in the hands of Karl Lagerfeld.

I didn't see Karl as often as I used to when I'd stayed with him on the Rue de l'Université in eighteenth-century rooms lit only by scented candles set on the floor between taffeta curtains, and slept under the ostrich feather canopy of his *lit à la polonaise,* while he stayed up all night drawing, writing, and reading. He, too, was an only child. He was as cerebral as he was gossipy. He'd adore and then loathe the same person in less than a week. He was critical of the living, enchanted by the dead, and thought his hands were ugly.

There had been tangos and waltzes and those fancy-dress balls, whispers behind his fan, long letters and longer phone calls, projects for movies that never happened, and always a deluge of clothes, an equal deluge of books—all eighteen volumes of George Sand's correspondence, of which I read only four. Laboratory samples of the Chloé perfume, bottles of the final scent. Clothes from Chloé and Fendi and all the other companies he designed for without credit, calling himself, proudly, a mercenary.

In 1978, I'd lobbied Alex and Leo to let me profile Karl for *Vogue,* and now I wrote about him with fearful regularity. After he joined Chanel in 1983, access to Karl became laborious as a hedge of colleagues and sycophants rose up around him, but when I got through, I found him the same as ever, and was rewarded, after an anxious wait, with whatever Chanel suits, bag, blouses, and jewelry I chose.

I wanted Inès and Nicole to understand that I was as close to Karl as they were. I put on a Chanel necklace that Karl had given me, and came down to lunch with three rows of pearls and glass cabochons clanging against my collarbone, my neck aching from its weight.

Hélène said, "It makes you look older than you are."

Inès laughed and said, "That really isn't necessary."

Embarrassed, I removed the heavy necklace; Inès put it on her golden retriever, Jim, and added my panama hat. I photographed the dog, dressed as me.

I'd marked myself as a rube. I wouldn't do that again.

Fashion was a game the true players didn't take seriously, a game that the icons didn't fall for beyond fulfilling the duty to represent their brand in public. The duty was noble and arduous, but it was also, they knew, a little pathetic.

To the insiders, fashion was work, separate from real life. The American notion of a lifestyle where gorgeous people lolled about wearing branded goods had no purchase on Nicole and Inès, for whom old sweaters, lace negligées, and espadrilles were more desirable than the latest thing. Inès was paid to be Chanel in public, but her white jeans were old and her sweaters shapeless.

Nicole's other best friend, Hélène Rochas, was more attached to her role as the figurehead of Parisian chic, but then she'd held the position for forty years. Hélène was impeccable in faultless shirts and skirts, good low-heeled shoes. At her dressing table she used a straight pin to separate her lashes, a nerve-racking process that gave her an alert expression. She wore her blond hair in a complicated style that demanded visits to a local hairdresser, who never quite mastered her directives.

I'd first seen Hélène and her dashing lover Kim d'Estainville in Sardinia when I was seventeen. I was on Irwin and Marian Shaw's boat as company for their son Adam, whom I adored but considered beneath my romantic attention, as he was eighteen months younger. The Shaw boat was called *Xantippe*, fifty-two feet long, expensive to run, and balky. Before it broke down completely and forced us all onto Sam Spiegel's yacht, we docked in Cala di Volpe, a new development with a Pucci boutique but nowhere to buy food.

Marian, Adam, and I were looking for tomatoes in an arcade so new that the plaster was still wet, when I saw a blond woman in a sarong with a dark man of such stunning allure that I gasped and grabbed Marian's hand.

"Not for you," said Marian firmly.

"Why not?" I whispered. He had black hair, blue eyes, and walked like a god. Dashing yet casual, intense yet cool. Handsomer than anyone, even Peter O'Toole.

"He's hers," said Marian. "She's a queen of fashion. She own Rochas. You know that boat that looks like a pirate ship, with all the sails and the mullioned windows in the stern? That's her boat." It was a galleon called the *Quattro Fratelli*.

Movie stars were wisps in the wind compared to people whose names were on products—perfume, clothes, alcohol. The owner of Martini apéritifs, Signor Martini, had welcomed us onto his yacht. Docked next to us was Fred Chandon, of Moët et Chandon champagne. And now Hélène Rochas, owner of the pirate ship, was the actual "Madame Rochas."

The couturier Marcel Rochas had married her during the German occupation of Paris, and named his first perfume Madame Rochas, after her. He died ten years later, leaving her a perfume empire. She'd gone on to launch Femme and Eau de Rochas, married and divorced a theater producer, and lived for years with the handsome Kim d'Estainville, an ex-paratrooper and a *Paris Match* journalist.

A few years before I met her, to the shock of all Paris, Kim left Hélène for their best friend, Pierre Bergé, Yves Saint Laurent's lover and partner. Yves and Pierre were the first couple of fashion, Hélène and Kim the first couple of society, and Paris hostesses wrung their hands over their fractured guest lists.

After Kim left her, the heartbroken Hélène sailed off on her galleon, Stavros Niarchos on his yacht *Atlantis II* in hot pursuit. She left the schooner for the yacht, for a while. Now she was in love with Patrick Modiano, a novelist whose books were always about France during the Second World War. He was mesmerized by Hélène's past as the wife of the foremost Parisian couturier during the German occupation.

Like all of our men, Modiano was married. Inès was in love with a married scientist. Nicole was married but besotted with Avedon. My Philippe was only technically married, since his wife was with the German director, but he acted married more often than necessary.

All of our affairs were supposed to be secrets, which made discussing them all the more urgent. Inès, Hélène, and Nicole had their views about Philippe. They knew his previous girlfriends, Clara Saint, who ran the press for Yves Saint Laurent and therefore ran Paris, and Colombe Pringle, who wrote for *Elle*.

Hélène was thirty years older than the rest of us, but wept as copiously as we did over the timid prevarications of married men. She talked to me for hours about her life and her tastes—only, ever, white flowers, she said. And every morning she produced her pack of tarot cards, which she read for herself, then for me. She'd use antiquated turns of phrase, for instance: *Querelle dans la maison,* quarrel in the home. She saw change coming.

Françoise Sagan arrived in a low sports car like one of her heroines, smoking a cigarette and calling for whisky. She looked like Woodstock, the bird in *Peanuts,* and talked birdlike in fast cheeps. She put up with two days among the weeping lovelorn women, until she could bear it no longer, announced, "You are a bunch of witless fools. There's more to life than men," and drove off to the local casino to gamble for days.

"Well," said Hélène, "she doesn't care about men anymore. She has a girlfriend."

After Françoise left, Nicole told me Kim d'Estainville was coming to stay.

"Is that all right?" I asked.

"We're all civilized," said Nicole, "and he's depressed. Pierre has left him for a younger man. And he's fun."

Kim arrived, a pink sweater from his shop Hemisphères tied around his neck. I was prepared to hate the man who'd betrayed my new friend, but Hélène seemed pleased to see him. Kim's socialite zest for a good time brought the household to life. Suddenly, we were off the sofas and on a local fishing boat headed out to a sandbar with a cooler full of very good wine, finally on holiday. When Kim left after three days, Nicole's husband was sorry to see him go.

Karl called Nicole, who passed the phone on to Inès, who giggled with him for a long while before she passed the phone to me.

"Aren't you bored in that house full of dreary weeping women?" he asked, as I caught my breath—wasn't Nicole his friend and Inès his muse?—and then he added, "but I'm sure it's better than being in a tower with that dreadful Philippe Collin."

"You know everything," I said.

"People talk."

"Well, when do I see you?" I asked, to pull the conversation back to the semblance of friendship.

"Oh," said Karl, "I'm not so much in the public eye right now."

"I'm not the public eye," I said, stung.

The *Atlantic II* knocked against the concrete seawall all night. Summer was almost over and I didn't want to go back to New York. I was comfortable with my new friends. I could write my second novel anywhere and most of the magazine stories I wrote were about people in Paris.

"I don't want to go home," I said at lunch.

"Jeanne Moreau's about to do a play in New York," said Inès. "Why don't you trade apartments with her?"

I made the call and it was done. It was as simple as that.

Jeanne Moreau's bed was beached in the middle of her living room, which was set between two silent courtyards behind the Rue de l'Université. All the luxury had been burned off her, her grand apartment gone, along with her house near Saint-Tropez. She was alone, fifty-nine, a star with nothing left to lose, doing *The Night of the Iguana* in English on Broadway because she needed money. Two dour Germans were in love with her, the writer Thomas Bernhard and the director Klaus Michael Gruber, who was the lover of my Philippe's wife.

Hélène sent white flowers, her signature. Karl sent an assault of color, late-summer asters in red and yellow and purple and bright pink, a little slap at Hélène's dictum about white flowers.

While Jeanne slept in my sleigh bed to car alarms and boom-box hip-hop on East 77th Street, I slept on her immense mattress in the eerie silence of the Rue de l'Université.

Philippe was glad that I was in Jeanne Moreau's apartment; it allowed him to feed his curiosity about the woman who'd mesmerized his wife's lover. He'd settle into a small leather armchair, look over at the bed, and tell me how depressed he was while I lit Jeanne's half-used Diptyque candles, and served him Grand Yunnan tea with gingerbread from the tea shop up the street.

We were terrified to touch each other. In the fall of 1985, the soot of fear pervaded every relationship. AIDS was a good reason to be a nun. I was thirty-seven and had a book to finish. I'd have the test when I was braver.

A young director wanted me to write a play for him about Shirley Goldfarb, the beatnik painter from the Café de Flore. Did I know Shirley Goldfarb had always wanted to sing? I remembered Karl's shoe show, Shirley perched on the mantelpiece, the audience convulsed with laughter. When Shirley was dying, the director explained, a young American named Madison Cox had organized a concert at the Théâtre de l'Athénée, so that Shirley could sing show tunes to an audience made up of Rothschilds, Yves Saint Laurent and Karl Lagerfeld, Hélène Rochas and Kim d'Estainville. The grandees had all cheered and celebrated her at her own gala dinner.

Madison Cox was the young man Pierre Bergé had chosen over Kim d'Estainville. A phone call to Clara Saint, and Madison Cox met me for tea. He looked like a young version of Yves, with thick hair that fell on his forehead and horn-rimmed glasses. He was an open, twenty-seven-year-old American with impeccable manners, studying landscape design.

Soon Pierre Bergé invited me to dinner—"It's good to have you back"—and described Madison as "*remarquable,*" while Madison stared at his plate. Pierre liked those words: *admirable, remarquable.* He spat out pronouncements that made him sound like Jules: *exécrable, abominable.* Men who get things done give brief verdicts. "Big mistake." "The real thing." "Piece of shit."

The play I didn't write about the woman I'd avoided at the Café de Flore brought me into the Saint Laurent fold, and Clara Saint was the first to welcome me. Her taste and her opinions informed Pierre's world, and she was as consumed with the betterment of her circle as she had been when I'd met her fifteen years before.

Hélène wanted to give a dinner for my thirty-seventh birthday, but it posed diplomatic problems. Over lunch at her apartment, between bronze snakes holding up alabaster *torchères* in a décor that combined Directoire and Art Deco, we dealt with the delicate issue of the guest list. Apart from Nicole, Inès, and Clara Saint, it was a minefield. The first person I had to ask about was the man who'd stolen her lover away.

"I've seen Pierre Bergé a few times with my new friend Madison," I said, choking on the fried parsley. "Would it be all right to invite them both?"

Hélène repressed a little contraction of her mouth. "If we have Madison, we can't have Yves—but he doesn't go out anyway—and if we have Pierre and Madison, Kim has to be at a different table."

I hadn't realized Kim would be coming.

I wanted to invite Karl, he was a very old friend, I said, but weren't he and Pierre fighting? Could they be in the same room?

The mouth pursed again. "As long as they are at different tables."

"My friend Anna Wintour is editing British *Vogue*, I think she'll be in Paris. Could I ask her?"

"Of course," said Hélène.

Philippe had been difficult in our Italian tower, but he was a friend of Clara and Pierre.

"And he's a very old friend of mine, of course," said Hélène. "But with or without his wife? She'd bring her theater director who had an affair with your friend Jeanne . . ."

"Jeanne's in New York. Let's not have the wife," I said.

"You're American," said Hélène. "We don't have to follow the rules."

I picked a cocoa-dusted almond from a silver bowl, glanced at the Marcel Duchamp *Mona Lisa* with its pun caption "L.H.O.O.Q.," and

Photo by Robert Siodmak

Feeding the seagulls on the Alster with my father, Hamburg, December 1952.

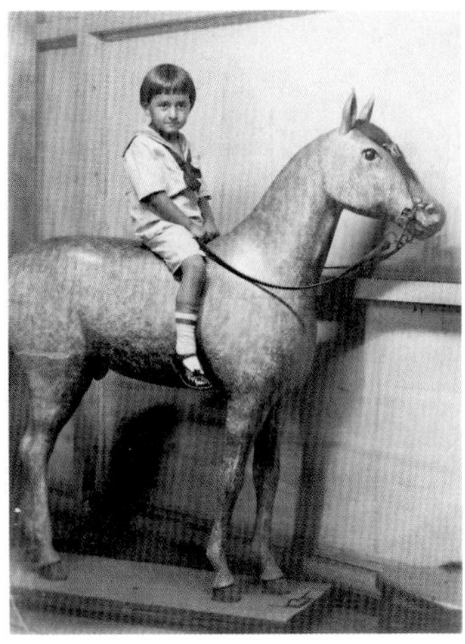

Jules Buck on a toy horse, St. Louis, 1922.

Joyce Gates (née Getz) as a Gypsy girl with George Sanders in the movie *Summer Storm,* 1944.

Joan Harrison, maid of honor, and John Huston, best man, with Joyce and Jules at their wedding, Beverly Hills, January 28, 1945.

Photo © Jules Buck

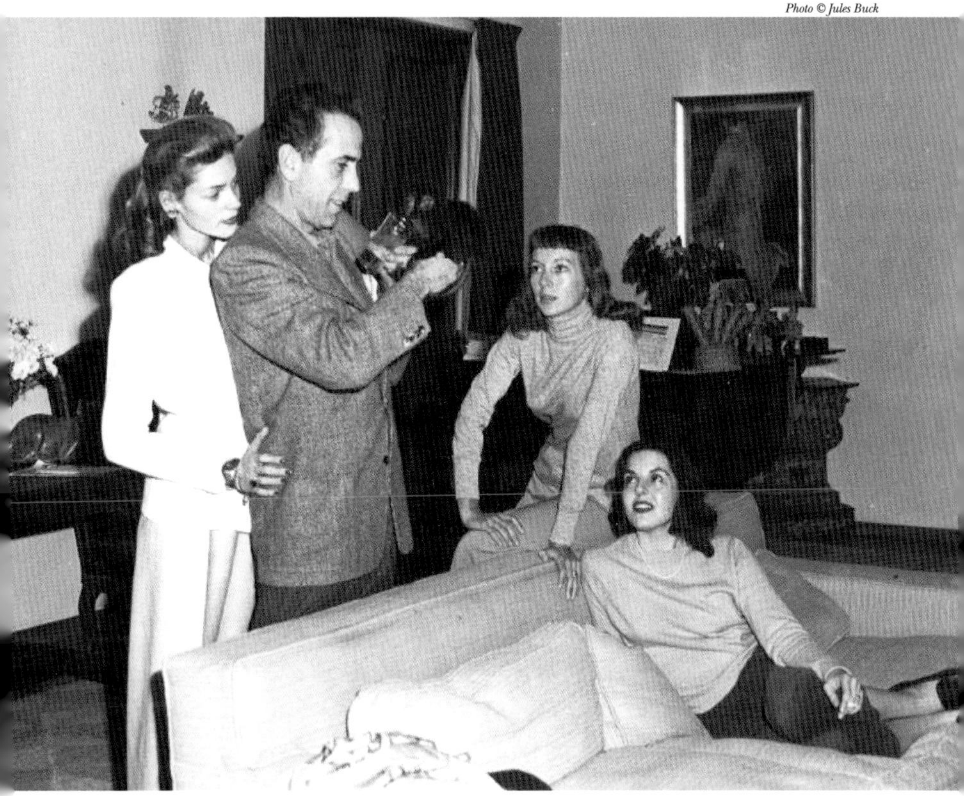

Lauren Bacall and Humphrey Bogart give whisky to John Huston's monkey, as Evelyn Keyes and Joyce look on, Tarzana, 1946.

Joyce with Kirk Douglas, Rome, 1951.

Photo © Jules Buck

Joan Harrison and John Huston, Hollywood, 1946.

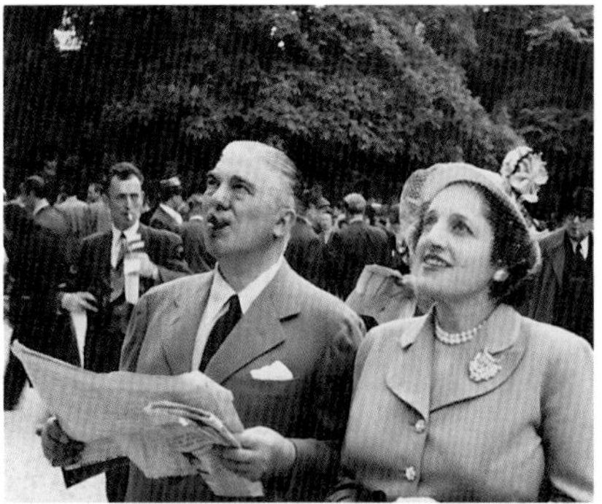

Morey and Esta Getz at Longchamp Racecourse, Paris, 1952.

Photo © Jules Buck

Joyce Buck, Paris, 1952.

Photo © Jules Buck

With Joyce in the grand salon at Le Palais Rose, 1954.

Photo © Jules Buck

Le Palais Rose, Le Vésinet, 1954.

Photo by Robert Siodmak

Photo © Jules Buck

My uncle Don Getz and Robert Siodmak, London, 1957.

Jules smoking an uncharacteristic cigarette under *Psyche and Eros,* 24 Groom Place, London, 1957.

Photo © Jules Buck

Above: Wearing my raincoat as a sack dress, London, 1958.

Right: Peter O'Toole and Jules on a soundstage at Shepperton Studios, 1964.

Photo © Jules Buck

Drawing at the coffee table in the library at St. Clerans with John and Anjelica as Joyce looks on, Christmas 1959.

Photo © Jules Buck

Ricki Huston with flowering branches in her hair in the red drawing room, St. Clerans, 1963.

Photo © Jules Buck

With Anjelica, wearing Christmas scarves and all the wrappings, St. Clerans, 1963.

Left to right: Jules; me; Derek Coombs; Joyce; Peter's sister, Pat Coombs; and Peter and Siân at the *Lion in Winter* première, London, December 1968.

Photo © Jules Buck

Fernand Léger's *Le Pont* hangs between two windows, 14 Chester Street, 1968.

Photo © Jules Buck

Globes and armillary spheres atop the bookcases, 3 Upper Belgrave Street, 1975.

Photo © Trinity Mirror/Mirrorpix/Alamy Stock Photo

With Peter O'Toole, arriving at the *Lord Jim* première, London, February 1965.

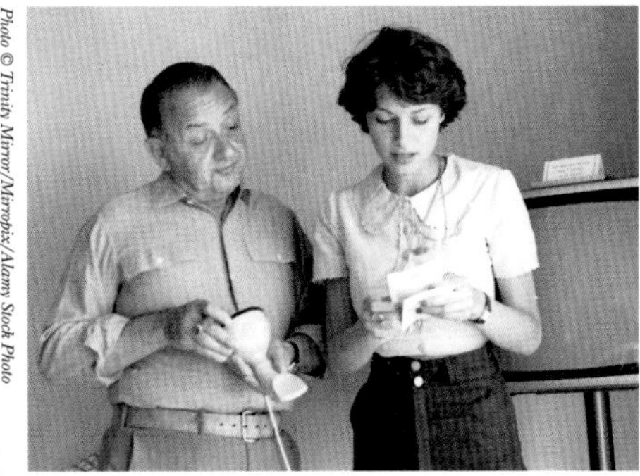

With Jules at the Majestic hotel, Cannes Film Festival, 1974.

Betweeen Loulou de la Falaise and Marisa Berenson, both wearing that season's cable-knit cardigan with fox collar and cuffs, Yves Saint Laurent, Rue Spontini, Paris, 1973.

Photo by Marit Allen

Above: The photo by Marit Allen that opened the door to British *Vogue,* London, 1972.

Below: With Paloma Picasso and Manolo Blahnik, posing on the balcony at Roebuck House, London, 1978.

The cover of Eva Gschopf's composite card, Ford Models, 1969.

Photo © John Heilpern

took in Hélène's Fernand Léger. It wasn't quite as good as the one that had once been about to be mine.

"How funny," said Hélène. "This dinner is going to bring together people who haven't spoken in years."

The dinner was at a small Italian restaurant, Beato. Hélène sat Madison on my left and Pierre on my right, in deference to my new circle. New friend Pierre over old friend Karl, Yves Saint Laurent over Chanel. That placement broke my bond with Karl, who was carefully seated at a different table with his muse Inès.

Anna Wintour arrived from London, pregnant and without her husband. Hélène sat her next to Karl. I saw their heads bend together in instant complicity and was relieved they were getting on so well.

From that night on, my Paris life was traced out. I would have dinner every night with the same group: Hélène and Pierre, now reconciled thanks to me; Madison, Clara, Nicole, and her husband; a pair of playwrights; the aged son of Paul Valéry, the poet. Philippe, a longtime member of the clique. After Philippe told me her story, I was fascinated by Charlotte Aillaud, Yves's favorite. She'd been a teenager carrying messages for the Resistance when the Nazis captured her, tortured her, and sent her to Ravensbrück; sometimes the sleeve of her haute couture jacket rode up just enough to reveal the number tattooed on her arm.

Charlotte Aillaud believed one did not bore people with one's problems, and set the tone for *le petit clan.* One did not discuss anything ugly, anything nasty. One tasted exquisite flavors, remarked on the hint of acetone in a pear sorbet, and for a whole spring, until the hangover headaches became unbearable, one drank peach-flavored champagne. One ate simple French dishes, *merlan en colère, boeuf mode en gelée,* choucroute, a monastic slice of foie gras with a few lettuce leaves.

Clara, keeper of the schedule, decided in which restaurant we would eat, at what time, and with whom. There were no strangers and no foreigners, apart from Madison, me, and Marian McEvoy, who like me was a former *WWD* correspondent. Every woman in a tight little jacket, Marian and I with floppy satin bows in our hair, only the most fleeting suggestion of Chanel, so as not to annoy Pierre.

I'd been accepted, inducted, subsumed into what they called *le petit clan,* a court where the ultimate accolade was to say someone was *de bonne qualité.* Good quality. Well constructed. Durable. Handmade. Of impeccable breeding and manners.

I dined out with *le petit clan* all over Paris, but I never saw a face I knew at another table. *Le petit clan* excluded strangers from its center and somehow from its periphery as well. If they weren't invited, they didn't exist.

Jeanne's play closed out of town in Baltimore, and she was coming home. I found another apartment through a friend of Clara's, a seventh-floor walk-up on the Rue Guénégaud, once a safe house for exiled Colombians where, legend had it, Gabriel García Márquez had written his first book. The floor was ancient red tiles, the bathroom a brick cube by the kitchen, the tub a deep footbath that emptied directly onto the street from a drainpipe on my balcony. The toaster was a primitive instrument to torture bread. In the hallway was a secret room to work in with a sawhorse table and a chair. The sun bounced off the golden domes of the Académie Française beyond the zinc balcony; I stood barefoot at the kitchen sink looking out over to the verdigris roof of the Louvre, eating Camembert with *saucisson* on a piece of fresh baguette, Paris in my eyes and in my mouth, in bliss.

Once visitors stepped inside my front door after the seven flights of stairs, they gasped and clutched at the backs of chairs for a full ten minutes. The last two flights were steep as ladders, and dangerous; the concierge polished each step with beeswax on Mondays.

But Madison, Clara Saint, Hélène Rochas, and Pierre Bergé all hauled themselves up the stairs to gamely eat my bad chili from rough Mexican plates that Hélène had given me. The ascent deserved better food, so I learned to cook *pintade aux choux rouges.*

Up the stairs they returned. There was snow on the zinc balcony, and ice in the Seine. Pierre sat on one of the single beds that served as sofas, and for once he sighed. He was clad in a new suit in a particularly acute shade of *caca d'oie,* his declaration of freedom. He couldn't officially leave Yves, but he'd taken a large suite at the Lutetia, redecorated his rooms, and carpeted them with wall-to-wall ocelot. He had gone to Arnys for new suits in the color that only he and I loved. More important, he was in the process of buying back the house of Saint Laurent from Charles of the Ritz; the money at stake was huge, and confident Pierre was quivering with nerves. Clara and Madison perched on the other single bed while Hélène sat in the one armchair.

A Vacherin sat ripening extra-fast in its open spruce box on the radiator, the *pintades* were jumping in their sauté pan, the red cabbage hissing in a pot. It was only two steps from the living room to the center of the kitchen, so I could attend to both guests and food. Three opened bottles of Côtes du Rhône stood on the big table, and I hadn't forgotten the Perrier.

"Pierre's worried," whispered Madison in the kitchen. "The buyback."

I thought of Dad buying back *The Ruling Class* from United Artists in 1972, and how that had gone. The paintings flying out the door to meet the payroll for the Western. I didn't want Pierre to lose everything the way my father had. I didn't want to see the house of Saint Laurent dissolve like Keep Films, I didn't want this new world of mine to vanish like the old one had.

I rummaged in the bedroom for a talisman and found a chain bracelet, once gold-plated, now partly worn back to base metal. It was thick, it was heavy, it would do.

I handed it to Pierre. "This is to make sure the buyback goes well. Carry it with you all the time and touch it for luck."

Pierre closed his hand over it. "Thank you," he said. "Thank you. I will."

"When everything's done and you've won," I said, as solemn as my father when he stood me in front of the Léger, "you'll give it back, but it will be a real gold chain. To show that you are Midas, and everything you touch turns to gold."

The novel filled the garret and kept me in a world I couldn't gossip about, or even discuss. The story was based on Maurice, the fleeting, beautiful man who'd lived in Pierre and Yves's guest room and was desired by all, men and women. What if the man you loved was the lover of everyone you'd ever known? I made the heroine's father a dealer in

Greek and Roman antiquities, a gay American in Paris, a softer version of Pierre.

I wrote barefoot every day in the tiny room from ten until four, when I bathed in the ridiculous little tub. Then I wandered into shops on the Rue Bonaparte, read the *Herald Tribune* and *Libération* in a café, and dressed for dinner in a suit from Saint Laurent, where my discount was now fifty percent. The heels on my shoes were so high that I couldn't put them on until I'd made my way down the polished stairs.

The *petit clan* dinners were perfect after a day of writing. Nobody cared what I was writing, what the advance had been, when the novel was coming out. They cared what lieder singer Pierre was bringing to his Théâtre de l'Athénée, what Clara thought of Patrick Modiano's new book, what Charlotte Aillaud thought of the new Patrice Chéreau play. They cared what things looked like. Hélène leaned forward, full of concern—"My darling, should you have such big glasses? They exaggerate the lines under your eyes."

The *petit clan* tethered me to its hermetic rituals, its mandarin proprieties, its dress code, its values. My panic about AIDS made me appreciate Clara's flat-earth doctrine about sex; she held that there was no such thing.

I told Jules and Joyce the stories on the phone, the dramas about placement at Hélène's formal dinner parties where the butler circulated with crystal glasses of *cerisette*—cherry juice and Perrier—to let guests know it was time to go home; Pierre's Monday night lieder concerts at the Athénée; Marian McEvoy and Madison and how we had lunch once a week, just the three of us, the "American Lunch Club," to take a break from the relentless French chic. Marian cooked offal, I cooked chili, and when it was Madison's turn in the perfect apartment that Pierre had given him, he presented the vanilla ice cream on top of a folded white linen napkin set on the serving plate.

"What about that Philippe boyfriend?" my father asked. I was too busy with the novel, I said. Philippe had disintegrated into the background cast of *le petit clan*. A friend of Inès's was my secret lover and came to me between five and seven. Unfortunately, five and seven in the morning, before he went to work.

The *petit clan* never knew about the dawn lover.

Anjelica did. She was the only person I confided in, pulling the phone through the garret on its long cord for our 6,000-mile conversation. She'd given Jack the Mafia script, John had directed the film, and now she won an Oscar for playing Maerose in *Prizzi's Honor.* The ceremony wasn't broadcast on French television, but we whooped with joy on the phone the next day.

~

The publisher of Paris *Vogue* invited me to lunch at Maxim's. "Maxim's," Pierre said when I told him, "at lunch?"

"Maxim's," Hélène said. "That's a little vulgar in the daytime."

The man, a plump prince of Polish lineage, unfolded his napkin, ordered two glasses of champagne, asked if I wanted to edit Paris *Vogue,* and added, "If you say yes, you could eat lunch here every day."

I told him that I'd been approached once before. "You were too young then," said the Polish prince. I suggested he meet Colombe Pringle, the clever journalist who wrote for *Elle.* I didn't want the job.

"You're an artist," he said. I picked at my coquilles Saint-Jacques. Yes, I thought, I am an artist in a garret who can borrow Saint Laurent couture any time she wants and would never be caught dead eating lunch at Maxim's. I might be a serious writer if I could finish my second novel and write a third one. I am American *Vogue*'s French-speaking creature, *Vanity Fair*'s French movie star correspondent. I don't want the play-pretend power of a magazine editor.

I have play-pretend bohemia instead.

"You're Ernest Hemingway!" Betty Bacall shouted once she'd caught her breath in the garret, and taken in the view.

I said, "Hemingway has nothing to do with it. I'm totally happy here."

"Yeah? Well, don't get too happy!" she said.

There was no danger of that. Bombs went off in department stores, malls, bookstores. The Chernobyl nuclear power plant in Ukraine exploded and released a mighty radioactive cloud, which, the French newscasters proudly announced, had entirely bypassed France, or as they called it, *l'Hexagone,* although it was over Europe and Scandinavia. No cloud was that discriminating or that agile. I warned my friends against fresh milk and vegetables, insisted they shower vigorously when they came home, leave their shoes and coats by their front doors, and eat only canned tuna fish. "You see death and catastrophe everywhere," said Philippe. It was everywhere.

One man after another grew tired, stopped going out, vanished. One night, after an hour at Régine's and two more in an African nightclub, Kim d'Estainville took a few of us to his secret place, an Italian restaurant that stayed open all night.

"But why are we going there?" asked Philippe. "It's four in the morning."

"You'll see," said Kim, as he parked his car.

The thick plaster walls were set with views of Venice. The banquettes were full. Thin men with scarves and knitted caps, pale faces with the hard red blotches of Kaposi's sarcoma, and leaning toward them, hunched, confidential, loving, their friends who were not sick, whispering, handing them forkfuls of food from their plates. Now and then a loud, defiant laugh broke through. Socializing in the dead of night, out of sight of the healthy.

Libération ran new speculations every day about the modes of transmission. Everyone felt at risk. I went to London for the AIDS test, certain I would be punished for my adventures, relieved, after ten days, to find out I was not. But too many friends were ill, too many were dying. Tina Chow called to tell me Antonio Lopez had died in Los Angeles.

Pierre bought back Saint Laurent perfumes from Charles of the Ritz for $500 million. After the couture show that July, Yves was cheerful enough for a dinner party in his garden.

In New York, my agent and my publisher were both excited that I was so close to Yves Saint Laurent, and pressured me to ask Pierre if I could write the authorized biography. I balked at the idea, but they were persuasive. I called Pierre. He was in Marrakesh with Yves.

"We haven't planned anything, but I promise you that the day we do, you are the first person I will talk to about it," said Pierre. "I give you my word."

I finished my novel, looked for a title in Yeats's poem "Leda and the Swan," fished "Daughter of the Swan" out of a different Yeats poem, and handed the manuscript to Pierre to carry on the Concorde to my publisher.

I dawdled in Paris for another year, rented out my New York apartment to Leo Lerman and Gray Foy when construction chased them from the Osborne, and then to Jay McInerney, whom I didn't know. The novel was done, and I was lost. I tried to start another, but I couldn't catch a feeling long enough to make it count. The *petit clan* were no longer the needed contrast to my life inside the book, and their rigid grace became a grind.

Hélène read my cards; she saw change. But then, she only ever saw change, and quarrels in the home.

Anna Wintour called to say that she was returning to New York to be editor in chief of *House & Garden*. "Si called me while I was on the delivery table!" she said. She had two children now. It was clear that American *Vogue* would be next.

Daughter of the Swan was coming out in September. Philippe said, "You're not with me, you're not French, you're not American, nobody knows what you're doing here. You should move back to New York. It's too hard explaining you to people."

My life was lines across continents, like the drawings of airplane routes in the back of in-flight magazines. New York was the halfway point between my friends in Europe, and my parents and Anjelica in Los Angeles. I'd keep the garret for the moment. It was cheap, and money was coming in.

At the end of August, I went to stay with Hélène in a house she'd rented above Saint-Tropez. Clara Saint tiptoed around the pool; her tendons had so contracted from a life in high heels that she could no longer put her feet on the ground.

I was jumpy about the launch of the novel, impatient with the French conversations about nothing. All the books in the house were closed off behind elegant chicken wire doors, and once I'd finished Bruce Chatwin's *Songlines*, there was nothing to read but the daily papers.

One morning there was no newspaper to be found anywhere in the house. Clara and Hélène looked blank. "Could I go buy some in town?" I asked.

"The butler will buy you whatever you want," said Hélène firmly. He brought back the new issues of *Vogue, Elle,* and *Marie Claire,* but no newspapers.

As I came into the living room before dinner, Clara turned off the television news.

"We'll dine early today," said Hélène, and led us out to the terrace.

The next morning, once again, there were no newspapers.

Friends of Hélène came for drinks. One of them leaned forward, her silver bracelets jangling against her navy blue serge trousers, and said, "You must be very sad that your poor godfather has died."

"What godfather?" I asked.

"John Huston," she said.

"When? How? Why don't I know?"

I asked Hélène, "Is that why you hid the papers?" She said, "We didn't want anything to upset you." Clara said, "It was to protect you." *Le petit clan* had one rule: Keep it light. Emotion and drama were unseemly. I was glad to get away.

Allegra came to the book launch in London, still red-eyed from John's funeral. I didn't see Anjelica until we were both in the dressing room of a Los Angeles photographer, Matthew Rolston, who was about to take a double portrait of us for *Interview.* I'd called her as soon as I'd found out, but it was still, in every way, too late. We stared at each other in the mirror. She'd been a star for over a year now, and she didn't feel the same.

"Your eyes aren't green like mine anymore," I said. "They've turned brown, like John's."

"My eyes were never green," she said.

Joyce and Jules had moved to a smaller, safer apartment on Montana Avenue. They introduced me to their new friends, Bob and Mark, who proudly showed me the pre-Columbian statues, furniture, and art books my parents had given them.

I wore borrowed Saint Laurent couture for the book tour, but had to return the purple satin suit early; Catherine Deneuve needed it for her own publicity tour.

Madison called from Paris. "Something's happened," he said, nervously. "I've fallen in love. I'm leaving Pierre. It would be wrong to stay in the apartment any longer. Could I stay at your place on the Rue Guénégaud?"

"Of course," I said. "The concierge has the key, and be careful on the stairs when she's gone at them with the beeswax on Mondays."

~

The reviews for my book were good this time, and Hollywood was interested until producers realized that the father in the novel was homosexual. No one wanted to touch that subject in a movie in 1987.

A year later, I was still in New York. I still hadn't started another novel; I was writing a script for Anjelica. Madison had moved to New York with his Greek lover, Konstantin.

Grace Mirabella learned from watching the evening news on television that she'd been replaced as editor in chief of American *Vogue* by Anna Wintour.

The London friends gathered in the loft where Anna and David Shaffer lived. Anna was collapsed into a chair, the sun was red at the windows. Her stomach hurt, she said.

My agent gave a dinner party for my fortieth birthday, forty people at tables decorated with dark dahlias. Pierre Bergé was on my left. "Go to the boutique and choose whatever you want, *ma chérie*," he said.

A few days later, Gita Mehta called. Her husband, Sonny, was the head of Knopf. "Sonny's in Frankfurt and he's bought the official biography of Yves Saint Laurent for Knopf," she said. "Your name's on the list of the approved interview subjects. André Leon Talley is going to write it."

"But that was my book," I said.

I screamed at Pierre on the phone, "How can you do this to me?"

"I don't know," said Pierre. "I don't know."

It was years before I learned the story. I was in Paris to interview Isabelle Adjani for *Vanity Fair*, when Anna Wintour asked me to write about the Saint Laurent couture. When I arrived at the show, Pierre was barking at the photographers to clear the runway, as ever, and my heart sank. Anna was sitting with André Leon Talley. I turned to bolt, but was intercepted by a team of PRs and diverted to a seat in the French section, between Anouk Aimée and Catherine Deneuve. Models in taffeta and grosgrain followed models in crepe de chine and *grain de poudre* as opera arias played. Thanks to Pierre, I now could tell Maria Callas from Montserrat Caballé, but I hated being there.

As I stood uncertainly in a mirrored hall after the show, Pierre erupted through a door, grabbed my wrist, and pulled me into an empty ballroom where he folded his arms and glared at me.

"I've thought a lot about what happened," he said. "I didn't understand why I'd given the book to André. Yves has refused to talk to him."

I shrugged. I could just imagine the scene.

"But now I know why I gave him the book. You gave Madison your apartment when he left. I cannot forgive that."

I pulled myself tall in my excruciating heels.

"Years ago," I said, "when I went to *Women's Wear Daily*, you said you hoped I'd remember who my real friends were. Well, I do. Madison is my real friend, and I chose him."

We walked away in different directions.

In the end, Madison went back to Pierre. André Leon Talley was unable to deliver the book; according to gossip I heard, Pierre Bergé had to reimburse Sonny Mehta.

"Your friends," said Leo Lerman. "Really."

CHAPTER TEN

On my return to New York, I played up Paris. In my black tights, perfect shoes, and tailored Saint Laurent suits, a Hermès shawl thrown over one shoulder, I dropped names no one recognized, threw off impenetrable French literary references, and presented myself as an imported luxury object. It was preferable to being seen as a single woman of forty who couldn't get started on a third novel. I resented being taken at face value, but that was all I was offering.

Without the *petit clan* to gather me in at the end of the day, I launched myself on secret love affairs that began in quiet restaurants in odd parts of town. I had the lingerie, I could pretend I'd had a wilder time in Paris than I really had. I could have been a courtesan, or the accomplished mistress of a demanding hedonist, and my American lovers could imagine they were the voluptuary playboys they'd always wanted to be. Of course they were married, and it didn't matter; I didn't want to keep any of them for myself.

I was playing a French game, but I lacked the splinter of French ice to keep my hopes cool. New York was too speedy to give me the empty days I needed to write fiction, too much of a marketplace for the sort of love affairs I understood. I adjusted my pace, gave in to my curiosity about the changing world, and set out to be a serious reporter.

In the press booth at the Democratic Convention in Atlanta, I asked a Washington columnist why Jesse Jackson had ended his speech by repeating, three times, "Chief Hold the Line." With a smirk of Beltway condescension, the columnist explained that what Jesse Jackson had said was, "Keep Hope Alive." My story, in the end, was not good. Despite my frantic research, the basic political vocabulary eluded me, as did the sequence of court cases and rulings that had caused a mob to stand outside the Omni Hotel, brandishing fetuses in glass jars.

I went to Prague for *Condé Nast Traveler* in 1988, and booked a train so as to feel my arrival behind the Iron Curtain. Before I left New York, Barbara Epstein suggested I stop in Paris to meet Antonín Liehm, an exiled Czech who ran the magazine *Lettre International.* He asked if I'd carry in a sheaf of papers for the playwright Vaclav Havel, who was in hiding in the countryside. The prospect of being a courier for a dissident made me feel like Lillian Hellman smuggling money into Germany, as played by Jane Fonda in *Julia.*

The papers were a loose sheaf of photocopied manuscripts; I packed them under layers of lingerie in my Ghurka bag, and set off on the eleven-hour ride on a hard train seat. The Czech border police unzipped my bag, and I began to sweat as I realized this romantic lark might be dangerous, but the sight of my lace bras and satin panties scrambled their intention, and they hastily zipped the bag back up, blushing furiously.

I handed over the papers to a woman who wanted to drive me to the country to meet Vaclav Havel, but I wasn't prepared to get that involved. I wanted do the things I knew how to do, tell Prague's history, see the castle and the Jewish cemetery, sniff the air and taste the moment. I introduced myself on the phone to contacts as "a friend from Paris" and met men in sunglasses in parks by the river who murmured about freedom and asked me back for coffee. The only vegetables I saw for ten days were jars of home-pickled cucumbers and peppers in their bare apartments, which told me about life in the Soviet satellite states. A year later, after the Velvet Revolution, Vaclav Havel became president of Czechoslovakia.

At a conference on Totalitarian Cinema in Moscow, there was even less food; the organizer tipped me off that I could buy contraband sturgeon at the cafeteria on the east side of the fifth floor of my hotel. We Westerners argued that Eisenstein was a genius; the Russians countered that he was a tool of Stalin, the real genius was Leni Riefenstahl; we argued back that she was a tool of Hitler. I asked the translator whispering in my ear what she thought; "You think I listen to this shit?" she asked. "I just translate."

I had a companion in these adventures, though he wasn't always with me. He was married, and still is, so I'll call him Ivan. He was even more curious than I was, an academic aware of every new book, every important film that no one had seen, every new composer, and, because of his ancestry, on constant alert for the shifts in the Soviet Union that would change the balance of power. 1989 was a year when history felt like hope. Ivan and I watched the Tiananmen Square protests on CNN together in June, and cheered the rumpled crew of revolutionaries who took over the Romanian television station in December. That November, as I was driving up a hill in Los Angeles after interviewing a movie star, the radio reported the fall of the Berlin Wall, and I listened to the hubbub and cheers; I was weeping with joy and with frustration to be so far away from the birth of a new Europe.

Jerry Brown invited me to come with him to his Yale Law School reunion that year; I accepted, but, loyal to my married Ivan, I demanded a separate bedroom. To apologize, I loaned Jerry my copy of Vaclav Havel's book of essays, *The Power of the Powerless.*

People kept dying. Friends in New York, in Los Angeles, in Paris. Kim d'Estainville died at the end of 1990. By 1992, almost 200,000 people in America had died of AIDS, among them my loving, gentle, beautiful friend Tina Chow.

Tina was an innocent, a subtle aesthete who'd be remembered for her style, for the crystal pendants she made, for the way she looked in photographs. I'd miss the urgent conversations we had about our lives as we ate tuna salad plates in delis, or primped in ladies' rooms between scenes of the beautiful life.

When I was forty-one, I became pregnant. My complicated secret would turn into a life. I wanted the child to have a real father, but for that, too many others would be hurt. I made the choice not to have the baby, and went back to work.

I lived from one adrenaline-filled magazine deadline all-nighter to the next, with pauses for naps and restorative shopping. The magazines paid well, but I was trapped in an ecology of splendor. Most of what I earned from *Condé Nast Traveler*, *Vogue*, and *Vanity Fair* went on clothes to wear to the parties for *Vogue* and *Vanity Fair* that Anna Wintour and Tina Brown threw in an arms-race escalation of launches, celebrations, and landmark events. Ladies with big hair and even bigger satin shoulders crammed through doorways festooned with buds and petals into rooms trellised and garlanded with more botany, swagged in gold lamé, lit with pillar candles. The tuxedoed men in our wakes checked each other out, then hit the leather bars in the meatpacking district for some real fun. The food was arch; one night, artichoke hearts heaped with caviar, and nothing else. A few models appeared, a few screen celebrities, but the cast was still the lacquered, slightly ageing media intelligentsia and old society names.

I prayed that something would happen to liberate me from the infernal cycle of writing profiles to pay for new dresses to wear to old parties, but I was passive in the trap. I caught the cleaning lady stealing, but didn't dare to fire her; instead I kept her on to iron the weekly washing in the basement laundry room.

Every so often I made an effort to find a more permanent man than Ivan, with terrible results. Single men in New York were looking for a sound investment; they thought I smoked too much and drank too little, and asked if I'd consider a nose job. A banker with a driver and a cook offered security, but after the cook insisted I eat the special salad she made for "any lady in his life," I succumbed to a rare parasite, the same one, I later learned, that had sidelined his last six girlfriends. He quickly broke up with me. I was in bed on heavy doses of parasite-killer when I heard that the editor of British *Vogue*, Liz Tilberis, had decamped to *Harper's Bazaar*, and called Si Newhouse to ask for the London job.

"We thought you didn't want to edit a magazine," said Si.

"I'd do anything to get out of New York," I said, too frankly.

"The job's taken, but we'll keep you in mind," he said.

I became American *Vogue*'s film critic, which helped limit the number of times I had to interview a star while feigning wonderment. It was liberating to write what I thought in my film reviews, and I was soon invited to join the New York Film Festival selection committee. Along with Richard Peña and Wendy Keys from the Film Society of Lincoln Center, Stuart Klawans from the *Nation*, and David Ansen from *Newsweek*, I set to choosing twenty-four films to play in the Festival from almost a thousand submissions.

The fact that I was *Vogue* and on the committee attracted a pair of enthusiastic but louche producers from San Antonio, Texas, who owned the rights to D. M. Thomas's *White Hotel*, for which they'd already commissioned and rejected some eighteen scripts. Great directors from around the world had tried their best: Bernardo Bertolucci, David Lynch, Emir Kusturica, Hector Babenco; and so had great screenwriters—Dennis Potter's script was as thick as a telephone book. Bernardo warned me against the producers, but I couldn't resist the challenge of dramatizing the erotic poem that filled eighty pages of *The White Hotel*.

The only way for me to adapt the book was to draw each thing that happened on a card. I turned my 857 bad sketches into 432 slightly better sketches, colored them with felt-tip pens, secured them together with a hair elastic, and took them the Arlington Hotel in Hot Springs, Arkansas, where I wrote the script in eleven days. I'd never enjoyed my work as much.

"Give them the drawings as well," my agent said when the script was done. "What are they going to do, steal them?"

It was never clear whether they stole them, or simply forgot the bundle of cards on a hotel room table. Intermediaries agreed that mine was the first usable script; D. M. Thomas praised it as faithful and brilliant. The enthusiastic producers immediately did what they'd done with every other script; they buried it. They hired Sally Potter to write another script, threw that one out, too, and hired Paul Schrader.

The more I asked for my drawings back, the more elusive the producers became. I never saw the drawings again, but I'd learned that pictures were as important to me as words.

"Big mistake, kid!" my father said at every turn of the story of *The White Hotel.* I wanted his advice, because when his instinct worked it was a laser, but he said "Big mistake, kid!" so often that I wished his opinion mattered less to me. He'll drive me mad, I thought.

Joyce found a niche redecorating the bedrooms of newly bereaved spouses, and the bedrooms brought in younger clients who wanted some of her expat chic. She was as beautiful as ever, her hair now white, and she used a tone of frosty charm to ask, 'Do you really like that lamp?" She was doing well enough for my parents to dine once a week at the Polo Lounge, where Jules always slipped a big note to the maître d' to secure their favorite booth.

Anjelica fell in love with Robert Graham. He smoked cigars, like her father; he'd been born in Mexico; he was a sculptor who worked in bronze. Anjelica had admired the nude torsos he'd made for the gateway to the 1984 Los Angeles Olympics. He'd done massive public commissions—a twenty-four-foot arm of Joe Louis in Detroit—and was working on statues for the FDR memorial in Los Angeles, and another of Duke Ellington for the edge of Harlem. Bob had thick gray hair and a neat goatee, and wore Chinese work jackets. He was kind and curious, happiest in his studio, where his dark fine hands worked women from clay.

They married at the Bel-Air hotel in 1992. Ricki's friend Dorothy Jeakins arrived, an old lady with long white hair in a wheelchair. She reached up to hand Anjelica the chain set with lava-stone faces that Gladys had spirited away the week after Ricki died. I watched the necklace go around Anjelica's neck, the pendant of rams' heads swinging over her white suit, the treasure I had craved since childhood. It was not mine to want; Ricki was her mother, this was her wedding day.

I got a cat that I named Sydney, and then a second cat, Igor, to keep Sydney company.

~

I was with the New York Film Festival Committee in Cannes, staying at the Splendid, a small family hotel in the shadow of the new Palais de Festivals, a block of stone that everyone called Le Bunker. Richard Peña summoned us for 7:00 a.m. breakfasts to dole out the screening assignments and fan us out across the Festival to look for the winners.

Uncle Don came to some of the screenings with me. He no longer had his suite at the Martinez, his house in Mougins, or his apartment above a sex shop; he'd found a self-catering hotel that had a garden.

We came out of Stephen Frears's *The Snapper* smiling, humming its fife-and-drum version of "Falling in Love with You."

"That's a happy film," said Don, "not a lot of those." He no longer looked like Marlon Brando. He didn't even look fat anymore. His pants were a little big. The heavy zipper of his thin windcheater was caught on his polo shirt.

The breeze was full of mimosa; it smelled like Coup de Vent.

"Would you take me to Nana's grave?"

"No, not today," said Don. He looked pained. I tried to distract him.

"Come see the Burkina Faso film. It's on my list. *Wendemi, l'enfant du bon dieu.*"

"I've had it with all that. I can't do it anymore," said Don.

Two tall women came over and invited him to a party at the German trade delegation, but fun, they said, with African musicians.

"I'm not going," said Don. "I'm just so tired."

"Are you okay?" I asked.

"Joanie," he said, "I'm seventy-three."

"Why don't you stop working and move to Cannes?"

"Who would I see? There's no one in Cannes in the winter."

At the end of the festival, after *Farewell My Concubine* and *The Piano,* over greasy croissants and bitter coffee at the Hôtel Splendid, I tried again. "Would you show me Nana's grave before you leave?"

"I can't," he said, and took a breath. "A few years ago some people got into the cemetery and desecrated a bunch of Jewish graves. They desecrated hers as well."

My breakfast rose in my throat. A Jewish cemetery had been desecrated in Carpentras, farther north in Provence, in 1990, but I'd never imagined the same thing could happen to Nana's grave. Being American hadn't protected her ashes; nothing could protect ashes from the hatred of strangers.

"It isn't even in the Jewish section," he said.

"Prove it," I said.

"I've got to put the car on the train back to London," he said. "I already paid for the ticket."

I followed him down to the street. His car wouldn't start. The mechanic who came with jumper cables said that *monsieur* had to drive the car for at least half an hour to reanimate the engine.

"Let's go," I said, and took the passenger seat.

We meandered to the western edge of Cannes, past pink houses, past traffic roundabouts, shopping centers, furniture warehouses, factories with funny names.

"Truth is," he said, "I haven't been there in a while. It's sort of difficult to find."

I pulled the map out of the door pocket and shook it open.

"So it's where, exactly?"

"Maurice Chevalier!" he remembered. "It's on a road called Maurice Chevalier."

On a fence across the road from the cemetery, among a display of ceramic flowers on a chain-link fence, I spotted a porcelain lily that would help make up for what had happened to Nana's grave.

He led me between black marble headstones under the hot sun, and pointed at a little wasteland of beaten earth six feet long and three feet wide. No headstone, no tombstone, no name, no flower. Rambling weeds.

"What was there to desecrate?" I asked. "There's nothing here!"

Don shook his head. "It wasn't safe. That's why I never wanted to put up any headstone."

I saw how tired he looked, how sheepish. Instead of calling him on his lie, I knelt in a rage on the beaten earth, pulled out the weeds until my wrists hurt, smoothed the soil with my palms. I didn't have a ceramic lily, so I spelled out Nana's name in stones. "Esta," the *E* a wide curlicue. The letters fit perfectly.

Don bent down with a grunt, placed a stone by the "Esta," straightened up with a longer grunt.

Birds were singing. The trees waved a little in the breeze.

"This is a nice place," he said, "pretty."

I made Don wait in his car while I stopped at the cemetery office by the gate, to ask how to install a headstone.

A one-armed man in a uniform opened a register with pages as wide as maps.

"When did Madame Getz die?" he asked.

"February 1973."

"Getz . . . *allée* 1, *carré* 6," he said, then—"This is irregular! She was buried in May of 1978. Madame, where was she for five years?"

I went out to the car and woke Don.

"Where was Nana for five years after she died?"

He stirred, sat up, ran his hand through his hair.

"Remember the smoked salmon?" he asked.

"The smoked salmon?"

"The one that I packed in my suitcase that got lost and ruined everything inside it?"—I nodded. Oh, that smoked salmon, of course—"Well, when I went down with Esta's ashes, someone gave me a smoked salmon."

"Another smoked salmon?"

"A really good one from Fortnum and Mason, to cheer me up. This time, I knew what could happen, so I didn't pack the salmon in my suitcase. I kept it in the Fortnum and Mason carrier bag. Esta's ashes were in a Pan Am bag, and I stowed them both in the overhead bin. When I landed at Nice, I took the Fortnum and Mason bag out of the bin, and I must have forgotten the Pan Am bag with the ashes. Well, the plane took off. The bag traveled around for a while. By the time it got back to the Lost and Found, I was in London, and then I had to go to the Coast, and, well, you know."

"How long was she lost?"

"She wasn't lost," he said patiently. "She was in the Lost and Found; it's just that it was never the right time to get her out of there. Your mother couldn't come down, and there was all that stuff going on."

I knew what "stuff" he meant. The end of Keep Films. "But we were all in Cannes in '74, and *Man Friday* was there in '75, and '76 you were selling *Caligula*—you mean, all those years we walked right past Nana in the Lost and Found?"

He didn't answer. I returned to the cemetery office.

The one-armed man had another problem. "She was buried in 1978," he said sternly.

"You just told me that," I said.

"A fifteen-year lease was bought on the grave."

So graves were leased.

"It expired in February of last year. We have written repeated letters to Monsieur Getz. In London, *n'est-ce pas?* Not one was answered. We are about to throw the bones in the ossuary."

He said it with relish. *Ossuaire.*

"It will be dealt with," I said grandly. "May I have the name of the best headstone company in Cannes?"

Don was standing by the car now. "I really have to get the car on the train; it's getting late," he said.

"You forgot to pay the rent on the grave!" I shouted. "You're dropping me at the headstone place next to the hospital first. I'm ordering a headstone right now."

I didn't wave to Don as he drove away.

The car missed the train, so he had to drive it back through France to the Channel ferry and on to London.

I called him when I arrived in London, but he was exhausted by the journey, still angry that I'd made him miss the train. "You'll catch me next time," he said.

In the friend's apartment where I was staying, I laid flyers out on the floor: grave designs, tombstone designs, varieties of granite and marble, types of incision on marble or granite, black, gold, or platinum-colored holders for flowers. Maybe just one ceramic lily.

I called Joyce in California.

"I can get a headstone put up so that Nana's grave isn't a wasteland anymore. But if you would rather I scattered her ashes by the casino, I can dig them up and hire a boat, but they say I need the signature of all living relatives for the permit."

There was a silence.

"But, Mom? Which casino? The one by the port was replaced by the Bunker, but there's still the winter casino on the other side. Isn't that the winter casino, near Golfe-Juan? And screw the permissions, I can just hire a boat. Isn't that what you want? Mom? Nana dancing on the Mediterranean waves forever?"

"Don't scatter her, please," she said. "All your grandmother ever wanted was security."

It's too late for that, I thought.

"Keep the grave," she said. "I need to know that she's somewhere safe."

~

Anna Wintour reached me the next day, breathy and confidential, to tell me to expect a call from someone who turned out to be Jonathan Newhouse, the head of Condé Nast International. He ran all of the magazines outside the United States, and wanted to talk to me about Paris *Vogue*.

I met him in Paris. Jonathan Newhouse was a slight man, a few years younger than me. Under a glaze of awkward composure, he seemed gentle, with the mischief of a shy boy who loves a dare. I didn't really read Paris *Vogue*, I said. Could he send me the previous year's issues of the magazine?

Rain pelted on the roof above my hotel room as I stuck Post-its onto pages of *Vogue*. I didn't want this job, I had hundreds more movies to watch for the New York Film Festival, but the gag lady in Chinese makeup from twenty years before enjoyed slapping the magazine, and the present version of me was happy to deliver honest opinions. Why couldn't anyone ever get the magazine right? By the time I'd finished going through the *Vogue*s, I knew how I'd do it.

We met, and I told him what I thought. There wasn't enough to read. French women were intellectual snobs, curious and educated; the magazine should be on their level.

"What about the fashion?" he asked.

Off I went. Pages and pages of women shot by photographers who were not Helmut Newton but clearly wanted to be. "When Newton shot girls smoking cigarettes in hotel rooms wearing suspender belts and stockings twenty years ago in Paris *Vogue*, it was shocking and new and interesting. It was necessary then, and now it's a cliché. French women know how to dress for an assignation. They want to know what to wear when they're not having sex."

He nodded.

"*Vogue* has to treat women with respect. That's what I'd do."

In New York, the committee went into the final selection process for the New York Film Festival. We watched movies starting at eight o'clock in the morning in the blasting air-conditioning of the Walter Reade Theater, eating Snickers and Raisinets from the concession stand; we watched more movies in the afternoon in Richard's office, and each went home at night with one last tape. I dreamed of Texas vistas and Denzel Washington.

At the end of August, my cousins Janis and Audrey called to tell me their father, my uncle Don was dying. I crossed the Atlantic and joined them at a hospice in Saint John's Wood. Don was tucked up in clean white sheets, his hair as soft as feathers, his frown lines gone. The lamp behind the bed made a warm circle on the wall. A pump was releasing morphine into his arm under the sheet. He looked happy, clean, safe. I held his hand.

"Thank you for always being there," I said, and then, "Your hair looks great." His eyes flew open. He still knew bullshit.

His driver arrived and introduced himself formally as "Jeremie, an ex-convict from Montserrat in the Western Caribbean." He sat down by Don's bed, and closed his eyes. "I'm just going to meditate a bit," he said.

Joyce didn't want to see her brother die, and missed the first three planes I'd booked for her. As Jeremie drove me to the airport to collect her, we saw a stand on the side of the road selling Easter lilies, odd flowers for the end of August. He bought a bunch for Joyce.

Don was gone by the time we reached the hospice; Joyce laid the Easter lilies on his empty bed.

Don was cremated at Golders Green to a tape of Louis Armstrong singing "What a Wonderful World": "I see friends shaking hands, saying how do you do, they're really saying I love you." That was Don. Friendship as love. His ashes went into a box on a shelf at the funeral home. Janis and Audrey wanted to bury him in the same grave as Nana, on the eve of the next Cannes Film Festival, so that all his friends from all over the world could say good-bye to him. I booked three nights at the Splendid for May of the following year.

I wanted to clean up my life. Two weeks after Don's death, I picked a fight with Ivan. That night I went to a *Vanity Fair* party and brought home one of the graduate students I'd refused to meet back at Sarah Lawrence. Brian De Palma had gone on to make baroque thrillers with plots as intricately twisted as instruments of torture. He affected the constant glare of a curmudgeon, but his girth reminded me of Uncle Don when he was young, and I found his bitter humor endearing. He wasn't married to anyone. I didn't have to be a secret, and nor did he.

I wasn't homesick for Europe anymore, so it no longer mattered that Brian De Palma was not a real Italian.

My sudden public status as his girlfriend brought invitations that made Brian snort with laughter. We saw movies instead, and ate dinner at East 77th Street. Sydney and Igor made his eyes water, so he'd take two Sudafed, and arrive with a good bottle of wine, some of which I'd try to drink. I didn't think once about Jonathan Newhouse or Paris.

Peter Eyre, my friend since Ricki days, said, "How delicious! Middle-aged love!"

I didn't feel middle-aged. I was only forty-five. Wasn't that still young?

Brian took me to Anguilla for Christmas.

"Don't tell him you've never been to the Caribbean before," Joyce said, too late.

Anguilla was flat and windy; a constant gale spiked crests onto the sea. Brian didn't want romantic walks on the beach, but sat still and silent, spinning the plot for a complicated new film in his head. I had to write another book.

We returned to a winter of seventeen snowstorms. While Brian burrowed into his script in his office, I listened to the hum of my Selectric at home. I wanted to write from a bedrock of experience, but that was impossible: I couldn't write about my five years with Ivan, they were secret. I couldn't write about my father; that would embarrass my parents. I couldn't write about a life that was nothing but deadlines and new clothes.

What was experience? I'd had adventures in high heels—one night in heels far too high to be climbing across a rooftop with Werner Herzog and Philippe Petit, but there was no novel where that story belonged. How many chapters would it take to explain Werner Herzog, who'd hauled a boat across the Andes for *Fitzcarraldo* and once ate his shoe on a bet? How many more to explain Philippe Petit, who'd walked a wire a quarter mile above the ground between the twin towers of the World Trade Center? And then to have such men be no more than the instigators of an expedition onto the roof of the Opéra Comique after the first night of an opera directed by Volker Schlöndorff—he would be another chapter, and he wasn't even a lover—an escapade of totally unnecessary bravado and panic on the roof of the Opéra Comique in a borrowed couture dress and spike heels brought on by a breakup, over the phone, with a secret lover.

~

In January, a large earthquake jolted Los Angeles, a 6.6 that lasted thirty seconds. My father called me a few minutes later, at seven in the morning New York time, while my mother waited in the car, to tell me they were safe. On television, I saw crashed freeways, gushing water mains, shattered overpasses.

Anjelica got through; she and Bob were fine, but this one was different, she said—not rolling like the usual quakes, but jagged and violent.

The phone lines went down. There were aftershocks all day.

Most of my parents' remaining treasures were rubble. The Etruscan pots in shards, the pre-Columbian dog chipped, the Chinese goddess damaged, the kitchen devastated, books everywhere, but at least their flimsy apartment building hadn't pancaked into the garage below, as similar buildings had in the Valley.

Los Angeles was still shaking from aftershocks when Brian flew out to inspect the damage to the house he had there. I called to tell him I missed him, and called again, and then again. He didn't want to hear it. I insisted he consider my feelings; he said, "Don't do this," but I did. He said, "That's it." And it was.

I didn't hear from him again. I'd been fired. I was stunned. Relationships with single men never lasted beyond four months.

Another snowstorm fell on the city. The mullioned windows tight against the white of East 77th Street. A snowplow grinding along the asphalt. I was alone again.

In front of me was my transcript for the profile I was writing of Mike Nichols, rendered in different colors of felt-tip: red for career, blue for family, pink for private life, green for money and success, purple for his insights. I needed color coding to find the story in the notes.

The Museum of Modern Art showed Carl Dreyer's 1928 silent film *The Passion of Joan of Arc.* I went with Louis Malle and my photographer friend Brigitte Lacombe. When the priest gives Joan Communion before she is burned at the stake, she takes the host in her mouth, raises her eyes, moves her lips. "Lord," read the titles, "tonight I will sup with you in paradise."

When I was a child in France they called me Jeanne d'Arc, which told me that one day I'd put on armor, gather an army to chase the English out of France, and preside over the dauphin's coronation at Rheims.

When we came out, I was still in tears.

"The Communion," I explained.

"But you're not Catholic," said Louis.

"I don't have to be," I said.

Brigitte Lacombe went back to photograph the scene for me, and gave me a print of Joan taking the host in her mouth.

The fourteenth snowstorm slapped at the windows, snowflakes thumped on the air conditioner outside, the heat hissed through the radiators, my study smelled of kitty litter. I sat at the desk with my back to the window, still in my ballet clothes after class, a cardigan over my leotard, leg warmers bunched down to my feet. The bunions had grown so prominent on both feet that I no longer wore shoes at home. A mug of coffee with cocoa was growing frigid on my desk, three previous mugs stranded nearby. The bathroom exuded the stench of ammonia and cat turd under a veil of sweet chalk.

In the hallway, Sydney and Igor batted at invisible beings several feet above them. I had three movies to review for *Vogue,* a big dinner to cook in ten days, a week full of screenings, and I had to rewrite the Mike Nichols profile so as to upset him. *Vanity Fair* was insisting I mention the wigs he wore to hide his alopecia.

I was boxed in.

The phone rang. It was Jonathan Newhouse, after six months of silence.

"Would you like to come to Paris to edit French *Vogue*?" he asked.

A clump of snow thudded onto the air conditioner. The only thing I knew was *Vogue.* Maybe it was time to run one of my own. Colors. Pictures. I could storyboard each issue on cards. I had a lot of cards left over from *The White Hotel.*

"Why not?" I said.

CHAPTER ELEVEN

The concierge at the Ritz apologized that I couldn't have my usual room at such short notice.

Jonathan received me at his apartment on the Rue Spontini, just a few doors down from the first Saint Laurent couture house, where I'd seen my first couture shows, and been received into the fold.

Jonathan was alone. In his kitchen was a plate of breadsticks, each one wrapped in prosciutto. I hoped he hadn't done it himself.

Paris *Vogue* needed a new direction, he said.

"I can do that," I said, rather too fast, "but I'd need a new staff." No more dour editors in kilts and navy blue shoes with dachshunds under their desks for me.

"Of course," he said.

I didn't admit that I couldn't even fire a thieving cleaning lady.

"And a new publisher. The whole thing has to be cleaned up," I announced sternly.

"We have to respect our advertisers."

"Yes, but we have to stand our ground," I said. Integrity. Division between editorial and advertising. No leakage.

I realized I'd have to deal with things I'd never considered before: advertisers, model agencies, makeup artists, hairdressers, brands, corporations, multinationals, production, distribution, print orders, paper suppliers, star photographers, star stylists, star agents, star fashion editors, star designers, star animal wranglers, star writers, star artists, star stars.

How did I even begin to structure all that? What were the rules? How did I handle obligations, imperatives? I had no idea. But if I took the job, I'd never have to write a profile of anyone again.

He cleared his throat and formally offered me the job.

Sometimes, when there's too much traffic in the street, the only way to get across is to close your eyes and hurl yourself in. "Yes," I said.

Then, to show off my true competence, I took him to the second film of Krzysztof Kieslowski's trilogy, *Three Colors: White*, so he could see how fast and legibly I took notes in the dark.

Back at the Ritz, I called Los Angeles to tell my parents.

"You said yes today?" asked Jules. "The same day he gave you the offer?"

"Was I supposed to wait?"

"You'd have more bargaining power," he said, "and maybe you need to think about what it means,"

What was I supposed to bargain for? This was providence. How could I argue with providence?

Joyce came on the line. "Darling, remember, you're going to have to wear shoes during the day. High heels, every single day. And what about your nails?"

I'd have a manicure, maybe more than one. I could pay my tax bill now. I could take care of them.

I went down to the underground temple of the Ritz health club to swim. In the dressing room doorway, I crashed into an American blonde wearing a terry-cloth robe. I'd seen her in the corridors of the American *Vogue* Paris office, done up in studded leather jackets with big shoulders, in tight leather pants, a va-voom fashion babe in control of her shit. Gardner Bellanger sold ads in Paris for American *Vogue* and was married to an antiques dealer who rode a Harley. Her face, the almost featureless oval of a Connecticut Wasp, was shiny with cream. We air-kissed. "Did you come in on the Concorde?" she asked. She took the Concorde all the time, she said.

The same Baroque music that played in the Ritz bathrooms was piped into the pool, underwater; I swam through Haydn's serenade wondering how I'd find a publisher. And then it was obvious. Gardner Bellanger. The Ritz health club had delivered my publisher in a bathrobe.

When I came out of the water, I saw Nicole reclining on a chaise longue next to the pool, *Egoïste* proofs on her lap, a bag spilling more papers by her side.

"Why didn't you tell me you were coming to Paris?" she asked. "Are you here with Brian?"

No, I was interviewing someone, but I couldn't say who.

"You're always so discreet," Nicole said, a little annoyed.

I settled in for a girlfriend chat on the chaise longue next to hers, and ordered a carrot juice. Nicole covered the papers on her lap with a copy of *Paris Match.* I'd helped her with *Egoïste,* been her champion, made calls, distributed issues around New York, labored for her over profiles of Norman Mailer, David Hockney, and Julian Schnabel. Now it was my turn to use her. In a sleepy voice, mere conversation, I asked her how she balanced ads and editorial.

"I didn't know you were interested," she said, and told me how she made her own magazine at her own pace. I noted that she shared her art director with Paris *Vogue.*

I flew back to New York on the Concorde. The caviar was followed by langoustines holding up basil leaves in their claws, looking like tiny Martian newscasters.

After dinner in his apartment, Si Newhouse pulled me into a corner, beaming. "You must be very excited to go to Paris and meet Karl Lagerfeld and Yves Saint Laurent and Pierre Bergé."

"I already know them all," I said, "but we can get past that."

~

It would be a month before my contract was negotiated and signed, my appointment announced. Under cover of deep secrecy, I learned how to read spreadsheets and how to use a computer. Jonathan agreed that Gardner Bellanger would make a wonderful publisher and arranged for her to be released from American *Vogue.* She and I plotted the renaissance of Paris *Vogue* on the phone as I sat with Sydney on my lap and Igor on my feet. Gardner had moved to France as an adult; her accent would never be as good as mine, but her command of the bewildering French business vocabulary was dazzling. She could think like they did.

Gardner talked me into a froth about the marvels we were going to work together, with the conviction of a zealot, the showmanship of a producer. "The star we're going to create is the magazine," she said. Her faith gave me confidence. With her, I could do it. The two French Americans would show the French.

The head of the fashion department was a good-looking German stylist named Jenny Capitain who'd once posed naked for Helmut Newton with a cast on her leg, a neck brace, and a cane. She was so nice that the French editors constantly overrode her. I was going to have to find a replacement with a hard French will. I'd need a new art director. I could do ideas, concepts, culture; but I hadn't seen more than a handful of fashion shows in years.

Jonathan encouraged me to steal away the fashion staff of *Glamour.* I met in secret with *Glamour*'s fashion director, Brigitte Langevin, a small woman with a halo of beige hair, the energy of a rat terrier, and a roster of talented fashion editors. She was willing to come to *Vogue* with two fashion editors, Carine Roitfeld and Delphine Treanton, two juniors, Alexia and Isabelle, and a model bookings editor, all from *Glamour.* I was eviscerating the most lively of Condé Nast's French magazines; power already felt a little dirty.

In his white apartment in a tower by the East River, Alex Liberman gave me instruction.

"Avoid, at all costs, Visions of Loveliness," he said.

"Why?" I said.

"They're cheap," said Alex.

"I'd like to revive the wonderful pages they did before the war," I said, "the illustrators, the artists."

"Forget the past," said Alex. "Only Today counts. Today and tomorrow."

The way he said it, "Today" had a capital letter.

To find what Today looked like, I bought every magazine there was and spread them in a glossy shale across the living room floor. French magazines, Italian magazines, insider magazines, art magazines with ambiguous covers—was that thing on the cover a pursed mouth or a sphincter? The only one I liked was *View on Color,* a Dutch professional quarterly devoted to forecasting color trends.

To prepare myself to be a boss, I bought two Soviet posters at Sotheby's: a Rodchenko from his series on the Russian Revolution, and a movie poster by the Stenberg brothers dominated by an enormous question mark.

My appointment to *Vogue* was announced in April. Americans were thrilled. The French were perplexed.

The first person to call from Paris was Clara Saint.

"Je suis sans voix," she said. I'm speechless.

I hired an assistant to answer the phones, put the bouquets somewhere, cope with the attention. The fax machine used two rolls of paper a day.

I polled my editor-in-chief friends, Tina Brown at the *New Yorker,* Marian McEvoy at *Elle Decor,* Liz Tilberis at *Harper's Bazaar.* Not Anna. My notebook filled up with advice. Button your lip. Every issue you do should be your first and your last. Don't make decisions until you have looked and listened. Fire first. Do the first six months without a budget. Don't ever fire someone in your own office, do it in theirs, so you can leave. Keep your own counsel. Act as if you have friends and not enemies. If anything feels icky, trust your gut, don't do it. Don't express yourself. Really? I asked. Yes, that'd be showing off. Control your natural tendencies. No instant reactions of outrage, one said. That would mean don't behave like Jules. Be nice and calm on the outside, tough in your center. That would mean, behave like Joyce. There wasn't one recommendation that indicated I could go on being myself.

Which brought up the unpleasant truth that unless I was absorbed in an idea and writing through the night, or alone in the dark with a man, or telling Anjelica the comic version of my adventures, I had no idea who I was.

I sat on the bed and meditated, Sydney and Igor against my thighs, purring. We'd been together every day, and until I found an apartment they'd be in a hotel, surrounded by strange walls and different shadows. Paris would be so much more gray, temperate, and damp, and I would have no time with them. A writer who never left his apartment on the Upper West Side offered to adopt them, so I carried Sydney and Igor to him in a Town Car, three months' supply of turkey-flavor Fancy Feast in the trunk, and bade them a brief good-bye.

Without my animals I needed a talisman; at an antique-jewelry store on Madison Avenue, I found a head of Mercury with diamond eyes made of labradorite, a dark blue stone with strange reflections. Mercury, god of communication, commerce, and trickery—the perfect ally. Until I could afford a chain, I hung it from a silk handkerchief around my neck. Those little diamond eyes could glare from my collarbone while I attended to the business of business.

I ate quickly without chewing and lived on cappuccinos.

The New York fashion shows began, the finale to the ready-to-wear schedule that started in Milan in March. I had to catch up on the Today of it all.

Wearing a secondhand man's raincoat from Burberry's, I darted through the Bryant Park crowd of fashion people with Jenny Capitain, sat down in the front row next to Grace Coddington, and took out my compact to powder my nose.

"Don't ever do that!" hissed Grace. I put the compact away. First row, on show. Don't show weakness. Smile. I glanced at Grace. No, she wasn't smiling. Set mouth in firm expression of—another glance at Grace—incipient disgust. Really? I looked at the other faces, front-row faces, second-row faces, PR girl faces, photographer faces, famous guest faces. Everyone looked miserable.

A miasma thickened in the tent as we waited in the half-light for the show to begin; I closed my eyes to isolate what I was feeling. A cold fug of anxiety, ill will, injured self-regard. Impossible, I thought, this is joy and beauty, this is fashion!

The show began. There was no danger of Visions of Loveliness here. Sad girls without makeup paraded in sad clothes, their hair lank and greasy. The year 1994 was the end of the grunge moment, a deliberate refusal of beauty, form, line. One collection featured dresses made of pale latex the color and consistency of condoms. Another show was all shrouds.

"The clothes look kind of droopy," I whispered to Jenny.

"Shoulder pads are over for years now," she whispered back in her German accent. I drooped my shoulders as far as I could. The pads in my Armani jacket weren't huge, but they were there.

More shrouds came out at the next show. What had happened to fashion while I wasn't looking?

"Tell me Paris and Milan looked better," I begged.

A Condé Nast statistician named Laure was dispatched from Paris to be my managing editor, and Anna Wintour invited us to sit in on the kind of *Vogue* business meetings I'd never yet attended. We arrived for the first meeting promptly at 9:00 a.m., but it was almost over. "It started at eight fifteen," whispered the assistant. The next day, we arrived half an hour early, but the meeting had been canceled. We arrived forty-five minutes early for the third meeting, but that one, oddly, had started two hours early and was now finished. The assistant was a little short with us.

Laure looked at me.

"We're on our own," I said.

Volker Schlöndorff had become the head of the Babelsberg film studios in Berlin; he came to see me wearing a new cashmere overcoat in an uncharacteristic shade of teal. I hung up the coat, gave him a coffee, and asked why he'd taken the job. "My girlfriend was pregnant, I was at a loss after I made *Voyager*, and I suppose I wanted to do something for my country."

"So you're a producer now?"

Volker crinkled his eyes and lit a cigarillo. "I don't direct, I don't produce. I host dinners. I go to ceremonies. I shake a lot of hands and I wear dinner jackets. Being the head of anything is a role. You have to look the part."

I'd have to look the part. My clothes would be seen, understood, and judged.

Jenny Capitain had sweetly said, "Don't shop before Paris, you'll get it all there." I hadn't worked in an office since 1978, my days were mostly spent alone at the typewriter wearing whatever I'd slept in, ballet clothes if I'd been to a class. I had no idea how to dress to be looked at every day.

If I turned up wearing Donna Karan, Ralph Lauren, or Calvin Klein, I'd look like an American invader. If I arrived in a new Chanel, I'd be announcing I was in Karl's camp. If I wore Saint Laurent, I'd look like a pawn of Pierre Bergé. If I wore Armani or Missoni, I'd be telling the French that I preferred Italian fashion, which was hardly politic.

Fuck it, I'd be English. I called Jean Muir, the Madame Grès of London, who had been making beautiful dresses since the 1960s. I'd buy my wardrobe from her, and the French, who didn't yet pay attention to British designers, wouldn't have any idea what I was wearing. I'd be mysterious, inscrutable, out of time.

Tina Brown gave a massive party for me at the Tribeca Film Center. There were four hundred friends, actors and writers, editors and painters, directors and layabouts, but not one designer. The designers would come later, they'd be new, they'd be today. Today was not here yet.

Tina handed me the microphone. "Being an editor in chief is the writer's best procrastination," I declared, very loud. I'd never have to write another profile, transcribe another tape, review another movie, attempt another novel. I'd wear a cashmere coat in an uncharacteristic shade of teal, and look like I'd once won an Oscar.

If the tents in Bryant Park were any measure, there were going to be some bad energies floating around. I'd been alone during the day for so long that the only shields I could conceive of were an amulet of Mercury and waving about smoking bundles of cedar in the manner prescribed by Native Americans. I packed some cedar smudge sticks.

~

Before I could start at *Vogue,* I had to bury Uncle Don. For his last trip to Cannes, he traveled in state in a suede carry-on bag, enclosed in a small pale oak box bearing a silver plaque engraved with "Donald Aubrey Getz 1920–1993." We landed at Nice during a total eclipse of the sun; I ran outside the terminal and opened the bag to the penumbra, to mark Don's return to the South of France.

At the Hôtel Splendid on the morning of the funeral, I placed the pink rose from the breakfast tray on the oak box. The fine white sand of Abadie II sparkled in the sun, birds sang, the trees were green, flowers bloomed on the graves. My cousins Janis and Audrey led a procession of Don's friends from London, New York, Los Angeles, Italy, and Germany, and I carried the box down *allée* 1 past the tombstones with Italian names to *carré* 6, where a pair of grave diggers stood by the freshly dug hole next to Nana's ashes.

"Nice place," someone said. But there's no one to see in the winter.

We repaired to the Colombe d'Or for lunch, and sat outside under the wisteria vines. La Colombe d'Or was a little fortress of Provençal peace, the peasant hut in the fairy tale, where French movie stars hid their love affairs, where rich writers liked to pretend they lived, where not everybody could get in. The walls were thick as bread, golden stone; inside were paintings that Miró, Matisse, Braque, and Chagall had traded for their dinners; ivy grew around a Fernand Léger mural, a Calder mobile hung over the pool, a giant bronze thumb by César by the front door. I could smell lavender and mimosa.

We ate ratatouille and crudités from little oblong dishes, and the different kinds of herring that Don loved, we drank rosé and cried a little and didn't say anything important because we couldn't really talk. Now that he was buried, he was dead all over again. We bought lavender essence at a shop up the street, to remember the smell of Provence.

That night, a huge party gathered Don's friends in the garden of the self-catering hotel, and then the festival began.

I walked past the little yachts in the old port. I had no role here anymore, no films to review, Uncle Don would not be at his corner table in the pizza place. It began to rain; I cut into a store full of fishing nets and hooks and bought a functional rubber slicker to keep me dry. I liked that it was bright blue, and ugly.

I got to work. Helmut Newton came from Monte Carlo to have dinner, shambled into Felix with his slightly comic elegance. He was seventy-three, his face unlined, his hair still thick, but his hug was inert. I was no longer his old friend, or his favorite pornographer. I was *Vogue.*

He didn't like the table.

"I'll have just water," he said. "French *Vogue* doesn't have the money to pay me properly."

"Have some wine!" I said.

"You can't afford it. I'll eat a salad. That way I won't break the French *Vogue* bank."

I'd heard him rage about *Vogue,* but I couldn't remember what slights the magazine had dealt him. He had four pages in the current issue, accessories photographed to shock: a woman's hands covered in jewels as she tore apart a raw chicken, an X-ray of a foot in a high-heeled shoe.

"Let's have the bouillabaisse!" I said. "I had it the other night, it was delicious."

"Are you sure you can afford it?"

"Stop that shit, Helmut, please. We'll have the bouillabaisse."

The bouillabaisse, when it arrived, was bad. We parted as acquaintances.

Just one more film to see, before Paris and the big day job. Patrice Chéreau's *La reine Margot,* a dark tapestry of scheming, betrayal, and poison at the French court in 1572. The Saint Bartholomew's Day Massacre filled the screen with corpses of naked men. King Charles IX sweated blood as he died a slow death by arsenic; Queen Margot couldn't bring herself to say "*Oui*" to Henri de Navarre on their wedding day, but donned a mask and prowled the streets that night to work off her lust on strangers. At the end, alone in a carriage, she cradled her lover's severed head on her bloodstained lap. I noted the earth tones of the costumes, the chiaroscuro lighting, Isabelle Adjani's blue eyes and pearl white skin, the men's choice of single pearl earrings.

The ruffs, I noted, everyone wore ruffs. "Bloodbath," I wrote in my notebook.

CHAPTER TWELVE

The mansion on the Place du Palais-Bourbon epitomized Paris *Vogue.* Built in 1791, it extended six regal windows across a stone façade, and its heavy double doors did not yield easily. It was welcoming and forbidding, bright and austere, expansive and cramped. Its grandeur remained undimmed despite the herd of messenger scooters parked outside.

It had passed from family to family for 150 years until a San Francisco heiress bought it, and sold it to Condé Nast in 1955.

I considered the mansion my third proxy palace, a successor to the Palais Rose and St. Clerans.

But the magazine revered as the diamond heart of couture, the byword for elegance and sophistication, the very essence of Paris and absolute icon of French perfection, was in fact an American import. Born in 1892 in New York, *Vogue* began as a general-interest magazine named after the French noun for "trend," which is also the verb for "sail," "drift," and "wander." The British edition was launched in 1916, at the height of the Great War, the French one in 1920. From 1968 onward, the word "*Paris*" was tucked inside the *O* of *VOGUE* so that the magazine could only be known as "Paris *Vogue*" to Americans, "*Vogue* Paris" to the French.

In a physical expression of *Vogue*'s identity as the pride of France but the property of the United States, the rooms one floor up on the left side of the 1791 staircase were for years the Paris offices of American *Vogue.*

The first editor of Paris *Vogue* was Cosette Vogel, wife of Lucien Vogel, who'd founded *Vu,* the newsmagazine where Alex Liberman began his career in 1932. She was succeeded in 1927 by Main Rousseau Bocher, an American who'd been one of her fashion editors; he left in 1929 to found his own couture house, Mainbocher, and dress everyone from Claudette Colbert to the Duchess of Windsor. One of Cosette's brothers, Jean de Brunhoff, created *Babar the Elephant;* another, Michel de Brunhoff, succeeded Main Rousseau Bocher as editor in 1929 and ran the magazine until 1954.

Michel de Brunhoff used Christian Bérard, Georges Lepape, René Bouché, and René-Bouët Willaumez for the drawings. Hoyningen-Huene, Horst, and Cecil Beaton invented fantastical settings for Paris *Vogue*'s monthly allotment of ten fashion photographs, which were shot on glass plates, retouched, and delivered to the engine driver of the Lisbon-bound train to hand over to the Pan American Clipper to cross the Atlantic to the mother offices in New York, with a refueling stop in the Azores. Clouds, neoclassical columns, and utopian arches turned debutantes and society matrons into flying goddesses, nymphs, and angels. De Brunhoff brought in Dalí and Chagall, Colette and Jean Cocteau, and on the nights when the magazine went to press, he held court until dawn at Le Vert Galant, surrounded by his artists.

The Nazis invaded Poland in 1939. The March 1940 issue of Paris *Vogue* showed two officers in brown boots marching in on a woman wearing a hat with a long black feather. They arrived in France on May 10, 1940, and by June 14, they occupied Paris. After the French government moved to Vichy under Marshal Pétain, Michel de Brunhoff closed down French *Vogue,* and its American publisher, Tommy Kernan, buried its vital papers in the woods at Vincennes.

Michel de Brunhoff spent the war anonymously putting together albums of French fashion in an effort to save haute couture for the world; couture now served the occupying forces. Maggy Rouff, Jacques

Fath, and Marcel Rochas dressed the mistresses of Nazi generals, the wives of collaborators. The foreign couturiers fled to New York: the Italian Elsa Schiaparelli, the Briton Edward Molyneux, the American Mainbocher. Others, like Chanel, shut their doors, though she had an affair with a German officer that she would have trouble living down. My friend Hélène's 1944 marriage to Marcel Rochas had made her famous, but it was also something one didn't ask about.

In 1945, six months after American forces liberated Paris from the Nazis, Michel de Brunhoff revived French *Vogue.* His friend Christian Dior showed his first collection in 1947, *Le New Look,* wildly decolleté padded peplums over rustling yards of skirts that signaled the return of social life, cocktails, and erotic rendezvous. A French teenager from Algeria sent De Brunhoff fashion drawings of such quality that he introduced the young man to Christian Dior, and Yves Saint Laurent's career was launched.

The next editor was a fiercely well-connected war heroine and a bluestocking. An ambassador's daughter who'd served in the Resistance and been a nurse in the French Foreign Legion, by the time she was twenty-five, Edmonde Charles-Roux had won the Croix de Guerre and been made a chevalier of the Légion d'Honneur. She had Communist sympathies and wore her hair in a strict bun, two marks of good taste in postwar Europe, and was fired after twelve years. The novel she promptly published, *Oublier Palerme,* won France's highest literary prize, the Prix Goncourt.

The magazine was split in two after she left, one editor in chief for fashion, Françoise de Langlade, another for features, Françoise Mohrt, neither with absolute power. Then came Francine Crescent of the canary yellow suits, who for twenty-six years made Paris *Vogue* a showcase for photographers by letting them do what they wanted.

The French advertisers could not support an issue in either July or January, so the June *Vogue* had to last until August, and December *Vogue* had to last until February. The shelf life of June was of no importance: bathing suits were never the core of fashion. But the December issue, fattened with ads for diamonds, watches, and perfume, lay around in drawings rooms for two entire months, and had to be an exceptionally rich feast. A so-called *Collector.* Francine Crescent and Françoise Mohrt invited Françoise Sagan to be the guest editor of the 1969 Christmas issue, which set the tradition of bringing in famous outsiders for Christmas. Françoise Sagan's cover showed two nude models sitting in a bed, entirely covered in tiny black beads, like dolls dipped in caviar and photographed, of course, by Guy Bourdin.

A parade of cultural legend guest editors followed Françoise Sagan, most of them from *le cinéma*: first Jeanne Moreau, then those icons of culture the French preferred to evoke by last name only: Fellini, Dietrich, Hitchcock, Polanski, Welles, Bacall, Huston, Kurosawa, Scorsese, Karajan, Rostropovich, Baryshnikov, Dalí, Chagall, Miró, Hockney. When Colombe Pringle took over from Francine Crescent, she aimed for global relevance. Under her, the Paris *Vogue* Christmas issue was guest-edited by His Holiness the Dalai Lama, followed by Nelson Mandela.

I'd have to find something to top that.

~

American *Vogue* had occupied the left-hand side of the mansion up until 1987. In the office on the left side of the main staircase of the mansion on the Rue du Palais-Bourbon, amid cheery green and turquoise upholstery, behind a small desk flanked by two assistants, a long-haired dachshund in her lap, the impeccable Susan Train had run the show since 1951 as the Paris bureau chief of American *Vogue.* Susan Train had the bearing of a Colonial Dame, which she was, the politics of a Democrat, and the wisdom to keep quiet about both in mixed company. Stalwart and unflappable, she had survived all the American *Vogue* editors in chief: Edna Woolman Chase—toques and tippets—who'd begun in 1914 and left in 1951, Jessica Daves—bad hair, lots of bracelets—from 1952 to 1963, Diana Vreeland—Kabuki hair, a tusk on a chain—from 1963 to 1971, Grace Mirabella—cheery beige cashmere—from 1971 to 1988, and now Anna Wintour, garden-party frocks and bobbed hair, blonder through the years.

Susan embodied the spirit of *Vogue,* its class and its style. As serene as Queen Elizabeth, she managed the flaps and drama caused by the arrival of American *Vogue*'s editors, its fashion editors, and its editorial director Alex Liberman, in January and July for the couture, in March and October for the ready-to-wear shows.

She went on attractive location in exotic countries with the photographer Henry Clarke so he could shoot models in evening kaftans perched atop mosques. She fielded the daily telexes from New York demanding a dress, a photographer, a model, a star, a location, a car, a different car, a different dress, a château instead of a house, not *that* château, the *other* château, visas for Yemen, customs declarations, tissue paper, dangerous wildlife, rare flowers, rarer flowers, bushes, buds, trees, photogenic children of impeccable pedigree. She flawlessly navigated the chasms of rage that roiled in the heart of every fashion player. Even the messengers were touchy.

Paris *Vogue* was an unruly autonomous duchy in the kingdom of Condé Nast, and sensible, diplomatic Susan Train struck the French as a well-dressed enforcer, an irksome intrusion at the Palais-Bourbon. By the mideighties, new magazines of *les Publications Condé Nast* overran the mansion, which forced the American *Vogue* offices to the Boulevard Saint-Germain.

Susan knew how to cope with the hierarchies of French bureaucracy without screaming, how to respect the by-laws of fashion protocol, and was a master of solutions that offended no one. She knew everything about the cut of fabric, and favored the way a *col Danton* stood up and away from her long neck. During my time in Paris as Guy Bourdin's gag lady, I'd glared at Susan Train across the fashion show runways, irritated that she was so classy, so grand, so old school, such a *Vogue* Lady. Later, I understood her discipline and intelligence. When *Vogue* and *Vanity Fair* sent me to Paris to watch the rich cheer at polo matches, try on couture ball gowns, or crunch down on birds the size of insects called ortolans, Susan arranged the logistics and kept saving my ass. Cars, hotels, irritable stringers, lost film, thank-you bouquets, last-minute rescues when Tony Snowdon's mischief turned cruel in Deauville, when I needed the seventy-ninth interviewee for my sixty-page essay on Italy, when I needed access to the stadium in

Cologne for the beatification of the Jewish nun Edith Stein—a piece spiked because the editor at *Vogue* would not allow the term "popemobile," and I would not budge—Susan came through. She knew my weak points, reassured me that my plane would land safely, and once produced an attic office where I could work in secret.

Over lunches of smoked trout at Caviar Kaspia, we discussed work and dentists, the Paris cast of characters, my latest boyfriend. For a few nervous months we examined the fact that she had fallen in love and was ready to abandon it all for a man who lived in Philadelphia. Susan stayed in Paris with her long-haired dachshund, *Vogue*'s vestal virgin, a friend I trusted and loved, a plumb line.

She was the first person I went to see. Cradling a small vodka in her white living room, the long-haired dachshund on her lap, she said, "Lovey, what you're doing is Mission Impossible." And then we both laughed.

But Susan was American Condé Nast, not French. I had no friends at Paris *Vogue*, and I'd arrived with only Gardner.

~

The manager of the Hôtel Lutetia announced, "You have our best suite," and showed me into Pierre Bergé's old apartment. His ocelot carpet still covered every room. The dining room still paneled in limed oak, the closets lined with Peter Marino's finest tongue-and-groove work, the travertine bathroom as big as a Mussolini ministry, the imperial bedroom, all mine now, at least for a while. Pierre's taffeta curtains still bunched stiff as tissue paper at every window, but his furniture had been replaced by a green living room set in a hybrid Provençal-BDSM style outlined in giant nail heads.

The Lutetia was the largest hotel on the Left Bank, a thick gray block of Art Nouveau built in 1910; much as I loved its Art Nouveau curves, I couldn't forget Pierre's aside when he'd moved in, that it had been the Nazi spy headquarters during the Occupation. Although the immense lobby had been redone in the seventies in brass and crimson, I could not cross it without remembering that this was where Charlotte Aillaud's sister had found her on her release from

Ravensbrück in 1945, among a crowd of concentration camps survivors.

That spring was the fiftieth anniversary of D-Day. Aged American veterans with medals and aviator glasses were all over the news, and the war was lodged in my head. All I could think of was the Occupation, the Resistance, and sabotage.

I wanted to meet the staff one by one before I began; Jonathan gave me his palatial office on the no-man's-land executive floor, one flight up from the entrance, one flight below the offices of Paris *Vogue*, where I didn't want to set foot until I knew who was who.

It was the first time I'd worn shoes indoors in daytime in sixteen years. I sat at Jonathan's desk overlooking a field of cut-glass ornaments, wearing one of my priestly Jean Muir tunics, Mercury at my neck. My new high heels hurt, but I kept them on. Bare feet would mark me as weak.

The first person was my predecessor Colombe's assistant, a tough Chinese woman named Mary, who informed me that she was really a filmmaker and would be spending her lunch hours editing Eric Rohmer's new movie. Paris *Vogue*'s staff were original, quirky, pleasant-looking men and women, not one anorectic among them. I took in what clues I could about them from anxious faces, checked shirts, flowered dresses, cotton scarves, bracelets, rings, medallions.

The first wave attempted to speak in English; I cut them off with a quick flow of French, laced with slightly outdated argot. Briefed by the first batch, the next visitors proceeded in French, some escalating into virtuoso deployments of the past subjunctive; I countered with the past conditional.

I told each one that I wanted to make this *Vogue* a place where the reader could play and find herself, which came out as a neat pun, "*rendre le Jeu et le Je à* Vogue."

I wondered how they saw me. Anyone who assured me of his or her loyalty too quickly would, I imagined, have said the same to the Germans in 1940. The ones who said they didn't know if they wanted to work for me were honest, and I saw them as brave members of the Resistance.

Fashion editors eager to impress, features editors determined to make it clear that the decision to stay or not was theirs alone, writers trying it on.

"I'm very good at testing spas," said one.

"Aren't we all," I said.

A tall writer leaned over the desk and announced, "I'm the best when it comes to talking about nothing!"

"This magazine," I said, "is no longer about nothing."

The art director who also worked for Nicole's magazine used a formal style better suited to the exquisite rarity of *Egoïste,* but the cover of the current issue showed Isabelle Adjani cringing like a beaten wife against a watery purple background.

"This isn't the message we want to convey," I said. I was a breath away from saying I wanted to see happy.

The photo editor—as distinct from the art director—came in with her Labrador.

"I hope you like dogs," she said. "He comes to work with me every day."

"I'm sure he's a sweetheart," I said, "but I'd rather not see any dogs in the office."

The gag lady had to exile the dogs. This wasn't going to be the old Palais-Bourbon from Bourdin days with a lapdog under every desk.

A fashion editor loomed over me, an aristocratic beauty.

"I don't think hotel rooms are the best setting for fashion stories," I told her.

"They're the cheapest locations," she said. "We can shoot in better places if you increase the budgets."

Budgets, I noted. Increase.

The company president, Gérald Asaria, an irritable man in pale checks, made a lemon face when I asked about budgets and sent men from *le directoire,* the business side, to harass me with questions. The beefiest member of *le directoire* shoved a piece of paper with empty squares on it across Jonathan's desk, and the way he stabbed his finger on the paper reminded me of the man in the cemetery office at Cannes.

"What is your *organigramme?* " he asked.

I squinted at the paper; the lines between the boxes suggested this was a diagram of the chain of command.

"I'll have it for you in the morning," I said, to make him leave.

I cheered myself by thinking that in a few days I'd be installed in Francine Crescent's old office in the glassed-in section at the back of the fashion room, my new Soviet posters on the wall behind me; I'd have a box of dark chocolates open on the desk, which I would happily share with my staff. I'd be powerful, in control, but generous.

Diamonds and watches were the magazine's best friends. The jewelers of the Place Vendôme were our best advertisers, so the jewelry editor was a key post. Franceline Prat was the most senior member of the staff, a woman in her late fifties with a remarkable brown mane of what my friend Valerie called "international hair." She raised her eyebrows at the sight of the plastic Swatch on my wrist. "I can help you get a real watch. Perhaps, a Cartier?"

"I'd love to buy myself a watch," I said, extending the word *acheter* so that she would understand that I bought, and thus could not be bought. She flapped her eyelids. Was I lecturing her?

Soon I was writing a check for 16,000 francs for a steel watch edged in gold while the saleslady looked on in astonishment.

My suite filled up with extraordinary bouquets from jewelers and makers of fine watches, and from Hélène, Nicole, and Inès, none of whom I had yet seen. Karl sent me a bouquet bigger than all the rest, and with it, instead of a dress or two, a small package with a note that said: "This is the most remarkable new writer in France, hope you like her."

I unwrapped five thin books of mystic poetry by Lydie Dattas. My friend from the lycée, the music teacher's daughter.

"How did you know I knew her?" I asked him.

"I could have guessed," he said.

~

The day before I officially took up my duties, Jonathan Newhouse called from London.

"When are you coming back?" I asked. "I thought you'd be here for my first day."

"Actually, I've moved to London. It's an easier place to work."

The next morning, I steeled myself to be a boss, put on a navy blue Jean Muir priest tunic, locked eyes with the diamonds on my Mercury medallion, called one of the VIP G7 cabs, swept in the door at number 4, Place du Palais-Bourbon, nodded at the receptionist, and climbed the second flight of stone stairs up to Paris *Vogue*, where I had not set foot in twenty-three years.

I strode confidently into the fashion room, threw out a general "Bonjour!," and headed for the glassed-in section at the back where I'd hang my Russian posters. Sitting at what should have been my desk was the jewelry editor Franceline of the remarkable hair. I stopped dead, turned, and shook every hand on my way out of the fashion room.

Where was my office? Gérald Asaria materialized in another checked suit, grabbed me by the arm, and marched me to the staircase. "Colombe liked to sit on the next floor," he said. He was on his way to the French Open at Roland-Garros and pressed for time.

Gérald pushed open the door of a narrow space no bigger than a child's bedroom. In it were two small desks.

"That's where you sit," he said, pointing to the desk with its back to the window.

"That desk doesn't have a chair," I said.

"Really?" said Gérald. "I never noticed. I'll send someone."

A disgruntled man in shirtsleeves arrived to verify that, just as I claimed, there was no chair at the desk by the window, and grumbled off to look for one.

If this was sabotage, then this was war, and I was most definitely a German. Shouldn't some advance forces have told me where my office was before I marched in? And not one lousy little posy to welcome me? I sat in Mary's chair until she arrived, and examined the bookshelves while Mary made calls.

Shirtsleeves returned, shaking his head, and declared, "There are no extra chairs anywhere."

"I think this wouldn't be so much an *extra* chair, as the editor in chief's chair, so you might make an effort to find it," I said, and went to the art department to look at the pages for the August issue. I didn't like anything, apart from two sittings styled by the jewelry editor's assistant Marie-Amélie Sauvé, one in Outer Mongolia or someplace that looked like Outer Mongolia, another in a studio. The rest were everything I would eliminate: six black-and-white pages of half-naked girls in a hotel room with veils, garter belts, cigarettes, one sitting open-legged on a bench, another lying on an unmade bed, the two of them making out against a door. Eight more black-and-white pages of a different model posing in a different hotel room, photographed by a friend I wouldn't be using. A color series that Jenny nervously explained as "Little Girl, Bad Girl, Fake Girl"—a model smoking a cigarette wearing a child's dress and kneesocks, a girl in a gold miniskirt sucking her index finger, wearing ankle socks with stiletto sandals, a black model done up like a transvestite, or maybe it was a transvestite.

I didn't know where to begin.

"The ankle socks!" I said to Jenny. Brigitte Langevin snorted in support.

"There were a lot of socks in the collections," said Jenny.

Back in my office, there was still no chair.

I called Gardner, who was also on her first day.

"My office is a closet in the back of the building," she said.

"Do you have a chair?"

"Of course I have a chair, but not much of a window. I hear you have a view of the square."

"But I'm running all over the place," I said.

"You do all the fun stuff," she said wistfully. "I started in editorial, I miss it."

"You're the producer, I'm the director, you have the power," I said. "But I promise you'll know everything I'm doing."

I still didn't have a chair, so I set off down the corridor to the offices of *Automobiles Classiques*. Its art department bustled with men moving pictures of cars around on a light box. The art director pointed to a black leather desk chair leaning against a wall.

"It's a bit broken," he said.

"I'll take it," I said.

"You don't have to carry it," he said gallantly. "I will."

Balancing in the broken chair, I sped into a stroboscopic world where people finished my sentences for me, agreed before I had phrased a full question, nodded as if I were always right.

What photographers would we use? No matter whom I chose, I was going to hurt strangers, acquaintances, and people I loved.

"I always knew that I was really *Vogue*," Mario Testino said across the tiny desk. "I am *Vogue*, and *Vogue* is me." He would have to be our mainstay. A tall, chubby Peruvian who favored silk ascots and an aggressive grin best construed as ironic, he'd been the star photographer at *Glamour*.

"Of course you are," I said. Everyone who worked for us had to believe that they were *Vogue*, that *Vogue* was them, to make up for our tiny budgets.

Couture was in a month, how many seats did we need, and what movie star did I want? "What about that British actress in *Four Weddings and a Funeral*?" I said. "She's beautiful and she's elegant and I think she lives in Paris."

"Do you have her phone number?" asked the booking editor.

"Never met her," I said. "You can find her."

"What about the guest editor for the Christmas issue?" asked the serious features editor Brigitte Paulino-Neto, a measured and judicious Portuguese woman, the one who'd expressed the most skepticism about my arrival. Everyone called her Paulino.

I couldn't top Nelson Mandela.

"What about Jackie Onassis?" I asked.

"I don't think we can reach her," said Paulino.

"I can," I said, and reached for my address book.

Jackie had sent me a letter of congratulations before I left New York. She hated publicity, but she was an editor and this was an editing job. Emboldened by *Vogue*'s need for her and by Paulino's astonishment, I dialed her home number. There was no answer; I sent her a fax, and went on to the next thing.

And then I was a pinball racing through the maze of offices—

tucked into antechambers, attics, rooms the size of linen cupboards, converted passageways—answering summonses from all sides. Gérald Asaria returned from Roland-Garros and called me to his office to meet the directorate gathered around a table like a secret society of gray suits. I was called into Human Resources to meet with an executive on confidential business. She was slim and fairly young, but her teeth were rebar and frayed concrete. She was concerned about the fashion staff coming over from *Glamour*; it was highly irregular, the new fashion director Brigitte was already causing trouble, and half the fashion room, she added, was drugged on tranquilizers.

I went to the café across the square to meet Brigitte Langevin's fashion editors, who stared in perplexity at my unidentifiable tunic and in disgust at my shoes, whose heels were too high for me, but not high enough for them.

Brigitte said I must use her husband, the photographer Marc Hispard, "Because he will do exactly what I want, we can't trust anyone else."

The juniors, Alexia and Isabelle, were young girls in tracksuits. The stars, Delphine Treanton and Carine Roitfeld, had both insisted on remaining freelancers. Delphine was dark, in her twenties, and had the irritable mien of someone who has better things than fashion on her mind. Carine was *Glamour*'s cool girl, five years younger than me. I took in a pointed face, freckles, thin lips, flat hair, and green eyes; how odd: our eyes were the same color, but hers glittered like the diamonds on the Mercury hanging around my neck.

People with green eyes recognize one another, a tribal thing. I looked into those eyes across and had the unbidden certainty that Carine would replace me in this job. So that's who you are, I thought. A neutral fact, it left me unmoved.

The *Vogue* fashion closet was in a basement across the square, where Vera Lungu, an old chain-smoking Romanian with hair dyed jet-black, explained that she was really an artist and only looking after the clothes to pay for her paints.

"We have to move *le shopping* nearer the fashion room," I told Jonathan on the phone as I went through my list—staff, budgets, chair.

"That won't be necessary," he said. "Paris *Vogue* is moving."

"We're leaving the Place du Palais-Bourbon? I only just got here."

"We have a new building big enough to house all the magazines. American *Vogue* is moving back into the Place du Palais-Bourbon, along with all the other international magazines. We have thirty-eight of them now," he said. "We just added Korea."

Don't be sentimental, I told myself. You're sitting in a broken secondhand chair in a child's bedroom.

"It's a new start," I said. "I can't wait."

"It's time you started firing the people you have to fire," Jonathan said.

I hadn't yet found the art director I wanted, but that sounded like an order to fire the one I had. I put on a Jean Muir coat of unremittingly black crepe, meditated cross-legged on Pierre Bergé's old bed, and, to forestall the hatred that would be added to the bad faith and ill will, unpacked one of my cedar smudge sticks. I felt the other side was better disposed toward me than this one, and it didn't seem odd to solicit its help.

I arrived at eight, long before anyone else, checked the fax machine on the curve on the landing, and found a fax from my father. He'd drawn a person sitting at a desk with a hat and a cigar, or maybe just a very large cigarette. A thought bubble read, OFF WITH THEIR HEADS! FIRE THEM ALL!! CHOP CHOP CHOP! I WANT BLOOD!

I crammed it into my bag, and called L.A.

"Christ, Dad, you can't send me faxes like that. Anyone can read them. I don't have a private machine."

"Well, you damn well should," he said. "What are you letting them get away with? Don't be a mug, honey. Remember, you're a pro."

I attacked the August issue fashion copy that was on my desk. Animism was rampant: skirts puffed themselves up, hair made itself light, the evening demanded satin, face creams brought themselves up to the taste of the day. I replaced the blather with active verbs and crossed out the adjectives. I felt like I'd weeded a garden when the copy chief came in.

"This is how we're going to do it from now on," I said. "Simple, direct, clean."

The copy chief looked at my red scribbles on her proofs and said, "I understand. You want it to be simple, for you."

"Simple," in French, means dim-witted.

"Clear," I said, "I want it to be clear."

Why had I handed her the word "simple"?

"I want it to be clear, but not *débile*." *Débile* means feeble. It also means idiotic. My *débile* to her *simple*.

At lunchtime, when Mary had gone to edit Eric Rohmer's new movie and the mansion was silent, I locked both doors of my office and lit the smudge stick. The flame on the cedar bundle burned bright, a sign of something amiss in the ambient energies. I waved the stick around, made up a cleansing chant that I kept to a low hum, and walked the narrow perimeter of my office, the smoldering cedar held over my ashtray.

The air grew thick with cedar smoke; I opened the windows to let it out, flapped the panes back and forth to clear the room, and wandered down to *Automobiles Classiques* to see if they hadn't by some chance unearthed a better chair. Two young men were laughing by the window. "Someone's smoking a joint in here," snickered one.

I hadn't thought about the smell.

At two o'clock, the executive from Human Resources scurried into my office. I was eating my lunch, a coffee éclair that the model editor's assistant had brought me from the pâtisserie.

"Did we have a meeting?" I asked.

She sniffed the air, asked the same questions she'd asked the day before, twice as fast and with repetitions, to trip me up. I felt my French deserting me under the interrogation. She leaned in to gauge how dilated my pupils were. She had no doubt who was smoking pot, and she was composing the first page of the dossier against me.

I tried to fire the art director in his office, but it was full of people. I tried to get him to my office, but Mary was busy on the phone. Standing a few steps above him on the staircase, I fired him in the most clumsy way possible.

My suite that evening was full of gifts from cosmetic companies, including a large copper-colored box that came with a garden's worth of flowers and a note from an old acquaintance who now ran Helena Rubinstein. The box was full of beautifully packaged lipsticks in every shade from pink and crimson to cyclamen and wine.

I'd humiliated a near stranger on a staircase, taken his job away, and now I was playing with eighty new lipsticks from Helena Rubinstein. The gifts would keep arriving no matter how many people I hurt. That wasn't how I saw the movement of grace through the world.

After that day, I wore the same black coat to give me courage every time I fired someone, without realizing that it was as blatant a warning as an executioner's black mask.

I had no time to read the newspaper that week, or turn on the TV. If a radio played I didn't hear it. I rose, meditated, bathed in the travertine Mussolini ministry, was in the office by eight thirty, and worked through till ten at night. I gave interviews to the British papers, to American ones. Promoting *Vogue* was easier than promoting a novel; I could say "we" instead of "I."

We proceeded without any art director at all. I knew what I wanted.

It was Friday of my first week. The features editor Paulino brought her chair into my child's bedroom and sat down. I held up a letter from Jackie Onassis's secretary. "She says Mrs. Onassis is not well, but will be in touch with me as soon as she's better. So there's hope for the Christmas issue."

"You haven't heard?" Paulino asked.

"Heard?"

"Jackie Onassis died yesterday."

Sadness for Jackie raced through me, I-had-no-idea-she-was-so-sick on its heels, a thought for her children, a kick to myself for having failed to register any news for an entire week, all of it so fast that I felt none of it. I discovered the snap decision.

"Her birthday will be the end of July. She'd have been sixty-five. Let's make a tribute to her in the August issue."

"Good idea," approved Paulino, a wise bird in black who was taking on the role of my professor.

I remembered everything I needed to know. "She won an American *Vogue* competition called the Prix de Paris back in the fifties. Let's find the text that won the prize, get it translated—by someone who doesn't use too many adjectives—have the photo editor find all the best—candid—pictures of her. And you'll write the introduction."

"The photo editor," said Paulino, "is very upset that you said she couldn't bring her dog to work."

"It's a fucking mastiff," I said.

"It's a Labrador," said Paulino.

Someone located the text of Jacqueline Bouvier's Prix de Paris essay, "The Men I Would Have Wanted to Meet," in a bound volume of 1953 American *Vogue*s on a shelf in Jonathan's office. The photo editor got to work.

The Jacqueline Bouvier essay was translated by the end of the following week. Laure the managing editor said I had to inform New York that I would be reprinting the text.

"It's ancient, are you sure?" I said.

"Protocol," said Laure, with a smile and a shrug.

A fax went off to New York.

Hours later, the New York archivist called me.

"You are not allowed to use the Jacqueline Kennedy Prix de Paris essay!" she said.

"Why not?"

"We hold the rights, and they are denied."

"That's absurd. It was published over forty years ago."

"Anna is using it in the *Vogue* August issue. She may allow you to use it in October, ninety days after our publication," said the archivist.

"It's forty-one years after your publication! This is crap!" I shouted. "I refuse to accept your restrictions!"

I sounded like my father on the phone to UA. Mary watched from her desk. The model editor, wide-eyed, pushed open the door between our offices to listen. People stopped in the hall outside my door.

"I'm sorry, Joan, that's the way it is," said the archivist.

I hung up and dictated a fax to Jonathan Newhouse in London.

"We'll fix this," I said to Mary.

Jonathan told me he'd tell Si Newhouse that Anna was being unreasonable.

Then his fax arrived. I needed immediate witnesses to the outrage. I called in the features editor, the travel editor, the copy chief, the photo editor, the entire art department, and Laure. The model editor tugged our connecting door fully open.

"Anna Wintour has denied permission for us to use the Jackie Onassis essay," I said. "I've appealed to Jonathan Newhouse, and this is the fax Si Newhouse sent back to him." I was trembling as I read aloud: "'I don't want to get involved in this, let them fight it out.'"

I looked around me. "So. We have no protection. And Anna Wintour wants to screw us."

I'd wanted rage, but the travel editor applauded, the art department boys shouted "*Hourah!*" The model editor ran in to hug me, her assistants cheered from next door, and then everyone in my room cheered as well.

"Vous êtes contents qu'on est baisé?" I asked. You're happy we got screwed?

The features editor leaned forward and said, "But now, we have the proof that you don't work for Anna Wintour. You're here for us, not for New York. Welcome."

I lost Jackie Onassis but I won a staff.

CHAPTER THIRTEEN

Hélène Rochas gave a dinner for Pamela Harriman and me, because, she said, "You are both American ambassadresses to France."

Well, she was.

Pamela Harriman, who'd married Winston Churchill's son, Randolph, during the war, who'd been the mistress of Stavros Niarchos, Gianni Agnelli, Prince Aly Khan, Bill Paley, Ed Murrow, and then Elie de Rothschild; Pamela Harriman, the stepmother villain of Brooke Hayward's memoir *Haywire* after she married Leland Hayward. Pamela Harriman, who then married the tremendously rich former diplomat Averell Harriman. Pamela Harriman, née Pamela Digby in England at the dawn of time, now, thanks to years as the most powerful democratic hostess in Washington, DC, Bill Clinton's ambassador to France.

"I know Averell Harriman's grandson," I said.

"Don't mention him, *ma chérie,* I think there's a lawsuit."

Hélène assembled a little group, two playwrights and one couple, for drinks at the American embassy residence on the Faubourg Saint-Honoré. I remembered how astute and cutting the playwrights were about theater, music, books; they would tell me what Parisian culture had become in the last six years.

Van Gogh's *White Roses* hung in the grand salon, the object of the lawsuit. Pamela Harriman wore a silk cocktail dress, had a ball of lacquered blond hair rising around a wide face, little blue eyes, weak pink lipstick; at seventy-four, she looked like a cheerfully reliable English girl, more a British Caledonian Airways air hostess than the most redoubtable courtesan of all time.

As we sat down to dinner at Lucas Carton, one of the playwrights murmured in my ear, "She once said there are no secrets to seducing a man, only enthusiasm."

The ambassadress of the United States welcomed me to Paris with a toast. I thanked her for the good work she was doing for our country. She said she couldn't discuss politics, so we lavished compliments on the lobsters *à la nage.*

"What have you seen?" I asked one of the playwrights.

"At theater? Nothing. But I adore *Alerte à Malibu.* It is wonderful, so American, so fresh, so amusing."

The entire table adored *Alerte à Malibu.*

Pamela Harriman inquired what *Alerte à Malibu* might be.

"Television!" said Hélène Rochas. "It's about lifeguards, and the star is a remarkably vulgar young woman. Vulgar, but very amusing."

"Blond, huge breasts, big lips," offered one of the playwrights, "very enthusiastic."

"You mean Pamela"—I shouted, and blanked on her last name as all eyes turned to me—"Pamela, Pamela, Pamela Anderson?"

The French nodded eagerly. *Oui, oui,* Pamela Anderson! The cultured socialites of Paris were fans of *Baywatch,* and now we had something to talk about.

I was not going to put Pamela Anderson in Paris *Vogue.* It had to be the most French of all French things, the summit of French achievement, the embodiment of France. The ads in the August magazines showed black leather corset miniskirts by Dior, fake Chanel by Céline, fur miniskirts by Chanel, a bag made entirely of crystal beads by Swarovski, a fake leopard coat to the floor by Dolce & Gabbana, sunglasses with gold stems by Versace, a fake panther jacket worn with a tutu miniskirt by Ana Molinari, along with big diamonds, gold watches, enamel bracelets that I couldn't imagine anyone wearing, night repair serums, tanning accelerators, and the Wonderbra.

I didn't want a floor-length fake leopard coat or a leather corset miniskirt. I wanted color and life. Back in my hotel, at night after work, I played with my gray Macintosh laptop, the first computer I'd ever had. I pressed keys at random, like a rat going at levers in a maze, and discovered that a computer contained millions of colors. I explored sharp transparent blues, yellows so bright they pierced my eyes, an infinite spectrum of rich purples that made up for the curiously unemphatic reds, the greens that were never green enough. I taught myself to modify the colors of the pixels that made up the patterned background to the desktop, and played with colors to wind down as compulsively as I'd crocheted when I was sixteen.

I wanted color. The fashion editors wanted edgy. Gardner wanted advertisers. The fashion editors winced when they heard the word *annonceurs,* those overlords who wanted to bleed creativity dry.

"We have to show the big names, they pay for the magazine," I said. Gardner wasn't allowed to tell me what to do, but I knew my responsibility to photograph the advertiser's wares.

"Real fashion is attitude," said Brigitte Langevin. She wore a white T-shirt, a tight beige skirt, and stilettos.

"Fashion is an attitude," said Carine Roitfeld. She wore a little sweater, a straight skirt, and stilettos.

"Fashion is the right attitude," said young Marie-Amélie, who was known as Mimi. She wore a white T-shirt and black pants, and the toes on her stilettos were the longest and most pointed of all.

The younger editors, Alexia and Isabelle, dressed as if they were on a handball team. They were all proud to be above what they called the diktats of fashion. They weren't bourgeois dupes who aspired to couture and diamonds. They were free women. They were *de gauche.* They were antifashion.

Paris *Vogue,* despite the best efforts of Colombe Pringle to radicalize it, represented power, patriarchy, property, and the supremacy of tradition. The Berlin Wall had fallen five years before, but the old binary left-right Marxist-capitalist reading still applied to everything.

The values of the bourgeoisie—tradition, family, church, marriage, ownership, wealth, reproduction, roots—easily shaded over into the nationalism that Marshal Pétain had invoked to save the pride of France during the German occupation, and slid into xenophobia and racism, all the way over to the hysterical, anti-Semitic, homophobic, Holocaust-denying, Muslim-bashing Jean-Marie Le Pen, leader of the National Front, who had once proposed concentration camps for people with AIDS.

On the other side was the freethinking, authority-hating, individualistic, tolerant, socialist position where marriage was an aberration, property was a crime, outward signs of wealth despicable—which shaded into a bohemian, existential, communitarian, fairly depressed borderline hippie view of the world that, when espoused by people with money and good clothes, was called *la gauche caviar*—the caviar left.

Women dressed to signify their allegiances: on the right, blazers over shirts, and, visible under the shirts, religious medals on a gold chain, a crucifix for Catholics, the dove of the Holy Spirit for Protestants, or gold charm cutouts of children, one for each child, to signal the successful repopulation of the mother country. The *gauche caviar* scorned bourgeois trinkets in favor of damaged trench coats, watches inherited from dead fathers, heavy silver bracelets inset with broken carnelians from the farthest reaches of the planet, hunted down in small wood-lined Left Bank shops, and sometimes a Palestinian scarf to signal general disapproval of Israel, but accessorized with a paperback by a Jewish philosopher, say, Alain Finkelkraut, to signal that they were not anti-Semitic, just anti-Israel.

The Hermès silk twill headscarf printed with images of reins, saddles, snaffles, spurs had signaled the supremacy of bourgeois values from the middle of the twentieth century onward, but was no longer worn on the head. The influx of Muslims filled the streets with women who covered their hair with scarves, shawls, and, in extreme cases, full veils. Too bad if it rained on bourgeois hair fresh from the hairdresser's; since there was no way to keep it out of the rain without a scarf, it became unfashionable for hair to look perfect. Sales of umbrellas went up, and raincoats began to spring hoods.

Yves Saint Laurent had long ago breached the division with his perfect wardrobe that included both the lefty trench coat and the suit for a mayor's wife. Other designers fell in one camp or another: Mugler and Montana made leather for hot lefty babes, Karl made Chanel lady suits that were worn with irony by the left. When Inès de la Fressange, his muse and emblem, modeled for the bust of Marianne, the symbol of France displayed in every mayor's office across the country, he promptly dismissed her, saying he could not be represented by a symbol of nationalist pride.

Only sex was beyond politics. Naked women were universal, and so was lingerie, and so was leather, and so was latex. Helmut Newton had for years been photographing women who embodied his prewar Berlin fascination with the night, but now fashion mined the wardrobes of prostitutes and dominatrixes. An editor at *Elle* had noticed rubber miniskirts on the hookers of the Rue Saint-Denis, and featured them in the magazine under the name "Sloogy."

Paris *Vogue* presented itself as seduction without distraction. Its paper was thicker than any other *Vogue*'s, its surface glossier, its ad pages thickened with advertorials. It was as dense as a brick, as slick as a freshly landed marlin, and almost perfectly empty.

I'd never found myself in the pages of Paris *Vogue*. Not that many had; the circulation was barely sixty thousand.

We had to take *Vogue* back from the concept of woman as object, turn *Vogue* into something other than an instrument of subordination, to vault over the glossy phalanx of press girls, the critical in-crowd, and reach a whole new audience, the reader.

I stole my art director from German *Vogue*. Donald Schneider was young, balding, with an open face and a thick Swiss-German accent. In the 1980s, he'd made the tableaux at Area, a New York nightclub part zoo, part haunted house, the first immersive experience outside of Disneyland. Every few weeks, Area became a fun house with a different theme: Science Fiction, Fairy Tales, War, Confinement. I'd loved its monstrous plush animals, its aliens, its mermaid with a fish-tail swimming in a pool that became, one week later, a vat of soup clogged with giant alphabet letters.

I needed a gag man, and Schneider knew that humor was the only way into this battlefield.

"The new art director is coming from German *Vogue*," I told Brigitte Langevin.

"German *Vogue*! It falls out of your hands it's so boring," she snarled.

"Well, that's who I've hired," I said, "Donald Schneider."

"And he's Swiss!" she hissed.

"I need some French clothes to wear at the couture," I told her, to make up for the Swiss art director.

"All you need is a Burberry trench, some jeans, and some T-shirts," she said, eyeing my black priest's tunic from London that had been pissing her off for weeks.

"Burberry is English, jeans and T-shirts are American."

"But it's a very Jane Birkin attitude," she said. "She's a French icon."

"She's English," I said.

"But the Hermès bag is named after her," said Mimi brightly.

"Prada," said Jenny. Italian. And Gucci. Gucci? The handbags? Yes, there was this young American designer who was a friend of Carine Roitfeld's, Tom Ford; in fact, she styled his shows, and he was doing wonderful things. Such as? Little sweaters, little skirts. And Jil Sander, Jil Sander was cool.

"That's two Italians, an American, and a German," I said. "Who is actually French?"

"Hermès," said one.

"Hermès is designed by a team," said Jenny. "There's Tomas Maier, he's German, and Tan Giudicelli, he's Vietnamese Italian."

"But they're going to hire Martin Margiela," said Brigitte Langevin, who was in the know.

"He's Belgian."

No one was French, Karl least of all. So they could all stop bitching about the two Americans at Paris *Vogue*.

Gardner eyed my silver compact when I powdered my nose. She lit her cigarette from my silver lighter. Once a fat girl, she'd trained herself not to eat, but at our lunches she knocked back the wine, while I cut my Perrier with Evian to tone down the bubbles.

"I can't drink," I apologized, "I get a hangover instead of a buzz, it slows me down and ruins the next day. I might have that Native American gene that makes it poison for me," I added. Deciding to enhance my pioneer ancestry with horse feathers from the Plains, I told her Grandpa Norman's story as if it were true, though I admitted I wasn't sure whether my great-grandfather was Blackfoot or Sioux, Navajo, Cheyenne, or Comanche.

"You need a shahtoosh," she said, flicking the fine beige cloud draped over one of her shoulders. She knew travelers who went to India to root out these precious shawls made of the chin hairs of Himalayan goats, and sent one my way. He talked in code on the phone. I bought two shawls, one dark purple, one rust. They each cost more than a coat. Here was the way to stand apart from the fray of commerce while wearing something rare and precious; no one had designed this, no one had marketed it, no one sold it in a store, you had to know the right person to get your hands on it. Here was exclusivity and privilege. Here was True Chic: It was antifashion, third world, and it cost a fortune. I didn't yet know that the shahtoosh was also illegal.

Very soon, Gardner had a silver compact like mine, and then an identical silver cigarette lighter. One day I used my Native American excuse to refuse the wine that Alain Dominique Perrin from Cartier offered me. "That's so strange," he said. "Gardner Bellanger has Native American blood as well, but she drinks."

It took a few weeks to secure a real chair. I'd ordered the biggest, reddest, most ergonomically complex chair in Paris, and set a four-foot inflatable version of Munch's *Scream* beside it to signal that I didn't take any of this seriously. But the role of editor in chief was beginning to stick, as if latex gloves were creeping from my hands up my arms to my torso, my neck, my face, suffocating me.

I needed a quick break. The beauty editor booked me into the Trianon Palace hotel next door to Versailles. From my window, I saw a herd of sheep standing in a great green field. I rented a bicycle, rode past the sheep, bumped along cobblestones down to the Grand Canal that spread out in a cross below the palace.

The trees striped past me, their low branches clipped into perfect horizontal lines. I left the path and took earthen *allées* straight as rulers through the forest, into an infinite unfolding of more land, more landscapes, thousands of acres of the seventeenth-century past to get lost in, with hardly a car in sight. For the first time since I'd arrived in Paris, no one was watching, and I was happy.

Geometry enfolded me. The Grand Canal was shaped like a cross, five miles around, its water reflecting the silver sky, its pale stone rim edged with a path of beaten earth. At the farthest end of the cross, I heard a *putt-putt* and saw a 1920s biplane coming in to land beyond a hedge.

The Grand Trianon rose above the cobbled road, and my heart beat as if I were coming home. The same pink marble as the Palais Rose, the same proportions, but bigger, with a portico and more wings.

I went down the stairs to the left, where my bedroom would have been if it were the Palais Rose. Past and present converged, just as I'd once willed them to while sitting on the steps at St. Clerans. I flattened myself against the stone and held my cheek against the wall to crawl back into my past, but the wall would not give. I pulled away. Stop trying child magic on old stone. Only Today counts, Alex Liberman had said. I got back on the bike and rode for hours to feel my feet, my legs, my hands. This was real; grass, sunlight, other people on their bicycles.

~

I decided I'd dedicate my first issue, September, to the French woman, *La Femme Française.*

No one could explain why so many French women had blond hair with black eyebrows, so I let the question drop. *Vogue* would define types of French women by their accessories—Le Trench, turbans like Simone de Beauvoir, sneakers—"*baskets*"—like Jane Birkin, shawls like Colette, hoop earrings like Béatrice Dalle, pearl necklaces like Chanel, push-up bras like Brigitte Bardot, Lacoste polo shirts like the newscaster Claire Chazal. The final accessory was the Handbag Shiv, like Charlotte Corday, who used it to murder Marat in his tub in 1793.

Brigitte Langevin's husband, Marc Hispard, shot clothes that women could maybe afford: a Burberry trench coat, of course, but in red—a black suit, a black sweater, a black evening dress, a black coat, a black sweater, a black pin-striped pantsuit, another black sweater, a red beaded evening dress, another black sweater, and a close-up of a model smoking a cigarette.

I stared at the photos on the light box. Delphine, the fashion editor who didn't like to be noticed, had done a beautiful job. But, I told Brigitte, I didn't want to see any more cigarettes in the magazine, and there were too many black clothes.

"Black! We need black! Black is all that French women wear!" Brigitte snarled.

"Exactly," I said, "they don't need *Vogue* to tell them to buy a black sweater. We're going to shoot colored clothes from now on. No more black in *Vogue*."

They already knew I hated dogs, now I hated black. I was hardly human.

At night I went to bed with mock-ups of covers for my first issue. The model wore black, but the cover lines were in red type. Black and white and red all over. I spread the printouts around me before I went to sleep. Whichever one I still liked in the morning would be the choice. Photocopies in my bed instead of a man. *Vogue* took up all the space inside my head, my heart.

Alex Liberman came to Paris for a final tour before his retirement, and Condé Nast threw a party to honor him, and to welcome me.

I pulled on a nylon mesh dress from Karl, and over it an old navy-blue shift that I'd bought at Ann Taylor for seventy dollars. They'd never be able to guess what it was, and I'd always had a good time in it.

Mercury's little eyes glittered from the medallion around my neck. He was my date.

The party was at Ledoyen in the leafy part of the Champs-Élysées on a slightly chilly evening in the endless late-June sun. The nonspecific famous blondes who filled the party pages of *Vogue* wore borrowed brocade suits and held flutes of champagne.

Gérald Asaria introduced me to two couples from L'Oréal, our biggest advertiser. "We'll be across the Champs-Élysées at Laurent for dinner after the party, if you want to join us," he whispered. I have so many friends here, I thought, I don't have to have dinner with advertisers.

My friends. We lined up for photographs. Manolo Blahnik, Tai and Rosita Missoni, Nicole, Inès, Hélène, Anouk Aimée, Peter Brook. Eric Rothschild with his wife, Beatrice. Betty Bacall had flown in from New York, just as she had for my wedding, to stand in for family. I asked her what she was doing afterward, but she had plans. So did everyone else.

Karl, Yves, Pierre. Loulou de la Falaise and Thadée. Clara Saint.

Karl and Yves exchanged a kiss; the photographers pounced to record the end of their long feud.

Designers I didn't yet know: the old guard, Givenchy, Pipart, Féraud; the younger ones, Lacroix, Michel Klein, Martine Sitbon; and the newest one, John Galliano, the strange English boy from Gibraltar, whose top was a smudge of torn pink net. There were the designers that Jane Gozzett had introduced me to when we were teenagers, Sonia Rykiel, Kenzo, Emmanuelle Khanh, even Jean Cacharel, master of the crepon shirts of 1965, but no Jane Gozzett. I hadn't found her.

As the evening wore on, the yellow pattern on the maroon carpet became more interesting. I was alone among strangers, and then I was alone among waiters. It was 9:00 p.m.

As the summer sunset turned to dusk, I stood at the curb waiting for a gap in the Saturday night traffic, and crossed to join Gérald Asaria for dinner with the advertisers and their wives at Laurent.

It was bad enough arriving at *Vogue* without a staff of my own. To make friends, I had to show this world that I shared its values. The next day, I bought clothes at Prada that everyone would recognize.

Gianni Versace showed couture at night—as Valentino had in the old days in Rome—fashion show as party, audience all dressed up. He always presented his collection on a platform built over the Ritz swimming pool, which was closed to hotel guests for a week so that fashion people could look at clothes for fifteen minutes. It was the first show of

Photo © Richard Young

My husband, John Heilpern, Tina and Michael Chow, and Joyce at our wedding reception, Mr. Chow, London, November 1977.

Karl Lagerfeld fitting my wedding costume, Hôtel Pont Royal, Paris, October 1977.

Right: Karl's sketch of my wedding costume, a skirt and blouse of antique mauve taffeta under a riding habit of equally antique mauve ottoman silk.

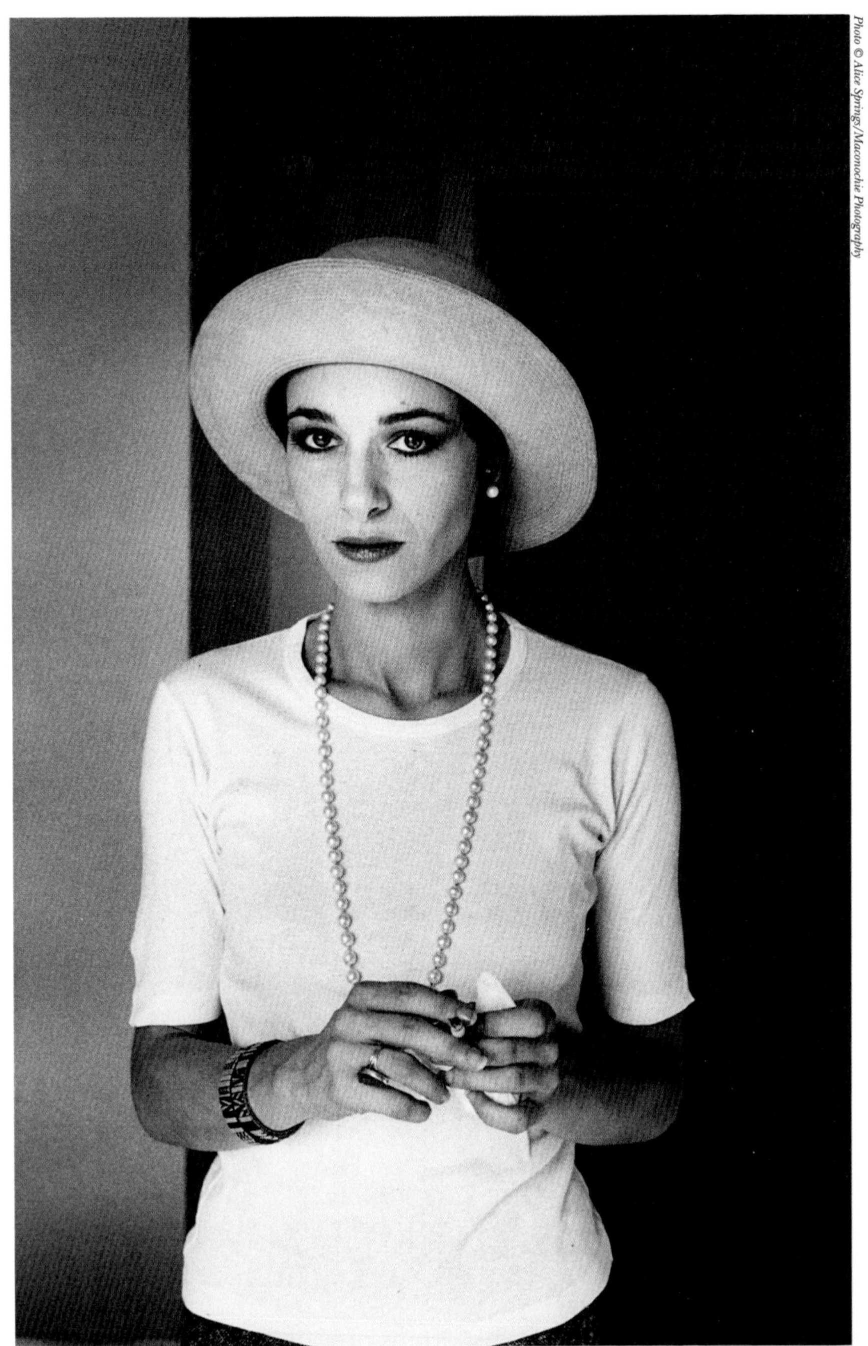

Portrait by Alice Springs, Chateau Marmont, Los Angeles, January 1983.

Portrait by Serge Lutens, styled by Marian McEvoy. I'm wearing an approximation of Ricki's lava jewelry, Paris, 1982.

Serge Lutens / Photo © Fondation Serge Lutens

Photo © Roxanne Lowitt

With Leo Lerman and Kathleen Tynan at the launch party for *The Only Place to Be,* Elio's, New York, July 1982.

Photo © Dominique Nabokov

With Hélène Rochas, Paris, 1987.

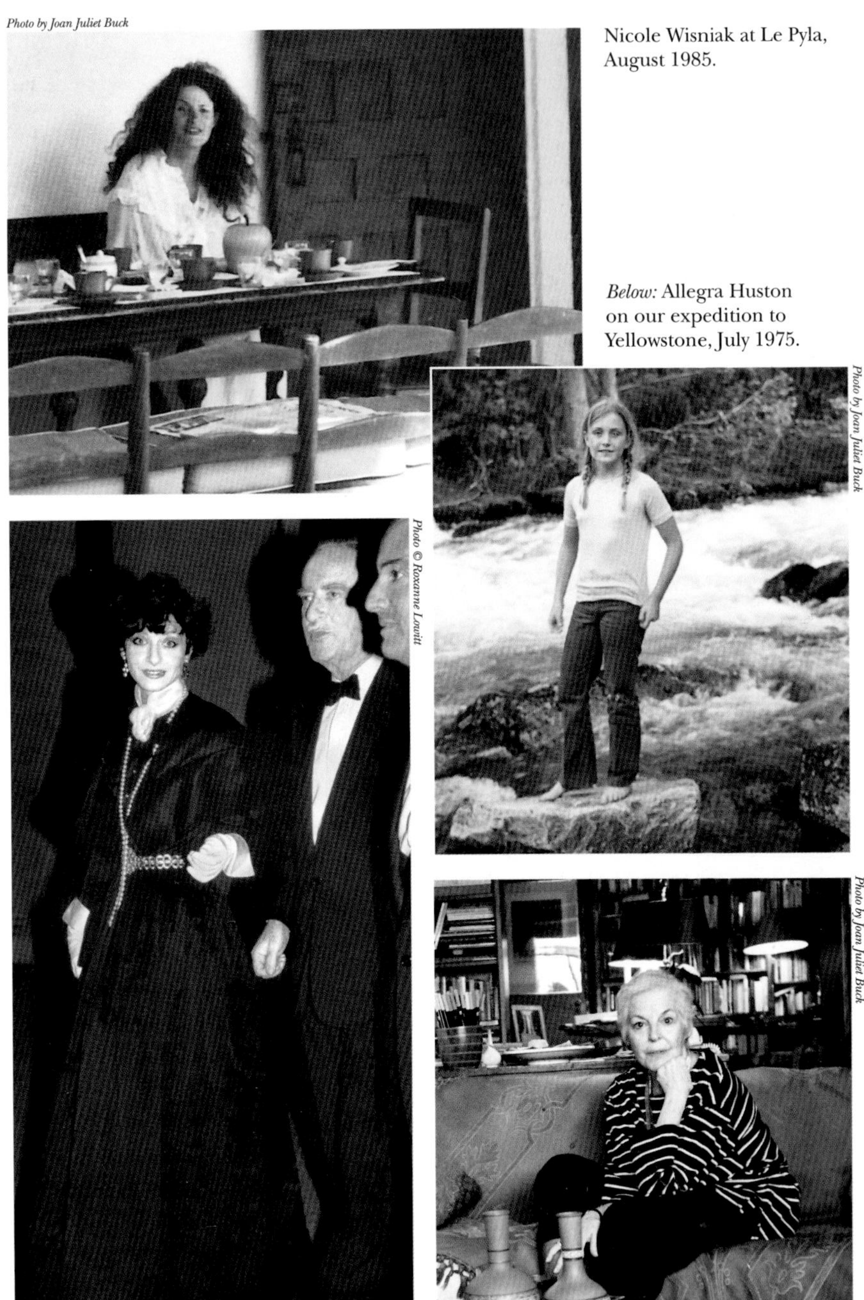

Photo by Joan Juliet Buck

Nicole Wisniak at Le Pyla, August 1985.

Below: Allegra Huston on our expedition to Yellowstone, July 1975.

Photo by Joan Juliet Buck

Photo © Roxanne Lowitt

In Karl's George Sand dress for Chanel, with Alex Liberman and Alain Coblence, the Met Gala, New York, 1984.

Photo by Joan Juliet Buck

Joyce in the living room at East 77th Street, September 1993.

Photo © Matthew Rolston

Portrait with Anjelica by Matthew Rolston for *Interview* magazine, taken in Los Angeles, October 1987.

Photo © Jean Pigozzi

On the dance floor with Norman Mailer at the party Tina Brown gave for me, Tribeca Grill, New York, May 1994.

With Yves Saint Laurent, Gianfranco Ferré, and Karl Lagerfeld, *Vogue* party, Paris, June 1994.

Photos © Roxanne Lowit

Photo © Jean-Baptiste Mondino

Above: Portrait for *Talk* magazine by Jean-Baptiste Mondino, 1999.

Left: Three faces of an editor in chief, Paris, 1994–2000.

Photo by Joan Juliet Buck

Photo © Jean-Luce Huré

Far left: Mantelpiece at 11 Rue Jacob, Paris, Christmas 1996.

Left: With Charlotte Rampling at one of the parties, 11 Rue Jacob, January 1997.

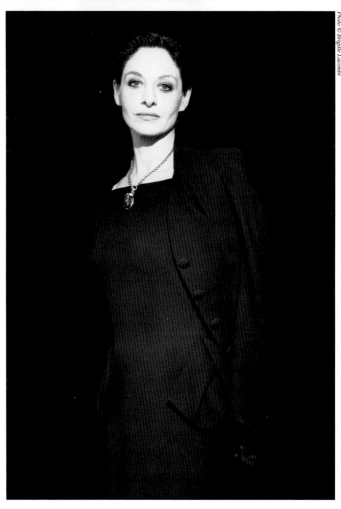

Photo © Brigitte Lacombe

Portrait by Brigitte Lacombe for *New York* magazine, 1996.

© Columbia Pictures Industries, Inc.

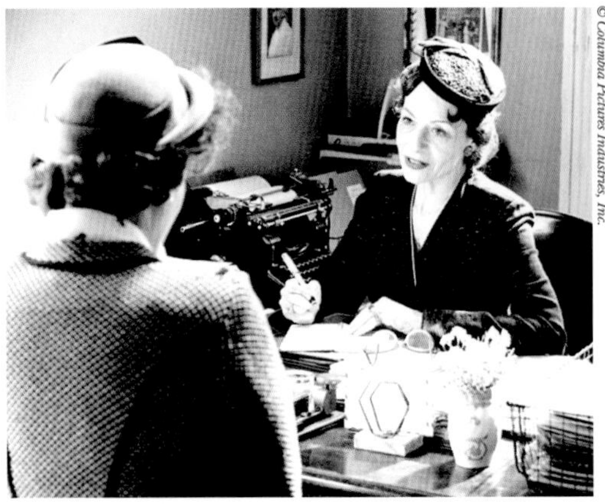

With Meryl Streep in Nora Ephron's 2009 film *Julie & Julia,* New York, 2008.

Photo © Brigitte Lacombe

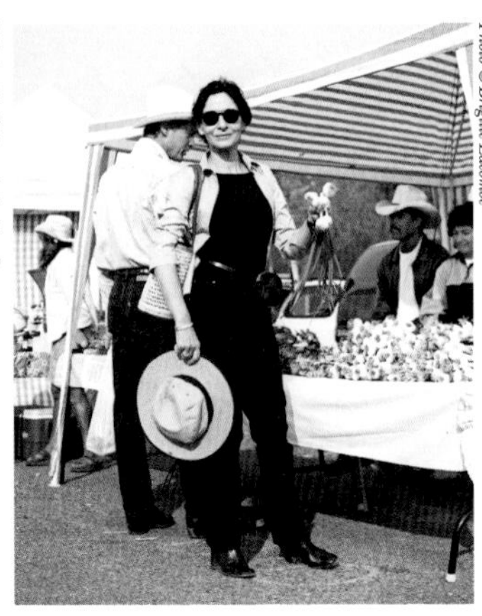

With Kim Moss at the Farmers Market, Santa Fe, 2002.

Photo © Coke W. O'Neal

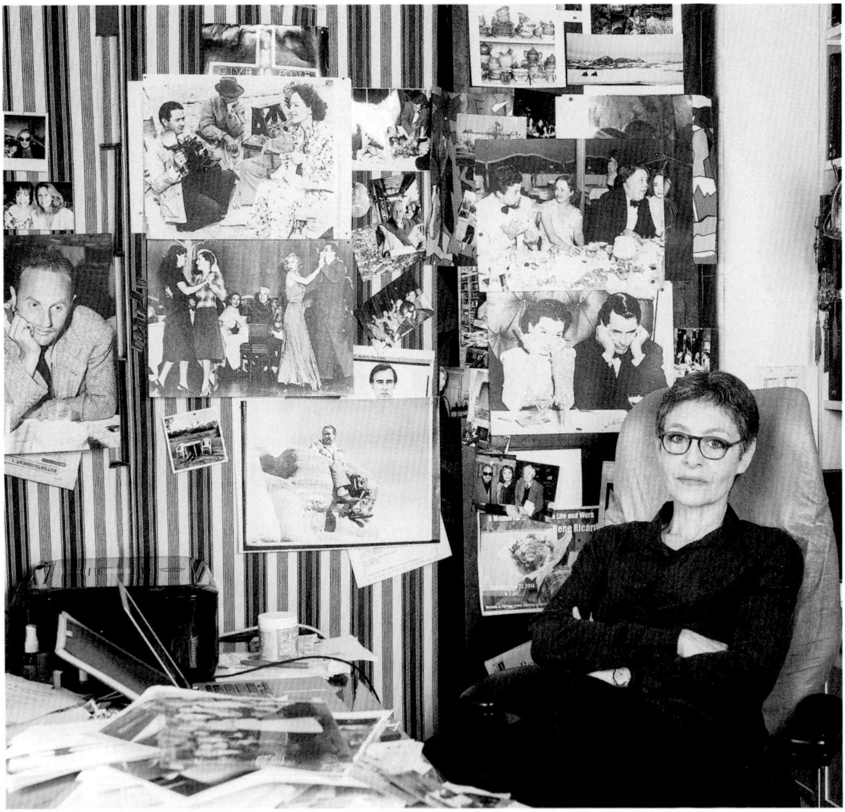

Hell's Kitchen, New York, 2014.

the July couture, my first couture show as editor in chief. We took our little gold chairs amid cries, hugs, kisses; the fashion press had been separated since April, and the reunion was ecstatic.

While a wall of paparazzi snapped the chain-mail dresses on the supermodels Claudia, Naomi, Linda, and Carla Bruni, Steven Klein shot the audience: Bryan Ferry, Marisa Berenson, Sylvester Stallone with his fiancée the rowdy model Janice Dickinson, Hugh Grant with his girlfriend Elizabeth Hurley, who was famous for having attended a première in a Versace dress held together by giant safety pins. Steven Klein shot a woman who embodied everything freakish about haute couture, a platinum-blond client from Germany who wore doll-like dresses thick with flowers, jewelry so big it looked fake, and a permanent look of ecstasy as she gazed upon clothes while clutching her son, a blond lump of nine in a white suit.

The Versace dinner was held in a dining room of the Ritz, with TV sets scattered around on high stands so the men could follow the World Cup semifinal. Sylvester Stallone and Janice Dickinson broke up before dessert, and Italy beat Bulgaria.

Anna Wintour gave a party for me at the Café Marly, a new restaurant set into a colonnade of the Louvre. The skirmish over Jackie Onassis was forgotten. Her cohosts were Franca Sozzani from Italian *Vogue*, an impenetrable blonde with Rapunzel curls, and sensible Alex Shulman from British *Vogue*, who gave me a deck of cards in a box labeled "Patience," the British term for "Solitaire." Everyone was relieved to see me in a dress they recognized. Prada spoke their language.

The burly directorate man took me and Gardner to inspect the new building, and Brigitte Langevin jumped in the car with us. In the grimmest, narrowest part of the Rue de Vaugirard, it was an ugly place made of horizontal concrete slabs with a sunken entrance that sank the heart. My office was an L-shaped wedge set behind a big front room where my assistants would sit.

"Look," said the directorate man, "you have your own private toilet."

Brigitte Langevin, more of a terrier every day, skittered past me to mark my private territory with a proprietary pee.

One month as a boss and I could no longer put a stamp on a letter or tell the difference between a receipt and a flyer. The dining room of my suite now had a fax, but it was buried under a mess of files, top-secret memos, financial reports, confidential lists of employees with their age, date of employment, salary, and, in some cases, the graphologist's report on their character, all hauled home for the sake of discretion. I had a letter from the producers of *The White Hotel* telling me to cease and desist about my drawings. I had papers from the French government asking for documentation as to my employment. One Sunday, as I tried to make sense of the mess, the phone rang; it was an American girl who knew me through someone in New York. "You need an assistant. I live here, I speak French, let me work for you," she said. I asked if she could come sort through the papers, right now. Within two hours, Mallery Lane had arranged the papers, filled out the forms, and photocopied my passport.

It was hot and humid the next day, a thunderstorm gathering. The mansion had no air-conditioning, my office had no fan; Mary said there wasn't one fan left in the entire building, so Danièle the beauty editor sent her intern out to buy one for me.

"Mary," I asked, "how's the movie going?"

"Still cutting," she said, without looking up.

"Are you happy working for me?" I asked.

Now she looked up.

I held the silence.

She opened her mouth to speak. A lightning bolt hit the statue of Justice in the center of the square behind me, and the mansion shook.

"No," she said, "I'm not."

I'd never had backup from lightning before.

Mallery began work the next day.

I asked the man who was good at writing about nothing to do an etiquette column.

"What should I say, since you don't want it to be about nothing?"

"The etiquette of condoms?"

He thought for two seconds. "I could compare them to white gloves," he said.

This was going to work.

I'd met Diane von Furstenberg's friend Christian Louboutin, a short and swarthy brat of thirty who had a street urchin's know-it-all, ready-to-rumble energy and such a precise vocabulary that he insisted his shoes be known by the archaic term *souliers* rather than the common modern term *chaussures.* He knew a great deal about everything, and even more about gardening; I gave him a gardening column in the magazine.

This was going to be fun.

Kristin Scott Thomas was found, and booked to pose in couture. I briefed the young fashion editor Alexia. "She's an actress, so don't embarrass her by putting clothes on her that are too tight," I said.

The day of the shoot, I picked my way to the studio across cobblestones, unstable in new heels that I'd imagined would not hurt because they were navy blue.

Kristin Scott Thomas stood on the no-seam paper wearing a tight white tweed jumpsuit from Chanel with legs that pooled around her ankles, a Louise Brooks wig on her head. She was close to tears.

"I'm so sorry," I said, tracking street dirt onto the no-seam paper to greet her. "This isn't fair."

"I hate the wig," she said.

"But you look beautiful. I loved the Romanian movie."

Her face relaxed. "You saw it?"

We had posters for the September issue all over Paris, on the sides of the kiosks, high up on poles along the avenues. There was Phoebe O'Brien in her black Galliano suit on the white cover with the red writing and a nice round number—50—for the best choices of haute couture. The bottom of the cover announced in huge letters "*La Femme Française.*"

"*La Femme Française?*" some people asked with little smirks, as if the words were wrong.

"Of course!" I answered, wondering if they had checked the model's name inside and seen she was Phoebe O'Brien, and Irish. What was the problem with proclaiming *La Femme Française?*

The issue sold better than any Paris *Vogue* had in years, but I kept getting these little "*La Femme Française?*" questions, as if I'd done something really sick.

"We died laughing over your '*Femme Française*' cover," an art director said years later.

"What was wrong with it?"

"La Femme Française!" He began laughing all over again. "It read like a rallying call to the far-right wing. It was as bad as if you'd put the words 'National Pride' on the cover. It looked like a poster for the National Front."

CHAPTER FOURTEEN

The September 1994 Paris *Vogue* vaulted over the in-crowd cabal of *mauvaises langues*, past friends of *Vogue* and friends of people who'd worked at *Vogue*, to reach readers who had absolutely no history with *Vogue*. It brought in an unprecedented number of new readers, presumably not all of them National Front. Gardner brought in an unprecedented number of new advertisers.

We moved to the grim new offices, where, despite the extra acreage, Vera and the *Vogue* closet were still assigned to purgatory on a lower floor.

I had to find a place to live. Ten thousand books and most of my furniture were heaving across the Atlantic in a container ship. A neat little *parisienne* who specialized in relocating executives took me around in her neat little car to show me apartments that were never as neat as she was. I wanted something romantic, practical, and generous, somewhere I could give parties. Lots of parties. She drove me from one sad place to another, until one day she took me to the Rue Jacob.

The narrow Rue Jacob had always been magic to me, each shop a door into the past, where cabinetmakers toiled ankle deep in sawdust, upholsterers still worked with horsehair and straw, taffeta came in shades of dawn and seascape. At one end was the Rue de Buci market, where fishmongers attacked giant red tuna with cleavers at tables in the street, the occasional country goat performed minor tricks on a stepladder, and, tucked in a doorway, there was the only place in Paris to buy both fishnet tights and sailor sweaters.

Behind the immense door, a wide carriageway led to tubs of pink geraniums and a tiny concierge standing in a cobblestoned courtyard. Beyond the glass door was a generous, smooth stone seventeenth-century staircase, the center of each golden step worn away, the balustrade carved into urns that rose up past an *entresol* to a high door lacquered the color of old wine. The agent fiddled with the keys while I told myself I couldn't afford this. She pushed the door open, and I stepped into a foyer, and then into a room that was a perfect cube.

Walls rose to a ceiling so high it seemed to float. "Five meters," she said. Was that eighteen feet? Seventeen? Everything was painted that fresh-start white, blank-page white, between-tenants white. The delicate paneling had been there since Thomas Jefferson and Benjamin Franklin lived up the street. There was a high *trumeau* mirror inset above a marble fireplace. Wooden shutters fit perfectly into the embrasures of the three windows. Double doors led to a narrow dining room, just as tall, that looked toward the top of the concierge's cottage, and on the cottage roof was a small, perfect cube that seemed to have landed from the Bauhaus.

Every room had public doors and secret doors, like a maze with safety exits. The uneven *parquet de Versailles* in the salon sloped up to the far corner, where I found a white sliver of kitchen, the *cuisine américaine.* The appliances were unused. The last tenant had been an American in charge of Euro-Disney, but he and his family had left as soon as they'd moved in.

I followed her into another room with the same high ceiling, but shadowy. "Your guest room," she said. Down the corridor was a second perfect cube, identical to the salon, its fireplace dark red marble, twice as ornate but boarded up. On the far side of a wall were the tops of trees, the garden of Delacroix's studio in the Place de Furstenberg.

Beyond a small door in the corner were two low, sliver-narrow rooms. I understood the apartment was shaped like a U when I looked out across to the dining room window. These little rooms had to be the attic of the concierge's cottage, under the strange white cube on the roof. The floors here were more skewed, almost torqued; I grew dizzy as I walked through. This is where my child would play and sleep, if I'd had him. Her. The child would be the same age now as I was when I moved to Paris, three and a half. The same story would have begun again.

The rent on all this magnificence was just two hundred dollars more than I'd paid on East 77th Street.

I walked the bumpy perimeter of the salon, I twirled in the middle and inhaled the new paint.

Two days later I was at a lawyer's office in the Rue Férou, behind the Place Saint-Sulpice. The lawyers were brothers, possibly twins, creepy and pale. They watched my every move.

I'd never signed an official property lease before in France. I'd only known sublets, arrangements with friends. I signed and signed, initialed each page.

I told them I had an enormous number of books.

"The building is very old, sixteenth, seventeenth century, and, of course, eighteenth, the floors are ancient," said one of the lawyers. "So please do not allow your men to stack the books in the middle of the salon."

"Will you be giving *soirées*?" asked the other.

"Yes," I said, "but only with very quiet people."

"Will you have any singularly heavy guests?" asked the first one.

"You must ask the more corpulent ones to remain on the periphery of the salon," said the second lawyer.

"I promise," I said. "Is the floor that fragile?"

The other lawyer drew himself up and pushed yet another piece of paper across the desk at me.

"Madame, we have to ask you to read this out loud before us, as your witnesses."

I read out loud in French: "I understand that I have been informed the apartment moves at night."

I looked up.

"Is it haunted?" I asked. "*Est-il hanté?*" in French, another of those vexing homonyms. "*Est-il hanté*" sounds like "*Est-il en T?*" Is it T-shaped?

"*Non, madame,*" said the first lawyer, "*il est en U.*" It's U-shaped.

"I know it's U-shaped." I gave a little laugh to show I knew they were doing the full Lacanian pun business on me. "Seriously, is it haunted?"

They shook their heads left to right in unison like windup toys.

"Now you must sign what you have just read," they said in unison.

I signed. I wrote the check, and then a second, a *chèque de caution*, and we shook hands.

I left, a little rattled. Well, of course it was too good to be true. That low a rent for that much eighteenth-century space in a building that went back to the Middle Ages and had a seventeenth-century staircase. The dream apartment. What did they mean, "It moves at night?"

Just to be safe, I stopped into the church of Saint-Germain-des-Prés. Maybe there was something I could arrange before I moved in. Some protective benediction.

In a little office, a woman with glasses and a bun was writing in a ledger. She looked up sharply with that "*Oui?*" that means You Are Disturbing Me.

"I'm renting an apartment near here," I said, "and before I move in, I'd like . . ."

She was perfectly still, watching me. "Yes?"

"Well, it's very old and a bit . . . I was wondering if perhaps a priest might come to, maybe, bless it before I moved in?"

Her nostrils flared.

"Madame," she said, "that is pure superstition."

She went back to scribbling in her ledger.

I backed out of the office and cut through the Place de Furstenberg to the Rue Jacob to look at my new apartment. I keyed in the code, climbed the stairs—how smooth they were, actually slippery, yes, very slippery. I turned the key in the high door and went into the perfect cube of the salon. In the blue hour before dusk, the distance between the walls felt regal, the distance between floor and ceiling felt as if my soul could expand to infinity. So what if the *parquet de Versailles* was warped and angled; that was probably what moved at night, as it settled onto its centuries. I'd put down a carpet. This was the romantic, historic, grand apartment that I deserved. That the job deserved, that the new me deserved. A fleeting thought of Upper Belgrave Street and the high ceilings under which Dad had lost his bearings and his luck. "Superstition," the woman in the church office had said. It's a shrink you need, not a priest, I told myself. Rise to this occasion. Spread out your arms. Soar.

~

My 1966 copy of French *Vogue* was faded, the glue on its spine had turned to brown dust, but I brought it to the office and opened it to Bob Richardson's Greek photographs. I'd make them the point of departure. Who'd want to shoot assignations in hotel rooms when they could show true love in all its drama? The fashion editors turned the pages, slightly irritated, and then paused on Donna Mitchell playing with beads on the beach, dancing in a taverna, lying on a rock as the naked man emerged from the sea at her feet. The photos had not aged. They had never seen them before. Mouths opened. Heads nodded.

"We're going to shoot with Bob Richardson?" asked one, cautiously.

"I think Bob Richardson is homeless these days, and insane," I said. "We're going to shoot with whoever we want to."

That wasn't strictly true. We were going to shoot with whoever we could get.

The Paris *Vogue* budgets had always been so tight that photographers shot what they wanted to make the portfolios that would get them the advertising contracts that would make them rich enough to indulge *Vogue* with a sitting they would do the way they wanted, to get more advertising.

We had to find a common purpose now. I'd figured out Today by playing with pixels on the Mac before bed. Today was the serial now, the millions of bright colors computers gave us beyond the primaries and the mauves, the Eurostar speeding under the Channel, the depth of—some—movies, the DNA code within our reach, the motion of music, the ambition of opera, the spell of dance, the sudden popularity of philosophy, the correspondences of the periodic table, the open borders of a united Europe, the sliver-flat Concorde and Jean Nouvel's fractured Fondation Cartier façade, the rise of women film directors, the opening of the former Soviet Union, and British designers and Cuban writers and African cinema, and all that would inform *Vogue* and *Vogue* would inform it in turn, the magazine would be at the center of Today, reflecting the glorious present in every page.

"So, no guest editor for the Christmas issue?" asked Paulino the features editor.

"Everyone here has the talent to make *Vogue* the rest of the year, why hand Christmas over to an outsider?"

The Christmas issue would be devoted to one hundred years of cinema, done in-house by the regular staff, with many guests. We'd be a movie studio and turn out our own films as glossy paper, the most important and essential films of the history of cinema, through our own lens of fashion and beauty. We'd begin with the Lumière brothers and Méliès, and go through to today. Everyone sparked to it. We'd remake masterpieces as fashion stories—*Metropolis, The Rules of the Game*, and *Terminator 2*.

"*Terminator 2*?" gulped Paulino.

"Masterpiece," I said, with my new finite crispness.

Chris Marker photographed the iconic gestures of cinema, Danièle Thompson wrote a screenplay set in the Trianon Palace, Alain Resnais compiled his list of essential films, Jeanne Moreau began her autobiography for the issue.

I ordered fresh sets of the same white cards I'd used to make my storyboards for *The White Hotel*, and began by drawing double-page spreads.

We reprinted Maxim Gorky's essay about cinema from 1896, written after he'd watched the Lumière brothers' *Arrival of a Train at La Ciotat*, the first film ever made. I particularly loved its beginning: "Yesterday, I entered the kingdom of shadows."

I asked Brigitte Lacombe to channel the Lumière brothers with her beautiful black-and-white. Isabelle Adjani posed for two photos, a long shot and a close-up. We did Méliès's *Journey to the Moon* as a comic strip narrated by novelist Michel Braudeau, the movie critic for *Le Monde*.

Delphine Treanton, who had spent a few years in a traveling circus, agreed to take on *Metropolis.* She shot in New York with Enrique Badulescu, a young Mexican Romanian photographer; Stella Tennant was our Maria, our Mechanical Woman, our heroine and villain. Thierry Mugler had once shown a metal robot costume that was perfect for the Mechanical Woman, the mainstay of the story, but US Customs impounded the Thierry Mugler robot.

Enrique sent his brother out to buy three colanders and two aluminum lampshades, and Stella became the Mechanical Woman with a colander on each breast and one on her head. Delphine and Enrique shot, without permission, in the vaulted passageways of Grand Central Terminal, and in front of the Unisphere from the 1964 World's Fair. Enrique's assistant left the exposed black-and-white film in the van in the heat; when the photos were developed, they'd been solarized. No matter. Solarization was perfect, a bit of Man Ray added to the homage to Fritz Lang.

Mario Testino remade Jean Renoir's *The Rules of the Game,* with cameo appearances by Dominique Sanda in a fur collar and Isabella Rossellini in a hat. They shot in a country château on a Sunday; I came to watch, wearing a skirt and moccasins. Mario shouted, "Don't ever let me see you in flat shoes again."

I decided to keep away from the sittings.

We did the Bond girls as a general idea of James Bond. Jenny Capitain dressed slick chicks in white fur and silver leather, Albert Watson photographed them from beneath a thick Plexiglas panel. Other photographers tried for years to reproduce the foreshortened contortions, without understanding how they'd been achieved.

The agent Eugenia Melian arrived with the wild young photographer David LaChapelle, once a protégé of Andy Warhol, who'd so far only shot portraits for *Interview* magazine. I paired him with the young editor Alexia Silvagni. He didn't like *Terminator 2,* he wanted remake *Blade Runner,* so *Blade Runner* it was. Models in reflective plastic and patent leather hauled around giant eyes, climbed ladders in five-inch platform soles, held up forceps dangling pale blue plastic innards over an eviscerated replicant, who on the previous page had carried on an urgent phone conversation into a Chanel pump.

There was no time to stop, or think, or be. Anjelica called me at the office.

"We never talk anymore. What's your life like?" she said.

I looked up at the model booker, the art director, two fashion editors, and the copy chief all standing in front of me. "It's like shooting a movie and going to the première at the same time, every single day. Would Bob like to photograph you for the movie issue?"

Bob shot Anjelica acting out emblematic movie scenes in the bright new house he'd built for her by the Venice boardwalk. She glowered and towered through Western, Thriller, Comedy, Sex, and for Martial Arts, she smote a watermelon with a samurai sword.

As a finale, I had a portfolio of male pinups: portraits by Brigitte Lacombe of Daniel Day-Lewis, Jeremy Irons, Gérard Depardieu, John Malkovich, Jean Reno, and John Travolta, who'd made his comeback in *Pulp Fiction.*

Delphine worked with Michael Thompson to turn the Dutch model Karen Mulder into Simone Signoret, Rita Hayworth, Ava Gardner, and Marlene Dietrich. The Dietrich photo became the cover, the image edged with white sprockets.

Each person involved surpassed what they thought they could do. The issue was fat, beautiful, astonishing.

I lugged the full dummy to New York to show Si Newhouse. On the walls of his office were the 1920 pencil drawings for the *Katzenjammer Kids.* If he really loved comics as much as I did, this was going to be the best fun in the world.

He went through the pages, slowly, and then more slowly.

"This is amazing," he said.

~

I returned to Paris in triumph, and then my belongings arrived. I was making sure the movers stacked the boxes of books along load-bearing walls when Jonathan reached me.

"I've made Gardner the new president of the company," he said.

"But she's my publisher! You can't take her away from me now. That's like taking away the engines on takeoff!"

"She'll do both," he said. "You two can do anything."

And we did. Some days it felt as if Gardner and I were standing back to back, fighting off enemies with broadswords. One photographer or another was suddenly exclusive to American *Vogue*; no matter. Schneider brought new portfolios to me, and we had a new photographer. The model we'd booked was suddenly on hold for American *Vogue*; no matter, let's look at the other head sheets, who have you seen this week? Carolyn Murphy, Phoebe O'Brien, Amber Valletta. Good. A dress we wanted was suddenly on hold for the cover of American *Vogue*; no matter, there were other dresses. The fashion editors would howl that that was the only dress, but Carine had Tom Ford in her pocket, Marie-Amélie had Nicolas Ghesquière in her bag, Isabelle Peyrut's boyfriend was Koji Tatsuno, and Alexia's mother, Irene Silvagni, worked for Yohji Yamamoto.

Every impediment spurred us into a new improvisation. I'd never had so many restrictions, I'd never had so many ideas. Each slice and bullet confirmed to the staff that I wasn't Anna Wintour's creature, and everyone got caught up in the excitement of thinking of another, better idea.

~

I distributed the advertiser Christmas booty to the staff as presents, stuck the faxes from my parents on the pin-board in the kitchen, and bought myself a pair of destroyed eighteenth-century armchairs from the antiques dealer downstairs. I stood my parents' old pub table on top of a library table from a Third Avenue junk store and climbed on top of both with a hammer and nails to hang my prints of Etruscan urns in rows up the wall.

I gave the first big party during couture. New taupe carpet softened the list of the floor. Isabelle Adjani peered in, fled, and called me from the street to say, "I can't go in, too many models."

Gianfranco Ferré arrived. The Christian Dior designer was a towering sphere in pinstripes, heavy enough to strain the fragile floor. Obeying the lawyers, I asked him to stay by the window to watch for whoever was coming. Everyone else milled and drank champagne and posed for each other's pictures. Betty Bacall was in town, and this time she didn't say a word about Ernest Hemingway. Carine and Mario Testino sat on the sofa in attractive poses. "You have so many things," said Carine. "You must see where I live, I have nothing."

All I could think about was sleep. I worked eighteen hours a day, fell into bed long after midnight, slept insensate in my vast bedroom, and rose in a fog at 6:45. I went to London to sleep nearly through entire weekends at the Pelham hotel, luxuriating in the British Sunday papers. The Eurostar made Paris and London into complementary suburbs of the essential idea of ParisLondon. Paris's gray to London's cream and brick, London's friendliness to Paris's rules; female, bitchy Paris to paternal, kindly London. The only place I felt at home was between the two, neither here nor there, not in Paris or London but in the liminal space of voyage. The terror I felt during the twenty minutes underwater in the center of the Channel was a small price to pay.

There was a week in early February that would be free of deadlines, so I gave myself a winter holiday in the Caribbean, at Cap Juluca on Anguilla, the only island I knew. As I was getting off the plane at Saint Martin, an old *Paris Match* photographer hove into view, over seventy but full of fun. He was joining a famous playboy on his yacht and asked me to come along for the week. I knew the yacht would be beautiful. There would be good white wine, fresh fish prepared by the chef, but also cocaine, weed, and more. There would be young women with smooth thighs and tiny bikinis, overall tans and little gold chains. There would be plenty of small talk and likely an invitation from one of the worldly seventy-year-olds to make even smaller talk in a cabin. It would be exhausting, competitive, and public; any sex would be just as exhausting, competitive, and public, because there is no privacy on a yacht, no matter how big it is. Sleep was more important to me than social sports, so I declined.

I gorged on sleep, woke at dawn from jet lag, ambled down the beach until the sun came up, and returned walking in the sea. I went through American novels like candy, and hired a horse from the local stables. The horse reared up when a snake jumped hissing from a bush, but I soothed it and rode on; eight months of learning to control people had also taught me to calm a horse. I rode him bareback into the sea until his hooves lost the sandy bottom, and hugged his neck as he swam with a thrashing paddle, his croup low in the water, vertical as a seahorse.

When I returned to Paris, I felt restored for the first time in nine months. I fell into my first normal sleep in the apartment on the Rue Jacob, and dreamed I was asleep in the lobby of Cap Juluca, where fine fingers gently brushed the hair from my forehead.

I opened my eyes in the dark. Where was the slight glow from the courtyard? The room was never pitch-black like this. I must still be in the dream. I tried to move, but the bedclothes held me tight. Someone was there, lying next to me on top of the covers. If I didn't move, would the feeling dissipate? I held my breath. I'd turn on the lamp. But the lamp was on the far side of whatever was on the bed. I marshaled my will, extended my left arm out of the sheets and across the dark to the lamp, groped for the switch, and turned it on. The click sounded like lightning.

I was alone. My heart clanged. You are imagining this, I told myself. You are the editor in chief of Paris *Vogue*. You can control a horse, turn down a boatload of ageing playboys, run a magazine. This is not happening, and it isn't going to scare you. I clicked off the light and willed myself back to sleep.

CHAPTER FIFTEEN

Yves Saint Laurent's friend Charlotte Aillaud gave a luncheon for me in her new apartment, a few houses down from me on the Rue Jacob. A thin edge of gray gold winter sunlight outlined the pale pink taffeta curtains. Hélène was there, and Pierre Bergé, who squeezed my arm with emphatic diffidence. Madison had broken up with the Greek illustrator, and appeared to be back in Pierre's world, though he was not at this lunch, where the real guest of honor was Yves Saint Laurent.

Yves had become bloated and vast. He was fifty-eight; his face hadn't aged, but his hair had turned to wood and rose from his forehead in hard ridges. He sat on my left, looking like a carved Austrian bottle stopper, gave out intermittent, uncertain giggles, and smiled sweetly. "Remember the time we danced all night at New Jimmy's?" I asked.

"All night," he said. "You wore an antique paisley shawl."

Lemon mousse arrived on eighteenth-century plates; Yves grabbed my hand with an urgent plea. "Do you remember my phone number?"

"Of course," I said, "how could I ever forget your phone number?"

"Would you tell me what it is? I have to call my maître d'hôtel to collect me and I can't remember the number."

I whispered his number in his ear, as if everyone else at the table hadn't known it by heart for forty years.

I longed to ask Charlotte Aillaud if she had ever felt a presence in her bedroom, but was wary of telling *le petit clan* that I had a ghost. Every night I woke in the dark to gentle fingers at my hairline. This is physics, I told myself, like a glass of water at an angle on a window ledge trembling as a truck goes by. Or physiology: the slope of the floor under the bed has made the balance of fluids in my body mimic the sensation of presence.

I got used to it. Whatever it was, it was company.

I told only my friend Martine Boutang and her husband, Pierre-André. Martine knew an exorcist in the Russian Orthodox Church, but she could never quite find his phone number.

I didn't tell anyone at the magazine. They'd think I was crazy, or, worse, superstitious, vulnerable. Franceline the jewelry editor would neigh and toss her mane of international hair; Jenny would be alarmed, but hide it; the young fashion editors would giggle; Schneider the art director would call in portfolios from people who photographed ghosts. The features editor Paulino and the writer Violaine Binet would know with Parisian certainty that I wasn't getting laid. And that was my shameful secret.

I could hide my private life and my secret alliances in New York where no one really cared, but in Paris my job meant being looked at. My most discreet liaison would be noticed, and presumably copied. The *Vogue* people mocked my unsteady gait in heels, but they copied my mother-of-pearl rings, the color of my lipstick, the shawls I'd copied from Gardner, who in turn had copied my silver compact, silver lighter, and my supposed Plains Indian great-grandfather.

At Gardner's mandatory 8:00 a.m. breakfasts under the gilded ceilings of hotel dining rooms, we sold the advertisers the concept of a new Paris *Vogue* full of *Je* and *Jeux*, and they sold us theirs: a fragrance with ingredients that went on forever, or a youngish designer who sat there reciting what new twists he'd bring to *la mode.* The designers were always men. The Ritz had excellent smoked salmon, the Crillon had magnificent pastries, the Plaza Athénée had cherry jam; I ate the smoked salmon, devoured the pastries, loaded my toast with cherry jam, paid attention as the advertiser listed "a point of ylang-ylang, California poppy, the dark mystery of datura, a hint of coffee for sparkle," and reacted with uncontained delight—"*Génial! Subtil!*"

Beneath the rare wood of aftershave I sometimes caught, creeping between the collar of a Charvet shirt and a pink neck, the lingering odor of bodies in the night. Well, you're doing it, I'd think, so people are still fucking, and you didn't shower, you dog. Some men dropped hints, but I had only the vaguest grasp of kinship patterns, the complex chains of exes, and didn't want to risk sleeping with an enemy.

At the Four Seasons Hotel on Via Gesù at the start of the Milan collections, heaps of gifts from the fashion houses awaited in my room, each one in the brand's signature shopping bag with the brand's signature tissue paper and an effusive handwritten note bearing the designer's inky signature. Shawls, scarves, throws, costume jewelry, the latest clutch, tote, pouch, and, from the less generous houses, small leather goods.

I tried to feel the Milan I'd known, the time of wonder when I subsisted on exotic fruit, skittered on pockmarked streets in high-heeled boots, lived for our nights in my narrow hotel room, when everything that wasn't Donald—all the fabrics, all the luxury, all the clothes—was merely lint. And now the lint was the star, silk, cashmere, leather. No trace of old passion could penetrate the barricade of Gucci panné velvet, Prada bags, Versace coats, the lists of shows and visiting cards and bouquets and white truffle lunches of this new life.

My new dark blue nylon trousers gave off loud scratching noises as I walked into the lobby of the Four Seasons; my T-shirt was the same color, and so was my cardigan, a penitent uniform of impeccable cut. Gilles Bensimon, the editorial director of *Elle*, whom I'd known a little too well when I was twenty, gave me a thumbs-up. "Jil Sander. Good. Now you look the part," he said. My hair was cut short to limit the time I had to spend in the hands of Philippe the hairdresser, though he'd insisted, for the sake of style, on a flap of hair falling over one eye. I looked like the dog in the ad for His Master's Voice.

I ran backstage after each show to hug the designer and cry, "You are a genius!" Gardner dragged me on a shopping blitz down Via Montenapoleone, along Via della Spiga and Via Sant'Andrea, through Corso Como—a shop, not a street—intent on rooting out whatever shirred sack of boiled twill—dress, coat, bag, or multipurpose tube—hadn't yet reached Paris. I insisted we go across the street from Caffè Cova to the knife shop Lorenzi, makers of scissors, razors, and fine dressing-table fittings since before Mussolini. In the old days, I'd peered in their window at displays of silver and horn, tortoiseshell and steel. Now I'd earned the right to enter.

I held a perfect object in my hand, two flat circles of rare wood ringed in brass that closed with a hook and opened like a clam to reveal a pair of mirrors facing each other, one magnifying, one plain. A beautiful object. "That thing costs more than a pair of shoes," said Gardner. I happily paid. This traveling mirror was going to be the hidden beauty in my life.

I wanted something to hold on to. My attention span had narrowed to the expedient focus of a darting predator. I looked at the mini versions of our pages in their plastic holders on the magnetic wall, half pages of front-of-book beauty and shopping and travel, six pages of one fashion story, eight pages of another, double pages of portraits, on and on across the wall to the next row, and the next. I had to think in heels, fast, and stick with first impressions. Brilliant. *Génial.* Ugly. *Moche.* Cool. *Cool.* Great. *Génial.* Lame. *Débile.* Fabulous. *Génial.* My vocabulary was as pointed and as tiny as my attention span. *Génial. Génial. Débile. Génial.*

Génial was expected. Everyone took *débile* personally.

I had ideas, but I couldn't bring a single one to life myself. The work didn't feel like real work. My medium was the talents of others. Carine and Delphine, Isabella and Alexia, Jenny and Brigitte Langevin; Schneider; Paulino and Violaine; the photographers, the writers, the art department. I thought of *Vogue* as us, I thought of me as us. We were a multiple entity in white wool coats and pointed shoes.

Now that I had the semblance of power, time had the shape and speed of a bullet train, but it was filled with waiting. The Paris collections made Milan look like a holiday; many more shows, many more obligations, fashion houses whose ads paid for our existence. The shows were short, the waits infinitely longer: an hour, two hours, sometimes more. Each magazine seated in clumps behind its front-row figureheads, rivals bunched next to one another surrounding runways covered in clear plastic. The fashion editors wished they were on sittings, I had photographs to look at, faxes to answer, proofs to read, but work was impossible in the front row; too many eyes and ears. So we discussed our watches or the new shoes on our feet, and then moved on to the shoes on the feet in the front row across the runway, and when we'd covered all visible shoes, we scanned the audience with actuarial zeal. What's she wearing? Is that real? Is that actress the new face of the house? How much are they paying her? And when there was nothing left to gossip about, everyone fell into a sullen private silence; witless from boredom, the occasional front-row editor would run a finger along her chin to check for hairs.

Then the runway would be cleared of its plastic cover, the music would begin, the lights would go on, the audience would don sunglasses against the glare, the models would walk the clothes at us, and my polarized lenses would reveal acute variations in shades of black. The culmination of six months' work for the designers, each show was a short paroxysm that lasted at most twelve minutes. Lights, music, girls, no plot.

Nylon. Satin. Tulle. Nylon. Bouclé. Mesh. Models with new breasts so flattened inside sheer nylon tops that they looked like sunny-side-up eggs.

It was a minimal moment: Helmut Lang showed pale clothes that slipped on a diagonal over the hip. An adventurous moment: Rei Kawakubo showed clothes in improbable volumes, carbuncles and growths. An excessive moment: John Galliano's models in tight 1950s day clothes vamped around a roadster in a concrete garage, the final dress an explosion of chicken yellow tulle. A classic moment: the advertisers showed safe suits for lady ministers to wear when giving speeches and attending the weddings of their children. Karl varied the Chanel tune like Bach turning out a new hymn each Sunday.

At Yves Saint Laurent, the editors who were prone to crying cried, though his shoulder pads were becoming a problem.

After each show, I ran backstage to repeat what I'd said in Milan, but in French, and repeat it again in English on camera for Tim Blanks from Fashion TV. *Génial, magnifique, historique.* Brilliant, magnificent, game-changing.

The shows began before I was fully awake and went on, without a break for food, late into the night, in abandoned factories on distant wastelands where young designers without backers presented ball gowns. The more the surroundings suggested overdose, depredation, slime and poverty—the four cardinal points of edgy—the happier the young editors were. The colder it was, the later it was, the hungrier I was. Sometimes I missed a fashion show to nap in the car. Sometimes, starved for plot and an ice cream cone, I went to a movie.

Toni Morrison was teaching at the Collège de France and needed shoes. I took her to Christian Louboutin's tiny shop, where she sat enthroned on the small sofa, her dreadlocks like a crown of gray snakes, every pair of flats in the store set out in tribute at her feet. A man watched her through the window, and came in.

"You have the Nobel Prize and you're buying shoes?" he asked.

"Every woman needs good shoes," she said.

I accumulated my own glut from Christian Louboutin, shoes with red soles but comfortable enough to wear when a perfume launch involved an obstacle course, most often in a hangar, through theater-set trees in fairy-dust landscapes, with real plants, fake vanilla pods, mountains of spices, all designed to convey *le headspace* and the ultimate meaning of the new fragrance, which we would then meet as a bottle unveiled at a lunch where the food, all too often, consisted of the same ingredients as the perfume.

In my apartment's sloping dressing rooms were racks of clothes ordered from advertisers, and garments that I'd bought in a hurry before lunch with an angry designer who'd not been featured enough in Paris *Vogue,* so that they could admire their product on the editor in chief of Paris *Vogue,* and keep on advertising.

Everything was PR except the brainstorming meetings around my desk, which were like a game of Essences in the back of Ricki's Opel on the way to Connemara. We tackled the essentials of a wardrobe as analogies. The inevitable black sweater headed the list; its essence was clearly coffee, so we'd show it with an espresso pot. A T-shirt was vitamin C; to avoid the obvious orange, we'd show it with a green pepper.

High heels, everyone agreed, were antidepressants.

"What color is Prozac?" I asked.

"Green and white," came the answer from all present.

Violaine wanted the Wonderbra; obviously, its essence was champagne. Franceline insisted on the Black Jacket. What was as protective, reliable, permanent, timeless? Easy answer. A man. How did we show a basic, essential man?

"We shoot a nice torso," said Schneider.

"Not a hairy one," said Alexia. God forbid. Hairy would be a fur coat.

David LaChapelle was shooting an ad campaign on Capri; we sent an editor, a model and clothes to join him. The model took against him and departed, but David called to say everything would be fine. "I have these life-sized dolls with me that I didn't use for the campaign."

I asked him to photograph the doll in the Givenchy dress that we needed in the magazine. But while David was photographing the doll in the Givenchy dress, the Capri police arrested him and put him in prison for public lewdness.

"But why?" I asked Schneider the art director.

"Well, the doll was one of those blow-up sex dolls," he said.

"How could the police tell it was a sex doll? It was wearing a Givenchy dress."

"The mouth," said Schneider.

After the collections, Gardner wanted to celebrate with another bout of shopping at Jil Sander and Prada, but I was snow-blind from clothes. All I wanted was an Empire mahogany bed from the antiques shop below my apartment. The shop owner, a mournful young man with a Russian name, said it would need a special mattress because of its peculiar proportions.

Allegra came for a few days, my first houseguest. She'd left publishing to work in film production at Pathé in London, where her boss was a young Frenchman with a Scottish name, Alexis Lloyd.

"Alexis wants to meet you, all his friends told him you're a monster," she said. "I think you fired them."

"I didn't fire that many people," I said, defensive.

In the guest room, I pointed at the tall mahogany bed, fresh from the upholsterer, its cover and bolsters printed with toile de Jouy pyramids and sphinxes in a pattern called Retour d'Égypte that dated from the time of Napoleon's first sighting of the Pyramids.

"Isn't it beautiful?" I asked.

"It's very small," said Allegra. I hadn't realized it was a child's bed. So that was why I'd bought it.

Allegra's boss, Alexis, came to meet me; he had a strong face on a compact body and was one of those exceptional Frenchmen who'd graduated from both the École Normale Supérieure and the ENA, where future leaders of France are formed. He sat in one of the destroyed bergères, I sat on the sofa, Allegra watched as we topped each other's stories until he got over the fact I'd fired his friends. We agreed it was no fun being a boss. Allegra, my younger semi-sister, had brought me a younger semi-brother.

I'd known Charlotte Rampling from a distance, liked her unpredictability and her skepticism. She'd been on view among the French for years, and as we became friends, she had good advice about shutting out Parisian judgments. We'd go to movies, have Sunday lunch at the Flore, eat pho at the local Vietnamese place; she came with me to bicycle at Versailles.

One winter night under the high ceiling at Rue Jacob, we sat eating lychee nuts with the Irish journalist Godfrey Deeny, hurling their pits into the blazing fire until the fireplace shot the lychee nuts back at us as burning pellets, and we chased them with wet towels. The next day Charlotte said, "I'm sending you something to protect you." I imagined some talisman, a faceted crystal, the kind of thing women exchange, but it was a metal fire screen. At last, I had a practical friend.

I told her that something touched my head at night while I was asleep. "Are you going to move?" she asked. No, I said, the apartment was too beautiful.

It was cold in Paris that June. I decided to bolt to Ireland for the weekend; the only hotel available was an eccentric place in Cork known for its cooking classes. Charlotte came with me; we flirted with a visiting chef, ate salmon and brown bread, walked through blue gray air to a seaside village where a striped lighthouse looked close enough to touch.

When I returned home early on Sunday evening, the lights wouldn't go on. I'd forgotten to pay the electric bill. It was still cold, so I pulled the duvet from the closet, opened it out on the bed, and went out to dinner with Charlotte and Rosita and Tai Missoni. I told Tai and Rosita about the ghost. They were old friends. They wouldn't think I was crazy.

Rosita said, "You're going back to a haunted apartment where there is no electricity? You're going to go to bed in the dark, holding a candle? Come sleep at our place."

I took Tai and Rosita back to the Rue Jacob so I could pack my costume for a TV interview in the morning to promote Paris *Vogue*'s first ever July issue, which we'd done as a comic book, entirely in drawings, cartoons, and manga. By the glow of the streetlights, I installed Tai and Rosita in the living room, poured them some tequila, lit candles in Nana's candelabra, and fired up some votives in round glass holders.

"Let's have a look at this ghost!" said Rosita, with a laugh. She'd raised three children and nothing fazed her.

"There's never anything to see, but come look at the bedroom," I said.

I took a glass votive in each hand and led her down the corridor where the glass on the framed photos reflected the glow of the votives. The door to my bedroom was ajar, as I'd left it.

"Well, where's your ghost, then?" asked Rosita. I held up the votives; the curtains were open, the room had a pinkish glow from the courtyard, the red marble mantelpiece was flecked with reflections from the flames. I turned and held the votives toward the bed.

On the duvet was a long indentation, the mark of a body, as if someone had been lying there. Was still lying there.

"Ah!" said Rosita.

The indentation was on the side where I always felt the weight, so fresh that as we watched, the feathers gently rose back into the fabric.

The next day, I paid the electric bill; when I came home the lights were back on. I ran to the bedroom, threw down my bag, pushed the bed against the boarded-up fireplace on the opposite wall, so that the mantelpiece now looked like a red marble headboard, but if I slept on this side of the room, I thought whatever it was might leave me alone.

It didn't.

At the next party, I showed some guests where I'd moved the bed.

"It's like you're sleeping in the Père Lachaise, very Jim Morrison," said a writer, "very nihilistic."

"So edgy," said a fashion editor.

My mother came to stay in time for the couture.

"The bed's a little short," she said on her first night in the guest room.

"I know," I said, "but isn't it pretty?"

I didn't tell her about my ghost. She'd say it was my imagination running away with me again.

The *Vogue* driver who carted clothes about for the fashion room volunteered to show her Paris.

"She knows Paris, but it would be great for her to have a driver," I said.

My new assistant Laurence was shaking her head behind the driver, no, no.

"It's a trap," said Laurence when he'd left. "*Abus de biens sociaux.*" Misuse of corporate assets. "They'll get you for that."

"But he offered," I said.

"Exactly," she said.

I hired a car and driver and made sure Joyce could shop wherever she wanted—Jil Sander, Missoni—without thinking about the bills. It was the first time I'd been able to buy her new clothes, not just scarves. When she came to the office, Franceline said, "Now, there's an elegant woman!" The long gold chain around her neck, the gold watch on a black band on her wrist, and her engagement ring were the only jewels that had survived Dad's shipwreck, but they were, in the words of *Vogue*, impeccable.

Joyce busied herself with improving the Rue Jacob; she collected fabric samples for the destroyed bergères, commissioned new lampshades for Nana's sphinx lamps, found a carpenter to build bookcases in the study, took pictures to the framers and rearranged the furniture with the cleaning lady. She was at home in the tall rooms, more than I was.

I took her to parties for perfumes and dinners for choreographers and artists. I discovered that if my luminous mother entered a room before me, clad in a blue gray Missoni column, her beauty, her smile, her dignity created such delight that when I arrived a few steps behind her, I was in the glow of the universal approval that she summoned. Beauty does make a difference. And grace.

Her French came back and improved. She was among French people, not in the backseat of a car in Los Angeles trying to tell me that my father had become a bear.

Designers sat next to her at dinners at the Ritz and were enchanted. She talked about statues with Gardner's antiques dealer husband, and she went out to dinner more than once with Docteur Jean Dax, who'd been our physician when we all lived in Paris and was now a widower. She came home from those dinners excited, happy, and confident, humming with unsaid new possibilities, and we'd sit and talk on the red sofa, smoking cigarettes as she had one last drink.

If only she could have the life she deserved, I thought, in Paris, here, being beautiful and appreciated, without worrying about money. I imagined that Dad would soon die, carried off by his rages and his unsteady moods, and then Joyce would move to Paris and live with me, but only briefly, because she would marry the handsome and compassionate Dr. Dax. He'd find the right thing for the neuralgia in her cheekbones and she wouldn't be in pain anymore, she wouldn't have to take the pills that removed her for days on end. It was a cruel fantasy. I'd have to lose my father for it to happen, but he was seventy-eight, deaf and intractable, mad; she was only just seventy and could tame a room with her smile.

Sometimes she stood for a long time at the open refrigerator door. It was a hot summer.

Vogue set David LaChapelle on the couture. He met us in the lobby of the Hôtel Scribe before the Christian Lacroix show, clad in a cowboy hat, a leather waistcoat over his bare chest, blue nylon surf pants unzipped up the sides, flip-flops on his feet. Joyce gave him the look she reserved for uncouth clients and took her seat next to me at the show. I apologized for the wait.

The clothes were all crinolines and décolleté, lace and ribbons, which fed David's idea to shoot the couture as an epic Marx Brothers orgy about French history. For his photos, a model was hoisted atop a giant gold crown in the garden of Vaux-Le-Vicomte, other models draped over miniature châteaux at an amusement park called Mini-France.

To prolong the ecstatic couture lunacy, we shot at the Musée Grévin waxworks in the middle of the night. It was fiercely hot when Joyce and I arrived at the museum at midnight. A model loomed over a wax Mozart as he played a real harpsichord. The crew moved on to Marie Antoinette's fainting fit during the Revolution and added our chaos to the drama. Cream cakes and vermeil forks were strewn among upended chairs under our hot spotlights, a wax Louis XVI stood back as a guard pointed a bayonet at our model Chrystèle in a hooded Grim Reaper dress, the swooning wax Marie Antoinette was flanked by models in ball gowns with makeup running down their faces in the heat. I checked the hand on the wax dauphin; it gave a little under my touch. I asked the crew about fans. There were none. There never were. Paris refused to acknowledge summer.

Charlotte's husband, Jean-Michel Jarre, was giving a July 14 concert on the Champ-de-Mars, a storm of electronic music. She handed me two tickets in the VIP section, but said there were no actual seats, so we'd need to bring our own. She'd be far away, backstage. Joyce bought a pair of folding aluminum chairs; we arrived as early as eager picnickers, set them up at the front of the enclosure facing the stage, and sat there eating sandwiches from Mulot, feeling a little American, a little suburban, as the enclosure filled up. The stage was high up in front of the Eiffel Tower, we'd be able to see, and, given the size of Jean-Michel Jarre's music, we'd hear. Joyce and I were the only seated spectators in the growing mass of people.

A woman in blue asked if she could park her bag under my chair. I nodded *bien sûr,* she pushed it under the chair and took up a position hard by me to guard her belongings. More people arrived. The place was crowded now.

As the first waves of electronic music swept the open space between us and the Eiffel Tower, a dark man in a brown jacket asked if he could put his bag under Joyce's chair. She smiled, *bien sûr.* It was a heavy duffel bag that seemed very full, and he set it under her chair with such care that I knew it must be precious to him; everything he owned in the world was probably inside that bag. No doubt he'd hover by his bag, flank Joyce on the right, matching the vigilant woman on my left. I readied myself for his company.

I looked away from the giant silver robots dancing around the stage to see that the man in the brown jacket was gone. Who would move to the back of the audience if he'd made it to the front? Wouldn't he stay by his precious bag?

"I'm just going to check on something," I said to Joyce, and wedged my way through the crowd looking for him. He was nowhere. At the entrance to the enclosure I found a man in uniform, and shouted over the music about the stranger who'd vanished, leaving his bag under my mother's chair.

He snapped to attention. "Show me, now. *Vite.*"

"What are you going to do?"

"We will take it away and test it. If there is nothing suspicious, we will return it before the end of the concert."

"Do you have time to do that?"

"It's a long concert," he sighed. A woman in uniform joined him.

Joyce was engrossed in the music. The uniformed pair knelt by her chair, slowly ran their arms in tandem under the duffel bag, rose without jostling it, and retreated slowly through the crowd.

The woman in blue on my left gave me a sharp look, and checked her own bag.

"Darling, what's going on?" asked Joyce.

"Can't hear," I said. "Nothing."

The man in the brown jacket would approach from the left, he'd approach from the right, he'd say, "Where is my bag?" Would I say, "I thought you were a terrorist"? I'd be American and offer him money to replace his belongings; I'd be French and scold him for trusting strangers.

The electronic music grew louder, French Air Force fighter jets thundered overhead, and the concert ended with sonic booms joined by the sound of July 14 fireworks magnified by a thousand speakers to shake the Champs-de-Mars.

This is when the bomb would have gone off, I thought, if it was a bomb.

The man in the brown jacket did not return.

Let's wait for the crowd to disperse, I told Joyce at the end. Let's wait for the police to return with this poor man's bag, I thought. No one came.

Back at home, I told her what had happened.

"Was it a bomb?" she asked.

"We'll only know if they try again, if a bomb goes off in the next few days."

I took her to the airport and watched her rise away from me on the escalator. She'd loved it all and accepted it all as part of the marvelous life she was so proud of me for having, she'd loaned me her beauty and her grace and made everyone nicer, and she'd been a most agreeable companion. I had betrayed my father and imagined a new life for her in the beautiful city. We had not talked about Jules; we had not talked about time or life or love or meaning or how much I wanted a man. We had floated and skimmed and appreciated. Had she kept me at a distance, or had I kept her away? I didn't want her to leave.

A week later, at rush hour, a bomb went off at the Saint-Michel metro station, killing eight people and injuring 117. A small gas canister packed with nails had been hidden under a seat.

CHAPTER SIXTEEN

Pierre Bergé invited me to dinner at his apartment on the Rue Bonaparte for our formal reconciliation. As I unfolded my napkin, a chain fell out, the fake gold chain I'd given him for luck eight years before, when he was buying back the Saint Laurent name.

"Pierre," I said, "you kept it!"

He took my hand in his and smiled.

"You didn't think I'd remember, did you?"

What he had forgotten was that the bracelet was to return to me transmuted into real gold, to prove he was Midas. I couldn't remind him; he was no longer Pierre, he was Pierre Bergé, an advertiser. I was no longer part of his clan, or anyone's.

I'd been at *Vogue* a year, but the Paris I knew had melted out of my grasp. I had no time to see my old friends Martine the book editor and her husband, Pierre-André, or Inès, Nicole, Hélène.

I had no connection to the exquisite life where Madison served vanilla ice cream on folded linen napkins. I gulped down café crèmes—they still wouldn't make cappuccinos in Paris—in whatever café was near a fashion show, I ate with business contacts at three-star restaurants, I wore the same expression of noncommittal enthusiasm that I'd so despised on poor Francine Crescent of the canary yellow suits.

I had to draw myself in around what I loved. I meditated when I remembered to, and on weekends I went back to the Trianon Palace hotel, alone, to bicycle between the trees, past thatched farmhouses, through farmland. I craved nature, reality, firm ground. Away from the foul diesel swamp of Paris, I was a child without a shell. I was what I saw, and what I saw was beautiful. Mud. The sky on water. A leaf that no one designed, a leaf I didn't have to praise.

The office closed in August, and it was time to visit my father. At LAX, Joyce looked immaculate, a Missoni shawl over one shoulder, cigarette in hand. Jules looked askew, nearing a rage. He grabbed my suitcase.

"It's got wheels," I said. "You can just pull it." The suitcase resisted him; they got into a tussle, and the suitcase won.

"He can't hear anything," said Joyce.

He pushed me away. "I fucking know what I'm doing," he said, and dragged the case on its side all the way to the car.

"He really can't hear," whispered Joyce. "He's had a *coup de vieux*."

"He hears me on the phone," I said.

"He has a thing on the phone that makes it louder."

I slept in their little study for three nights. Dad kept thanking me for taking such good care of Joyce, I kept shouting back that he should have been there too. "Try writing it down," said Joyce, and handed me one of his legal pads and a felt-tip. I printed out words, mainly "YES, YES, YES," and "VOGUE'S FINE."

Anjelica was away; I went to a spa in Tucson to have myself checked like a machine, and then for a few days to Corsica, alone. When I went home, Paris was on edge, not the same thing as edgy. A bomb concealed in a trash can exploded at the Arc de Triomphe at the end of August, wounding sixteen people.

Jules called; Joyce was having tests. She wasn't well.

In September, a nail bomb in a pressure cooker exploded at an outdoor market. Another bomb was dismantled the next day; two days later, a car bomb went off near a Jewish school.

The August issue had sold well; the September issue was a triumph. In my office there were flowers from contented advertisers, faxes of congratulations from Si Newhouse, and, on my wall, mini-printouts of the twenty-page sitting Mario Testino and Carine had done in Seville.

Jules called with Joyce's results. She had lung cancer. But, he said, he liked her doctor. I had ten minutes to take in that my mother was probably going to die before I went to the meeting with Jonathan Newhouse and Gardner. I sat down, shaking.

"Times are hard," he said. "We have to shut down *Glamour, Maison & Jardin, Automobiles Classiques,* and *Vogue Hommes.* This is the only way for *Vogue* to survive." He didn't look as grim as his news.

Gardner, as president of French Condé Nast, would have to oversee the dismantling of the company.

"I quit," Gardner said.

"My mother has cancer," I blurted out.

Gardner didn't quit. The impending closures were secret, for now; there were rules to be followed, union procedures, labor negotiations.

Joyce began chemotherapy; she had rules to follow, antidepressants to take, procedures to endure.

For the next nine months, I rocketed between Paris and Los Angeles as if crossing the street. I didn't want Joyce to know I was worried about her, and pretended I was just dropping by Montana Avenue on my way home from the Met Ball in New York, on my way to the *Vanity Fair* Oscar party in L.A., and if there was no public event, I'd make one up. I'd arrive high on Sudafed and thick with jet lag, drop my suitcase at Anjelica and Bob's house in Venice, bring Mom shawls and scarves, the latest Paris *Vogue* or a first-bound copy of the next one, sit on her bed, take her to chemo, fill the refrigerator with specific dark leafy greens, buy a juicer, show Dad how to use it, slip him a check, pick up her medications, gawp at the price—how could anyone in America afford to be sick?—take them to their favorite booth in the Polo Lounge, tip the headwaiter, bring Joyce back to the Polo Lounge for tea with Bacall, buy more carrots, and two days later I'd be on Air France again, hurrying the plane back to deadlines, strategic discussions, the Christmas issue.

This year, the Christmas issue would celebrate seventy-five years of *Vogue.* The writer Sonia Rachline went into the archives with the intern Olivier Lalanne, a handsome boy with thick eyebrows, whom Paulino and Violaine affectionately called Mowgli, after the hero of *The Jungle Book.* Photocopies of pages going back to 1920 covered the conference room table, bound issues lay open on my office floor. Susan Train interviewed every surviving member of the original staff to produce the first history of Paris *Vogue.* In the old issues, I kept returning to a 1932 portrait by Hoyningen-Huene, a woman—a lady—in three-quarter profile, wearing a fur-edged jacket, white gloves, and a hat with a delicate egret feather; she was the embodiment of class, the kind of grace that could tame a room. Madame Jean Bonnardel. No one had ever heard of her; she'd been in *Vogue* a few times in 1932, had created no scandal, written no book, starred in no play. She had just been very beautiful for a while, and then she was gone. I ran her picture across two pages to open the issue; Madame Jean Bonnardel was my love letter to Joyce.

Our slug brown building on the Rue de Vaugirard was like a freighter full of dark news. Gardner and I sat in secret meetings with the lawyers over lists of employees to calculate who might accept the offer to leave, who had to stay at any cost, and who might come to *Vogue* from a dead magazine. It felt like I was picking over bodies on a battlefield, taking the best armor, grabbing rings.

Jonathan was right, the times were bad. The government wanted to raise the retirement age, decrease benefits, reform pensions. In October, the strikes began, short strikes at first, then longer ones. There were demonstrations almost every day. The trains barely ran, the metro and the buses went on strike. The streets were clogged with idling cars. Those who had motorbikes carried their helmets through the office as badges of self-sufficiency. Everyone else walked, pale and nauseous from the pall of exhaust. At the end of November, gas, electricity, and the post office went on strike. Two million workers filled the streets of Paris. I walked home past cars stuck at dead stops in the freezing rain, dressed for luxury during social unrest in a cashmere-lined raincoat in a taupe color that Hermès called *marron glacé,* watching my *marron glacé* suede moccasins bull's-eye one puddle after another. I lay on the couch dizzy from diesel fumes and called

Jules in Los Angeles to see how my mother was doing. Not well. "Carry on regardless," he said.

I carried on regardless. The *plan social* was *mis en place*, the bad news confirmed, the blade fell on four magazines: *Maison & Jardin, Automobiles Classiques, Vogue Hommes,* and *Glamour.* The next morning the business pages carried headlines about the mass closures, and I went on a talk show to promote the seventy-fifth-anniversary issue of Paris *Vogue*, primed to ward off questions about the high-handed ways of Condé Nast. No one at the talk show had read the headlines, so I was free to deliver gay chatter about the perennial glamour of *Vogue*, and explain that the seventy-fifth-anniversary issue was as precious as a Cartier cigarette box, and would be as prized.

The Christmas stock of chocolate-covered cherries in brandy arrived at the pâtisserie; I bought an enormous box to cheer Jules, as if they would make a difference. In Los Angeles I draped new Missoni scarves on my mother's head, and cried on Anjelica's shoulder in the house in Venice. Bob sat in the living room, tequila in one hand, a cigar in the other, alive with ideas about his commission for the new cathedral downtown, Our Lady of the Angels. He would set the bronze doors with bas-reliefs of animals and symbols that were worshipped before Christ. Over the doors, he would set a golden tympanum with the Virgin standing on a crescent moon, like our Lady of Guadalupe, but not your regular Virgin Mary wafting in veils. "She's young, she's a virgin, she's a girl, she's mixed blood. She's like everyone. Her arms are bare. And when the sun shines through the hole in the tympanum above her, that will be her halo. "

~

At the beginning of 1996, *Vogue* was alone, five stories above the echoing brown marble lobby on the Rue de Vaugirard. And then it was January couture, summer clothes for the winners of the world.

"We have to do something about our PR," Gardner said. "The advertisers are asking if *Vogue* is closing. We have to show them we're just fine."

A couture mink coat with an immense collar from Yves Saint Laurent was beyond my clothing allowance, even in the winter sale, but I had to make a big gesture. I bought it on the layaway plan, over five months. Gardner did the same with a circular mink cape from Dior. I found her cape a little bumpy, she found my collar overstated, but we sailed into the couture shows glossy in our new furs, and silenced our enemies.

Backstage after the Chanel show, Karl touched my collar with a quick, but loud, "So, you have your grandmother's fur now?"

Fashion was a frantic carnival to counter the gloom. John Galliano's first couture show for Givenchy was held in a football stadium. There were toreador hats, golden epaulets, floor-length white coats, bias-cut burgundy gowns, kimonos, his tropes; Galliano took his bow in a beaded Plains Indian vest. At a Louis Vuitton party, supermodels wove between steamer trunks the size of houses, dodging live camels, panthers, tigers, and dancing bananas. Naomi Campbell strode about on roaring bare thighs. I danced such a vigorous boogie-woogie salsa with someone's husband that I was winded. "You're putting too much into it," said the husband.

Three thousand miles away, my mother was dying.

Joyce didn't feel condemned; she sounded positive, almost joyful on the phone. For their fifty-first anniversary, Jules took her to dinner at the Bel-Air hotel. The new owners of the Beverly Hills Hotel didn't want old-timers in the Polo Lounge. Joyce didn't seem to mind; the antidepressants were working.

Vogue sold well. The covers were bright, the pages sparkled with invention.

The summer was hotter than the year before, and worse in the ugly new building than it had been in the mansion. Grumpy shirtsleeves had been swept away in the *plan social*; his resourceful replacement produced floor fans and set them behind plastic trash cans filled with ice to make third-world air conditioners. Movie stars provided some relief. Sam Irons was an intern; his father came up from Tuscany on his Harley to see him. Forearms bulging like Bluto, Jeremy Irons arrived bearing trays full of coffee éclairs. Charlotte took her shoes off and distributed ice cream cones from office to office, barefoot.

And then I got the call that my mother had to go into the hospital.

The flight attendants on the Air France flight to LAX knew me well by now. I opened my precious wooden travel mirror before we landed, and saw thick sad eyelids, eyes like slits, cheeks fat from the pizza and the éclairs I'd stuffed down to keep the panic away. Smile. Try harder. Smile.

Joyce was in bed. Jules dried the dishes. The thin doors on the kitchen cupboards were warped open over the gold rims on Nana's good china that had survived the earthquake. The blinds ran vertical with clacking chains, and didn't meet. It was hot, but Jules wore one of his long-sleeved polo shirts and looked like he was on a break from a meeting with distributors. I was sweating in my sleeveless blouse. We whispered about what the move to the hospital meant. Tonight he could hear clearly.

"Is this it?" I asked.

He started to answer, but then mimed turning a dial and said, "Let's change the channel."

I could do that. "It's Anjelica's birthday tomorrow."

"We should send flowers," he said.

"I already have, from all three of us. Lilies."

"What's Bob doing? I like Bob."

"He's making the doors for the cathedral of Our Lady of the Angels. And the Virgin Mary to go on top of the doors."

"That's one hell of a big job he's got there," he said.

I lay on the bed next to my mother. Her back hurt. The cancer had gone to her brain, her liver, her spine. She was on the far edge of life. She opened her eyes and smiled at me. I stroked her shoulder. She was going to talk to me now, talk to me about the important things.

"You have beautiful arms," she said, "but you have such lousy luck with men."

Bob and Anjelica's house filled with birthday flowers the day Joyce moved into a blue room at Saint John's in Santa Monica. I was missing the couture shows, but FedEx delivered page proofs from Paris. I bought a Frappuccino at Starbucks, left it on the roof of my rental car while I looked for the key; brown streaks poured down my windshield at the first red light.

I set up at the foot of my mother's bed to work. She lay resigned, bald, very quiet. Morphine dripped into her right arm.

"What are you doing?" she asked. I brought over the proofs to show her. Watches with gold faces, with steel faces, rare complication faces with quarter moons, rose-gold faces, mother-of-pearl faces. The watches had metal bands, gold bands, lizard bands. It was not a year for crocodile.

"Watches, those bloody watches, why is it always watches?" she asked.

"It's our Watch Special, we have to do it twice a year. Look, do you see that all the hands are set at ten past ten, on every watch? It's so that the faces on the watches will look like they're smiling."

"All I want is ten more years," she said. "Why can't I have ten more years?"

She was hairless. She was gentle. She was bemused. We did not talk about anything except time, in the form of watches.

The birthday party was still going on at Anjelica and Bob's when I returned.

Joyce was moved to a bigger room. I ate a banana in the doorway. Jules was anxious, nearing a rage. The doctor gave me a prescription for Xanax. "For you," she said.

"It won't make me sleepy?" I asked.

"Not in the state you're in," she said.

Jules panicked that my mother's jewelry would be stolen from the apartment and sent me back to Montana Avenue. "Take it, keep her gold chain, her engagement ring, her gold watch. Just don't wear them to the hospital." They were waiting for me, perfectly safe in the drawer. I almost fainted and called Anjelica to come collect me. She arrived, her car full of her birthday flowers for Mom's hospital room.

I called Gardner from a restaurant. She screamed, "What's the delay?"

"I'll be back when I'm done," I said, as if waiting for Joyce to die was a job.

I sat by the window and went through more Paris *Vogue* proofs. Unruly pages flapped on the table, the chair, the floor.

"I'm so messy, I'm sorry," I told her. "You're so neat."

"I'm not neat," she said. "I'm leaving a big mess."

"No, not at all," I said. What mess?

"Don't let the cats out," she said later that afternoon.

"You don't have cats," I said. She smiled.

It was July 13, a Saturday. The doctor had said it would probably be today. My father rose from his chair when I came in, and left the room. I sat down and took her cool hand. An hour passed, less, more.

There was no real sound. No rattle. Her eyes opened wide in wonder, as if she recognized something she'd been waiting for, tears sprang from the inner corners of her eyes, and she was gone.

I took a tissue and touched it to each of her eyes to soak up the tears, and I folded it into a small square. I had to keep these clean, intact. I opened my wooden traveling mirror, placed the tissue damp with her tears inside it, and snapped the clasp closed.

My father came in, looked at the bed. I left him alone with her.

When I returned, we held each other.

"We have to bury her in France," he said, "in Cannes with Don and Esta, that's where she has to go."

He wanted a rabbi. "A sophisticated rabbi, not one of those Beverly Hills clowns."

Sophisticated: A rabbi who could give her a Jewish send-off and forgive the fact that her body was to be cremated, against Jewish law, so that her ashes could fit into an overnight bag to go to the South of France to join her mother and her brother in *allée* 1, *carré* 6, *tombe* 27, at Abadie II.

The man from the mortuary had just the rabbi, a British cabalist from Bristol. His office was under the intersection of two freeways. Clad in pale tweed, almost redheaded, he walked with sticks.

Jules leaned on the desk and announced that he loved England so much that he'd become British. "My daughter who lives in Paris is still American."

"Could you tell me a little about your wife?" asked the rabbi.

"She was the most beautiful woman in Hollywood when I met her, and she is even more beautiful today," he began, but suddenly John Huston was part of the description of my mother, and then his voice lowered to a whisper so that the rabbi had to lean forward across the desk to hear something about Kirk Douglas, and the captain of the *Coral Sea*, and a whole jumble of names and places, and the rabbi leaned and listened but as the stream of words continued unabated he sat back in his chair, folded his arms over his paunch, and, instead of looking at Dad, he looked at me.

Dad kept talking, and then he began to cry. He blew his nose, swam upward, fists simian on the table, and asked for the toilet. The rabbi rose on his two sticks, showed him to the men's room, came back, and said, "You want to take care of your father because you feel sorry for him, and you worry that he is crazy."

"He's manic-depressive to begin with, and now the grief . . . and as for money . . ."

"He's crazy. If you bring him to you, he'll make you as crazy as he is. Take care of him at a distance. Protect yourself. Don't fall into his hell to rescue him."

"I won't," I lied.

On the way back to Montana Avenue, Jules said Joyce's obituary had to run in the London papers. London was home, that was where they'd been important, at the hub of things, that was where they'd been glamorous, that was where she'd be remembered.

I called London, faxed the information to the *Times*, and rounded up Siân Phillips and Betty Bacall to write about Joyce for the *Independent*.

I hired a car and driver to take us to the cremation, and sent him to pick up Jules first. I was still outside waiting for the car when Bob and Anjelica came out of their house.

"Don't you want to come with us?"

"No, I'm waiting for Dad."

"But you're going to be late," said Anjelica.

The car company said the driver was waiting outside Carroll & Company in Beverly Hills while Mr. Buck did some shopping. "Have him get my father to the Little Chapel of the Dawn immediately," I screamed, scrambled for the rental car, and drew up at my mother's cremation under a crusty mantle of spilled Frappuccino.

The rabbi spoke about Joyce Buck's beauty at the service in the Little Chapel of the Dawn.

I spoke but cannot remember what I said; I saw her long gold chain hanging low on my gray dress, saw the faces of her friends frowning attentively. Anjelica deposited a rose on the coffin. Dad sat collapsed in the front row.

We scattered across the back deck at Shutters on the Beach like shells after a storm. Anjelica, Bob, my parents' old friends the Bernheims, the new ones, Bob and Mark. Nick the driver. Dad had taken to him.

I had to get back to work. I'd missed the couture, but that meant I'd see the photos with a fresh eye.

Jules and Nick the driver took me to the airport on the afternoon of July 17. As I was checking in at the Air France desk, Jules produced his TWA Ambassadors Club card from his wallet. He had a lifetime membership.

"You should be flying TWA," he said urgently. "Change your ticket."

I couldn't do that, I said, I lived in Paris. *Vogue* had a deal with Air France.

"I'll get you the TWA card," Dad said. "It lasts forever."

My seat was in the nose of the 747; I put on a big sweater and curled into a nest of pillows and blankets. This was not like mourning Ricki. It was simpler, a more fundamental sorrow that embraced me as I embraced it. My mother. I had the right to cry.

We took off at 4:30 p.m. Los Angeles time. Forty-five minutes into the flight, the ginger ale fell off my tray as the 747 took a sharp left turn and headed north.

I walked through the plane, wadded tissue in my hand, crying, moving from first to business to coach and back. Members of the cabin crew were crammed in each galley, like clowns, stuffing their mouths with cakes, cookies, chips. I stared at them, they stared at me, nothing was said.

For twelve hours I wept for my mother, the beautiful, fragile, witty, unreachable Joyce. A French diplomat was at the little counter between first and business class where Air France set out the sodas and the pastries; I asked him how to import ashes into France.

The plane landed at Charles De Gaulle an hour late. I came through the doors of the baggage hall into the main concourse and into a crowd of thousands of silent people, as still and stiff as zombies. I'm hallucinating, I thought.

"What's happening?" I asked the driver when he found me in the crowd. "Why are so many people here?"

"It's the plane that disappeared," he said.

I looked up at the board behind me.

TWA 800, it said. Delayed.

"They think it blew up," said the driver.

My private sorrow seemed a paltry personal thing next to 230 people blown up in a 747 over Long Island on a summer afternoon.

At the Rue Jacob, every message on the answering machine was someone asking, "Are you alive?" People thought I'd been in New York.

Charlotte came over with food; we crouched in corners of the sofa under the high white ceiling, holding plates, not eating.

"He kept telling me I had to take TWA. He wanted me to change my ticket."

"Even if you had," said Charlotte, "you wouldn't have been on that flight, because you weren't in New York."

Sensible Charlotte, the colonel's daughter.

I kept the folding mirror by my bed. The tissue with Joyce's tears was stiff and warped inside, scored on one corner by the lid. The last and purest moment of her life, now a thing. At night I was pulled into a dark river, not of dreams, but a sense of mother beyond any experience I had of Joyce, an essence that she'd never shared with me in life. Her impersonal, chthonic, eternal core. The phantom in the room left me alone; I was pulled far deeper than whatever level it came from.

One morning I looked at the folding mirror, clamshell-closed on the table. In the space of a week, it had become a holy relic that I was afraid to open. I found two Yahrzeit candles at the supermarket on the Rue de Buci, set them on the salon mantelpiece, put the closed mirror between them, and lit the candles with a prayer. They burned all day and through the night, they were burning the next morning when I left, and when I came home late from *Vogue,* they had burned out.

The summer twilight turned the Paris sky cobalt and all the streets to clear blue stone, mother of all sorrow. The French call it the blue hour. That was the title of my mother's short story that I'd found at Chester Street, and never seen again after I read it in front of her. All I could recall of it was the longing inside it, the delicacy, and such heart that I'd been shocked to see how much of her there was under the elegant impassive smiles. The only story she ever completed. Too much to do for Jules, too many rooms to decorate, too many dinners, too many smiles. Or was it too many things she couldn't say?

A corner of the tissue stuck out between the discs of the closed mirror, and now I was afraid to touch it. It felt as if I'd stolen evidence of a great secret in her dried tears. The hour was still blue when I opened the mirror, forced myself to pick out the buckled tissue, and held a match to it. I had to let her go.

Brief flames quickly ate the tissue. And she was gone.

I had to get ready for my father's arrival.

CHAPTER SEVENTEEN

Paris closed for the summer. I had one week to clear my head before my father arrived, so I went to a spa-clinic in northern Italy run by Dr. Chenot, whose cure began with a magnesium sulfate purge and went on to Chinese medicine, electronic acupuncture, herbs, and esoteric remedies.

"You must drink seawater three times a day, with every meal, to balance your electrolytes," Dr. Chenot said, holding up a clear phial that looked like a syringe. "This is *sérum de Quinton.*" He broke off one end between his fingers, turned it over a glass, broke off the other end, and shot a stream of seawater into the glass. "Drink," he said. "Saltwater is blood." I drank.

Jules arrived in Paris with Joyce's ashes in a carry-on bag. I had special dispensation to meet him at the door to the airplane, the way the head of customs used to in London. He liked that. He hadn't been in Paris in sixteen years.

He sat on my red sofa, thin in his khaki suit, and as I handed him one of the Heinekens I'd bought for him, he cleared his throat, gave a contrite smile, and said, "I forgot my lithium."

"It's August, no one's here, not even Dr. Dax, Jesus, Dad!" I sat at the desk to call around. "Eskalith, right?"

He nodded and looked up at the ceiling. "Great proportions, but the angle of the floor is worse than the rake at the Old Vic when Peter played Hamlet."

"What's the dosage?" I had a friendly pharmacist on the phone.

He looked over at the bergères, now upholstered in yellow brocade rampant with buds, fronds, and birds.

"Did your mother choose that?" he asked.

"Yes," I said.

"She was already sick." He sighed. "That's not a good yellow, it's too bright against the gilding on the wood."

We could talk for hours on the phone, but face-to-face we had only two subjects: speculations as to the nature of luck, or the things around us—rooms, furniture, paintings, objects, watches. If I didn't keep him engaged with what we could see and touch in the outside world, he went into his World War Two monologue, and I stopped listening. He had hearing aids now, small as peanuts with antennae.

He looked at the marble mantelpiece headboard behind my bed and muttered, "What kind of joke is that?"

~

I put him in the guest room, where new bookcases rose almost to the ceiling. He sat on the edge of the high mahogany child's bed; his feet didn't reach the ground. Under his open shirt, he was naked. "Cover yourself," I said.

I knew he needed to be touched and held, and took him for a week at the Royal Evian spa on the French shore of Lake Geneva, where he could be massaged every day.

He didn't like his hotel room; I gave him mine.

The local lake fish had a wonderful name, *omble chevalier,* but it tasted of mud.

"I'd love some Reblochon," he said. "They don't allow it into the States." He carefully cut the crust off the cheese and let the taste of the past melt into his mouth.

I set a glass phial of *sérum de Quinton* seawater on the table.

"What's that syringe?" he asked.

"It's not a syringe, it's seawater to restore my electrolytes," I said. "Want some?"

"You're drinking seawater? That's how sailors die!"

He finished off all the liquor bottles in his minibar and was shouting drunk when I came to collect him. I turned Nurse Ratched and tipped the room service maids to replace the Stolichnaya and Ballantine's in the minibar with water.

"There's nothing but Evian water in there!" he said, slamming the minibar door the next day.

"That's because we're in Evian," I said, "where the Evian water comes from."

We veered between best behavior and fits of temper. I had no idea how to be with him; there were so many of him. He was weak, lost, immobilized with grief; he was a vampire for attention, binding me to him with the unrelenting monotone about the Second World War, a few decibels short of intelligibility; he was a meek servant asking for a break; he was a malevolent imp darting through the hotel, causing havoc; he was a screaming baby throwing things on the floor; he was part of me, he was the person I trusted above all others, he was the person I hated.

I found him in the lower lobby, screaming in a phone booth. An American in the next booth leaned out and said, "He reminds me of my father."

The man was a doctor. I explained: bipolar, lithium, drunk, deaf, bereaved. He wrote me a prescription for something called Haldol that I was to give Jules when he started having what the man called "a psychotic episode."

"He doesn't have those," I said. He simply started creating—"creating," the English euphemism—creating a fuss, creating a disturbance, creating a scene.

"Don't let him out of your sight," said the doctor. "The bottle should last two weeks."

He lost a crown from a front tooth; I took him to a dentist in Geneva who said he needed fillings, more crowns, root canals. "I didn't want to waste time on my teeth, with your mother sick," said Jules as we left the dentist, and then he held up his wrist. "Since we're in Geneva, let's pick up a new band for my watch." He was wearing the watch his friend Charles Collingwood had left him in his will. "Remember, it's the one Ho Chi Minh gave him? And it's an Audemars Piguet, it's a very good watch."

I'd always had trouble picturing that moment in Hanoi when the leader of the Vietcong presented the CBS newsman with a very good gold watch. Off we went to get a band for it.

"Watches, those bloody watches, why is it always watches?" my mother had said as she was dying. Now I knew why.

"The Rolex," he said, as I paid for his new band, "it's still at Beverly Loan."

"What's that?"

"It's very classy. Very discreet," he said.

Back at the hotel, we found the *Independent* with Joyce's obituary in it, and her photograph. He settled by the billiard table to read it. Siân wrote about a moment, after her wedding to O'Toole, when Joyce was asked, in an after-hours Dublin pub with rotting stairs, if she had ever read *Finnegans Wake*, and she'd said, "No, but I think I may be in it."

Betty Bacall wrote,

> She was always beautiful, intelligent, generous. She had grace, integrity, a great gift for friendship and, to top it off, wit. We were friends for more than fifty years. I remember, as we waited in the wings of the Lyceum Theatre to audition for a play called *Franklin Street* (by Ruth and Gus Goetz), looking at this girl—Joyce Gates (her stage name)—hoping we would not read for the same part as she, with her beauty, was sure to get it. As it happened we were both cast in the play, which was directed by George S. Kaufman. We were seventeen years old.

"Betty's wrong, Joyce was sixteen," said Dad, and then he read it over again. A raucous Russian family gathered around the billiard table and started fencing with the cues.

"Let's get the fuck out of here," he said. We drank Evian water on the terrace, looking across the lake at Lausanne and Vevey. The French say lake water is *lénifiant*, calming. I hoped this was the real him.

"Do you want to come live with me in Paris?" I asked.

"Honey, you have to live your life. I'll be fine."

We flew to Nice with Joyce's ashes in the carry-on bag, and a cab took us up to the Colombe d'Or. Neither of us had ever stayed there before, but a blond woman welcomed us with tender hugs, as if we'd come home. It was my old friend Danièle Noël from London, who was now married to the son of the owners of La Colombe d'Or.

Jules took in the mural by the pool. "Fernand Léger," he said, proprietary. In the dining room, young French movie stars sat in pairs, lovers exhausted by their afternoon in bed. Famous people being private in public.

I did anxious accounts in my room. Six thousand dollars for Evian, probably another six for ten days at the Colombe d'Or, then the airplanes, the cars and drivers. It was going to be $15,000 at least. I was spending as if I were rich, but what was money for if not to cushion pain?

The next day at breakfast, he was raging again; ringing cell phones had kept him awake all night. I was beginning to see why his friends had avoided him for years. I had to stop loving him and then hating him. How had Joyce coped?

"Do you need some help?" asked Charlotte from Saint-Tropez.

"I do. I think I'm going a little mad."

Danièle found a room for her in the annex, and she drove up from Saint-Tropez, seven hours in the August traffic. It was as simple and practical as giving me a fire screen as protection from flaming lychee nuts.

She'd known Jules in London, and treated him with the same teasing respect as she had in his good days. We ate long dinners outside, under the wisteria.

Late at night Charlotte and I talked. How could anyone bear to be married? I asked. To be subject to the other person's moods, all day, every day, every week, every month, for years? Wasn't it better to be alone?

Now Jules wanted a French rabbi to say the Kaddish over Joyce's ashes at the grave. I found three local rabbis, but each one scolded, "You have cremated your mother? That is forbidden."

“But our grave is full of ashes,” I said. Travelers pack light.

On the day of the burial, Charlotte drove back to Paris in her big old Mercedes, Jules and I got into a big new Mercedes and were driven to Abadie II. The one-armed man I recognized from the cemetery office held open the gate for us. The headstone was engraved with Nana’s name and Don’s name; I’d have to add an extra piece of marble for Joyce’s name.

We took the bag out of the trunk, I cut through the strings sealed onto the box, to find my mother’s ashes contained in a canister shaped like a cocktail shaker. Two gravediggers set the canister into a new hole at the foot of the grave. The birds didn’t sing, the August afternoon was dense and sunless. We’d forgotten to buy flowers.

Jules and I took turns reading the Kaddish from his bar mitzvah Bible; I’d never seen it before.

It was done. Joyce was buried with Don and Esta. As the car took the rise out of the Avenue Maurice Chevalier, I asked whether—when the time came—he’d want to be here with Joyce and Don and Esta.

“I hate the fucking South of France!” he said. “I’m never coming back.”

“Then why did you want her buried here?”

“You have no idea how miserable I was when we lived at Coup de Vent, no idea. Your grandfather and his cousin were making twelve million a year, they kept me running around to try to raise money for pictures, you know she didn’t wear a bra or panties, she was a tease, I was away two months, men were all around her, Esta wanted her to marry one of those big New York Jewish guys.”

Two months, I thought, the summer before I turned five, the summer of lightning and fireworks, and then: What big New York Jewish guys?

I didn’t ask out loud. He didn’t tell me. He’d never told me how he felt before, and now he was silent.

He went home to Los Angeles. “Nick the driver will pick you up at LAX, but just this once,” I said.

“I like Nick,” he said. It was a hint. He needed help and he needed company. Fifty-one years with my mother, and now nothing. Donald Schneider, the art director, said he had a friend in Los Angeles who would help, a Japanese woman named Paula. I arranged to pay Paula to watch over Jules and hoped for the best.

The September 1995 issue came out. Cruelly, Paris *Vogue* was revitalized, fed with the blood of dead magazines. *Glamour*'s beauty editor Sophie Mazeaud joined us, and Pierre Merlin their copy chief, who kept the old formality at bay and helped me cull the adjectives. The features department worked like a chamber orchestra: Paulino revealed a talent for comic essays, Violaine could match Colette on the sensual pleasures of life, the intern Olivier was good at everything. Human Resources said that Olivier had overstayed his internship and had to leave; I sent him to interview Catherine Deneuve, and put the words "*Catherine Deneuve par Olivier Lalanne*" on the cover, which made him an instant star at the magazine, and Human Resources ordered me to keep Olivier at all costs.

Olivier's interview with Catherine Deneuve did not mean Deneuve got the cover, which went to Juliette Binoche. Catherine Deneuve called to yell that she could not be seen inside a magazine with another actress on the cover. I couldn't yell back at Catherine Deneuve, so I decided that no actress would ever be on the cover again. From now on, we'd only use models. "Actresses can be *in Vogue*," I told the staff. "They can't be *on Vogue.* We're not here to give the reader celebrities, we're here to give the reader ways to see herself."

The fashion department was rocky. Jenny Capitain held on, Brigitte Langevin peeled off, Delphine turned out imaginative and beautiful pages, but did not want to be a star, unlike Carine and Mario Testino, who produced fashion pages that pleased them immensely. Mario endlessly declared, "I am *Vogue*," but try as I might, I couldn't understand what the particular magic of his bright pictures might be. Carine's style relied, as far as I could see, on little more than straight hair, tight skirts, bare legs, and high heels, but her influence on fashion was decisive. She styled Tom Ford's sexed-up Gucci collections as morning-after chic, and everyone copied it. She wore white patent stilettos, and soon white patent stilettos were the rage.

Through various Condé Nast machinations, I inherited a new editor from Italian *Vogue.* Debra was a New Yorker and rarely smiled, but she had taste, had started at American *Vogue*, and was savvy. I made Debra my right hand. The French fashion staff snarled at her.

The weeks of dawn-to-midnight fashion shows were such a mind-crushing marathon that I insisted we review them together, fed and rested, to make a magazine that was not just whims and favors but reportage. I brought in an old-fashioned carousel to project slides from the collections on the wall as editors and assistants from fashion, beauty, and features sat at the conference table. As the photos came up on the wall, editors would fill plastic sleeves with the choices for their stories. The laborious communal process convinced the fashion editors I didn't trust them, and the carousel was much derided around Paris. I had a hard time finding a fashion director.

Jonathan wanted me to hire a man from British *Elle*, Marcus von Ackermann, a fashion director who had the reputation for balancing the needs of a magazine with the demands of advertisers. His eyes were small and close-set, his clothes cashmere, and he carried a briefcase. He loved, *loved* luxury. Von Ackermann, he said, was a Sudeten-German name, but he was British. He didn't speak French. "I don't need to," he said. "Everybody speaks English."

He struck me as cautious, grim, and a snob.

"He doesn't speak French," I told Jonathan, grasping at reasons to reject Marcus.

"We can buy him lessons," said Jonathan. "You need the security of someone reliable."

Jenny left for *Mirabella* in New York, and Marcus arrived in the fashion room. I'd traded a pretty German for a Sudeten-German. The French editors liked his New Balance sneakers.

Vogue left the dreary Rue de Vaugirard and moved back to splendor. The new offices were set behind a portico on the Faubourg Saint-Honoré, across the street from the British embassy and the residence of the American ambassador, flanked by luxury boutiques. The fashion editors, Left Bank girls, had never seen so many strangers shopping for expensive ready-to-wear.

Gardner's office was creamy and palatial, with a glass conference table. Mine was down a long corridor, bigger, not as sleek, and bright as an operating theater under its fluorescent ceiling. My half-moon desk matched the oval conference table that took up the center of the room. They were both a little ugly, a little catalogue; to make the office mine, I brought things from home: an antique Soumak rug and the poster for the 1953 movie *Love Nest*, on which Marilyn Monroe rose like a pinup arrow in a red bathing suit and high-heeled sandals; discreetly below her were the words "Produced by Jules Buck."

The *Vogue* closet, *le shopping*, and its guardian Vera were now where they belonged, on our floor next to the fashion room. The traffic of clothes in and out of *le shopping* made fashion a constant presence, not just ideas flashing past on runways or the small selections brought in for each shoot. I visited the racks several times a day.

I wore Joyce's chain, her watch, her necklace of antique turquoises. "Your mother, now, there was a chic woman!" said Franceline the jewelry editor, looking at the watch, adding, "Boucheron?"

Gardner wanted a face-lift; all I wanted was more sleep, but that was impossible, so I swam at the Ritz pool and exchanged half-naked greetings with Pamela Harriman in its changing room. I no longer smoked. I took the herbs. I carried the glass phials of the *sérum de Quinton* in my bag to down a shot of seawater after every meal.

On Dr. Chenot's orders, I ate vegetables, started dinner with fruit, gave up coffee, discovered maté, alternated maté with green tea, shunned the Nespresso machine in the secretary's office, where a vivacious trilingual Italian named Loredana now ran my *Vogue* life. I was forty-eight and had great arms, but now there was maintenance to be done. Jil Sander gave me a small Pilates reformer and a trainer came to me three times a week. Once a week I went to Françoise Morice, whose treatment consisted of pinching her clients' faces, to excellent effect. I had new clothes that fit, was thin enough to borrow couture samples, even from Chanel, where Karl's models had not yet attained puberty. The shoe problem was solved when Donna Karan made suede clogs on high rubber wedges.

"Those clogs are ridiculous," said Gardner.

"But I can walk again," I said.

~

My old married boyfriend Ivan came to see me in Paris. I hoped he would break the nun spell of *Vogue*, and kept quiet about the hand that stroked my forehead in the middle of the night; I thought of it as my Canterville ghost, a smitten dead marquis, and was relieved it did not get between us in the night. But as Ivan got out of bed in the morning, he fell forward onto his hands and knees with a yelp.

"What was that?" he asked. "Who kicked me?"

The ghost in daylight? Perhaps it didn't like men.

"It's the slope of the floor," I said.

A few weeks later, in the middle of the night, I was woken by screams and the sound of blows. I sat up in bed to listen. In the landlord's apartment eighteen feet above my head, I heard a thump like someone falling, the slide of a body along a wooden floor, and then a thud as it hit a far wall.

I ran down to the courtyard to try to catch any movement in the windows above my bedroom. One floor above the dim glow of my bedside lamp, the closed glass reflected the stillness of the autumn moon. Centuries of silence engulfed the little courtyard.

Back in my bedroom, I took out the smudge stick and an abalone shell, set them on my bedside table, and lit the bundle of dried cedar. I blew on it to reduce the fire to embers, but flames shot up from the cedar sprigs, bright and hot, and filled the room with smoke. I pulled the window open to let it out, and watched the fire turn to ash. In the morning, the table was scorched under the shell.

I had to see the bedroom above mine, find out if it had a wooden floor and marks on the wall. I left the landlords a cheery note asking if I could visit that evening, and they invited me to come upstairs at 18:30.

Their front door was identical to mine. They were both thin, formal, dry. Their living room was the same perfect cube. Their furniture was sparse. We drank wine from tiny glasses. I asked if both apartments were really identical.

"It was built for prelates visiting the Abbaye de Saint-Germain," said the wife, "and to prevent jealousy between cardinals, the apartments had to be exactly the same."

"Then your bedroom is above mine?" I asked.

"Oh! *Non,*" said the husband, "we sleep in the dining room."

"Could I see that room above my bedroom? I'm so curious!" I gave the editor smile.

"That room? We never go back there," said the husband. "We keep it locked."

"Why?" I asked, but they were evasive.

~

The theme for the December 1996–January 1997 issue was Music. To prove how cool Paris *Vogue* could be, I brought in the photographer Jean-Baptiste Mondino, who had the angry street cred that *Vogue* lacked. Mondino had a shaved head and, one editor said, was hairless all over.

We did our best, but the issue didn't dance.

The day after the Christmas Music issue shipped, I woke to an image of my mother's blue bed jacket folded on her pillow. It was not quite a vision, a distant snapshot, an astral Polaroid. I knew I had to see my father, took a long weekend off, and went to Los Angeles. Paula warned me that he'd lost his hearing aids.

At the apartment on Montana, he sat in his green leather chair, the one he always specified was Regency, collapsed inside a polo shirt. On their bed, her pale blue bed jacket was neatly folded on the pillow next to his, exactly as I'd seen it. Flotsam in the drawers. Nothing of hers in the closet. Paula had her clothes, he said, I was to go to her place to choose whatever I wanted. The vertical blinds flapped on the high flat windows. He'd be moving to a smaller place soon.

"I want to show you something," he said. He'd spread photographs all over the living room, big prints on tables, on the sofa, on chairs, in piles by subjects, by the men in the pictures. Never posed, often looking away, sometimes alone, sometimes caught in conversation with Joyce. I'd never seen most of them.

"Your mother had affairs," Dad said. "She slept with every one of these men."

He's gone mad, I thought.

He handed me a photo of her, very young, at a party with a man who looked like a turtle. "She's in Paris, that's Claude Terrail," he said. "He owns La Tour d'Argent."

She'd told me about that affair, back in 1982 in Los Angeles. Maybe he wasn't mad.

There were pictures of the captain who'd moved the aircraft carrier *Coral Sea* to please her. There was a young Kirk Douglas in a bathing suit, with Joyce in Rome. A rotund man who owned a trade paper in London. Joyce with someone called Serge, no idea who he was. "Beware of men called Serge," she'd told me once. A thin man, thin mustache, the air of a happy poodle, the husband of her friend Lorraine. Her friend's husband?

Mad with grief, I thought.

Ian Bedford in a dinner jacket on a damask sofa next to Joyce in a cocktail dress. "Look at their expressions," Dad said. I'd always thought they looked merely polite; now I could see their lips were swollen, their expressions tender, dewy, unfathomably moved. Do photographs tell any truth you're looking for?

"She'd stay out late, three-thirty, four, even when I was in town," he said.

That would be why she took those long naps in the afternoon. Or was she only exhausted by the life of a producer's wife, lunch, lamp shops and upholsterers, hours under the hot dryer at Vidal Sassoon?

I sat on the floor next to him, dizzy as he handed me photograph after photograph. I couldn't speak, and if I had, he couldn't hear me.

Now he held another photo of her, the photo that embodied the careless allure of innate elegance, the one of her in her striped sailor sweater at Coup de Vent. The only photograph of my mother where she wasn't smiling. I reached for it, but he held it just beyond my grasp.

"When you were all at Coup de Vent, I came back one morning from one of those trips your grandfather sent me on, and she told me she'd met an American who wanted to marry her," he said.

"I had my camera with me, I always did, the good Contax. She said she was leaving me for him, and that she was taking you with her. He was at the Carlton hotel, waiting for her call. I said, 'If you want a divorce, that's fine, but I keep Joanie.' And that's when I took the picture."

The photographer's revenge.

He handed me the photo. I wasn't looking at elegant allure, now all I could see was a frightened woman, her left eye more open and almost twice as big as the right one. Her mouth half open, but in horror and astonishment.

I knew he wasn't making it up. He'd caught the instant my mother had to choose between what she wanted to do, and what a good person would do. The instant she became trapped in the swimming pool at Coup de Vent, her butterfly net held over a grasshopper. The instant she gave up the nameless lover from New York to be a good woman who doesn't abandon her child.

If she'd stayed for me, she would have held me tighter afterward.

But she kept her word, stayed with my father through the champagne years, stuck by him as the Dom Pérignon became splits of Korbel. And she smiled, and smiled, and smiled till the smile made her cheeks hurt so badly that she had to be drugged to go on.

Towers of Joyce's clothes rose across the floor in Paula's apartment. I retrieved two green vases she'd loved, six pewter ashtrays from Rome, the coat she'd looked so good in during the spring of 1973. Did he tell you she slept with everyone? I wanted to ask, but instead I wrote Paula a check to watch over Jules for two more months.

Everything I knew about my mother had been twisted into a new shape, but the shape fit what had been in my head since Coup de Vent.

Back in Paris, I called Dr. Dax to ask for an analyst, any kind of analyst. I had to talk to someone. Dr. Dax asked how my father was holding up. Mad with grief, I said, and thanked him for the name of an analyst, a woman I saw for several years without ever getting to the heart of anything.

Jules moved to a smaller apartment in Los Angeles; the good furniture was shipped to me, along with the Fernand Léger carpet that I didn't dare walk on, and a small Cubist still life by Alfréd Réth, his last remaining treasure. The Rue Jacob apartment became so full of their things that it looked like Upper Belgrave Street.

He included two dolls, large felt dolls made in Italy in the 1930s, a boy in a kilt and a Little Red Riding Hood. "They were the only things your mother ever bought with her own money when she was a child actress," said his note. "She saved up for them for years."

He arrived in Paris for Christmas with a briefcase full of new prints of old photographs. He was thinking of having an exhibition. I took the child's bed in the study for myself and gave him my bedroom, figuring he was so full of ghosts that he wouldn't notice if another one touched his forehead at night.

But something attacked him in daylight, outside the front door.

We were on the way to meet Charlotte at the Brasserie Lipp. He'd been standing by the stairs while I locked the door, and as I turned I saw him jolt forward and fall down the ten stone steps to the landing. He rolled like a soldier, arms over his head, and ended curled into a ball. I raced down after him.

"It's like I was kicked," he said, unfolding himself slowly from the curl.

"I'll cancel lunch," I said.

"Fuck that, we're going to lunch. Get me some codeine."

His thick winter coat had softened the fall.

"I was just standing there," he told Charlotte, "and someone I couldn't see kicked me in the ass, right down the stairs."

Charlotte looked at me.

A London friend, Valerie Wade, produced a feng shui man. Maybe feng shui would have something to say about the inexplicable events at the Rue Jacob. He came with his girlfriend, who was, he said, a Reiki master. Jules took her to the bedroom to show her his briefcase of photographs while the feng shui man explained auspicious corners.

"I think there's something in the bedroom," I said, "it touches my forehead at night, and I'm almost sure it threw my father down the stairs yesterday."

"Let's ask my girlfriend," he said.

The girlfriend was absorbed in Dad's photographs of Cary Grant, Gary Cooper, Clark Gable, and W. C. Fields, spread out across the duvet. Dad's head was down, and he was mumbling.

"Darling," said the feng shui man, "Joan thinks there might be something in here that—"

She turned to us, her face blank, and interrupted him with automatic, neutral words: "A little girl was tortured in this room during the war."

I caught my breath. She'd said it so simply, so fast. She returned her attention to Dad, who hadn't heard a word.

No eighteenth-century marquis, but a child tortured fifty years ago. The ghost of a little girl who hated men, who attacked men, but who played with my hair at night, gently, as if I were her doll, a doll of the dead.

I found a new apartment within days. I went to tell the landlords I was leaving, and try to find out more about the room.

"My family bought the building in 1929," said the owner, "but that's all I know. And they're departed now."

"Don't you know anything about, say, what happened here during the war?"

"I wasn't born," said the owner, offended.

"There was an old lady"—her husband cut in—"living up the spiral staircase at the back. She was here before the war, even before that cube went up on the roof."

"Have you ever tried to open up that cube," I asked, "to have a look inside?"

"There's no access," he said.

"You could pierce my dressing room ceiling, or make a hole high up on the bedroom wall."

"That would be very expensive," said the husband. "Why spend all that money to find out something of no importance?"

~

Hermès decreed 1997 "The Year of Music," which validated the music theme of our Christmas issue, still on sale when they threw their party at their factory in an industrial suburb. Musicians coaxed harmonies from lengths of silk and strips of leather, from belt buckles and chains. To preserve the purity of the aural experience and avoid the percussions of metal on china, the dinner plates were made of bread crusts and the utensils were wood. The main course was pig's ears; conceptually disgusting, but as deliciously crunchy as pork crackling.

~

I couldn't wait to move. "How can you give up Rue Jacob?" people asked.

I said the neighborhood had changed. Saint-Germain-des-Prés had always been a place of high stimulus, where you flirted in the cafés and filled your mind in the bookstores and the music store, where you could buy more books, more magazines, more music late into the night and seven days a week at Le Drugstore. The march of luxury was obliterating books and music; the perpetrators were our advertisers. Giorgio Armani was remaking Le Drugstore Saint-Germain as an Emporio Armani; the record store Raoul Vidal had become a Cartier boutique; the bookstore Le Divan was a Christian Dior boutique overnight. Half of Arthus-Bertrand, the august purveyors of government medals and decorations, was now a Louis Vuitton. The *gauche caviar* of Saint-Germain-des-Prés railed at the march of commerce; because of my job, I said it was the march of progress.

"The Left Bank is finished," I declared in private. "The Champs-Élysées has always been commercial—and you can still buy music and videos and books late at night at the Virgin Megastore."

I didn't like the side I was now on; I didn't like that when I arrived at a table of *Vogue* people, they stopped talking and readied themselves to please the boss. They knew I didn't want to hear anything that wasn't praise. There were few people I felt easy with apart from Charlotte, and my friend Martine, who began each phone call with a welcome, "Come to dinner tonight." I wanted anchors from the past, school friends. I learned that Jane Gozzett had died shortly after I'd arrived in Paris. I found Lydie Dattas, now the mystic poet admired by Karl. She'd married the son of a Parisian circus family, and for a while she'd had the lions she wanted as a child, though they were circus lions. The lions and the husband were now gone, lions first.

Lydie wrote her poetry in a *loge de concierge.* Her life was so spectacularly austere that I felt the impulse to ask her forgiveness for having run off, like the heroine of *Les Malheurs de Sophie,* to play with the beautiful children in beautiful clothes in the beautiful garden. I was afraid I had become one of them.

The special cab company always had a car waiting for me. I looked at what people wore with a critical eye, as if they had access to as many clothes as I did, as if they didn't have to think about other bills first.

I had the wardrobe of a very wealthy woman, racks of things I had worn once, coats from Jil Sander for every possible climate, a teal blue astrakhan Gucci trench coat—a gift from Tom Ford—jackets bought at Saint Laurent out of loyalty to the past. Each time I went on TV, I liked to wear the same red Prada suit until our new PR said: "You have to wear something different for each television show."

"Why?" I asked.

"Because that red suit makes if look like it's always the same interview," said the PR.

So I bought more clothes. My job was to be seen wearing the latest thing, or, better still, the thing no one had yet seen. I owned a profusion of outfits so dense that no joy, no event, no memory could stick to any one thing. They flashed by like landscape in a train window, the way days at *Vogue* did. Because I gave myself no time to play, I never got my look right. My old New York clothes looked meek and emotional among the new things, like old friends with whom I used to laugh and cry.

Before I moved from the Rue Jacob, I gave most of the clothes away, with first pick to Lydie, who didn't care who'd designed anything as long as it kept her warm.

I gave the mahogany child's bed to Charlotte. I didn't need it now that I understood the impulse that had made me buy it.

I kept the folding traveling mirror that had held my mother's last tears, but kept it shut in a drawer.

Eric Wright, who worked with Karl on his Fendi collections, loved my giant rooms and asked if he could take over my lease. I hesitated because of the ghost, but rationalized that Eric was gay, so it would probably leave him alone.

The new apartment reassured me. It was a normal French apartment in a normal nineteenth-century elevator building in the familiar neighborhood from the good times, on the Rue de Cérisoles, a short, anonymous street in the heart of what was called the Golden Triangle of Luxury between the Rue François 1er and the Avenue George V, around the corner from the Hôtel de La Trémoille. It had all the rooms I needed, and more.

When I went to visit the antiques dealer on the Rue Jacob, I'd look up to see painters busy stippling the inner shutters of my old apartment, painting the ceiling, but never a sign of Eric Wright.

A year later I ran into Eric at the Milan shows.

"I never see you in Paris anymore," I said.

"I'm never in Paris anymore," said Eric. "I'm in London or Milan or Rome."

"How's our apartment?"

"Oh honey," he said, "that's the reason I never sleep in Paris anymore. That apartment is so haunted!"

CHAPTER EIGHTEEN

It was as if by dying my mother had transferred some of her beauty to me. I'd seduced, but in camouflage as an androgyne, in priestly robes or clothes for my father's son: shirts and trousers, jackets, a man's wardrobe. Now I had license to be beautiful. I wanted dresses. Dresses to show strangers the lines of my body. Dresses to be a woman in.

I put aside the sports bras that I'd used to compress my breasts, and bought French ones that presented them instead, and silk stockings with garter belts from Sabbia Rosa, to wear out to dinner. I left home without underpants. I looked at my body as I dressed. Maybe it wasn't just for dancing or sex; it had an existence in the world and an effect on people. I tilted my head when I listened, I let a man's words subside into a long silence before I answered. After our breakfasts and lunches, advertisers and foreign Condé Nast executives now lingered to banter, much to Gardner's annoyance.

Except for Ivan's brief visit, I'd lived like a nun for three years, but the day I moved to the Right Bank, the silk stockings summoned Bertie into my life. He was an elegant playboy of sixty with a brat's appetite for fun, and, of course, a wife and children in London. His grand accent sounded like a put-on, but he read books and he liked to laugh. It was good to speak English in private.

Loredana came in to deal out the deck of invitations. Dinners, balls, premières, operas, ballets, seated dinners, and promotional ratfucks that went by the term *buffets dînatoires.* Advertisers celebrating new products that would be waiting on the dinner plate, or handed over in a beribboned bag at the end of the party.

"I'll go to all of them, but not alone."

Loredana's face lit up. "You have an *ami*?" she asked.

I wasn't going public with Bertie.

"Let's make a list of every man I know."

Her pencil was poised. "Single?" she said hopefully.

"It doesn't matter. Sometimes wives are away. Some of my friends have wives who won't mind lending them to me, as long as they come home with the gift."

~

"I met Madame Claude this weekend," said the jewelry editor, Franceline, at the Monday morning meeting. Madame Claude was a legendary madam whose girls were the most luxurious of whores, the kinds favored by heads of state, sleek beauties with long legs who sometimes went on to marry titans of industry. The whisper "Madame Claude girl" clung to a few elegant wives. Madame Claude was the dark side of glamour, and the mention of her name derailed the meeting.

"Wasn't she in prison?" asked Paulino.

"We absolutely have to shoot the Graff diamonds this time," said Franceline. "I can't let them down again."

"What was she like?" asked Violaine.

"She must have some stories to tell," said Olivier.

"God, I'd love to meet her," said the new beauty editor, Sophie Mazeaud, whose braided hair made her look like a naughty child.

Buñuel's *Belle de Jour* was forty years old, but the bourgeois wife who moonlights in a bordello still had us transfixed. In the film, Catherine Deneuve embodied the contradictions of female lust: soberly dressed in Saint Laurent Rive Gauche, Puritan buckles on her Roger Vivier shoes, panting to be used and abused by strangers. I had banished the photos of models in garter belts by hotel beds from Paris *Vogue,* but I had to admit how potent that seduction was.

"Let's put Madame Claude in the September issue," I said. "Franceline, would you ask her to lunch with you, me, and Sophie?"

I wanted Madame Claude to meet us away from prying eyes, in what I imagined would be a familiar environment. Loredana booked one of the small private dining rooms at Lapérouse, where, since 1766, notables had disported with courtesans on red velvet divans that were still in place, and waiters still knocked on the doors as if something more than food was being consumed.

Madam Claude was a small woman of seventy-four in a canary yellow suit. Her hair dyed blond, her face tiny, her lips a thin seam. She sat down slowly. "My bones are like glass," she said.

She'd invented the term "call girl," she said, because she did not have a *maison,* but sent her girls out to meet the men. Sophie was the scribe, but we all had questions. What were Madame Claude's criteria for beauty? A tall Grace Kelly type was easier to place—I loved that, "to place"—than an Ava Gardner or an explosive redhead. The most popular girls, she said, had the sporty solidity of the newscaster Claire Chazal. She rejected any girls who were not perfect, anyone with short thighs—"though I made exceptions for those who had a big name and needed a little gift to fix the roof on the family *château.*"

No one with an accent, so no *Marseillaises,* no Belgians, no Canadians. Few French girls, because they were never on time. No one over twenty-five: "That's the age when women develop *manies,*" she said. *Manies*: habits, tics, peculiarities. Individuality.

Her girls never wore perfume, only light scents that would not stick to a man; carried three deodorants at all times, for the mouth, the armpits, and what she called the *foufoune.* And they always brought a wig.

"A wig?" I asked. Quick escape, disguise?

"In case they can't get to the hairdresser."

Madame Claude wanted her girls to be classy, discreet—adjectives I'd heard all my life. They had to give the man their total attention, never talk about themselves, and, if conversation flagged, confine themselves to "Oh" or "Ah." Once she'd taught them grace and manners, eradicated minor but irritating physical flaws, she took care of their culture.

"I made each girl buy a subscription to *Historia,* the monthly history magazine, so they'd always have something to say about Napoleon or Talleyrand."

This was the *Belle de Jour* mother lode, the etiquette book for the better class of whore, and I had a new word. *Foufoune.*

The *foufoune,* however, was no longer in fashion. One of the editors explained over lunch that she'd eliminated her pubic hair. "Everyone's doing it, to be like the porn stars," she said.

~

In 1997, old haute couture houses absorbed new London designers to become young again. Christian Dior took in John Galliano—playful, dreadlocked, from Gibraltar—who was replaced at Givenchy by Alexander McQueen—angry, bald son of a London cabdriver. The younger French designers, Jean Paul Gaultier and Thierry Mugler, retaliated with couture of their own. Each couture show was a spectacle of epic fantasy in a space as large as a stadium. The skirt of a Galliano Dior dress was so long that for our cover we posed the model on a ladder to show off the tumbling multicolored organza above the words *Le Big Bang.*

Jean-Paul Goude wanted to photograph Thierry Mugler as a centaur, which meant hiring a horse. "The horse should be wearing stockings," said Jean-Paul. Someone made horse-sized stockings.

"There's a bit of a problem," Jean-Paul said from the studio. "The horse got excited when we put the stockings on him."

"Stockings," I agreed, "are an erotic charge."

"It's got a hard-on as long as my arm, and it won't go down."

"Take the picture of the horse with his hard-on, we can always erase it."

"The stockings don't look so good," said Jean-Paul. "They're taking them off now. Oh Christ. The horse still has a hard-on."

"Shoot it," I said.

When Jean Paul's photomontage came in, Thierry Mugler's

bulked-up torso rose from the body of a horse trailing a giant penis. I sent it to Jonathan Newhouse for approval or veto. It was only a horse, but it was still a hard-on.

"I like it," he said, "but you'd better get Thierry Mugler to sign off on it."

I took a copy of the photo to Thierry Mugler's office, where an assistant took me past the workrooms to a locked door beyond which was an elevator that rose to a massive metal door with a dial on it, like the door to a bank vault. And then we were in Mugler's safe room, a workroom like all the others.

The designer stood erect and buff; tattoos and a buzz-cut beard made black patterns on his skin. I laid the copy of the photo on a table. He looked at it. I gave him a felt-tip.

"Can you just sign that it's okay?" I asked.

He leaned down and began to scribble. Soften lines in the face. Soften shadows around the nipples, which, I now noticed, were tattooed black. Fix the chin line. He was looking only at himself.

"Thierry," I said, "the horse."

"Oh," he said, "it looks fine."

"The penis," I said.

"Oh, it's fine." He drew a circle around the horse's penis and signed "OK Thierry Mugler."

~

A froth of luxury coated everything, and the demands of inanimate objects began to eat my soul. Tides of things engulfed my office every day, flowers from designers happy to see their clothes in *Vogue*, from models grateful for the cover, from relieved advertisers. Perfumes, makeup samples, small leather goods, artistic fan letters, vanity publications by designers, silver picture frames, books inscribed to me by people I had never met, books inscribed to me by friends that I would never have time to read. Editing meant deciding what things, in the daily whirlwind of products—clothes, accessories, shoes, watches, spas, face creams, underwear, jewelry, bikinis, images, attitudes, hotels, restaurants, vacation spots, films, songs, artists—were worthy of being featured in our pages. The editors in various departments did their job of sorting through the raw material, but I was too curious, too much of a flea market rat, not to believe that if I had a look, I'd find the one treasure no one had noticed, the key that would make all the difference.

From my early relationship with my toys, I knew that inanimate objects had feelings. Each gift wanted admiration, approval, love. The needy swag scattered across my conference table made me feel guilty that I couldn't respond to each thing. The best I could do was hand over that thing to a less spoiled, less busy person who would take good care of it. I distributed everything but the flowers, and the bottles of new shampoos.

But I was caught in a romance with things, and wanted the ones I didn't get. I waited for Karl to cover me in gifts the way he had when I got married, and was still perplexed that he'd greeted my arrival with the slim volumes of mystic poetry by Lydie Dattas. He was shaped like Santa Claus, and I expected him to act like Santa, but he'd known me too long to be interested in what I'd look like in his clothes. I hated myself for wanting more. I had a clothing allowance and could buy what I wanted at a discount; that wasn't the point.

He handed me barbs, not favors. I had still not asked him to take photographs for *Vogue*.

"He's your friend, you should have lunch with him," said Gardner.

Karl's new apartment was at his old address on the Rue de l'Université; he'd moved from the annex to the palatial main building. I waited for him for an hour, fidgeting on a sofa as big as a barge, staring at the overscaled platinum-lined dome lampshade above me in a mounting rage. Would he keep Anna Wintour waiting like this? Karl swept in from someplace—his bedroom, his library, his photo studio—complaining how busy he was.

"Are you showing me what you think of *Vogue*, or is the contempt personal?" I asked.

"But you're my friend," he said.

"Then act like it," I said.

We proceeded to a lunch table set with stiff linens and interesting plates; he acted like my friend, I acted like his friend, and then we were friends again. We talked about our dead mothers; I told him how worried I was about my father. By dessert I'd I asked him to take photographs for the magazine. His last Chanel ready-to-wear collection was full of long thick wool dresses edged in constructivist patterns that evoked the period I loved, Moscow sometime between 1912 and 1925. I tried on the samples at Chanel; he told me which ones would be mine. "I'll have Manolo make me red boots for these," I said.

"You want to look like a Hungarian folk dancer?" asked Karl.

~

At a dinner in a château for a tycoon and his second wife, I asked the man on my left my usual question: "What have you been doing this week?"

"I just bought the company that publishes this funny little magazine called *Historia*," he said. "Do you know it?"

"Madame Claude told me she made all her girls subscribe to it," I whispered.

The guest of honor's second wife called out to him across the table. "I haven't seen you in such a long time! What have you been doing?"

"I just bought this funny little magazine called *Historia*," he said. "Do you know it?"

"Know it? I love it! I've subscribed to *Historia* since I was eighteen!" said the tycoon's wife.

~

Charlotte Rampling took me to a lunch party on the Rue du Bac. Standing between two doorways was a short whiskered man who looked like a drunk teddy bear. His first words were: "That Gardner Bellanger's a real bitch."

"Not really," I said. "She's just tough."

"Everyone's talking about you two," he said.

Someone said he was an agency man. "ICM? William Morris?" I asked.

"CIA," they said.

He was the chief political correspondent of the *Herald Tribune*, and more or less single. I added his name, Joe Fitchett, to the list of party escorts.

Paula reported from Los Angeles on my father's doings, his near misses and sudden rages; she carried a bottle of Haldol with her for the tantrums. I thought the motion picture home might be a good place for him, full of old actors, directors, producers. But his old friend Walter, who ran it, said Jules didn't have enough American credits to qualify for admission.

Barred from the Polo Lounge for being an old-timer, insufficiently American to merit a place among his peers, of course he lost his temper. I hired a lawyer to get Jules a green card to make him a legal resident in the States. "An American born in America of American parents needs a green card, " said the lawyer. "This is a first."

My friend Randall Koral said it was time for me to get on the web, and opened Internet Explorer on my laptop.

"Look up something you want to know about," he said. I typed in "Jules Buck." The first entry was in the "List of names deleted from new edition of *Katz's Encyclopedia of Film*."

"It may be time to get him out of L.A.," said Randall. "No one in France has ever even heard of *Katz's Encyclopedia*."

~

Paris *Vogue* was selling well, but the fashion room was a place of misery. The new designers were experimental but despondent Belgians, and most of the clothes coming into *le shopping* were laser-cut white nylon. Marcus had still not learned French, and was obsessed with having Princess Diana in the magazine. She was on the cover of *Vanity Fair*, shot by our own Mario Testino. I said no: we couldn't have Princess Diana in Paris *Vogue* without having her on the cover, and Paris *Vogue* would look like *Paris Match*.

Helmut Newton wanted to use crash-test dummies as models for his haute couture photographs.

"I've seen some very beautiful, very elegant dummies," he said. "I could pose them as if they've been killed in car crashes."

"Absolutely not!" I yelled. "No!"

"Don't shout at me!" shouted Helmut. "You are such a spoilsport!"

A week after his July couture show, Gianni Versace was murdered on the steps of his house in Miami.

The upper ranks of the fashion world convened in Milan for the funeral. The bar at the Four Seasons was thick with bodyguards. Valentino's partner Giancarlo Giammetti said, "You do everything to become someone, and then they shoot you because you are someone."

The funeral seemed a tiny thing crammed up by the incense-smoky altar inside the dinosaur skeleton of the Duomo. Fashion notables took their places in the nave.

"Let's stay with the press, on the side," I said to Gardner.

Cell phones rang one after the other, then together, like bells. Bodyguards fanned out around the altar to guard Elton John as he sang "Candle in the Wind." Models in sunglasses and black minidresses took Communion. Outside the Duomo, walls of onlookers stood thick around the cars, shouting out famous names, as if this were the Oscars.

At Versace's apartment on the Via Gesù the butler stood at attention, stiff and frozen; his name was Gianni, too. Jonathan, Gardner, and I were early, alone with Alex Shulman and Anna Harvey from British *Vogue*, and Princess Diana. Diana was tall, her arms a touch big in her sleeveless dress, turquoise on her eyes, mouth long and curling like an animal on a rock. The butler served canapés laid out in a checkerboard, black caviar, gray caviar. Princess Diana took a black one. Jonathan asked, "Which kind is the best? Which kind is the most expensive?"

"The gray," said Diana. Jonathan took a gray one.

No one arrived for a long time. "We knew we were in Italy because we got a police car up our back," Diana finally said. "It chased us all the way from the airport."

~

My father called me as soon as his green card came through. "I think I'll come live in Paris with you after all," he said.

I'd been expecting that. "I'll buy new sheets for the guest room," I said.

"What am I going to do with him?" I asked Karl.

"Take him to my house in Monaco for a few weeks in August," he said. "No one's using it."

La Vigie, a pretty little Grimaldi palace high over the Monte-Carlo Beach Club, was on loan from Princess Caroline, but Karl now preferred the bracing Atlantic air of Biarritz, where he'd discovered a whole new style of house, half-timbered and rustic, that gave him a fresher feeling. "I think palaces are finished," he said. "Have mine."

Jules arrived in Paris at the beginning of August, this time with a full supply of lithium, new hearing aids, and his photographs. I'd put the Cubist still life over the bed in the guest room. "Hang it over the couch, where everyone can see it," he said. While I nailed it onto the living room wall, he shifted his weight from one foot to another. "The floor's level here," he said. "That's good."

He'd spent time with Bob Graham in the last year, and set out the gifts Bob had given him, small bronze heads and figures, wax maquettes for a Roosevelt memorial in DC, small plaster sketches, drawings, prints, photographs of nudes. "His studio's really something," he said. "Bob's working on this statue of the Virgin Mary for the cathedral downtown."

"How's it coming?" I asked.

"She's young and she's beautiful, but her arms are too long," he said. "I tried to tell him, but he wouldn't listen."

When he was tucked into new sheets across the hall from me and I could hear his sleeping breath, I felt I held him safe from the L.A. traffic, and I wasn't incomplete anymore.

I gave a dinner party for his eightieth birthday, and Gardner's fifty-fourth; they were born days apart. She came in a dress as flimsy as a nightgown, with her husband. She'd lost more weight in preparation for her face-lift. I gave her a tote bag from Hermès and a thick silver chain from India. Instead of a cake, there were two pyramids of *macarons* from Ladurée.

Karl's chauffeur met us at Nice airport in a Bentley that Dad took to at once, and drove us up a steep winding drive barred by two security gates; the chauffeur stopped at each one to call the butler in the house. He said that he was entirely at our disposal "during the day," and repeated "during the day," so we'd understand.

Massive bouquets from Karl waited for us in our rooms, where chairs heaped with picture books were set up as bedside tables. The butler explained that he would serve dinner at seven, and then he and the cook would go home. I realized I'd be locked up with my father in a palace on top of a cliff, with no escape after sunset.

The Xanax left over from the year before got me through the days. That, and the London papers. They were full of Princess Diana, now just Diana, now just Di, Di with Dodi Al-Fayed, out there on a yacht on the Mediterranean in the blue water at our feet. Every day the *Mail* and the *Express*, the *Sun* and the *Daily Mirror*—on holiday, I had no shame—had new pictures of the lovebirds on the boat. Swimming, sunbathing, hugging, kissing, going ashore shoes in hand, returning on board barefoot. Italian gossip magazines and *Paris Match* had more pictures. I wanted the fairy tale, the princess romance. The few moments sitting beside her in Milan had left me with the fan's conviction that I should have a life like hers, with a wealthy swain on a yacht, swimming in the thick deep water off the side, the smell of Bain de Soleil, burning yellow mattresses on the teak deck, sex in the cabin, everything I'd always been too clever for, everything I'd had too much taste for, everything I'd rejected. I was becoming like Marcus. Suspended in borrowed luxury, I wanted teenage dreams. I didn't want to be locked up with my father.

Bertie called from some absurd island to say he missed me. I cannot spend another summer like this, I thought, missing you when I don't even like you that much.

My father didn't want to see anyone; he was happy talking about the good days. "Remember the crazy nights at Le Pirate when the waiters threw everything from the tables onto the rocks, everything? The plates, the glasses, the evening bags, the gold lighters?"

At night, after he went to bed, I watched the fireworks over the Monte-Carlo casino. Pink and blue stars, muffled bangs across the water, glitter flashing, twinkling, sparkling out of reach. I was five and back at Coup de Vent and my mother was falling in love with an unnamed American from New York.

I brought my father back to Paris two days before *la rentrée,* when work would start again.

Early on the Sunday morning, Marcus called me, sobbing, "Diana's dead."

I couldn't speak.

"Last night. Dodi's dead as well. They were in a car that crashed in the underpass by the Alma."

Paparazzi had chased their car into the crash. "They chased us all the way from the airport," she'd said in Milan. The soft tall white body, quarry.

At the office, Donald Schneider saw the bright side. "That's so great that you didn't let Helmut photograph the couture on the crash-test dummies; can you imagine if we'd had those in the September issue? How did you know?"

I didn't know. Until the day before, I'd wanted to be Diana.

Gardner returned from holiday with her new face. The doctor had winched her skin so tight and injected so much in her lips that her mouth was folded outward, the soft tissue exposed. One evening, during a fashion conclave when all the stores on the Avenue Montaigne were open, one person after another exclaimed, "What has she done!"

"Nothing at all," I replied. To say she'd had a face-lift would be to agree that she'd gone too far. I was loyal to my colleague.

The September issue was out, dedicated to "The Power of Women," with "Beauty According to Madame Claude" right there on the cover. The PR couldn't keep up with the demands for interviews, the invitations from talk shows. Pierre Bergé called to yell so loudly that the only word I could make out was *couverture.*

"Yves's dress had two pages all to itself!" I said.

"I don't care about the dress! How dare you put Madame Claude on the cover? You don't put a pimp on the cover of *Vogue*! She's evil!"

I thought I'd done something knowing, something French. I had no idea what the real stories were behind Madame Claude, and no one enlightened me.

But there was a flurry of invitations to lunch from men I barely knew. I was flattered by the attention and imagined that, on some invisible level, my selfless devotion to Dad had paid off with oblique rewards.

A talk show host, a sexy mouse with long front teeth, got to the point over miso cod in a Japanese restaurant: "Have you been to Les Chandelles? It's just reopened."

"And what kind of food does it serve?" I asked.

"It's not a restaurant," he said. "It's a sex club."

"Thank you, but no," I said.

Other lunches with other men followed, at the Bristol, the Ritz, the Crillon, Le Voltaire, and Noura. The ones I knew through *Vogue* were lit with a brighter spark than when they were pitching designers or fragrances. One or two mentioned that they'd liked reading about Claude. Not Madame Claude, but Claude; they knew her personally. They all eventually came to the subject of sex clubs, new sex clubs, classic sex clubs, kinkier sex clubs. "You've never been to Les Chandelles? Really?" they asked. One volunteered that porn stars made love better than other women; another that his wife was totally bare down there, as was his girlfriend. The *foufoune* was a thing of the past. Another had invested in a laser hair-removal system, though he said it only worked on black hair. For once my fashion editors and the advertisers were in agreement.

I had no interest in having sex in public with business acquaintances, but, thanks to Madame Claude, I had Paris by the balls.

~

Karl's constructivist Chanels weren't alone; the ready-to-wear collections for 1997–1998 also had workhouse suits and sad clothes lit up by abstract shapes in primary colors that looked like the founding artistic movement of the twentieth century. There were dresses in saturated colors, experiments with grain and photographed patterns. The Christmas issue that year was dedicated to art.

Delphine, inspired by Rodchenko, had Michael Thompson photograph the models as heroines of the October Revolution. David LaChapelle put one of his models in a glass tank to be a Damien Hirst shark, did a Christo on a house in Queens, and made his own Jeff Koons, a girl in a Dior corset holding a pair of china fruit baskets overrun with white china cats.

Karl took dark giant Polaroids of the costumes from Oskar Schlemmer's 1922 *Triadic Ballet,* which we had borrowed from the Schlemmer foundation. Vera from *le shopping* spent two nights sewing silver buttons along the arms of a Sonia Rykiel sweater to match a Schlemmer costume. Francesco Clemente, Annette Messager, and Ed Ruscha drew, painted, and played with clothes. Donald Sultan drew the gift pages. It was a glorious game of pastiche and make-believe, and every one of our contributors played with joy, except Mario and Carine.

Mario and Carine found our imaginative effusions hard to take; I'd forgotten that not everyone is good at charades and that some people don't even want to play. Their careers were taking them into the smoother realm of American Condé Nast; Mario shot for *Vanity Fair,* Carine was featured in American *Vogue* striding through Mario's favorite *allée* in the Tuileries.

Carine tried to demonstrate our fundamental aesthetic differences by showing me her apartment. "You have so many things, you must see how I live. I have nothing," she said, using the exact words she'd used before. Her nothing was infinite square meters of fine parquet overlooking the Esplanade des Invalides, the most expensive real estate in Paris; she lived with a man everyone called Sisley, who'd made a fortune with silk shirts called Equipment. She took me around the way a child shows off her room, proud that there was nothing to see. No books in the living room, nothing on the tables, nothing in the kitchen. Everything in her apartment was hidden behind closet doors.

"I don't like mess, it's confusing. I only have a few things," she said. "Straight skirts, plain sweaters," and then she showed me her straight skirts, her plain sweaters.

Fashion was her element, which made her immune to the lure of beautiful things. That was her strength.

My apartment was full of things, and most particularly full of Dad, who padded around in his socks from the living room, where he read, to the library, where he watched French television, which he professed to understand. He had only scorn for CNN. "I didn't move here to watch Lou Dobbs," he said.

He sorted the new prints of his old photographs on the dining room table, moved them from left to right and right to left for hours. I looked at them closely, for once. As the years went on from Hollywood to Paris, to London, he'd lost his focus. The St. Clerans photos were all a little fuzzy. Many of the shots I knew were missing; the pictures of Joyce with the other men that he'd shown me in Los Angeles were gone, and so was the one of her with her eyes open too wide at Coup de Vent.

"Didn't you want to show these to a gallery?" I asked.

"No, these are private," he said. "These are my life."

Olivier the intern found a copy of *Katz's Encyclopedia of Film*; it was the edition that still had an entry for Jules Buck.

"Mais c'est une légende, ton père," said Olivier. Your father is a legend. Yes. Now safely nestled into my life in Paris, he could be.

~

Mode et Art was a triumph. Fashion was thrilled to be called Art, Art didn't mind being called Fashion. Flowers and chocolates came into the office, and gifts, enough wampum to spoil everyone who was on the staff, and many who weren't. Loredana wrapped for days behind closed doors, keeping in mind that Paulino liked leopard prints and Veronique the photo editor liked clocks.

I set up a fat Christmas tree in the entrance gallery of the new apartment, bought old-fashioned silver balls and glitter garlands, and green plastic ropes of lights from Prisunic that Jules found a little vulgar; to limit his interference with the decorations, I set him up in the library with a new videotape of *Singin' in the Rain*, put the Christmas Oratorio on the CD player, and went at the tree. I'd carpeted the rooms in a dark rust red called *coq de roche*; the third bedroom was now a dressing room, and in the library were only the books with titles that guests might recognize. I hid the Jung and the anthropology in the bedroom, but left the pornography in the back hall bookcase, to cheer anyone who went exploring.

It turned bitter cold. When Jules went out for his morning walk, he left a note by the front door: "I'll be back in an hour, if the ice holds."

A few days before Christmas, I gave my first Christmas party for the staff, with cases of champagne and a baked ham *à l'américaine.* The tree glowed and sparkled over a mound of presents, and everyone from Paris *Vogue* came to eat and drink and sit everywhere and smoke cigarettes and gossip and get a little drunk and open their presents and try to catch the gist of Dad's stories. I gave Gardner Tibetan turquoises; she gave me a Navajo cuff. We knew better than to exchange the office swag.

~

For Christmas Day, I hauled the rest of the presents out of the dressing room, set out another baked ham, chilled more champagne, and finished cooking my red cabbage for my friends. Charlotte brought her new man, Jean-Noel, Alexis brought his parents, Pierre-André and Martine brought foie gras made by one of her authors. We played charades, in English. Jules sat holding his glass, watching the game, telling only a few stories, an open box of *griottes* on the table in front of him. He wore a new black cashmere sweater; his new gray cashmere muffler was draped on the back of his chair. Bertie was in the Seychelles with his family.

I wanted the illusion that I had a rich boyfriend who cared, so I bought myself a pair of fake diamond earrings, big enough to look serious, discreet enough to look real. At the January Valentino couture show, the fake diamonds acted like magnets on Anna Wintour, who ran up to hug me and kiss each cheek. She'd never shown such warmth, and whispered, confidential and girlish, "Who gave you the earrings?"

"You know how it is," I whispered back. "Diamonds never come from the person you wish had given them to you."

CHAPTER NINETEEN

My father didn't want to go to the Fernand Léger show at the Pompidou museum, but Betty Bacall came with me. I had no idea if I'd find the painting, but around a corner in the third room, behind a rope like all the rest, there was *Le Pont*: my checkerboard plane, my circles, my poplar tufts. While I gazed helplessly at my lost inheritance, Betty slipped into the bookshop to find me the catalogue with the best reproduction. I gave the page with *Le Pont* to the photo department with instructions to print it full color, on foam core, two meters high. The painting was only an idea now, and could be as big as I wanted; I wanted it huge.

The reproduction of *Le Pont* came back too big to fit in my elevator; I carried it up the stairs, invited Dad into the living room, pulled the brown paper off the panel, and turned it to face him.

"Look," I said. "It's back." *Shazam!*

Dad gave it one glance. "Wrong size," he said, and left the room.

I leaned it against the wall. Every time Dad walked past it, he gave an irritated shrug. I'd overdone it.

~

Bertie wanted to spend the night, but I didn't like to have sex in the same apartment where my father slept, so I insisted he get us a room around the corner at the Hôtel de La Trémoille. When I returned in the morning, my father was holding open the door; he gave me a wink and asked, "How was it?"

I had to divert his attention to someone else, who had to be a woman, who had to speak English, and who had to be wise enough to put up with all the impossible things about him. I'd pay her to spend time with him, go to museums with him, have lunch with him, and take him to the dentist several times a week. Aneeta Clark was from India, had grown up in London, and lived in Paris with her second husband, an American who worked in telecoms, and her daughter, Joti. Aneeta was a little younger than me, had long glossy black hair, and was ready for the challenge. "I'm really an art restorer," said Aneeta, "but why not?" She'd have to look at many photographs, I warned, but some of them were interesting.

He took to Aneeta at once and called her "my assistant."

The next time I had to spend the night with Bertie at the Trémoille, I told Aneeta she had to find Jules an apartment.

The rent was more than I'd wanted to pay, but it was in an Art Deco building on the Avenue Matignon that overlooked the tented booths of the stamp market that his friend Peter Stone had written into *Charade.* He had light and space, his photos, his TV, and his tape of *Singin' in the Rain.* I gave him the Art Deco standing lamp, he put his Fernand Léger rug on the floor. He was happy.

Now that we weren't living together anymore, I could see him only on the weekends, and gave up bicycling at Versailles. For Sunday lunch, we made ourselves at home at the bar of the Bristol Hotel and spread out on the sofa with the London Sunday papers; at the bar of the Ritz we minded our manners and folded the papers into neat quarters, but still devoured the miniature coffee éclairs from the stand of petits fours, and called for more. After lunch, I'd walk to the office to catch up on work; my weekdays belonged to the demands of others.

Martine thought I should have a more interesting man in my life than Bertie, and introduced me to a philosopher who was, she said, the Real Thing, not just a TV talking head, though he was that as well. He was a Nietzschean hedonist with the face and body of a Caravaggio bruiser; at forty, he'd already written thirteen books expounding on the fully realized sensual life. I was almost ten years older than he was; after our first night, he faxed me Baudelaire's line "*J'ai plus de souvenirs que si j'avais mille ans*"—I have more memories than if I were a thousand years old. This could be interesting, as long as he wasn't implying that I was a thousand years old.

He wrote compulsively, and soon forty fresh pages of philosophy with a thousand commas awaited me every evening in the fax at home. He would not talk to me unless I had comments informed by a careful reading. His hedonism was as compulsive as his typing; he lived with a woman in the Normandy village where he'd been born, but exercised his libertine prerogative all over Paris. He loved three-star restaurants, drove an old Mercedes, but hated the rich. One evening, as he zipped me into a leather dress I'd bought in the Hermès sale, he asked in a tight voice, "What's that on the label?"

"It probably says, '*automne–hiver* 1997–98.'"

"That's not what it says."

He picked a fight at dinner, and drove back to Normandy. I looked at the label when I took off the dress and saw the retail price, an incriminating 25,000 francs, five times what he earned in a month.

That was the end of the philosopher, but I still had my fake diamond earrings, and Bertie, who wasn't aware that he'd given them to me. Dad was safely in his Art Deco apartment, spending his days with a quick, attractive woman from London who understood him. Everything was pretty much in order.

"You know, I cook, too," said Aneeta. We started to concoct menus for dinner parties every few weeks, and they were better each time.

Aneeta turned out Italian or Indian feasts for forty or fifty guests whenever there was something to celebrate. I hired a *maître d'hôtel* and two waiters to circulate with food and drink, bought too many Baccarat wineglasses in a grand pattern that belonged in a château. So many cases of Comtes de Champagne came in from Taittinger for the *Vogue* parties that there was always champagne left over for the next one.

Parties for photographers or writers, Herb Ritts or Jim Harrison, parties for issues, parties for any excuse to bring together Paris *Vogue*'s favorite actors and photographers, designers and artists, old friends and new ones, bohemian aristos, Spanish dancers, Sydney Picasso, Roman Polanski, Barbet Schroeder and Bulle Ogier, Manuella Papatakis and her mother, Anouk Aimée, and a new young photographer, Taryn Simon, whose ambivalence about *Vogue* made me like her all the more. Gardner came with her husband, Patrice; Jonathan Newhouse came with his wife, Ronnie, if they were in town. I never invited Bertie; the writer was stuck in New York. I did it happily alone.

Guests lounged on the sofas eating like Romans, sat on the floor to eat off a low Indian table the size of a double bed, or perched formally in the gallery at round tables hung with rust or violet cloths, and long after the waiters had left, they returned to the serving table for more dessert. Aneeta always filled a punch bowl with pomegranate seeds; they lightened the impact of the chocolate mousse, but it took her the better part of a day to peel them.

The bigger the parties, the easier they were. I wasn't at the dining table with five or seven people that I had chosen in function of a common language—English, French, or Italian—I didn't have to administer flattery or praise, or feed them gossip as choice as the dishes. Guests at a big party acquired velocity and volition, found a common language or two, delighted in one another. I didn't have to perform or control; I could enjoy the pleasure around me and didn't have to stay in any one place too long, and they all took care of my father.

He was, each time, the star.

Jules developed his own method with the parties. He'd kept away from social events for twenty years, but since Aneeta—his assistant—was cooking, he felt a proprietary interest. He'd arrive a few minutes before the waiters, follow them around telling them how to light the candles—the chic candle that year was a thick pillar with three wicks, tricky to light—told them which china to use, checked that the silver was polished, made sure the vases didn't sit directly on the polished tables. His inspection completed, he'd station himself in the kitchen to chat with Aneeta until she could stand it no longer and sent him out the door. That's when he'd grab his coat and leave.

The first time he vanished before dinner I worried he'd wandered under a bus and died. Sweating over her saucepans, Aneeta reassured me: "I'll bet he's gone to that café where he says the *Paris Match* people used to hang out." She was right; he sat at La Belle Ferronnière across the street for an hour or two, preparing his entrance.

He'd return when the party was in full swing, at nine thirty, ten o'clock. He'd stand absolutely still on the rust red carpet in the gallery, framed by the open doors of the living room, waiting until someone caught sight of him and rose to greet him; he'd look a little surprised, touched at the attention, allow his coat to be slipped off, be led into the room like a king, allow someone to give up their seat for him, and receive a plate of food and a glass of wine. As he started on whatever fine dish Aneeta had made that night, he'd hold up his fork—one of the good silver ones—and explain, "Aneeta's actually *my* chef, but I have her cook simpler things for me at home."

His stories were as unintelligible as ever, but my guests strained to listen. They wanted to know about *The Ruling Class* and *Quoi de Neuf Pussycat?* They'd catch the word Huston or Gable, Monroe, or Garbo—Garbo, I'd think, what picture did he do with Garbo?—and sometimes he'd tell a man about his love affair with Joan Crawford when he was a young photographer and she was already a star and they made love on the beach and she scratched his back so hard that he still had the scars. Jonathan Newhouse brought his full attention to Jules's stories and fell under his spell. He was my boss, so Dad took care to articulate.

Thanks to *Vogue,* I'd given back my father his life as I imagined it.

And now, on each of his visits to Paris, Jonathan made time to visit Jules in his apartment, where he learned that their fathers were both named Norman. One Norman had run the *Times-Picayune* in New Orleans, the other Norman had run a cigar store at 1441 Broadway, but the shared name made Jonathan feel they were related.

The photographs weren't a problem for Jonathan, and he loved movies. At the dinners he held each ready-to-wear season in Paris for the editors of his multiplying international *Vogue*s, Jonathan always gave the same speech; holding a microphone and summoning Marlon Brando's *Godfather* rasp, he told us that we were all family, that family was important; and he'd conclude with a knowing little chuckle.

Gardner called Jonathan *l'actionnaire,* the shareholder, though "owner" would have been more accurate, as Condé Nast was a private company, but she liked the roll and pomp of *l'actionnaire.* As *président-directeur général* of the French company, she reigned supreme from her vast office, where she relentlessly convened the entire staff to toast advertising triumphs in champagne provided by whichever brand was most generous that year.

She relaunched *Vogue Hommes* as a biyearly publication, and hired my friend the Irish journalist Godfrey Deeny as editor in chief. Then she fired Godfrey.

"I can edit *Vogue Hommes* myself," she declared. "It's not that hard."

"It's not a good idea for the *président-directeur général* to edit a magazine," I said.

"Don't you forget I started in editorial," she answered. "I know what I'm doing."

Then she hired Richard Buckley, who did know what he was doing. He was also Tom Ford's boyfriend, and the acid expression he wore above his fine turtlenecks suggested he suspected he'd not been hired entirely for his talent as a journalist. I loved his clarity and his bitter humor.

~

I put the words "100% CACHEMIRE" on the cover of the August issue, and it practically sold out. The unprecedented occurrence was, I knew, due to the implication that somewhere inside the magazine was a piece of real cashmere.

In July of 1998, Tina Brown left the *New Yorker* to start a magazine of her own with Harvey Weinstein. Jonathan called to say that if I wanted to propose myself as editor of the *New Yorker*, the job could be mine.

I thought about the *New Yorker* editors. The legendary Harold Ross, the all-seeing gnome William Shawn, the irreproachably tasteful Bob

Gottlieb, and then Tina. Tina with her unstoppable drive, her raging appetite for buzz. Tina, protected and shored up by the devotion of her husband, Harry Evans, who'd changed British journalism as editor of the London *Sunday Times.* I wasn't one of them.

I thought about the amount of copy that went into the *New Yorker* and how many times I'd have to read ten-thousand-word articles about important matters, I thought about how little English I'd read in the last four years, I saw myself hunched over a desk until midnight, choking on words. And would they pay enough for my father to have his own place, or would I come home to an average apartment at the end of a long day to find Dad shuffling his photographs around the dining table, complaining about the cold? And no beauty outside, only honking and bustle, and what, we'd have Sunday lunch at the Palm Court? How would I find a New York Aneeta? And what about his abandoned green card?

I knew pictures, I knew color, I knew how to mold fashion to fit crazy concepts in *Vogue,* I dealt in images and first impressions, I panicked that luxury had eroded my mind.

"So," asked Gardner, "anything you want to tell me about?"

"I'm thinking about the Christmas issue," I said.

"Is that all?" She cocked her head knowingly.

"It's everything," I said.

Jonathan called to ask what I'd decided. "I'm staying in Paris," I told him.

It was around then that Gardner began to hate me.

~

It was going to be the greatest Christmas issue ever. The pictures had to vault us into the infinite future on the far side of the next century. The only way to think about 1999 was to think about the year we'd all been waiting for, 2000, when the world would change—if it survived the precarious jump from the prefix 19 to the prefix 20, when the Y2K glitch might fry every computer on the planet. Scientists were unraveling the human genome, Michel Houellebecq's fairly pornographic novel *Les Particules élémentaires* blamed everything on sex, *Sliding Doors,* playing on the Champs-Élysées, explored the butterfly effect, and Darren Aronofsky's film π was about to open.

The carousel slideshow revealed a faint pulse of science in the collections. Prada's white dresses with black lines and red dots could be Geometry. What were those excrescences on Rei Kawakubo's clothes, if not Biology? The Dutch designers Viktor and Rolf had made a suit that looked exactly like a cell in the process of dividing itself. More Biology!

"What if we did Science?" I asked at my conference table. There was a dead silence.

Francis, the man who was so good at writing about nothing, hissed, "That's the worst idea I've ever heard, and if you go ahead with it, I'm quitting."

Francis embodied the past; I was on the right track to the future. Why stop at Science? We'd take on Quantum Physics in the pages of *Vogue*.

My scientific knowledge came from poets and mystics. I'd known, since I'd read the Roman Lucretius at fourteen, that the world was made up of only two things, atoms and the void. He'd written that solid objects were accidental agglomerations of atoms, that nothing was stable and all was flux. Now I read *The Dancing Wu Li Masters* by Gary Zukav, a twenty-year-old book about quantum physics that confirmed my view of life. At the subatomic level, Zukav explained, particles were not particles like dust particles but more like tendencies to exist. The trace that an electron leaves on a photographic plate is a track made up of a series of dots that look like snapshots of the progress of a planet, a baseball, or a particle whizzing through space. Quantum mechanics says that these dots are merely records of past interactions, not the flight path of a single electron.

Each particle could be either a wave or a particle until the moment it was observed, when the fact of being observed condemned it to a single identity, that of wave or that of particle. But the other—unobserved—potential spun off into its own existence, unseen, unrecorded. *Vogue* was the observer that defined everything it chose to look at. Reality was what *Vogue* said it was.

I went ahead with Science, and Francis quit to open an antiques shop. Others caught my enthusiasm. Caroline, a young fashion editor, had a degree in advanced mathematics, the photographer Eric Traoré had a degree in physics. A video of the Mandelbrot Fractals set played on a loop on the television in my office.

Delphine and Michael Thompson explained Euclidian geometry with a Prada dress, Archimedes with a model in a bathtub, Isaac Newton's gravity with a model under an apple tree. Marcus and Herb Ritts took on biology: the Viktor and Rolf cell-division suit, a Paco Rabanne dress of iridescent plastic scales to show the first vertebrates, a Ralph Lauren crocodile jacket for the first reptile, a Givenchy dress of parakeet feathers for the first birds, an actual Thierry Mugler couture gorilla suit for the first primates, and a Primavera goddess dress for the advent of Homo sapiens, or, as we liked to think of the species, Pretty Girl. I commissioned Duane Michals to shoot seven principles of quantum physics. Todd Eberle photographed Charles Jencks's quantum garden, a journalist went under Geneva to observe the building of the Large Hadron Collider at CERN that would eventually find the Higgs boson, known as the God particle. We did optical illusions and cloning, and found scientific *raisons d'être* for silver sequins, silver fringes, silver streaks, and silver stars.

I asked the company's administrator François Dieulesaint to get computers for everyone on staff and set them up on the Internet.

"Non," said François.

"The model editor and the fashion editors are constantly on the phone to New York. Everyone needs email."

"If they have computers, they'll be playing solitaire all day long," said François.

"Computers will save us money!" I said.

"Save us money? Marcus had a six-hour conversation from Milan on his *Vogue* cell phone!"

"We all work on our cells."

"It was in the middle of the night, to a number in South Africa. He must have been having phone sex with his South African boyfriend."

"It's none of my business," I said. But every time I looked at Marcus, I thought: Phone sex. Every time I looked at François Dieulesaint, I thought: You're monitoring my calls.

~

Si Newhouse wandered into my office during his annual visit to Paris and mumbled an invitation to edit *Architectural Digest*, at some time in the future. I had no interest in shuffling around photographs of empty rooms, but Si had brought Anna Wintour back from London to edit *House & Garde*n before he gave her American *Vogue*. Did I want American *Vogue*? Could I bend American *Vogue* to ideas about physics? Would it be fun? Did I want to keep watching fashion shows and handing out judgments on luxury products, but for higher stakes? Did I want power? No, no, no, no, no.

Jules was troubled by fleas in the floorboards of his Art Deco apartment.

"Fleas?" I asked Aneeta. "He hasn't got an animal, and it's cleaned twice a week. "

"I've never seen any fleas," she answered in a voice grown weary.

Jules came back to my guest room while the exterminators went in. He went home, found more fleas, and returned to my place while the exterminators tried again, and then again. Finally, they sent me a letter.

"We have exterminated at your father's apartment three times. Upon a fourth visit, we sent the dark specks that your father indicated between the floorboards to a laboratory for examination. They are grains of Nescafé."

The grains of Nescafé would always be fleas to Jules, so he moved to a new apartment behind a green hedge on a street that sloped down to the Seine on the far side of the Place de l'Alma, where he had a balcony and a view of the Eiffel Tower.

He returned the Art Deco standing lamp—"Honey, you know I've always thought Art Deco was shit." I gave him an armchair and a settee. Aneeta toiled to assemble bookcases from Ikea. Painters were summoned; the estimate was high.

"Why do they have to do so many coats?" I asked Aneeta.

"He says his office in London was Napoleon green, that's what he wants," she said.

The living room came out the darkest olive green; Aneeta pointed out the whisper of teal in the glazing. The *bouillotte* lamp that had been mine was his again; its ormolu shone like gold against the Napoleon green.

Soon, documentary makers and film historians began to come to Paris to interview him about how he'd shot *The Battle of San Pietro.* They'd watch the video, he'd say, "See, men walking left to right—staged, to show where they will be in the next shot. See, men walking right to left up the mountain—to establish where they will be when the artillery fire goes off."

"You can't capture reality," he'd say. "You have to shape it."

~

We titled the Quantum Christmas issue "Archives of the Future." It was bold, strange, and much written about, though with some perplexity. Paulino reported that the scientific community applauded our achievement, but the fashion world did not. A *Wall Street Journal* reporter asked if I spent a lot of time with designers, and I carelessly answered, "I don't have dinner with those people." "Those people" felt dismissed, even the ones with whom I regularly ate dinner. Before Christmas, my conference table, usually a garden of thanks, held only five small bouquets. Not enough presents came in to distribute to the staff, but I'd had a star named for each of them, and handed out the star certificates at my party at home, which that year felt a little sour.

"You have to stop showing off," said Gardner, who hated the Quantum issue. "And you should never have given that interview to the *Wall Street Journal*." I thought she was being jealous, but began to wonder if the spell that quantum matters exerted on me was perhaps evidence of a maniacal hubris, if I were perhaps as mad as my father.

~

Circulation had almost doubled, ads were coming in, the magazine was making money. I'd closed my eyes to the possibility of the *New Yorker*,

I didn't want *Architectural Digest* as a springboard to American *Vogue,* I'd chosen Paris, and now I had to do that thing called making a life. Paris *Vogue* had been my substance for five years; the transient men, the philosopher, Bertie, the passing visits from Ivan, none of that was real. When a man advanced on my apartment and attached himself to my days and nights, I let it happen.

Joe was the political journalist who looked like a teddy bear. He drank too much, but he listened to my father; he knew about his *O.S.S.* TV series, and wanted Jules to know that his college roommate had been the son of the founder of the CIA. He introduced me to people from "the Agency," spies or former spies who ran their hands along the underside of restaurant tables to check for bugs before they sat down, a gesture I found thrilling.

Very quickly he moved in a toothbrush, a change of shirt, a dinner jacket for a party. Then came books and overnight bags filled with papers. I was invaded by a bon-vivant teddy bear. There was no sex, which was a relief. He drank himself to sleep each night, washed down his pills with rum, and snored so loudly that the apartment shook as I lay sleepless, but he loved my life so much that I could love it, too. He loved my status, the glamour, the openings, the dinners, the beauty of the models. He insisted I take advantage of every opportunity, and made sure that Eric Rothschild invited us to Lafite, where he knelt at the foot of a vine. Then Alain Dominique Perrin of Cartier flew us to his château near Cahors. Joe planned weekends in London and Vienna, and came with me to New York. I was as busy as a real human, and worn out.

As for sex, like a bored Parisian wife, I spent a few hours now and then with men I'd known before, in the privacy of good hotel rooms, where I acted out the photographs I'd banned from *Vogue.*

I hadn't bicycled through Versailles in more than a year, the Pilates instructor no longer came in the morning, I forgot to meditate. Without silence, without solitude, without discipline, I lost myself on the surface of things.

Joe wore a nautical cap to the Sunday lunches with Jules, who no longer wanted to go the Bristol or the Ritz; we ate at a Lebanese restaurant where Joe expertly ordered the *mezze* he knew from Beirut. Jules called him "the captain," but he would never look directly at him, and kept the lunches short.

When Allegra visited us, she found Joe's false notes interesting; a month later, Anjelica came to stay, hated Joe on sight, and lay in the guest room counting his snores. I could tell she thought he was grotesque, and because I did, too, I turned defensive and starchy. We floundered in frosty small talk. When we parted, it was for two years of silent ice.

At the office, Franceline said, "We're all so relieved you have a man in your life." Gardner and her husband liked him. I couldn't get him out of my apartment.

~

Paris *Vogue* was copied and obeyed. The Art issue had told designers they were artists, now the Quantum issue told them they were mad scientists. *Le shopping* filled up with dresses shaped like beakers, made of thrice-boiled wool, hung with schizophrenic spiderwebs or linen origami squares the size of dinner napkins. Chemistry was applied to fabric to make wrinkled tops that sprang from the fist and crinkled across the body like lichen. A Martin Margiela evening gown was a black-and-white photo of a sequined dress printed onto a cotton panel, hanging to the floor from a T-shirt. Portly lady architects and fashion editors wore pleated Japanese polyester that opened like fans at their hips, and the sexiest garment was a tight nylon scrim that rubbed the nipples raw. Parisian ladies, cloaked from shoulder to knee in shawls made of silk and cashmere, looked like tarpaulins in shop windows during a change of display.

The Quantum issue had decreed indeterminacy, and indeterminacy it was. Doubt was a sensible reaction to world events, but not a rousing rallying cry. Fashion lost its forward thrust, died, and turned into loose scatterings of separate things.

The survivors were leather goods: handbags, safely self-contained entities, candy, instant advertising for any brand. Bags were as easy to market as perfume: no one had to fit into them. There was no limit to the potential clientele base for handbags, which were now called It Bags. The editors of the many international *Vogues* compared their It Bags at fashion parties, handed them around, stroked them like kittens. A beaded baguette, an eel-skin clutch, a miniaturized Chanel.

Bags began to take the place of clothes. The heavy handbag twills woven with the initials of Dior, Vuitton, and Gucci were made into unwieldy jackets and coats. Burberry used the instantly recognizable plaid from the lining of their trench coats for shirts and dresses, skirts and scarves. We photographed the monogrammed creations and titled the story "Logomania." Standing at an airport baggage claim in my brand-new Louis Vuitton raincoat, I watched piles of Louis Vuitton suitcases circle around the carousel and wondered why I'd chosen to look like luggage.

~

Tina Brown called to tell me I was the "Queen of Paris." "You know that's bullshit," I said. She wanted to send a writer to interview me for her magazine, *Talk*, at the end of August. "Paris is empty at the end of August," I said. Then I gave in. Joe was excited.

At a loss for local spectacle, I took the journalist to Joe's favorite restaurant, a den of pimps and arms dealers; he arrived dramatically carrying the door to his car hooked over his shoulder. "Little traffic accident, *rien de grave*," he said, and handed the door to the waiter as if it were a winter coat.

Jean-Baptiste Mondino took the pictures for the story. My wrists heavy with borrowed ruby and sapphire bracelets, I posed wearing a plain gray T-shirt to prove that accessories had taken the place of fashion, holding my satin-shod foot in my hand to prove how limber I was.

Joe was not mentioned in the piece. Karl was quoted saying that I looked tough, but I was in fact very fragile. "Fragile" is not a good word. Despite the lack of any evidence, *Talk* magazine called me the Queen of Paris.

"You should never have done that interview," said Graydon Carter, editor at *Vanity Fair*. "Don't you know Condé Nast hates Tina?"

~

A luminous display on the Eiffel Tower counted down the days to the year 2000. A Ferris wheel went up in the Tuileries and glowed like a target behind the Place de la Concorde obelisk at night. Between the trees wrapped with lights along the Champs-Élysées rose twenty-one smaller Ferris wheels. We bought flashlights and candles and took cash out of the bank in case Y2K was a real thing. On Christmas Day, while I was playing charades with Aneeta, her family, my father, Alexis, and Joe, a hurricane came through Paris at a hundred miles an hour, pulled the awnings off façades and the façades off buildings; out in the fields around Versailles, it blew down ten thousand trees.

Barbara Walters asked me to be a presenter of the Paris New Year's Eve celebrations on ABC; I said I had to take my father to the country. We went down to Joe's house in the south, at Gordes, where the stone houses were built like beehives.

Dad talked for thirty hours straight. The snatches I heard almost drove me mad.

"I told Zanuck you can't cast Jodie Foster. She has a face like a ferret!"

"Zanuck died before Jodie Foster was born, Dad."

"What's the difference?" asked Joe, on his third bottle of wine.

There were black truffles on sale at the outdoor market; I decided to attempt a New Year's Eve dish I'd eaten at Hélène's. I interleaved sliced potatoes with sliced truffles inside a baking dish and put them in the oven. They emerged burned, yet somehow still raw. I rescued some truffle slices, and made a bad omelet. As Dad and Joe sat stupefied before the millennial fireworks on television, I went out into the cold garden, and wished I were in makeup under hot studio lights, talking about fireworks on network television.

~

The invitation to the costume ball said "*Un Conte d'hiver*, A Winter's Tale." It was to be held in January at the Hôtel Lambert, the mysterious Rothschild mansion on the eastern point of the Île Saint-Louis, in celebration of the marriage of Violaine Binet's sister Sandrine to Philippe de Nicolay, the son of the late Marie-Hélène de Rothschild.

Marie Hélène de Rothschild's ball at Ferrières in 1971 was still talked about as an unmatched night when society and movie stars, costumed as characters from Proust's *À la recherche du temps perdu*, had ignited the ultimate constellation of elegant glamour. I'd admired the photos of barons, debutantes, and Burtons dancing into history with feather fans; I'd longed to go to such a ball, and now the invitation was in my hand. Joe was even more excited than I was.

A Winter's Tale. I told Joe, somewhat cruelly, that he had to go as the bear that chases Autolycus off the stage in Shakespeare's play; I'd go as the embodiment of Winter. Karl loaned me a couture ball gown of pale chiffon with an overlay of silver. I hired a white wig to accentuate the wintry aspect of the costume, and found a pair of evening heels in a suede that looked like hoarfrost on rose petals.

The bear suit was too grotesque for Joe, but he gamely said he'd make his entrance wearing the bear head over his tuxedo. I hired an SUV for the evening, and off we went to the Hôtel Lambert on the Île Saint-Louis. Voltaire had lived there with his mistress, the marquise du Châtelet, and called it "a palace fit for a philosopher king."

Snow fell over the courtyard of the Hôtel Lambert, and only there, a private snowfall for the ball. I wrapped a misty tulle shawl around my shoulders and set my frosted rose petal slippers on a carpet laid across the flagstones. Joe put on the bear head and followed me between the tubs of orange trees. The bride and groom greeted guests between blazing torches at the door. Pearl necklaces fell to her waist over a dress of stiff gold and red brocade, around her neck rose a half-moon ruff as bright as a fallen halo, and on her head was a diamond diadem topped with a star. The groom, in a doublet of crossed blue ribbons, puffed shorts, a cape, and a velvet cap, looked like a jester.

The steps were so thick that the Hôtel Lambert seemed to be made of children's building blocks. Inside, in the crush of barons, bankers, and ladies brocaded into costume, I glimpsed tapestries of ornate processions, banquettes of garnet velvet thick with faded gold braid, framed enamel pictures rising around cabinets inlaid with ivory and gems, walls of incised Córdoba leather, each object from the sixteenth century, the seventeenth century, no later.

Joe removed the bear head and took off after the bankers. I made my way up the stairs, and stopped at the little studio *Vogue* had improvised so that Kate Barry could take portraits of the costumed guests; I sat at a table in the Galerie d'Hercule under the ceiling by Charles Le Brun and rested my feet on a chair. I'd arrived, but not really. I sat with *Vogue*'s society editor Emmanuel de Brantes, who'd chosen to come as a Napoleonic general instead of a character from Shakespeare. I was as little in the play as he was, in my pale pink chiffon and tulle, my wig from the wrong century.

I looked at the women in black with stiff white ruffs around their necks and pointed velvet caps outlined in pearls, the girls in décolletés edged in fur with pearls wound in the braids around their heads. I saw emerald pendants, young throats left bare, old wrists bound with bracelets. The men wore lace collars tumbling over velvet and sashes, wrinkled linen shirts the color of tea, their waists wound round with fringed silk above their breeches. Many men in velvet caps with feathers, and often with a single earring, like favorites at the court of Henri de Navarre. "Don't you dare take my photo," hissed one banker in a pink velvet cap, a double pearl hanging from one lobe.

I'd seen this scene before, these close rooms, these thick flagstones, these earrings, these ruffs, these damasks, batistes, velvets. Apart from the groom's jester suit, every costume was a shade of red—garnet, ruby, blood. As if the entire ball had been costumed by one person, intent on telling a story.

"It all looks rather art-directed," I told Emmanuel de Brantes.

"Everyone hired from the same place," he said. "They're all in costumes from *La reine Margot*."

The last film I'd seen at Cannes before I went to Paris to take up the job, Patrice Chéreau's film about the Saint Bartholomew's Day Massacre. My first Rothschild ball was costumed as a bloodbath.

CHAPTER TWENTY

One winter day as my father and I stood on his street, he was exceptionally clear. "Sometimes I can't remember," he said. "Everything is normal, and then I don't know what I was thinking anymore. Like a great blank just flew over me and settled there."

I hugged him tight, patted his new gray cashmere scarf.

"You'll be okay," I said. "Look how great you look! Let's go have lunch with Joe now."

"No," he said.

"No?"

"Do me a favor, honey," he said. "Go for someone you really like. Do it for me, please."

~

It was 2000 at last, and now each *Vogue* had to start its own website, and do it by March. Gardner and François Dieulesaint convened a focus group so strangers could tell us who we were. I stood behind a two-way mirror to watch eight civilized French women, aged twenty-five to fifty, well dressed and recently coiffed, sitting in a room with piles of our *Vogue*.

Once the moderator had closed the door on them, each woman pounced on the piles of *Vogue*s, grabbed as many as she could, retreated to a safe spot, and set to devouring them as if her eyes were teeth.

I watched as they turned the pages, and caught the exact moment when each one fell into a trance under the spell of *Vogue* and burrowed into a private world, as if the magazine were a drug. I realized I was making a drug.

At the next annual conference of International Condé Nast editors at the Cipriani in Venice, I gave a passionate speech explaining that I'd understood the truth about *Vogue* from watching a focus group.

"*Vogue* is a potent drug that women get lost in. We are making more than magazines, we are making the most addictive substance there is—the dream. There's a huge responsibility in making dreams."

At the lunch, some of the Condé Nast people looked at me oddly. I calmly broke open my phial of seawater, poured it into a glass, and slugged it down.

Jonathan found a present for Jules in a Venetian antiques shop, and handed me a fine wooden cane with a T-shaped handle, wrapped in marbleized paper. "I hope he likes it," he said.

~

Gardner wanted Condé Nast to extend into custom publishing by producing the Air France women's magazine. We pitched my ideas to the head of Air France, and in the early months of 2000, while building the website, I also became the *directeur de la rédaction* of *Air France Madame.*

I stole the web editor from *Elle,* Tina Isaac, hired a journalist named Isabelle Lefort to edit *Air France Madame,* and we set up their offices on a street next to us, the Rue d'Aguesseau. The website could trick out Paris *Vogue* into endless visuals, and, I hoped, show the clothes we'd called in that hadn't made it into the magazine. *Air France Madame* had a page devoted to ways of fighting off jet lag in every issue. Its first cover showed a travel-weary model in a raincoat, sitting with her bare feet in a bowl of water.

Stiff-legged as a stork in my heels and new suits, I crossed the Rue d'Aguesseau six, eight times a day to work with Tina and the website programmers, with Isabelle and her staff, inventing new ways to show things.

To Jules, airlines were as solid and reliable as watchmakers, and he was unreasonably proud of my new connection to Air France.

"Aneeta has been working up some ideas for you," he said. "Please come take a look." In his living room, Aneeta gave a little cough and handed me a deep pile of typed menus.

"I don't have that many dinners coming up," I said, looking through them.

"It's for Air France," said Aneeta.

I looked over at Jules.

"Oh for God's sake, honey, you've taken over Air France, and Aneeta's going to be the executive chef. You know that."

I looked back at Aneeta.

"He said you were going to put me in charge of all the Air France catering," she said, reddening.

"I'm only doing the magazine," I said, "sorry."

~

Sleep deprived from Joe's snores, I worked seven days a week, ate too much and then too little. I drank the seawater. My skin began to itch, and I scratched at my arms, my neck, my legs.

Fashion was still dead. Marcus von Ackermann shot his pages at new resorts in exotic locations, and brought back photos of models wearing palazzo pants in hotel lobbies, their hair as big as bundles of wet sheets. He said he was aiming for the look of the photos Henry Clarke had taken for Diana Vreeland's *Vogue*.

"Well, you missed," I said.

I needed someone better in the fashion department.

"You can't get rid of Marcus. It'll look bad," said Gardner.

"*Vogue* is looking bad, I have to get rid of him. And he still hasn't learned French."

Carine invited me to lunch at her apartment and served me beluga caviar. She spoke in a high, thin pitch, without emphasis, as if reciting words she'd learned by heart, to announce she wasn't going to work for the magazine anymore. She wanted to do other things, maybe work with Jean Paul Gaultier. God, you're a bad actress, I thought. I came out onto the great empty Esplanade des Invalides and wondered how I could mend this.

Mario Testino invited me to lunch to tell me he couldn't be seen in Paris *Vogue* in the company of second-rate photographers. Who was this Taryn Simon? he asked. Who was Tim Walker? He would concentrate on American *Vogue* instead. "You don't know what it is to be an artist," he said.

Over *poireaux vinaigrette* at Tante Louise, Jean-Baptiste Mondino declared, "I'm not working for *Vogue* anymore unless you fire Donald Schneider."

"Don't give me orders," I shot back. "Donald stays."

The magazine shed more editors, more photographers. I was an inventor, not a manager; I didn't know how to coddle people's hopes or manage their ambitions. I only knew how to get a willing crew to make fun things. I'd carried *Vogue* through on my own energy; and now my energy was gone.

Nonetheless, I was given a new long-term contract that would keep me with *Vogue* forever and make me secure for life. I signed, feeling I was being entombed. Was I only in it now for the money, the expenses, the dress allowance, the discounts? But how else could I take care of Dad?

"Let's have lunch, just you and me, on Sunday," Dad said. "You're not happy, and I don't like it." But I couldn't that Sunday, and the next Sunday I was away.

I tried to turf Joe out of my apartment, so I could at least get some sleep, but once again I failed.

~

Jonathan loved games, particularly the Portobello Trust quiz night, which happened every two years. I went to London with Joe, who headed straight for the bar.

Jonathan introduced me to his friend whom I will call Harry Stein. I felt I knew him already.

There was something of an arrogant animal about him, that familiar look, seedy and polished, of a media figure from the 1960s. His pale linen jacket was slightly stained, his blue shirt strained over a belly that had grown since some haberdasher had made it for him, because, stained and rumpled as he was, he looked rich. His hair was cut priestly short, his glasses had thick frames, his mouth was wide. I was attracted to the confident and irritable atoms that spun off him, I recognized something I wanted. He was a London American, and divorced.

"Harry's my best friend," said Jonathan.

"No, my best friend's Gilbert," said Harry. The petulance was interesting, the put-down bold. No automatic reciprocity here; the man had no time for a linear scenario. Who was Gilbert?

"You bankers stick together," said Jonathan. "It's a different mindset."

Banker. Red flag.

"I'm not really a banker," said Harry.

I smiled.

"I'm a catalyst," he added. "That's why the bank keeps me on. Even though I'm crazy."

That's honest. And crazy, what's crazy? Don't people say I'm crazy, just because I'm enthusiastic? The Quantum *Vogue* was a bit of a leap, but wasn't it fun?

He sat on my right at dinner and refused the wine. Like me, he drank only water. Joe was already incoherent with drink.

"When I was growing up in Ireland . . ." Harry began.

"That's my line," I said.

"It's mine," he said firmly, "always has been."

"I grew up in County Galway," I said, stretching the truth.

"So did I," he said.

"What do you mean by 'County Galway'?"

"Near Loughrea," he said. "What do you mean by 'County Galway?' "

"Near Loughrea, between Loughrea and Craughwell."

"That's impossible," he said. "That's John Huston's house."

"That's the house. He was my godfather. I grew up with Anjelica and Tony at St. Clerans." How I loved saying that name, St. Clerans, to someone who knew it.

"Where were you?" I asked.

"Five miles up the road from you." I remembered talk of the rich American family with children older than us, a German name. Stein.

"You're one of those Steins from up the road that I never met!"

"I was older than all of you. I already had a life."

"You knew St. Clerans. You knew Ricki."

"I remember Ricki," he said.

The exchange felt like a homecoming.

The quiz was beginning. Jonathan said, "Pay attention." I got to work. Joe, well past his whiskies into his wine, was no help. Our team was ahead, and then we weren't, and then we lost.

A small, pale man came to the table with a blond, slightly cross-looking wife. He exuded neatness, caution. He had to be the other banker.

"This is Gilbert, my best friend," said Harry, "and this is Janet, his wife."

Jonathan summoned the waiters to bring more chairs.

Gilbert's impassive face took in what was going on. I realized how close I'd pulled my chair to Harry. I felt unstoppable. The jacket I wore was half a couture suit from the days when couture showed off a woman. I wanted him to see the shape of my body, my waist. My card was already in my hand when Harry asked for my email.

I went back to Paris and tried, once again unsuccessfully, to get Joe to move out.

A producer called from the *Charlie Rose* show; Charlie was coming over in two weeks, Charlie was doing a Paris special with the *New York Times* correspondent and a French architect who'd won the Pritzker prize. Would I be on the show, and have dinner with Charlie afterward? Of course, I said.

I didn't tell Joe. In my mind, he was out.

Ten days later, Joe found out about Charlie Rose, both the show and the dinner, and insisted I had to include him; he had important things to tell Charlie.

"No," I said.

"How can you do this to me?" asked Joe.

"I'm doing it," I said. "It's no."

That was all it took to move him out. Joe's currency was connections. All I had to do to make him leave was withhold one big name.

~

Before the show, Charlie Rose asked me what I was going to do after Paris *Vogue*. The question was part of his formula, but it stuck with me. I didn't have an answer.

Vogue's fashion pages had turned brown and sad. More fashion editors had scattered in the wake of Carine, leaving only juniors and freelancers. Delphine barely talked to me, furious at the time I spent with the website and *Air France Madame*. No photographers wanted to work with Marcus, so the warhorse jewelry editor Franceline had to do most of the sittings. The underlying Parisian entropy had engulfed us. I had discreet meetings with fashion editors from other magazines, but not one wanted to work with Marcus.

A male fashion editor, Xavier, insisted I see him; he announced I had to hire him to replace Marcus. I didn't want Xavier, who struck me as a gossip and a fantasist. "That's not possible," I said. "No."

I took a long weekend in London, ostensibly to see my friend Valerie and read the Sunday papers in bed at the Pelham hotel. I let Harry know I'd be there. We had things to talk about. And he didn't drink.

The hotel receptionist mistook Harry for a minicab driver. He handed me two books by W. G. Sebald, and drove us to an East London restaurant that specialized in arcane organ meats, and there he tackled a plate of tripe while I nibbled on roasted pig's skin.

"How is it?" he asked.

"Not as good as pig's ears," I said. "Ever tried those?"

He was an eccentric, but that meant he could play. We talked about London, his London, north of the park, mine, in a small circle around Belgravia. The old days, his and mine. Groom Place. Chester Street. "Have you ever been back there?" he asked. I hadn't.

He had none of the cautious rigidity of a banker, but there was that thing I'd seen at the Quiz Night, the know-it-all glow of a polymath who could talk about anything and never lose the thread. The charisma of real stars, an implacable self-regard.

I thought I was keeping my distance, assessing him, but I was falling. On the Eurostar I looked at photos of Harry's apartment in *World of Interiors.* The pulls on his dressing room closets were casts of his children's hands, so he had a heart and was perhaps even sentimental. Along the top of the bookcases in his living room ran a line of life-sized rubber rats. You had to grow up in Ireland to have that crazy practical-joke irreverence. He appreciated the startling image, the skewed perspective. He's like me and Anjelica, I thought. Ricki would have liked him. He's got the wild imagination I need, but he's stable, he's a banker. An American in London, and five miles up the road from St. Clerans. Practically family.

We spoke every day, emailed; he sent me photos of him missing me.

And then he came to Paris. The first kiss was at the Place de la Concorde; his mouth tasted of cigars, mine probably of cigarettes.

We set off up the garden part of the Champs-Élysées, along the dusty walks where I'd rolled my wooden hoop. He walked beside me, kicking up small clouds of the fine sand. He had something to tell me. His mouth was so dry that the words stuck together.

"I don't drink, I don't do drugs anymore. Once, when I was at a low point, I took the Minnesota Multiphasic Personality Inventory test." As we walked, he explained that this was the test used to diagnose a number of conditions, ranging from anxiety and paranoia to schizophrenia and manic depression.

"My father is a manic-depressive!" I exclaimed, delighted. "All the best people are manic-depressives!"

If he were too, I could deal with it. I knew what to do for Dad—make sure he had three meals a day and got his sleep. Lithium in the right dosage, Haldol for the episodes.

We spent the rest of the day in bed. There was no problem there.

Later he declared my CD player lame: "Bose, no highs, no lows"—how manic-depressive that sounded—and bought me a better one.

Everything had come together. There was going to be a fairy-tale ending.

He went back to London, and I went to my father's apartment to give him the good news.

"I've met someone, a friend of Jonathan's, who grew up near St. Clerans. He's a banker and he's called Harry Stein."

"Stein, he has to be Jewish," my father said.

"He is."

"Oh honey," said Dad, "I'm so glad."

~

I introduced them the next time Harry came to Paris, on a Sunday, at the bar of the Bristol. Harry strode in, imposing but casual in his cobalt blue shirt, his wrinkled linen jacket, his black jeans. Jules, impeccable in his blazer with the real gold buttons that you'd only know were real if you saw the stamp in the back, sat in the bergère, relaxed, regal, at home. He owned Paris. He owned me.

They talked about photographs. Cartier-Bresson, the Maison Européenne de la Photographie, the photographs that Harry collected. Harry was letting my father know who he was, what he could afford, and that he would take care of me.

Harry paid for lunch and went to the men's room.

"He's tall," said my father with appreciation, and then, "He's a true gent."

He wanted to bring Harry back to his apartment, where his box of photos from the war was waiting to be opened. Harry deflected him with: "I want to come back when it's just you and me, and I can have a real look at them."

"I like a man who takes his time," said Jules.

Harry went once more to the bathroom; my father turned to me and said, "At last. This is the man for you. I'm so relieved."

"It's only just begun," I said. "Whoa."

But if this was real, I wouldn't have to edit *Vogue* for the rest of my life.

He set about improving my life with decisive speed and the rationale of a banker. The Paris real-estate market was heating up, he said, I had to own something here, at the very least as an investment. He'd persuade Jonathan to give me the special loan that Condé Nast gave its top editors. No man had stepped into my business before. I was uncomfortable to be pushed to be demanding.

"Wise up," Jules said. "Let him take care of you."

Between phone calls and visits to Paris to see me, Harry sent me drafts of a letter for Jonathan asking for an apartment. I put them together, rewrote them a little, took a deep breath, and posted it in an envelope. The thrust and speed of decisive action made me nervous; I felt like Nana in the convertible, looking over the precipice and screaming at my father to drive slower.

Jonathan answered that he was not opposed to the idea. I began looking at apartments.

The haute couture once again washed over us, *défilés,* cocktails, dinners, movie stars fanning themselves with paper fans that had been set out on each gold chair. The theme of Galliano's collection for Dior was Wedding and entirely shown on couples, models marching down the runway in pairs, boy-girl, boy-girl, boy-girl.

I told Gardner the Christmas issue's theme would be Theater.

"Theater?" she snarled.

"Spectacle, show, costume, disguise, illusion, you know—theater!" I said.

Harry came to Paris to see me every week, and each time he felt more solid. He showed no interest in models or fashion shows, so it had to be me he wanted, not my world.

"Do you close the magazine in August?" he asked.

"For three weeks," I said.

"You're spending them with me. That's when I go to New York—there's no one there in the middle of August, so it's at its best. You'll join me at the Carlyle; I keep a suite."

I said I'd like to go to New Mexico to see Allegra in Taos, and watch her dance in a charity marathon with her boyfriend, a river rafter named Cisco Guevara.

"Great!" said Harry. "Let's do that as well. We'll drive through the desert in a white convertible."

He added, "At the end of August, you're coming with me to stay with Gilbert and Janet in Provence. You met them at the quiz. He built himself a seventeenth-century mansion from scratch in a valley full of lavender. It's his life's work. It's the only place on earth I'm happy, and I want you to be there with me."

I wouldn't be locked up somewhere with my father, I wouldn't be enduring restorative treatments in the spa in northern Italy, I'd take off for America with my brilliant banker, drive through the desert in a convertible, and finish in a valley full of lavender to share the only place on earth he was happy.

Aneeta was staying in Paris for August; I hired a young Polish girl, Johanna, to relieve her, rented a room for Johanna above Jules's flat, and rented a bank vault to keep the Cubist still life safe from thieves.

I convinced Jules that he didn't have to write Harry a note to thank him for taking me on holiday.

"I just want him to know how happy I am," said Dad. "If only your mother was alive to see this. Americans are more solid in London than Americans in Paris. Look at us."

"Paris hasn't been so bad for us this time," I said.

"When are you marrying Harry?" he asked. "Don't marry him in America. I want to be there to see it. This is the man I've been waiting for."

"Stop, it's too soon," I said.

"If you're going to New Mexico to see Allegra, do you think you could stop by Los Angeles? You could go into Beverly Loan and pick up the Rolex. I'd like to have it back now."

"What's another plane ride?" I said. "Of course. You should have your Rolex."

~

A chartered Air France Concorde taking German tourists to New York caught fire on takeoff and crashed near Charles de Gaulle Airport. Gardner was landing in another Concorde, and saw everything from her window seat. She sounded shaky on the phone that night.

But when she called me into her office the next day, she was imperious and angry. François Dieulesaint stood next to her, arms crossed, her witness.

"How could you do that?" she shouted. "Are you out of your mind? Why did you offer Marcus's job to that man Xavier?"

"I didn't offer Marcus's job to anyone!" I said, but she had her bone, the crime I had committed, and she would not let it go. I called Xavier, put the phone on the speaker, and asked him if I'd offered him Marcus's job.

"I wish you had," said his voice on the speakerphone.

"But did I?"

"I went to a dinner with friends after our meeting, and I told them that you did."

"But you know I didn't!"

"I wanted it to be true, so I said it. That's how much I want to work with you."

I hung up and looked at Gardner. Her lips were pursed. François Dieulesaint stood impervious as a bollard. She was the boss.

"You are going to call Jonathan right now to explain what you did," she said, cold.

I felt my blood speed up as I called Jonathan.

He believed me. "Have you found an apartment yet?" he asked at the end of our conversation.

"Not yet," I said, "but thank you."

I hung up.

"What was that about 'not yet'?" Gardner asked.

"I'm buying an apartment," I said, recklessly. "I haven't found one yet."

Her face contracted around a blue green rage. White face, cigarette in hand, sapphires winking on her neck, she screamed, "Don't you dare ever do that again!"

"Dare do what?" I said, and I let my own rage rip. "You accuse me of something I haven't done, you refuse to believe the evidence, you're still staring at me like I took a shit on the carpet!"

I didn't care that she'd seen one Concorde blow up in front of her as she was landing in another. I didn't care she'd had a fireball in her eyes at 4:20 the day before. I wanted to throw another one at her right now, and annihilate her. I had a better life waiting for me.

"You just heard the guy tell the truth, and all you want is the lie. It's as if"—I cast around the office for some sin I could lay on her, I saw the heavy sapphire choker around her neck, caught François Dieulesaint's eye, and went on—"as if I were accusing you of taking kickbacks from the jewelry companies in the Place Vendôme! How would you like that? It's just as absurd! How would you feel if I believed that? How would you feel if I told Jonathan that?"

Her contracted face went smooth with fear. I seemed to have scored a bull's-eye.

"Right! See what it feels like to be accused?" I shouted, adding, "You can go to hell!" and left, slamming the door.

I'd shouted before, but never as loud. The electricity still crackling inside me, I walked down the long hallway to my office. I had a protector now, a man of substance, the chairman's best friend, and I was meeting him in a few days in New York.

CHAPTER TWENTY-ONE

Harry met me at JFK carrying a black rubber rat just like the ones running along the top of his bookcases. "I buy all my rubber rats in New York," he said, handing me my rat wrapped in a wet hotel towel, "and instead of flowers, I'm having a girl come in to set up a Fu garden on the coffee table for you."

His mouth tasted of cigar. He'd been in New York a week, doing, he said, not much. His rooms were dusty. "I hate the maids here, I never let them in," he said at the door to his suite.

My suitcases choked the bedroom. I'd brought far too many dresses from the Prada fall collection, crepe-de-chine afternoon gowns in which to sparkle like Carole Lombard.

I unpacked the $900 white satin nightgown I'd bought from Sabbia Rosa, an insane indulgence, but our hours in bed deserved the best, and if it tore, that would be an offering to love.

We did not make love that night.

His New York routine was set: breakfast in the dining room at the Carlyle, midmorning Frappuccinos at Starbucks, dinner at the Post House next to the Lowell Hotel. He took me to the place he bought his rats, a joke store on Park Avenue South, where he found a pair of rubber snakes and decided we'd send them to Jonathan and Ronnie at their holiday address in Spain.

"Will they get the joke?" I asked.

"Of course they will. Spain's full of snakes!" he said.

The white satin nightgown lay untouched in its tissue paper. Harry sat on the bed next to me, turned my face in his hands, and said my features would age well. With my face between his hands, I could imagine I had a great many years ahead of me in which to age well. I could forget I would soon be fifty-two.

He would meet me in Taos, he said, and it would all be so beautiful.

I was patient. He was older than me, closer to sixty. It had to be tough up there.

I went alone to Los Angeles to retrieve Dad's Rolex from Beverly Loan; as pawnshops go, it was a nice one, like a small department store for jewelry and cameras. I flew to New Mexico, where Allegra was waiting for me by a hut in a pasture in front of Taos Mountain, smiling, straight-backed in a blue dress. She seemed to own the town, the mountain, the sky. "You'll be the mayor of Taos in no time," I told her. I'd come to consider power a natural attribute, and I could imagine no other reason to live in such a remote place.

She installed me in a bed-and-breakfast she'd chosen, and went home to Cisco, her river rafter. I waited in the garden of the bed-and-breakfast as Harry missed one plane and then another, and another. "It's hell to get to Taos," he said on the phone. Allegra took me to buy shell ankle bracelets made by Pueblo Indians for their dances. In her house, she gave me three blue vases shaped like teardrops that had been Ricki's.

Harry drove up in a white convertible, two days late. The angry busyness I had found so attractive in London was still there, exacerbated by the exhaustion of the trip. He needed a nap.

At the restaurant where we dined with Allegra and Cisco, Harry snorted when the waitress said they didn't have the license to make a margarita, and turned angry when she said he couldn't smoke indoors.

"He's a tad moody. I'm sorry," I said to Allegra.

"I thought you said he didn't drink," she said.

The next morning, Harry and I walked through Taos Plaza, past adobe walls, houses as solid as the earth. Harry's head swiveled until he spotted what he was looking for, and dragged me down an alley and into a bar.

"Just one margarita, to get it out of my system," he said. "Like having a Starbucks in New York."

"But it's ten thirty in the morning," I said, "and you said you didn't drink."

"It doesn't matter what time I have it. You can't be in New Mexico and not have a margarita."

After the margarita, he needed a nap. He napped before lunch, he napped after lunch; he napped the next day while I went riding on Pueblo land with Allegra and Cisco. He napped before dinner, and after dinner he snored. He apologized for being so tired. He was a little low, he said. He hugged me. He was happy to be with me in New Mexico. But just wait for Provence, he'd be happy there, we'd be happy there.

We watched Allegra and Cisco dance the western two-step marathon amid a throng of dancers primed to dance until dawn, the way people danced during the Depression. Allegra shook the hem of her flounced skirt, Cisco danced with his hat on.

Tony Huston materialized in fringed buckskins, rolling extra syllables into every word. He had a talk with Harry, Galway son to Galway son. "I remember your father. He collected paperweights," said Tony.

"It's a famous collection," Harry said.

We left the dancers in the middle of the night and drove south to catch a morning plane. As dawn rose, Harry pulled the convertible into the Santa Fe Railyard and parked between locomotives. "You know, the Atchison, Topeka and Santa Fe never stopped in Santa Fe," he said. He knew trains.

I leaned back against a wooden post and watched the sky turn pink, mauve, indigo. The train engines were painted ochre with maroon lettering. This truly is the ass-end of nowhere, I thought. The absolute end of the line, so far that even the line named after it doesn't reach there.

The rooms in the Carlyle were as dusty as they'd been when I left.

A porno cassette popped out of the DVR. This Prince Charming business wasn't working out; it wasn't even charming. A young woman who was the Fu garden expert wiped the dust from the coffee table before she set moss across its glass top, and on the moss, miniature trees, pagodas, and a circle of mirror to represent a lake. "Remarkable," I said to Harry.

I flew to Paris, he flew to London, we'd meet on the plane to Marseille in two days. In my hushed, hot apartment, I carefully set the dancing shell ankle bracelets and Ricki's three vases on my parents' table from San Simeon. The Wild West and Maida Avenue, come to roost at the Rue de Cérisoles. If I stopped to add up the events of the past two weeks, I'd have to come to a conclusion, so I kept busy and went to see Jules.

He didn't look any the worse for having been in Paris without a holiday. He looked, in fact, pretty good. He wanted to know all about the trip. He so wanted the happy ending. I didn't tell him the suite at the Carlyle was covered in dust; I said we'd run into Joan Didion and John Gregory Dunne at breakfast there every day. I didn't tell him how many planes Harry missed on his way to Taos; I told him Allegra was thriving in New Mexico.

"And Harry?" he asked.

"He's a little moody," I said.

"These things take time. Be patient, he's a good man. He's the one, and this trip to Provence"—and here he touched his finger to his nose—"is very important. It's going to change everything. I see a diamond ring. He's going to propose. Yes, I see a diamond ring on your finger."

He took my hand in his. The little hairs on his knuckles were still black. I undid the strap of the watch he was wearing, the plain everyday Juvenia Eterna, and fastened the big gold Rolex with the gold face on his wrist. "And now you have it back," I said.

He held the watch so the crystal caught the light.

"It was in there for ten years," he said. "Thank you."

I packed a small bag for the five days in Provence. The satin of the nightgown glowed through the creased tissue paper, which was still fastened shut with the gold sticker from Sabbia Rosa. I tucked it between my bathing suits. There was no problem between us. He was simply tired all the time.

The next day at noon I joined Harry on the plane to Marseille, and he gave me a loving hug. We landed, were driven along hot winding roads, came to the valley full of lavender, and there was the seventeenth-century manor house, built yesterday. A Cambodian butler waited for us on the steps.

Janet materialized at the bottom of the stairs, a little constrained in a printed dress from Gucci. Despite the millions, the billions of pounds Janet had been born into, despite the wealth of her first husband and the even greater wealth of Gilbert, despite the respect she commanded for her legendary generosity and taste that had almost single-handedly funded the Tate Modern—despite all this, I felt superior to her. Her Gucci dress was from the summer collection, and almost out of date. My Prada dress was from the fall collection. I felt the fashion editor's contempt for her, and also a twinge of tenderness for her vanity, because she had bought it one size too small.

"Welcome!" said Janet.

"Love the dress," I said.

We went up the stone stairs and crossed a landing on floorboards a foot wide, held in place by wooden pegs just visible under the waxed surface.

Janet showed us into a vast bedroom. "I've given you a room of your own as well, Joan, because we all know how Harry is," she said, and opened a door into a second bedroom where I caught a glimpse of bird wallpaper.

She would probably have a lot to tell me about how Harry was, if I asked. My dignity was in pretending that I already knew.

On each bedside table was a small box of chocolates, the top of each chocolate painted with a different number. Harry set his computer on the desk and sat down; I sat on the bed and started with chocolate Number One. Number Three had caramel and sea salt inside; it was sweet, salty, a touch sour, perfectly calibrated.

In the guest bathroom, the box of Q-tips was open and partly used, the shampoo bottles half full. I liked that Janet had not tried to make the guest room into a hotel.

A German art dealer and a blond princess lay on massive white marble daybeds by the swimming pool. The art dealer was sulky, but the princess was genial. Gilbert was in Geneva at a memorial service for a fellow banker, and would arrive in a day or two.

As I slipped into the swimming pool I knew I should be at the spa in northern Italy putting body and mind back together, instead of waiting for things to improve with Harry. This was where he was happy. Give it time, I thought. Your impatience ruins everything. Stay in the fairy tale.

We ate lunch on a flagstone terrace under a grape arbor. Bulls stood in a field that stretched into the distance. Nearer to us was an elaborate maze, a low one, barely three feet high. Harry and Janet gossiped about people I didn't know. I dropped art names with the art dealer, the princess dropped fashion names with me.

Harry went up for a nap; I stayed by the pool and told myself to listen to the crickets, pay attention to the smell of rosemary and lavender rising through the late afternoon. Enjoy the beauty of Provence. You can't have everything, but here, you can have beauty.

Maybe Harry's dark moods would pass. In the room, he turned toward me on the bed and said, "It's nothing to do with you, I'm just very, very tired."

The dazzling conversation he'd launched at me in the first weeks was replaced by silence. After dinner that night, the art dealer, the princess, Harry, and Janet sat down to play cards. I whispered to Harry that I'd be waiting for him, but I left the white satin nightgown in its tissue paper. Harry fell heavily on the bed, threw an arm over me, and began to snore.

The art dealer left the next day, the princess left, two more guests arrived. Adrian was a famous London restaurant critic; his girlfriend Nicola, whom he called "the blonde," bore such a resemblance to Princess Diana that she'd played her in a television miniseries. Janet's two daughters arrived that afternoon, effusive blondes in their early twenties.

"So, are you happy yet?" Janet asked Harry.

"Yes," Harry said. I couldn't see it.

As we got into bed, I said, "I have to leave tomorrow."

"I know I'm being uncommunicative, but it will pass," he said.

I liked the girlfriend role, but it was a one-woman show. Big, clever, charismatic Harry had dissolved.

"I really have to rest up properly before work starts," I said.

"But Gilbert hasn't even arrived!" said Harry. "You'll love him!"

"I have four days before *Vogue* begins again. I should go to my spa."

"You're not fat at all," he said.

"It's not about losing weight, it's about relaxing . . ."

"I thought you said you loved me," he said.

"But I do," I said. I didn't know what I felt.

"Then give me just this. This house gives my whole year meaning. Gilbert will be here tomorrow. He's exceptional. You'll get on so well with him. You're very similar. That's why I like you."

Coaxing, flattery. I said I'd stay.

"There's a good girl," he said, and went to sleep. Timidly, I put my hand over his back, as if he were a manatee of uncertain temper. I'd fled a teddy bear for a manatee that spent most of its days asleep.

We were all out by the pool when Gilbert arrived, small and neat in swimming trunks and tiny goggles. He dove into the pool without noise and swam methodically, such a number of laps that everyone stopped watching. He had been born in Egypt, made his fortune in Geneva; his life was now London. I tried to see what was Egyptian about him. His gestures were precise, disciplined. His body was slim and compact, tanned and freckled.

At lunch, Adrian launched once more into the story he'd been telling about hanky-panky at the last house he and Nicola had stayed in, in Tuscany. He'd worked his material overnight to improve it for Gilbert, raised his tone to a comic disbelief, and there were more details about shirt buttons and spaghetti. Gilbert laughed. Adrian was pleased.

Harry went for a nap; Adrian and the blonde went for a nap; Gilbert and Janet went for a nap. The sisters went shopping. I wandered into the maze in the garden. The hedges only reached to my waist, and the path out was as quick as the path in.

"Your maze is easy," I said to Gilbert at dinner.

"It's the kitchen garden that's complicated," he said. "It's built according to Pythagorean principles."

He set out to explain mathematical correspondences, harmonic principles, and the golden mean. I told him I bicycled in the outer park of Versailles under rigid lines of trees, around the basin shaped like a cross, and asked, "Does Versailles clear my head because of the way it's laid out?"

"Yes, absolutely," he said.

He was reconstituting Montaigne's library book by book, and had Montaigne's own annotated copy, from 1653, of Lucretius's *On the Nature of Things*, one of the books I loved. We talked about Lucretius's theory of atoms and how, in the first century, he'd written that nature had exhausted herself. Something hooked and fastened there; something sparked. Here was an interlocutor, a fellow student, a guide, maybe a teacher. And he was neither spoiled nor insane.

A banker with a soul? I knew there was no such thing. Up the table from me, in one of his thunderstorm blue shirts, was the living evidence.

Gilbert took us to Arles. On the way, he pointed out the stand of cypress trees he had planted on his neighbor's land, to mask the lights from oncoming cars at night.

We stood in the courtyard of the hospital where van Gogh had been interned, and then Gilbert led me down a narrow street into a bookstore, where he handed me a book. "For you," he said. It was a short biography of Le Nôtre, the genius who'd designed the gardens of Versailles. It was called *Portrait d'un homme heureux.*

"Portrait of a happy man," I said. "That's you."

We had lunch on the terrace, under the grape arbor. I sat next to him again.

Gilbert climbed a ladder to cut a bunch of Muscat grapes from overhead; the butler brought a bowl of cold water to rinse them in.

"Montaigne wrote that life should be an end to itself," he said, and handed me a stem of shining grapes.

There were blackberries for dessert, picked wild in the fields. They tasted rich and ripe, particular. Gilbert tried to describe the taste to me, I tried to describe the taste to him, softness with an afterbite. The only thing as good as a blackberry, we agreed, was the dark chocolate with caramel and sea salt in chocolate Number Three.

"Number Three! Yes!" he said.

"The best thing in the world!"

"I have Janet put them out in every room—did you eat yours?"

"I tried them all, but I'm only in love with Number Three," I said.

Harry looked over at us.

"Aren't you glad you stayed?" he said, a little too loudly.

"Oh, she wasn't leaving, was she?" asked Janet.

Adrian and the blonde looked up, alert to trouble. Maybe before the weekend was over, they'd have a better story from this house than the hanky-panky in Tuscany.

I could feel the outlaw urge to change horses, to align myself according to my preference. I was being pulled to someone who fascinated me, adjusting my receptors to capture as much of him as I could, turning like a radar dish to capture, captivate, receive; mirroring and gazing and listening and, yes, it looked like fawning.

"My skin hurts," said Harry as he lay on the bed after lunch. "It hurts all over, so I'll ask you not to touch me right now."

I haven't touched you except for a timid hug last night, I thought, you asshole.

"I just need a little sleep," he said, "a little nap."

I itched to go downstairs to see what Gilbert was doing, but I forced myself to stay next to Harry on the bed, and looked at a book until my eyes closed in the afternoon hum.

I awoke to thickened air and a sense of guilt. I imagined lunches in Paris where Gilbert and I would talk about Lucretius and Montaigne, maybe dinners, maybe more. I thought about being rescued from my life. I thought about being freed from having to pretend to be powerful. I thought about being freed from Paris *Vogue.* I swung my legs over the bed and woke Harry.

"Let's go look at Gilbert's kitchen garden," he said, and added, with a little sneer, drawing out the syllables, "I hear it's Pythagorean."

From ground level, we couldn't see the concentric circles at the core of its magic. Nasturtiums climbed up trellises, small eggplants and gourds were trained on sticks, tomatoes grew apart from the rest. We walked back out to the pool and past the strange marble beds.

"Gilbert has perfect pitch in everything," I said.

"No, he doesn't!" said Harry. "In London he has some perfectly awful pieces of furniture. He made all his money himself, you know"—with a tone of pity in his voice, as if Gilbert had spent years breaking stones on a sunbaked highway—"so maybe all this is because he waited so long to get what he wanted. He only started building this house five years ago. He didn't invest in mistakes, he waited until he knew himself before he committed."

"He lives better than anyone I know," I said, as we walked back toward the house.

"Joan," shouted Gilbert from his balcony, "in the front hall is a paper package. In it are two small boxes of chocolates. One of them is for you."

One of them? I thought. Just one? Small?

"Is it Number Three?" I shouted back.

"Yes!"

"Oh my God! Thank you!"

That night when I changed for dinner I put on real makeup and a long red dress. It was time to show Gilbert I could look good. A hair dryer applied to the hair instead of a twisted scarf, dark powder around the eyes, something on the lips. I looked better than I had in days.

We sat down for drinks on an unfamiliar terrace off the living room.

"You look really nice," said the blonde, resplendent in white. Janet, in a checked dress, looked cross again. She was tending the barbecue grill; we could hear it hiss nearby.

Gilbert came down in a fresh linen shirt, walked past me as if I did not exist, nodded at Adrian and the blonde, smiled at Janet and Harry, and said a few words to the girls.

"I'm going to cook the lobsters!" said Janet, and headed off.

Gilbert sat down with a drink. He gave me a polite nod.

The butler announced dinner.

Everyone rose.

"Where's Joan?" asked Gilbert.

"Right here," said the blonde. "Right there!"

Gilbert's head turned.

"I thought you were someone I didn't know," he said. "A new dinner guest."

Once again I sat on Gilbert's right, and the blonde sat on his left. There were no other guests, just the eight of us.

"I really didn't recognize you, I'm sorry," he said.

"I don't always look like me," I said.

Gilbert ate slowly. After dinner he led us all past the kitchen into another garden, this one his secret garden beyond the kitchen, where stones cut like monoliths were set into thick gravel. He turned up the music full throttle; the sobs of Callas singing *Tosca* floated up to the moon over the white stones. Harry put his hand on my shoulder, human again.

"His office is like this as well," he said. "Space age. *2001*."

Janet put a video of *Reversal of Fortune* into the player after dinner, but no one paid attention to the movie. That's Barbet's movie, I wanted to say, that's Jeremy, those are my friends, pay attention, but the entertainment was just background noise. Adrian and the blonde peeled off first; the older daughter stayed up, waiting for a phone call.

Harry lay on the bed in his shirt, snoring, a thriller open on his belly. I wanted to make as thick a wall as I could between us, without the drama of retreating into the room next door. It was hot, but I put on a toweling robe from the bathroom, tied it tight around me, and curled down to sleep.

There was no moon that night, the shutters were closed, the room was black. I fell through the dark into deep sleep.

A voice was calling for help. Black sleep held me down. The voice let out a scream.

It was Janet, outside the door. "Gil-bert"—two broken syllables—"it's Gil-bert."

Harry heaved out of bed, bare-assed in his blue shirt, balls flapping as he followed her down the hall. Barely awake, I picked Harry's jeans off the chair and followed, the bathrobe as tight across my waist as when I'd tied it there.

Gilbert lay in the center of the floor of his dressing room, in his dressing gown.

The wooden panels of the room rose up around him like a palisade. Janet retreated to the hall.

"I put him on his side," she said. "I know that much."

Harry picked up Gilbert's hand and put it down again. I handed Harry his jeans and knelt next to Gilbert's head.

I didn't know what to do or why I was alone with him in the middle of the room. I took Gilbert's right wrist and held it in mine; I had never touched him before. I couldn't tell whether his hand was warm or cool, whether what I was feeling was his hand or mine. Was that my blood beating under my skin, or his pulse? I pulled his head and shoulders up on to my thighs and rested them there.

Janet called out, "You're the one person here who speaks French. Do something."

Harry threw me my cell phone. I dialed 117, asked Janet for the full address of the house, asked her to tell the security guard to light the drive and gather in the dogs.

I sat, Gilbert's head on my lap. The dark floorboards stretched out forever on every side. A thin hope that everything was fine floated up near the ceiling, but down on the floor there was only weight and unutterable stillness. Trapped between sleep and waking, I cradled a mystery.

He seemed, on my lap, young, strangely ageless.

Harry came over with a hand mirror and held it under Gilbert's mouth.

We had no way of knowing.

Now there were firemen in the room, firemen in boots and heavy gear. Their leader, a woman, motioned me to leave. I slipped my legs from under Gilbert's torso, waited until she had him firmly in her hands, and scrambled to my feet.

"Get my latex gloves out of the bag," she ordered.

I handed her the gloves and went to Janet in the corridor. We sat on a bench like children.

"This is a nightmare," said Janet. "This is not happening. Tell me it's a nightmare."

It was as thick and slow as a nightmare.

Then the doctor was there, another woman. She pushed away the firemen and settled on the floor with two paramedics. They activated noisy pumps, held up bottles.

"This isn't happening," said Janet.

Maybe I was still asleep.

The doctor stood up and came over to Janet.

"Madame, your husband has been dead since we arrived."

There was no more possibility for it to be anything other than what it was.

"What should I do?" Janet asked me.

Sleep fell off me; I knew what to do.

"Get your daughters," I said. "Take them back to your room with you."

"I don't want to wake them," she said. "They need their rest."

"You need them more."

"Can you take care of everything?" she asked before she went down the hall to get them.

"Of course," I said. I didn't see Harry anywhere.

The security guard said, "Madame, we have to move the body to a room with air-conditioning, because with this heat it will decompose by dawn." I nodded.

He led the paramedics into the coolest room, and returned with papers for me to sign.

"Voilà, Madame," he said. They were forms for the morgue.

I signed. I didn't know Gilbert's date of birth or his nationality, but I signed.

The butler stood by my side. "My last three employers all died," he said. "Do I still have a job?"

"Of course you do," I said. "Nothing changes."

"*Merci*, Madame."

I still had my phone in my hand. There were things to do to make tomorrow easier for Janet. There would doubtless be a private plane to take the body to London. There would be permits needed. Would the permits have to be issued by his country of origin, or his country of residence? I needed to speak to ambassadors. The British one, the Egyptian one, the Swiss one. The only one I knew was the American one, but I had the number of his house in the Hamptons. It was four thirty in the morning in Provence, ten thirty in Southampton, just after dinner, when I reached the summer house of the American ambassador, Felix Rohatyn.

I was pacing through our room, waiting for Felix to come on the line, when I passed behind Harry, who sat at the desk on his laptop. On its screen I saw a photograph of Gilbert's corpse lying on the guest room bed.

You are mad, Harry, you are quite, quite mad, I thought. Leaving you is the next item on the list. Just not quite yet.

"How are you?" asked the American ambassador, on the phone at last. "How was your holiday?"

"Someone's just died," I said, "here in the South of France. I need your help," and to prove I wasn't asking for charity for a hiker, I added there would be a private plane for the body, that I wanted to make sure there was no problem with permits, and could I—please—have the home numbers of the British, Egyptian, and Swiss ambassadors, so that they could expedite matters tomorrow, on a Sunday.

"Who was he?" asked Felix Rohatyn, cool and formal.

And now, I could not say Gilbert's name. His death was not yet real enough for it to be anything but a secret. We were in the gray place. All my little efforts to stanch the finality suddenly seemed a terrible parade of ego, an unsolicited flourish of competence. Telling Felix would make Gilbert's death public and real, the people at his dinner table would talk about it, the secret would be out—and wasn't there the billionaire equivalent of getting to the bank vault before the certificate was signed? But I'd signed the certificate. And the vault was probably taken care of a long time ago.

I whispered his name.

"No!" said Felix. "Not Gilbert de Botton! I know him."

I'd let the secret out.

I sat on the bed in the second bedroom to absorb what had just happened, away from Harry. I'd wanted to know Gilbert. Instead I'd sat on the floor in my sleep, holding his dead body. My mind couldn't encompass what had happened, I couldn't cry, I could only wonder.

Harry was asleep when I walked back through the bedroom. This was no time to join him.

I dressed, and packed my bag. I'd be leaving soon, that day, at some point. I was done here. And now I had to go down to the kitchen and help the help.

My shoes clacked past framed dried flowers as I took the back stairs in a daze. I would ask for some coffee, then there would be phone calls. I had to take care of things. I had a pen in my hand.

The butler, his wife the cook, and one of the maids stood in the kitchen, dressed for the day. It was seven fifteen on the morning of August 27. No one could speak. A young local girl dressed in her own maid uniform pushed open the door, ready for the day. "Bonjour!" she shouted with gusto.

All eyes turned to her, but no one said "Bonjour." There was no way to begin. The young maid's eyes went from the butler's face to the cook's to the first maid's, but still no one spoke. Her expression went from surprise to suspicion, to fear, to anger, and then to rage.

"Qu'est ce que j'ai fait?" she asked. What did I do?

We only ever think about ourselves. She thought she'd lost her job.

The cook opened her arms and said, "*Monsieur est mort.*"

I told the butler to proceed as he would normally, set the table for breakfast on the terrace, make the coffee extra strong. I sat under the matchstick awning, a tray of coffee and a plate of toast on the table in front of me. Adrian and the blonde would be coming down. The time inched toward eight, past eight. I didn't want to be there, but someone had to tell Adrian. I couldn't stand the thought of the Cambodian butler trying to explain, and breaking down, or of Adrian wafting through the day all quips and jokes until he ran into a wall of what had happened.

He came across the flagstones, espadrilles flapping. Big smile.

"You look a little rough," he said as he sat down.

And now it happened to me. I couldn't speak.

I pointed at the coffeepot.

"So how did you sleep?'

"Gilbert died," I said, but not loud enough.

"Gilbert what?" he said.

Oh no, I can't say it again, I thought. Please just get it.

"Christ," said Adrian, when I repeated it. "Christ."

Harry came down an hour later, and then Janet. I took up a position by the Rolodex in the kitchen, collecting numbers for the names Janet gave me, people who had to know.

Half of them had already heard the news from the American ambassador to Paris, thanks to my ridiculous efforts to make it all right.

By noon I could no longer stand upright. Harry walked me to the bottom of the stone stairs, told me to take a pill and get some sleep.

"You're like a pioneer woman, crossing Indian territory in a covered wagon, taking on all comers, making firewood out of anything and shooting your dinner," he said.

Had I told him about my great-grandmother Juliet, who gave birth in a covered wagon in Mexican Hat, Utah?

When I came down in the middle of the hot afternoon after a Xanax nap, the climate had chilled.

"You're so fucking competent," said Harry.

I had to break up with him, but not while more important things were happening.

The widow's iron hoop of respect had settled around Janet. None but her daughters dared sit near her. Only Harry enveloped her in hugs; Adrian, the blonde, and I pecked at her cheeks.

The butler asked more questions, the security guard stood to attention when he saw me.

Two private jets came from London that evening. Professionals had intervened, as I should have guessed, to sort out all the permits. I stood with the security guard at the barrier of the private part of the Nice airport, my bag at my feet.

Janet, Adrian, the two girls, the blonde, and Harry climbed into the first jet; a coffin slid into the second one. The jets taxied away, one behind the other.

I turned to the security guard. "Where do I find Air France?" I asked.

"In the main building," he said, and cocked a thumb over his shoulder, "over there."

I looked down at my bag. "Could you drive me there?" I asked.

"You can walk," he said. "I've got other things to do."

CHAPTER TWENTY-TWO

I'd left for my holiday with Harry in a blaze of triumphant expectation; I returned too rattled by Gilbert's death to grasp the damage done the day that, rich with the certainty of a better life, I'd told Gardner to go to hell. There is a price to pay for temper, and I had no protector now.

I left all the clothes I'd taken to Provence in the suitcase, as if everything inside it were tainted.

At *Vogue* the next morning, Gardner was cold. Jonathan had told her everything. "I had a terrible holiday as well," she said. It was August 28, the *rentrée* had not begun, most of the staff were still on holiday.

"I'm going to the funeral in London tomorrow," I said. She pursed her lips, which were thin again after a summer away from the doctor's needle.

Harry picked me up at Waterloo, a sweating stranger giving off a buzzing irritation. The funeral was in a small Jewish cemetery in North London. Janet and her daughters, Gilbert's son, Alain, his daughter, Miel, their shock bounded by formality. Jonathan, Rothschild bankers, a rabbi, Hebrew, earth. In the car on the way back from the cemetery, Harry grew agitated and ran into a greasy spoon café to find the men's room. I wondered if he had a prostate problem.

We had tea in the lobby of the high-luxury hotel at Hyde Park Corner that had once been Saint George's Hospital, where my grandfather had died at the end of another summer, forty-three years before. There was a pattern of blackberries on the teacups. I told Harry that he and I had been an experiment, and the experiment had failed.

"Your picker's broken," he said, and saw me off at Waterloo station.

I tried to call him from the Eurostar to ask what he meant about a picker; the screen on my cell spelled out "No Connection Possible."

I was still in shock, the shock would not let me go, and now I stammered. Consonants rose up like gates in the middle of words, I'd try to charge through the *t*'s and *p*'s and *d*'s and fail.

"Just cut it out!" Dad said as I stuttered through telling him that Harry was over.

"I'm not doing it on pu-pu—pur-pose," I said.

Paulino came into my office, frowning and sympathetic. "Work won't start till next week. Go to Versailles for a few days," she said. "Get back to yourself, it does you good out there."

"Do you think that's okay?" I asked.

~

"We haven't seen you in a long time!" said the concierge at the Trianon Palace.

The park was deserted in the middle of the week; I rented a battered bike from the stand inside the gate, and rode past the long regiments of lindens, hoping the regular shadows of their perfect alignment would bring me back to reality. I went as far as I could on the Allée de Bally, and stopped to dry my eyes by oaks felled in the Christmas hurricane, now sawn and stacked in an open field. I sat on a tree trunk and cried. I didn't know why I cried until I was singing the Habanera from *Carmen*, "*L'amour est un oiseau rebelle*," off-key, loud, for the sky turned upside down, for the Harry myth exploded, for Gilbert dying on my knees, for the way my heart had opened straight to death.

I stood up, got back on the bike, and headed down an unfamiliar path through the woods. A wall rose on the far side of a moat, the outer boundary of Versailles. The bicycle chain jumped its sprockets; I knelt to put it back in place and then I noticed a small bridge that led to a tall portico with an open door I'd never seen before. I crossed the bridge and found myself in an instructional garden center, with shops that sold seed catalogues, wheelbarrows, and toys. There were people here, French families making the most of the last week of the holidays.

A sign said LABYRINTHE, the French word for "maze"; another maze. I chained the bike to a post, and bought a ticket at a wooden hut.

"It's harder than you think," said the woman in the hut, "when it's time to get out, I'll ring a bell. The first bell is a warning, the second is to remind you about the first, and when you hear the third bell, we're closed."

"Oohhhh!" I heard from behind the tall spikes, and followed French parents and children into a tight maze of dying cornstalks, to a small clearing where they'd stopped to stare at a panel of poetry set on an easel made of logs, illustrated with a crudely drawn ant and an even cruder grasshopper. It was one of La Fontaine's fables.

The parents, once French schoolchildren, recited in unison, and so did I: "*La Cigale ayant chanté tout l'été / se trouva fort dépourvue quand l'hiver fut venu!*" The grasshopper, having done nothing but sing all summer, found herself without provisions with the arrival of winter.

I was the grasshopper: I'd spent everything I earned. The Napoleon-green apartment for Dad, the room above it for the Polish girl Johanna, his improbable cab service bills, the dentist, the doctors, the trips, my trips, too, my rust red carpet and fine linen window hangings, my Baccarat glasses and Art Deco silver, the dinners, Aneeta. I had no savings at all, and summer was over. But I had a job.

I proceeded through the cornstalks from one fable to another. I knew them all. Each one was a cautionary lesson and a stinging slap. *The Ant and the Grasshopper:* improvidence is bad; *The Fox and the Crow:* boasting is bad; *The Tortoise and the Hare:* speed is bad. Or was it showing off that was bad? I'd wanted Versailles to console me, but instead it scolded me.

It was getting late. My feet were throbbing, my head hurt, I was sick of being lectured by panels with bad drawings. In the distance the bell rang once. I walked back to *The Grasshopper and the Ant,* and tried the path I'd come in on. Wrong turn. Back to *The Fox and the Crow.* Dead end. The bell rang again. I ran to *The Tortoise and the Hare,* but there was no way out. The bell rang a third time.

This maze was no more than a construct, and I didn't have to obey its rules. I pushed my way through the rustling stalks, pulled apart one high wall of dying corn after another until I was outside. All I'd had to do was refuse to play the game, and I was free. I got back on the bike, but the wooden doors into the park were shut and locked. I pushed; they had no give. I was shut out of Versailles.

The only way back was on the side of a busy highway; the bike shook with every passing car as I pedaled for the hours it took to return to the hotel.

In Paris, I retrieved the Cubist Alfréd Réth still life from the vault and hung it back on the living room wall. I finally unlocked the bag I'd taken to Provence. The white satin nightgown had vanished, along with the white knight who was going to rescue me.

I found an apartment big enough for me and Jules, with a room above for Johanna, but I didn't make an offer.

I was half present, numb, and clumsy. I stammered. Everything seemed too heavy or too light, too important or not important at all. *Vogue* was a jangled wire. My new assistant was a fearful sort, and my stammer did nothing to reassure her. In meetings, I'd lose my French and stumble on words. I didn't want to go into the fashion room; Marcus was more opaque than ever, a visitor in a white cashmere jacket. Delphine was angry that I spent my time across the street with Tina for the website, with Isabelle for *Air France Madame,* but they were the only ones not contaminated by the poisoned air of *Vogue.*

I tried to pat the Theater issue into place, felt unsure of my choices, and invited Gardner to sit in on my meetings, where she attacked the editors at my conference table. I went to her office to ask her to stop, but my words came out, "P-p-p-p-please d-don't d-do that." She rolled her eyes and went back to reading the trade paper on her desk.

Paulino said, "Something bad is going on." The managing editor, Laure, twisted her hands around her Filofax; she was worried about Franceline, and Schneider, and Marcus.

"What's wrong with them?" I asked.

"Gardner's been taking them to lunches, more than once, and that doesn't feel right. You should see each one of them in private."

Only Schneider was free to have lunch with me; at Tante Louise, he gave his Swiss grin and said everything was fine. I didn't tell him that, at that very table, over the same *poireaux vinaigrette,* Jean-Baptiste Mondino had told me to fire him.

Samia, the Algerian credits editor, took me aside to give me a circle of turquoise beads.

"Protection," she said, "against the evil eye."

"What evil eye?" I asked.

I withdrew. I'd tell my timorous new assistant that I had a confidential lunch date, and hide in a distant bistro alone with a book. I ate my dinners alone at André around the corner from home, mesmerized by the tarragon leaves set into my *oeufs en gelée.*

I thought I was going insane. Wasn't manic depression hereditary? My doctor prescribed what he claimed was a very weak antidepressant, but the first pill turned my head to ice and set a python writhing in my chest. Another doctor called it a vasovagal reaction and handed me a Xanax.

Over coffee at La Belle Ferronnière, Marcus said, "I'm quitting. Jonathan's made me fashion director of Japanese *Vogue.*"

I was too disoriented to start putting together the pieces of the story that was unfolding at *Vogue.*

"Offer Marcus's job to Carine Roitfeld," said Gardner. It was an order.

I was in a cab in the Place de l'Alma the next day when I reached Carine.

"I don't want to be your fashion director," she said. "All my girlfriends have their own magazines. The only job I'd want at *Vogue* is editor in chief."

Her green eyes had told me that the day I'd met her.

As calm and detached as a suicide, I relayed Carine's message to Gardner, exactly as she'd said it.

And then I cried in bed all weekend. I'd lost my will. Fashion had turned to poison, Paris *Vogue* had become a prison, but if I quit, I could no longer take care of my father.

The Milan collections for spring–summer 2001 were beginning on Monday, and Jonathan wanted to see me at Caffè Cova at 4:00 p.m., before the Prada show.

I watched lightning bolts shoot from the screaming yellow air and hit the car park at Linate Airport, and, yes, I knew they were meant for me.

And then Jonathan said "sabbatical" and told me to vanish for two months. He said I'd still have my job when I returned, but I knew what "sabbatical" meant.

I went off with your best friend because I thought he'd save me from you; that failed, and now I'm lost. In my panic I summoned up the guardian angel from the book I'd read when I was seven, *Les Malheurs de Sophie*; the angel was protection, the angel was nineteenth-century Catholic judgment, the angel was confirmation of my guilt. Here was my punishment for every wrong thing I'd done since I'd gotten the job, every person I'd fired, every sin of omission, every act of exclusion, and my greater—my greatest—sin, that of superficiality. I sat completely still. Every second counted, because every second was the last second of being who I'd become. To make this pink linen napkin last forever in just this shape, this cup always brimming with foam, this sugar cube half unwrapped, this spoon at this angle on the tablecloth, stop time in this turn of now, expand the stillness of this second to fill the room and stop the next one coming, to stop the next thing being said. I was amazed at how I could stretch out inside time and stop it, until I couldn't anymore, and I heard the next words.

"This is where you're going. They have very good therapy there." Jonathan handed me a piece of paper with "Cottonwood" written on it in neat capitals. My refusal to go, it seemed, would constitute quitting. If I went, if I obeyed, I'd get the severance, and I could take care of Dad.

I'll need the therapy to get me over losing my job. How thoughtful. The angel has come to take me away from the beautiful garden where the flowers are rotting and the fruit is poison. It was such a pretty life.

Others liked it, my father liked it, I never asked for it, not directly, all I said was, "Why not?" when you offered it to me, and now you're taking it away, and now I'm ready to climb the stony path in—where is this, Arizona? "I'll go," I said, "but why?"

He leaned forward and said he didn't want me to end up like one of his London editors who'd died of a cocaine overdose after an orgy with hookers in 1995.

Cocaine, orgy, hookers: this wasn't some therapy place. Cottonwood must be a drug rehab.

"Are you mad?" I asked.

He smiled indulgently. I tried to get his eyes to meet mine.

"I don't do drugs," I said. "I don't even drink. You know that."

He gave me the smile that says, "Everyone knows addicts don't drink."

"But who'll run the magazine while I'm away?"

"Gardner can do it. She started in editorial."

I gave him the smile that says, "Everyone knows she drinks," but I couldn't say the words. How vulgar it would be to defend myself by calling Gardner an alcoholic, when I had what I wanted. I didn't think of everything I was losing, the angel wouldn't let me grab at material things, the angel had given me the escape I'd been longing for.

"This will be our secret, no one will know you've gone there," he said. Of course he wouldn't talk. I took his hand.

"Either you're my friend, or you're setting me up. I choose to believe you are my friend," I said.

You can't complain about being exiled from Hell.

And I got back into my car and told the driver to take me to Prada, because the show had to go on, even if it was over for me.

Gardner arrived at the Prada show, her face as smooth as an egg, her lips newly plumped, immense. Can't she tell that mouth makes her look like someone hit her? I wondered. She didn't like her seat; I made room for her next to me in the front row. At the show, I stared at the shoes. At my hotel, I stared at the presents. The next morning, while everyone went to the fashion shows, I lay in bed feeling my sudden freedom; and then, instead of taking a plane to Paris, I went to the Brera museum to stare at Raphael's *Betrothal of the Virgin*. After Gardner had called me for the third time, I let the driver take me to Linate Airport.

The phone was ringing as I came into my apartment; it was my predecessor Colombe Pringle, who'd already heard the news and wanted to know more. I told her there was nothing to know and took the phone off the hook.

"What do you mean, you're going away now, didn't the shows just begin?" asked Jules, who knew the schedule. I invented a two-month biking holiday in Laguna Beach. "Like Versailles but longer, and in the sun." He looked at me across his table and shook his head. "Why don't you tell Jonathan, 'Fire me now, asshole.'"

"I'm too tired to be fired right now," I said, "and as far as I know, I'm not fired."

"You are so naïve, honey," said Dad.

I told Aneeta I had been ordered to go away, without details. She'd look after him.

My lawyer told me not to go, but I had my justification ready.

"I always knew that when *Vogue* ended, I'd have to become normal again, and this is what I need," I told him, "and this gets me the severance."

Martine and her husband thought I should do as I'd been told. I didn't want to call Charlotte with this; she was beginning a new film on location. Anjelica and I had not talked in over a year. A countess offered me her island near Tahiti, but added that she was worried about the estate manager and needed me to report back; I declined.

I wondered if Joe had invented the story as revenge. I told him the story at a café, searching his face for signs of his betrayal, but found only concern. "That man you went off with is a notorious piece of shit," he mumbled.

I huddled over files from the office with my new assistant at the Bristol Hotel bar. She was distraught. "This is the second time this has happened to me," she said, "maybe I have bad luck." Maybe you bring bad luck, I thought. And if I couldn't blame her, I wondered if there wasn't some object at home that I could blame, that I could throw away to bring my world back to rights. I put the silver bracelets Gardner had given me into a plastic bag, took them to the Champs-Élysées, and dropped them in a trash can.

I told myself it wasn't so bad. Condé Nast was sending me away on a plane, as they had done for almost thirty years. I was being sent to Arizona. This was an assignment. I was going to report on what it was like to be in an American rehab. I'd need notebooks and pens for that, lots of new felt-tips to take notes. And my camera. I packed less cashmere and more denim than usual, and some Missoni to keep my spirits up, a bright cardigan, a long zigzag scarf. I knew what I was doing. I knew how to pack. I'd watched an explorer do it once. Plenty of supplies, well wrapped, and marked. Boxes of the glass phials of the *sérum de Quinton* seawater, the pills that smelled of horse manure from Dr. Chenot, magnesium and B_6, Shalimar deodorant spray, oh, sunglasses, it's Arizona. A bundle of cedar from Taos. A sheet of six Xanax to sleep on the plane and get me through the first nights of jet lag.

I was going to find out if I was crazy like my father.

In the cab through the freezing early-morning drizzle on the way to the airport, I heard, "I see friends shaking hands," . . . coming from the radio . . . "saying how do you do, they're really saying I love you." It was Satchmo singing "What a Wonderful World," the song we'd played at Uncle Don's funeral. That had to be a good sign.

I could cry on the plane for thirteen hours straight, and only the Air France attendants would see; I'd cried on the flight to Los Angeles many times before. No one in fashion would be flying west during Paris ready-to-wear, they'd be watching clothes go by in stables, in variety theaters, in underground storage units, in tunnels, nunneries, museum annexes, Communist party headquarters, slaughterhouses. I'd be alone in first class in a navy blue seat with foie gras and a little container of sevruga, because even in first class you don't get first-class caviar.

I wasn't alone. In 1A was a designer, in tears because her jewelry samples had been stolen at the airport. In 2A was Jil Sander, who'd lost the right to her name after Miuccia Prada's husband bought her company. I crouched in my mysterious disgrace in the row behind her, and behind me sat my old friend Gilles Bensimon, on his way to photograph Madonna. He quickly figured out he wasn't flying with the lucky, and kept to himself.

The rehab was outside Tucson, off a dirt road called Silverbell, and I hung on to that name. Silverbell. How bad could that be?

The first thing confiscated in the room they called the Intake was the little sheet of Xanax. The Guerlain deodorant was next: alcohol. "I'm going to drink it?" I asked, haughty as a duchess. "Your roommates might," said the woman in charge. "Roommates?" I asked, but she was shaking the phials of seawater out of their box. "I take those three times a day to balance my electrolytes," I explained. She put them out of reach, ran the cedar stick under her nose. Gone. The antioxidant pills went next, the magnesium and B_6, then the cell phone, then the camera. She let me keep my pens.

I peed in a cup, let a nurse draw my blood, and was put to bed in a room they called the Detox, where the walls were made of molded plastic, and there was plastic under the sheet.

When I woke, before dawn, I went outside. A woman with a mustache was sitting on the porch, smoking and writing in a journal. I could just make out a saguaro cactus in the dark behind her.

"I'm a train engineer," she said. "I drive trains all through the night, a hundred cars at a time behind my engine. They're called shooters, because they don't stop till they reach the end." She was in for gambling.

I hadn't yet been assigned a room and was still in the Detox when the director of the rehab called me in. She held up the results of my blood and urine tests.

"Why are you here?" she asked.

"Orders," I said. Could I tell her I was just playing the game through to the end?

"Well, you can leave now, your tests are clean. There's no reason for you to stay."

"I'm supposed to vanish for two months. Let me stay here. Please."

"I've never heard that before," she said.

"I have nowhere else to go."

She thought for a moment. "There may be some useful groups for you," she said. "Are there alcoholics in your family?"

"Just the usual amount of heavy drinking."

She didn't smile.

"My father is manic-depressive. It's hereditary, isn't it? Do you have the test for that here?"

"The condition is now called bipolar, but yes, I can schedule a Minnesota Multiphasic Personality Inventory for you."

"That's the one!" I said. The test Harry had told me about, the impartial arbiter that would assemble my answers into a complete inventory of my personality. I'd be able to define myself at last.

The morning group meeting was held in a circle of tubular chairs on an acrylic wall-to-wall carpet in shades of teal, sky, and mauve. I didn't know what to call the people there: inmates, patients, addicts, customers? All ages; faces without defenses or the defenses etched deep as scars; checked shirts, sweatpants, noisy hi-tech parkas. First names only, and not all of them the real names. Each one in turn stated a wound: survivor of childhood rape, alcoholic, junkie, bulimic, suicide, gambler; there was one pill head, another who said he was a garbage head. A rage-aholic, a handful of codependents. I stated "no label," and "no label" stuck.

Cottonwood had no classification for me, so I was put in a room with three suicides, pleasant middle-class women who'd come unstuck from the proprieties of marriage. "I'm codependent," announced the one who put rollers in her hair every night before bed. They gave us Benadryl to sleep, but a flashlight ran over our faces every hour through the night.

You could receive faxes, but not phone calls. You had to call from one of three pay phones in the nurse's station. I soon found out that *Vogue* had canceled my calling card, and relearned to call collect, sitting in a plastic chair on the linoleum floor across from the counter where nurses handed out meds to everyone but me.

A New York friend sent the *New York Times* clipping that said my disappearance was the biggest news of the European ready-to-wear, which confirmed that I'd missed a dreary season. Joe faxed printouts of fashion website chatter. One reported I was getting "endless quantities of sun in Australia" and concluded:

> It's like in the old days of the Soviet Union, when TASS announced that a member of the Politburo has gone to the Black Sea for a cure. Well, you know, sometimes they did come back to the Kremlin, but very rarely.

I spoke to my sad assistant, who was very lonely in my outer office. "There are a lot of nice people working there," I told her. "You could make friends."

"I'm defending you," she said, and faxed me Gardner's memo that announced Emmanuelle Alt as Marcus's replacement as fashion director, and welcomed Carine Roitfeld as creative director of the entire French Condé Nast group. Under Gardner's leonine signature was an equally leonine handwritten line that read: *À Nous les belles Françaises.* Here's to the beautiful French girls.

"She wants to make *Vogue* French again," said Paulino when I called her. "She made fun of your accent in the meeting."

"I have an accent?" I asked.

As the days went by with their regular hours and kindly therapies, the shock of Gilbert's death subsided and the guardian angel from *Les Malheurs de Sophie* withdrew. I stopped thinking that I had to atone for the sin of success and began to understand that I'd paid for my freedom with a ludicrous incarceration, but still I couldn't think beyond the confines of the world as *Vogue.* If Jonathan was stupid enough to believe I was an addict, I told myself as I walked a brick path between patches of sand and dwarf palms, he deserved to be punished by losing me. Without me, Paris *Vogue* would subside back into a catalogue of indistinct black clothes, nipples, and cigarettes, and, boy, would he be sorry. I was still trapped.

To soothe myself, I did the only thing I knew how to do, and took notes. I was Nellie Bly undercover in the madhouse, the alert, inquiring subject, not an object, not a victim. I took notes in the lectures that outlined strategies for coping with addiction. They might work for cigarettes. I forced myself to read the entire texts of inspirational posters down to the last line about "Him," copied down the Core Feelings listed on whiteboards—Happy, Sad, Fearful, Lonely, Ashamed, oh yes, I could see that one, Grateful, Angry. I peered into the booklets of Christian sermonettes in the same spirit of inquiry as I greeted the Jolly Ranchers that were the currency of friendship. I'll have that red one, thank you.

In that autumn of 2000, my universe came down to the fake adobe walls and Formica surfaces of the bare-bones rehab and its desert campus where woodpecker-scarred saguaro cacti rose up here and there to declare that this was postcard Arizona, and not a Twilight Zone full of lost souls. Outside the perimeter of what they called the campus was a patch of desert marked with sobriety maxims engraved on stones. It was the rehab version of the fables of La Fontaine in the maze at Versailles, but here they called it the Spiritual Path.

It rained in Tucson that fall, and it was cold. One of the employees, who were all called techs if they weren't therapists, said that all this rain made the desert north of town bloom with blue flowers, but the cacti on the campus were bare. The only way I'd see blue flowers was from the minivan that took us to kickboxing class somewhere in Tucson.

Everyone cried in public most of the time, and, to my relief, so did I. Tears were encouraged. Breakthroughs, they said, came through breakdowns. Quiet sobs rose above the scratch and crackle of parkas. Every man, woman, and teenager was raw, open, their psyches altered only by new antidepressants. I was prescribed no meds, but after an emergency visit to the dentist, I was allowed to gargle with Listerine to the open envy of my new friends. The nurse kept the bottle locked up behind her, and watched me at the sink in case I swallowed.

I'd looked for people I might recognize. Celebrities. Wasn't I on assignment? Maybe someone else was there by mistake, like me, merely to fulfill a contractual obligation. I saw tattoos; a braided beard, a shirt rolled up over an elbow crook with slits and gaping sores; I saw engineers, a pilot, construction workers, wives, southern guys in business. For the young girls, it was heroin. The southerners liked beer. The soldier had a dent in his head from the last time he'd tried to shoot himself. The airline pilot had an anger problem. The TWA loader, a stocky woman with short arms and a pug nose, knew for sure that a US missile had brought down TWA flight 800. The tall Apache was in for unspecified. The boy who'd been a courier for a Mexican drug cartel and was facing eight to twelve in a federal pen after rehab said he'd never touch heroin, but he liked crack.

My snobbery was consoled by a few aristocratic British addicts pulled in by Cottonwood's thriving London outreach program, and again when the wiry man with the tragic face turned out to be a Los Angeles talent agent, the gentle older man in an olive-green suit a legend of jazz, the braided beard a rocker worshipped in the heartland. They weren't famous to me, but famous enough in their own spheres to prove I had not been thrown onto a compost heap. The jazzman had a CD coming out; the rocker had been taken off a tour; the agent represented a friend of mine.

I was in a small group under a therapist called Dan, who had a gravelly Brooklyn voice, and something of Uncle Don about him. He let things come at him, and didn't push the Christian subtext of the twelve steps; like all the therapists, he was a former addict.

I suspended my disdain for the 12-step pablum, and had to concede that in many ways I did believe in a Higher Power, though without the capital letters. A lowercase higher power, barely magic, powerless but ever present. The guardian angel, watching me for missteps; not such a benign presence.

My ex-husband read in the *New York Post* that I'd slugged Gardner at a fashion show and faxed me the Page Six clipping. I called him collect.

"I didn't slug her!" I said. "I was in shock by the time she turned up at the Prada show. I made room for her next to me on the first-row bench."

"No good deed goes unpunished," said John.

"The only person I've ever punched was you, when we were married. But we were fighting."

"I wouldn't bring that up," said John; his lawyer training.

"Noted," I said.

My own lawyer had seen Page Six. I was irked he hadn't let me know.

"Are you completely sure you didn't slug her?" my lawyer asked.

"I've never slugged anyone in my life," I said. "You have to make the *Post* retract the story."

"You're a public figure," he said. "They can say what they want."

"Editing *Vogue* makes me a public figure? I don't exist anymore. I'm hiding in a rehab."

"I told you not to go," said my lawyer.

"I had to become a human being again. I had to get back with real people."

The real people were not my little in-crowd, but the engineers, pilots, wives, southern guys, angry daughters, twisted Los Angeles kids, and all of them had tattoos, except the Apache who wouldn't make eye contact. The boy who'd called himself a garbage head was caught sucking the Freon out of an air-conditioning unit. The bulimics hogged the toilets after each meal. I was fascinated by a cluster of obese women in housedresses and watched them as they heaved along the walkways on reinforced sneakers. There was one in particular who had a halo of yellow cotton-candy hair and always wore baby pink, the sad wife of a miner. I was fascinated by the solid expanse of her bosom, a cube from shoulder to shoulder, neck to waist. I wanted to grab hold of her and hang there.

We enacted therapeutic rituals on the blue carpet of the big meeting room under the close supervision of recovered addicts with masters in social work. There came a day when I was asked to hug the miner's wife. I was afraid to break the space between us, but when I put my arms around her shoulders and let myself settle onto the solid volume of her breasts, I'd come home.

I hadn't touched anyone that size since my grandmother, and as I hung on to the miner's wife, she became Nana. My body remembered how I'd clung to her, I could smell the Pond's Cold Cream on her fingers and the raw ground beef she tried to feed me, I could feel the greasy sparkle of her star sapphire. The bosom was all those places where Nana had been my rock. The rooms in the Hôtel Prince de

Galles and the nights in the villa above Cannes and the days in the Palais Rose, and Nana's tiny apartment on West 54th Street. I could feel the love I'd felt, the need for that safety, for that bulk, and I wept with gratitude. I remembered her in her bath, the water too hot, her breasts floating like zeppelins.

But as I clung there, a reproach came in, a proviso, a disturbance in the gratitude; the love changed color and it was my twentieth birthday, Nana and I crammed into a booth at the Brasserie on Park Avenue, when Nana said, "If your mother had married a handsome man, you would have been beautiful and you wouldn't have all these emotional problems."

I pulled back from the pink bosom, away from the kind blond woman who was crying along with me, and went to think about it on a chair.

I called Jonathan collect in London. "I'm resolving my problems with my grandmother, which is wonderful," I said, "but I don't think my problems with my grandmother have anything to do with my performance at *Vogue.* Could you please explain why you ordered me to rehab?"

He said he'd send me a letter.

Once a week I called my father, and though I kept the inventions about my biking holiday in Laguna Beach short to avoid too many lies, he'd barely listen and quickly put Aneeta on the line.

"He's being a bloody trial," she said. "When the hell are you coming back?"

"You know I have to get through this charade," I said.

"Do you really?" she asked.

~

The Minnesota Multiphasic Personality Inventory test was administered by a large computer in a small office. The 567 questions went on forever. I liked answering the questions. I liked accounting for myself with full honesty, with only a few preemptive evasions.

I was careful to answer "True" to number 427, which stated: "I have never seen a vision."

"I often feel as if I can read people's minds" sometimes felt true, but I knew how to avoid the straitjacket and answered "False."

Some questions posed subtler problems. "Someone has been trying to poison me" had been true a few years before, when the first banker's housekeeper fed me the special salad that she used to eliminate all his girlfriends. I was holding on tight here; it wasn't true anymore, so I could answer "False" without betraying the objective fact.

But one question stopped me altogether. Number 311 read:

"I often feel as if things are not real."

I stared at the words.

I didn't slug Gardner, but the *New York Post* says I did. Everyone thinks my father is rich. Jonathan believes I'm an addict or an alcoholic. I don't know if Gilbert was dead or alive when I cradled him on the floor that night. What were the probabilities of anything being real? I decided I'd better pretend everything was real, and say "False" to that one.

It would take a while for the results to be processed. I tried to be less nervous.

The rain stopped and the wildlife came out. The barrio boy who was looking at six to eight in a federal pen caught a big snake just south of the swimming pool. It wasn't poisonous, but it was long and fat, with scales that shaded brown to beige to white. He held it between two sticks; a few of us followed at a safe distance while he carried it away into the desert and released it on the Spiritual Path. He tossed the snake by a stone inscribed: "We admitted we were powerless, that our lives had become unmanageable."

I went back to get a sweater from the room I shared with the three suicides, and from the open door I saw a long beige and brown and white snake lying across my bed. I shrieked and bolted for help; two of the heroin girls marched in to confront the snake, I followed behind them. They stopped in the middle of the room.

"That the snake?" asked one, pointing to the bed. I peered from behind her shoulder. It was the Missoni scarf.

~

There was no television anywhere at Cottonwood, but we insisted that even if we were temporarily unable to vote, we had a right to see democracy in action. The addicts were generally Democrats and the drunks mostly Republicans. A chunky rabbit ears set was installed in the lounge for election night, and we stood in front of it, trying to see through the static, straining to hear. We went to bed with the election unresolved, and when we woke up it was still unresolved, and it stayed unresolved for months. Reality was unstable.

The Minnesota Multiphasic Personality Inventory released its diagnostic. I was trembling hard on the way to the director's office, and stopped twice to pee. And then I was across the desk from her, and she was holding the results. She handed them to me.

"These results are so normal as to be abnormal," I read. "The subject however shows some evidence of paranoia, answered True to 'People are plotting against me.'"

"That's it?" I asked. All this madness in my life, and I wasn't even crazy?

"You're not bipolar," she said. "Are you sure you want to stay now?"

I wasn't finished here, I said. I signed up for kickboxing. I signed up for Adult Children of Alcoholics, Sex Addicts Anonymous, Codependents Anonymous, and Anger Management.

In the codependent group I learned that taking full responsibility for other people was nothing more than emotional blackmail. I was given tasks to curb my goody-goody reflexes. One day, in the controlled environment of a ritual exercise, I managed to tell a man, "No, you can't have my bandanna."

I rose at five to get the first, fully caffeinated brew in the cafeteria and follow the rocker, the jazzman, and the agent to the flagpole to watch the soldier raise the Arizona Republic flag above the meeting room. They were my friends, and hard-core addicts. For the agent, it was cocaine, and, he admitted, hookers. The rocker liked everything. For the jazzman, it was pills. He recited their names like love music: Percodan, Percocet, Hycotab, Hycomed, Lortab, oxycodone, Norco, hydrocodone, and, last, most beloved, OxyContin, which he liked to crush and dissolve in a glass of vodka, and called "The O.C."

"You getting bored with Acquaintances of Occasional Drinkers?"

asked the rocker, who despite his hillbilly satanist mien was cheerful and kind.

"Why don't you stop farting around with the soft stuff and come to the real meetings?" said the agent.

"Yeah, man," said the jazzman, who was not black but called everyone "man." "Come taste the real thing." And he did his funny little surprised double take.

The agent gave the time and the address: "Narcotics Anonymous, six p.m. tonight in the lodge."

I humored them. Their lives had been shaped by their drugs, and they were my friends. And since this was reportage, I should find out what the real addicts experienced.

I took my place in the circle of people in the lodge. More noisy parkas. The outside speaker stood up. That night it was a large woman with flat hair to her hips and a shiny face. Her parka was sugar pink. She was probably fifty pounds overweight. I sighed. This pathetic middle-of-nowhere addict, nothing to do with my infinitely complicated pattern of circumstance and loss. Humoring my pals by listening to yet another confession about substances. My fingers twitched around the felt-tip in my pocket, but I knew I couldn't take notes.

"I was a poodle groomer," she began.

I rolled my eyes.

"And I was doing coke," she continued.

I sighed.

"I was doing the coke and grooming the pups, and doing the coke. And then I was grooming more pups to pay for the coke and all my money was going to the coke, and I wasn't earning enough with the pups. And then I thought—instead of grooming the pups, why don't I deal the coke?"

She was talking about me. Me and *Vogue*. The spell of *Vogue*, British *Vogue*, American *Vogue*, Paris *Vogue*. This woman was me. All those clothes, all those outfits, all those pretty things to make life beautiful, weren't they drugs? This woman and her coke were me and *Vogue*, me buying the clothes, buying the parties and the famous names and the access to everything that glittered and shone and was superior and wonderful, and it cost me so much that I didn't have time to write anything except more pieces about the clothes and the glamour and the parties and the famous names and everything that glittered and shone and was superior and wonderful, I was an addict and servant to illusion until the day I understood that, instead of getting high on it, I could deal it. From magazine writer to editor, from addict to dealer.

I jumped up from my chair yelling, "That's me! You're me!"

The circle in the lodge applauded. The poodle groomer smiled and continued the tale of her descent into addiction while I fidgeted, flushed with insight.

After the closing ritual prayer about acceptance and change, I took the agent's arm and the rocker's arm and kissed the jazzman on the lips, and we marched off to the cafeteria for decaffeinated tea and ice cream sandwiches under a neon light.

"I understand everything now," I told my three friends, "the poodle groomer and I are the same person! Her cocaine is my *Vogue*! I'm addicted to *Vogue*!"

"That's just the first step, man," said the jazzman. "Watch out for relapses."

The next day, Dan summoned me to his office and smoothed out a fax in front of him.

"I have to read you this," he said in that voice.

It was from Jonathan in Australia, addressed to "the primary therapist" for Joan Buck. It began "*I write to you as your employer, as well as a friend who cares deeply about you.*" Dan raised an eyebrow.

This was presumably a Cottonwood form letter conceived to standardize an exchange of grievances, and divided into thirteen points. Jonathan expected me to look deeply and fully into myself, and so on; he expected me to come back to Paris *Vogue* as a team player and respect Gardner's authority.

Point 12, presumably the flashpoint drug slot, addressed the issue of Camel Lights: "*I expect you to have a healthy lifestyle and not behave in ways which could jeopardize your physical or mental health. (I understand you smoke and accept this.)*"

Dan read the whole letter in a newscaster-neutral version of his voice. I sat paralyzed by the fear of letting my rage show.

"What do you think?" he asked me.

"What do *you* think?" I replied.

"I think it's a shit sandwich, and if you eat it, I'll be very disappointed."

Shit sandwich. I liked that. I wasn't going to eat no shit sandwich.

Someone handed me a poem. It read, in part: "I want to know if you can disappoint another to be true to yourself . . . If you can be faithless and therefore trustworthy."

That's impossible, I thought. I'm a trouper, I'm a pro. I don't disappoint people, I always come through. I can never disappoint Dad. He said stop acting, I stopped acting. Write, he said, I wrote. Wasn't I right to have created the aura of a golden life around him in Paris? Who did I have to disappoint to be true to myself? What was that stupid poem?

That night I couldn't sleep; I left the room where the three suicides whimpered through their Benadryl stupor, and went to lie on a bench and look up at the stars over the desert. Stars in the sky, where they belonged. I looked up at the stars and knew that I belonged nowhere, not New York, not Paris, not London, not Los Angeles where I was born. My dream life was over. Before I could find a home, I'd have to stop obeying other people and a guardian angel from a children's book.

The next day, I sheltered from the rain next to a guy called Mike. "You ever do theater?" he asked. "You're always dancing around."

A day later, in the group in Dan's office, I said, "My turn," reached into the basket full of inspirational booklets, turned to the date, November 19, and read out: "What a wonderful world it would be." Satchmo's lyrics, Uncle Don's music. It was time to leave. I'd been there forty days.

I said good-bye to the director. "You did this to yourself," she said, "because you didn't dare say you were bored. You kept giving them more, and the more you gave them, the more you despised them."

The jazzman hugged me. "Don't relapse," he said. "You hate yourself so much for relapsing. And when you relapse, that's when you die."

"No chance," I said. Forty days of approval had put me in a pink glow. The woman from Intake returned all my potions except the Xanax, because it was a real drug.

I went to Sedona, wrote a hundred postcards of red rocks to tell everyone that I'd be back in December, and bought a remarkably ugly red Polartec jacket printed with steer heads. Woman of the West, wild and style-free.

I was at a friend's in New York when Jonathan reached me to say, "There have been changes at *Vogue*," as if I didn't know that Emmanuelle Alt had replaced Marcus, that Carine was creative director.

I was succinct. "I'll see you when I've spoken to my lawyer."

"I should give you a going-away party," he said.

"Not a good idea," I said.

I tried to get some Xanax for the jet lag from the friend with whom I was staying, but he was reluctant. I'd just come out of rehab and might very well be an addict.

Before I went home to Paris, there was Gilbert de Botton's memorial service in London, three months after his death.

CHAPTER TWENTY-THREE

The Pelham was my London home, but my room this time was part of an incomplete expansion, isolated between floors on a steep staircase to the street, a room that was nowhere.

Jet lag, no Xanax, no sleep. In the December dawn over the Lycée Français South Kensington, I saw where I'd waited for the number 14 bus after school, Dino's Pizzeria, the tuck shop where my father bought the candy bars for me to make friends with, the street where I'd watched Roman Polanski shoot *Repulsion.*

Joel Rosenthal, an American jeweler I knew from Paris, would escort me to the memorial; he was Janet de Botton's friend, Jonathan's friend. I waited for him to come down from his room at Claridge's, dressed up in my new Prada clothes I'd had sent from Paris, swaying slightly on my platform shoes.

Joel handed me a diamond ring, in a shape that was his trademark, the stone a cushion set on an insubstantial circle of stardust. A famous magician had given it to a supermodel for their engagement, but the engagement was now off.

"Wear it tonight," he said.

It fit. I held out my hand to see how it sat on my finger. Here was the diamond ring my father had seen in my future, but things are never what they seem. Diamonds never come from the person you wish had given them to you. I wondered how much it was worth. What if I kept it? Could I be untrustworthy? Jump in a cab at the end of the evening, vanish into the night with a stolen ring, sell it, and live off the proceeds in some distant jungle?

The service was held in London's oldest synagogue on a deserted street in the financial heart of the city. I saw Janet, bejeweled, her girls, Gilbert's children. Harry arrived, scowl first. I looked the other way.

The synagogue was tight and dark, full of tall British bankers. I was given a seat apart, on the side of the lectern. At the end of the service, the rabbi said, "I must ask you not to linger outside, but to disperse quickly. We are not loved, we must not be a target."

We dispersed quickly and gathered at Harry's Bar. Friends of Gilbert's, people I hardly knew, thanked me for what I'd done the night of his death, and commented on the beauty of my diamond ring. I understood that Joel had put it on my finger to deflect attention from my story.

I closed my hand into a fist when Joel hailed a cab for me, but he held out his hand. Slowly, I pulled off the ring, and gave up the last piece of stardust.

On the plane to Paris the next day, coffee was served in newly designed mugs decorated with romantic black-and-white photos of Paris, each mug bearing a different picture. I wanted every one of them. I was Nana, stowing ashtrays in her handbag, souvenirs of Europe. It was all going to be over so soon. I asked the flight attendant to give me a full set, and she did.

I set my eight new coffee mugs on my kitchen table. Nothing had changed since I'd been gone, but I no longer had a job, and this was no longer my home.

I went to see Jules. He was sitting on the daybed in the Napoleon green living room, watching the video of *Singin' in the Rain*. He glared at me; I hugged him. "Your hair looks like shit," he said.

"It's over," I said, "*Vogue* is over."

"I knew that," he said.

Aneeta took me aside to say, "We've gone through a lot of Haldol. He keeps having rages. He wants to see Dr. O'Brien every day. And the only thing he'll eat is pistachio ice cream."

My friends from the magazine came to see me at home and report on all the changes. Richard Buckley from *Vogue Hommes International* took me to dinner to give me all the gossip. I wanted food as soft as pistachio ice cream, so we went to Le Soufflé.

"So," he asked, "do you want to know what they're saying? Fashion people are stupid, you have to remember that. Feel free to laugh."

"Go ahead."

"They're saying you and Gardner were lovers until she dropped you because you're an addict. People saw syringes in your handbags. One editor said you opened your Fendi tote and the syringes just rolled out. Clear-glass syringes."

"That's my seawater," I said. "*Sérum de Quinton,* to balance my electrolytes."

"If you just took drugs like everyone else, you wouldn't be in trouble. So they say she dropped you because you're an addict, and then a ghost came to you and told you to kill her, so you followed her to Milan and tried to kill her. That's why they got rid of you."

It hadn't occurred to me that I was going to be labeled an addict by anyone but the cabal that wanted me gone from Paris *Vogue.* But the story hung on visual clues, the Sapphic connotations of my short hair, the phials of seawater, the ghost of the Rue Jacob. Eric Wright must have talked about my haunted apartment. The attempt to kill Gardner was the only thing that didn't fit.

"And why did I slug her?"

Richard laughed. "When Gardner walked into the Prada show she'd had her lips blown out so huge that the fashion TV cameraman said it looked like someone had punched her in the mouth, and his boss said it was probably you."

~

The announcement of my departure was drafted in New York for release on December 7. On the sixth, Paulino told me that Gardner had made her translate it into French, without the lines about my contribution to the magazine and the 40 percent increase in circulation during my tenure. I called the PR in New York to make sure the full text was enforced, made a cup of tea, and asked the cleaning lady to come in early the next day and stay until evening.

"There are going to be bouquets coming in all day," I said.

The doorbell rang only twice that day: one bouquet from a nice PR, the other from an Italian designer's husband. At seven thirty that evening, the cleaning lady asked, "Can I go home now?" I thought I'd broken through to a more cogent view of life, but still I waited for floral tributes, even to my failure.

Empty days, while everything was worked out. I didn't have the anxious baying of the magazine in my head anymore, or its advertisers, staff, and contributors. I had sums and trivia, laundry, repairs, maintenance, and a gag order. I wore only jeans, desert boots, and the offensive Polartec jacket printed with the steer heads, proof of my newfound authenticity; but it was just another costume, another pose. In case anyone was watching, I went to have my hair done at Carita twice a week, and then I went home through the cold gray streets, longing for American sunshine.

I dreamed the office was a spaceship with curved white walls, a place where I trespassed. I went back one last time on a cold December Sunday to empty my bookshelves and my desk, under the vigilant eye of the general manager François Dieulesaint, who kept his coat on as I hauled books into boxes. "There are two copies of that one," he said as I held a book of Peter Lindbergh's photos. "They're both mine," I said.

~

Charlotte and her boyfriend, Jean-Noël, invited me to a dinner. Aneeta was cooking, so I went to see her in the kitchen.

"I can't believe you left me alone with that maniac for a full two months," she said. "I can't do it anymore. I'm done. Johanna's there, and you can take care of Jules from now on."

A friend knew a woman who was good with old people. Corinne was eager and enthusiastic, had red hair, and there was a lot of her. We discussed terms: she should spend about six hours a day with him, take him out a bit, make sure he had his hair cut, his nails done, and then there was the dentist. Eat meals with him, try to interest him in something beyond pistachio ice cream. Johanna upstairs would take up the slack.

"Do you want me to fuck him?" Corinne asked, matter-of-factly.

"I hadn't thought about it," I admitted, "but you don't have to."

~

I had to find what there was beyond the promises I'd made to Dad, to Paris *Vogue*, beyond my addiction to brightness as pathetic as the poodle groomer's addiction to cocaine.

I didn't know where to start. I was offered jobs, consultancies, advertising gigs. Chanel asked me to work on a campaign; Cartier offered another. My lawyer told me to refuse everything until the exit contract was signed, and I was relieved. I didn't want to advance the agendas of advertisers; I wanted to find substance.

Paris *Vogue* was moving my things back to America, but there was as yet no destination. In New York I'd be sealed into the persona of former editor in chief of Paris *Vogue*; I'd spend my time having my hair done, finding ways to get new clothes to conceal my loss of status. I didn't want to be watched. In any case, I couldn't afford a place in New York City big enough for me and Jules, and I was not going to put him in a home in Queens.

"Where shall we move, Dad?" I asked. "Where do you want to go?"

"L.A. would be nice," he said.

Two cars. No, just one. Whoever I found for him would already have a car.

For Christmas, I gave one last party, decorated a tree, pawed through the accumulated loot of six and half years to find presents: mother-of-pearl caviar spoons, Chanel cushions, bags, boxes, vases, small leather goods still in their logoed boxes. My actor friends came, my artist friends, my writer friends. Old friends. Many people brought foie gras, more fresh foie gras than anyone could eat.

My father sat on his chair, regal. He knew it was the last time he'd be the honored guest at the Rue de Cérisoles. He was so charming, so well dressed, so impeccable, that a divorcée babe mistook him for her next benefactor, and insisted on taking him home in her car. Charlotte said, "Let it happen."

When I asked him about it the next day, he answered a different question. "When the time comes," he said, "I want to be buried with your mother at the Père Lachaise."

~

Karl had been silent, but after Christmas, Nicole Wisniak made sure that he called me. He asked what he could do.

I was still attached to things, and could only think of treats.

"You know how I never accepted any couture while I was editing *Vogue*?" I said. "Now would be a great time for you to give me something."

He thought that was a wonderful idea, and invited me to lunch.

I hadn't seen him in more than half a year. I climbed his palatial staircase at the Rue de l'Université and, bidden by the butler, waited for him at the dining table set up on the landing.

He came from behind me and sat down, on time.

"How do you think I look?" he said.

It was horrifying. He looked like a cadaver. I wanted to scream.

"I lost ninety pounds," he said.

I took my place among clients in the front row at the Chanel show and ostentatiously marked the outfit I wanted, a sheer blouse and long skirt fit for a 1930s debutante intent on renouncing the world. Millicent Rogers, say, just as she was moving to Taos. Another costume for another romantic idea.

Allegra came to stay with me as I wound down the apartment. I took her to the most eccentric section of the flea market, the Marché Paul Bert, where I bought a leather screen and antique dishtowels. Allegra circled two battered leather armchairs, and then bought them.

"How are you going to get them back to Taos?" I asked.

"You've got a container going to America; they can travel in that."

"What if I go to New York, or Los Angeles?"

"Well, at least they'll be in the continental United States."

I had no reason to be in one place rather than another. I remembered the dawn, five months and a lifetime ago, at the ass end of nowhere in the Santa Fe rail yard, leaning against the maroon and yellow locomotive with "Atchison, Topeka and Santa Fe" written on its side. I had no agenda other than to find a place where Jules could be safe. Allegra needed her leather armchairs in Taos, an hour up the road. That was a good enough reason to move to Santa Fe.

"How would you feel about New Mexico?" I asked Dad. "I could get a pretty nice house there, and we could find a new Corinne, we could be in Santa Fe."

"New Mexico? Live in New Mexico long enough and you start seeing flying saucers. Fuck New Mexico."

The contract was still being negotiated, no money was coming in, Dad's expenses had not gone down. I sold his Toulouse-Lautrec poster, Nana's silver candlesticks, a set of chairs: I sold the monogrammed raincoat and my custom-made rust red Hermès Kelly bag to pay the bills, and went to New York to see what was happening. When I came back, shaken by machinations that could only come from Gardner, I'd agreed to leave Paris by the end of February.

~

Corinne said Johanna had run out of Haldol to give Jules. I ordered a new prescription, this time for two bottles, one for her to carry and one for Corinne, and called her to check that she'd picked it up.

"I gave them to Jules," she said.

"It's for you to carry," I shouted, "it's not—"

I ran to Dad's apartment.

There he sat in his green leather Regency chair, at the round table he and Mum had given me when I was twenty, its top scorched from the cedar I'd burned that ghost night at the Rue Jacob, the marks hidden by a table carpet bought at the antiques fair in the Place Saint-Sulpice. In front of him was one of the tall beer glasses they'd been given as wedding presents, and next to the glass were two plastic bottles of Haldol, and one spun on its side, light and empty. In the glass was a dark yellow liquid.

That's what despair looks like: a tall glass of Haldol to end it all.

"What are you drinking?" I asked, casually, my voice steady.

"Ginger ale," he said.

"Oh, I love ginger ale," I said, and reached for the glass. "Can I have some?"

He covered the glass with his hand.

"Don't drink it, it's bad," he said. "It's gone off."

"Then I shall have to throw it away," I said, like a nanny, and swept the full bottle of Haldol into my hand, plucked the glass off the table, carried it to the kitchen, trembling, and emptied it in the sink.

"I'm going to America to find us a wonderful place to live. I promise it'll be nice," I said.

"Los Angeles," he said, "or, if it's really nice, Santa Fe."

~

I went to New Mexico first. Richard Buckley and Tom Ford had a house in Santa Fe, where Tom had grown up. Allegra came down from Taos and stayed with me at La Posada, an inn full of local ironwork. The crouched brown buildings were dreary under March snow, the sky lightless. There were quirky gift shops, older ladies with dangling earrings, strange white Sikhs in white turbans. No one would be watching me here. Richard found me a Realtor, who assured me there was not one house to rent, only to buy.

Los Angeles had to be a better idea. I stayed at the Chateau Marmont. The hotel manager, Phil Pavel, was also an actor. We sat in the lobby and discussed plays. I had an invitation to the *Vanity Fair* Oscar party, hardly a touchstone of reality, but it might yield a job, a contract, a future.

I wanted to see Anjelica; Bob Graham made peace between us, and we reunited over dinner, just the two of us.

"You in a rehab, that's rich," Anjelica said. "Tell me again how that happened."

"I'm not entirely sure," I said.

I was having breakfast in the garden of the Chateau Marmont when Carine Roitfeld arrived. She had yet to be named editor in chief of Paris *Vogue*, but it was imminent. The fashion people sitting at the tables between us stiffened and chirped, anxious to see what would happen. They knew I was a homicidal addict.

I crossed the garden to Carine, and hugged her.

"Watch out for Gardner," I whispered. "She's a lying bitch."

Carine hugged me back. "*D'accord*," she said.

~

I drove around to sense what neighborhoods would be safe for Jules to walk around in, but the desultory search was interrupted by a call from his landlady in Paris.

"Your father was naked in the staircase again today, Madame, and the day before, and last week. You must come back to Paris."

I went back.

"I think he's had a stroke," said Corinne. I called Dr. O'Brien, who put him in the American Hospital for a scan and tests. His brain, said the doctor, did not show the lesions of Alzheimer's, but the shrinkage of dementia.

"Don't pay Dr. O'Brien, he's a wonderful guy," said Dad from his bed in the American Hospital. "I've given him one of the Monte Carlo apartments, and the boat. You don't need them."

I took Dr. O'Brien to lunch to straighten him out.

"You don't have to worry about my bill," he began.

"Oh, but I do," I said.

"No, really, your father's taken care of it," he said, a little shyly.

I took out my checkbook. He shifted in his seat.

"There are no apartments in Monte Carlo," I said. "There is no boat."

"Really?" he asked. "Are you sure?"

I went to London to look for anything left of Dad's former security, a silly hope. Dad's old accountant Nymie Libson, who knew all the secrets, had died; I filled in his son John.

"He told his doctor in Paris that he'd leave him one of his two apartments in Monte Carlo, and a boat!"

"Jules," said John Libson. "Oh Jules."

And then my exit contract was finally signed, I had my severance, and I was free to go. "Lovey," said Susan Train, who was now in charge of my return to America, "your things have been with the movers for more than two months. It's costing the company a fortune. Don't you have any idea where you're going?"

"Not yet," I said.

~

Johanna showed me a large check that Dad had written to her while I was in London. At least she hadn't cashed it.

"It's to buy him a bicycle," she said.

"A bicycle?" I asked. "With two wheels?"

"He wants to use it to go down to Monte Carlo," she said, "to look at his apartments."

I fired Johanna, confiscated the checkbook, and conferred with Corinne. He needed to be somewhere supervised. Corinne knew of a home of superior quality, La Villa des Sources, near Versailles. The guests I saw there—or were they customers, clients, inmates?—were well dressed, many of them spoke English, the public rooms looked like a nice hotel, and the private rooms overlooked beautiful gardens.

He might not mind it too much; I brought him to see for himself.

"Classy," he said. I was relieved.

"It's only until I get our house," I said. "And then I'll come back to get you."

On cue, the Realtor from Santa Fe called; she had the perfect house. Allegra went to look and reported that it had two wings and a walled garden. It would do, and I could deliver her armchairs almost to her door.

Corinne moved Jules into the Villa des Sources with his favorite things: his photographs, his books, his tape of *Singin' in the Rain*, the photograph of him and Joyce on their wedding day on its Lucite stand.

I had to sort through his apartment, choose what things were going to the movers, so he'd have them in Santa Fe, what to discard. Much of the furniture was useful currency to pay for my French lawyer; various things would go to Corinne, many to charity. I asked Susan Train to bring her taste and her good sense to the task.

"You have to tell me what to keep and what to throw away," I said. "Please just sit in that chair and say 'Yes' or 'No.'"

She sat with her back to the window, lit a cigarette, and prepared to edit Dad's leftovers. I held up one thing after another. Household objects, *objets de vertu.*

She called out "Yes" or "No" with the elegance of Diana Vreeland choosing photos.

I kept his first Hollywood address book, the one with Marilyn Monroe's home number.

~

I left for New Mexico. Now that Jules was installed there, the Villa des Sources looked less attractive than it had before, but he wouldn't be there for long.

The house in Santa Fe was on a dirt road—he wouldn't like that—and had a raised kitchen as bright as the set for a cooking show. His wing had two bedrooms; later I'd find a woman to live with us, for him. His room had a skylight; he could watch the sun move across his bed in the morning, down the side, and along the dark red floor tiles. I pictured him sitting in a chair by the hollyhocks in the garden, face turned to the sun, smiling. He had to like it here. The colors were so strong.

I hired a bed for myself, leased a yellow car, met new people, and waited for the containers to arrive.

Corinne called. Jules had had some episodes at the Villa des Sources, and he'd thrown his cane, the one from Jonathan, at one of the attendants. The man was unhurt, but the cane was in pieces.

"Should I come back?" I asked, panicked. "No," said Corinne.

I went on waiting for the containers to arrive. The ship had barely set off across the Atlantic when Jules began to will himself to die. Corinne called at dawn; he was in hospital, in a coma. His heart, she said. I flew back to Paris.

I slept on the floor of Charlotte's study, on the mattress from the bed I'd given her. She'd put the mahogany frame in storage; it was too high and too narrow to be useful. I took the subway to the hospital, which was in the suburb of Suresnes.

The hospital hallways didn't smell of ether and alcohol the way they used to; the new disinfectant smelled faintly of shit, or perhaps the halls smelled of shit, and I pretended it was a new disinfectant.

His head looked very round on the pillow. His eyes were shut. Was this a coma? Outside his window I could see the Longchamp racetrack where Nana and Poppy so loved to go, where they all went to the races in the old days.

I sat by him; after half an hour, he opened his eyes.

"It's a miracle," said the nurse.

"Good hospital," said Dad, after he'd had a drink of water. "Much better than the American one."

"How are you?" I asked.

"Tired," he said.

I didn't know what to do, so I did what I'd seen in movies, and wet washcloths and put cologne on them to make compresses for his forehead. I held his hand and rubbed his knuckles. Every day he was a little more present. I brought the English papers, read him the latest news and scandals, the reviews. Soon he was well enough to sit up in a chair and read the *Herald Tribune* for himself. His glasses, his newspaper, water. I brought him some things from his room at the Villa des Sources.

"I'm so glad you and Anjelica are talking again," he said. "I like Bob. You have to tell him something. That Virgin he's making for the cathedral. Her arms are too damn long."

A few days later, the nurse who brought his lunch said, "*La glace à la pistache, c'est pour plus tard.*" Pistachio ice cream, that will come later.

"You've got them trained," I said. He winked.

I told him about the house on the old-fashioned road in Santa Fe, told him how the light from the skylight would move across his bed, how tall the hollyhocks were in the garden. I didn't mention the desert dust that settled on everything.

"We could get a dog, a yellow dog," I said. "They do yellow dogs in Santa Fe."

"No mutt," he said. "Fleas."

I told him I was writing again, but this time a play. He wanted me to get a job.

"Work with Tina Brown," he said. "I like Tina."

I went down to the hospital garden to take a call from Jonathan.

He wanted Jules to know he loved him. I didn't answer. He asked about the cane. "It's gone," I said.

I bought sweet things from the vending machine, and went back upstairs.

"Jonathan sends his love," I said, as if that were good news.

"Why are you talking to that asshole?" Jules asked. "He can drop dead."

He didn't want to walk; he didn't leave his room. He had bedsores. It was unclear what had been wrong, but he was getting better. He wanted to write something. I gave him a pen and paper, but he drew lines, not words.

I was by his side for weeks. Susan Train called from her holiday. "Lovey, you can't keep sleeping on a floor," she said. "Have my bed." I took the weekend off and moved to her apartment. Corinne took over for two days.

When I came into his room at the hospital on Monday, my father's wrists were tied to his bed with leather straps.

"He was a little agitated," said the nurse. I asked to see his doctor and fell asleep on a chair in the corridor waiting for him.

He'd turned violent on Saturday, midmorning, said the doctor. "The straps will be removed when he is calmer."

As for his physical state, "*Il n'y a rien à faire*," said the doctor. He had no diagnostic.

It wasn't really happening. He wasn't a devastated old man with bedsores and a shrunken brain on the verge of his eighty-fourth birthday; this hospital room was a movie set, its view of the Longchamp racetrack a matte painting, added to tie up past and present.

I sat by him and tried to think. There was nothing wrong with him, not in his body. It wasn't a disease, it wasn't the heart; his heart had always been strong. It was disappointment. And the moment the word "disappointment" came to me, I knew I'd let him down.

"I'm sorry," I said in his ear.

He didn't answer.

He'll be better soon, I thought. The containers were about to arrive in Santa Fe, I had to meet the movers, to fill the house with our things.

"I'll be back in ten days," I said, "and you'll come home with me to Santa Fe."

He turned his eyes to me and made the motion "Cut."

"Cut," the way a director does at the end of a scene. Cut. The hand straight, up and down, fast. Cut. Like scissors. Cut. He knew the hospital room was a set.

"You'll love the house I found," I said. We had a home to go to.

"Go away now, leave me alone, and shut the door," he said. "Go away. Leave." I came closer to him. "I said leave now, leave me alone, and shut the door."

I left. I'd ask around in Santa Fe, I'd find the perfect person to keep him happy.

~

It was July 13, the fifth anniversary of Joyce's death, when two forty-foot containers arrived on the dirt road in Santa Fe. It took five days to move everything in. There were too many books to unpack and no shelves, so I asked the movers to take them to storage. They left one book behind, forgotten; the last edition of *Katz's Encyclopedia of Film* to carry an entry for Jules Buck.

On the morning of July 18 came a call from Paris to tell me my father had died.

I didn't hurry. There was no reason to anymore. A friend had come to help me make the place look nice; I let her. I could leave the next day. I called the obituary pages of London newspapers; the last edition of *Katz's Encyclopedia of Film* had all the information I needed.

I napped on the Air France flight from Los Angeles to Paris, and dreamed of Dad standing in his pale polo shirt and his gray trousers, happy and spry.

"Look, I have a new watch!" he said. "It's a Juvenia Eterna."

I woke in a sweat, wondering what watch I had to retrieve from what pawnshop. And then I stopped trying to picture a watch, and saw the words in Latin: Juvenia Aeterna. His new time was eternal youth.

In the hospital morgue, Jules's face was thoughtful. I gave the attendant the blazer with the real gold buttons for him to wear in his coffin, slipped one of his calling cards in the breast pocket, the one with nothing on it but the name Jules Buck in copperplate script.

"You may meet some new people," I whispered.

Charlotte said, "Your father only dies once. This time you stay in a hotel." I checked into the Lancaster off the Champs-Élysées, near the Virgin Megastore, where I went to find music for his cremation.

I wandered between wooden boxes full of slim clear plastic cases. "Which one do you want?" I asked, and my hands went to a CD, the 1943 Broadway revival of the musical *A Connecticut Yankee in King Arthur's Court*. His favorite book. One song was titled "You Are from Another World." That'll do, I thought.

The obituaries in the London papers were extensive and fairly accurate, but still, he'd want the *New York Times*. I asked Betty Bacall for help.

"Just call the *New York Times* obit department, say you're Lauren Bacall, and ask them when Jules Buck's obituary is running."

"Done," said Betty.

I'd give him one last party with all his favorite foods, and tequila, because tequila turns sadness into something higher, and wine just makes people weep. The hotel's owner, Grace Leo-Andrieu, was happy to let me take over the hotel garden for the lavish celebration to honor Jules Buck. One last grand illusion.

Flowers came in, all the flowers I could have wished for. The concierge said, "The guests are asking what all this is for," gesturing at the new bouquets on his counter, the waiters rushing into the garden with ice buckets and more bouquets. "Would it be all right if we made photocopies of your father's obituaries to explain?"

"Of course," I said. You couldn't explain me in Paris, but a brace of London obituaries would explain my father.

The cremation was held on top of a hill in Suresnes, in a chapel lined with sunflowers, to a full house. Everyone who'd ever listened to him, everyone who was a friend, was there. John Libson came with his wife, Maxine, to represent London, and to read the Kaddish.

I handed Charlotte the slip of paper that I'd asked her to read.

Charlotte rose to the lectern, the paper in her hand, and said, "Joan asked me to read something, but I'm not going to do it." She paused. I froze in the front pew. "Now that I've looked at it, I realize I know it, so I'm going to sing it instead."

And she sang the Twenty-Third Psalm, unaccompanied. Her voice, poised and steady, light. Her gift, a performance for Jules. No one had heard her sing before. I was too moved to cry.

The garden at the Hôtel Lancaster filled with guests; the stars came out for him, and friends and pretty girls, and kind boys and men who'd strained to listen to Jules's stories through the nights at the Rue de Cérisoles.

I nudged John Libson when my father's doctor arrived.

"That's him," I whispered.

John Libson looked at the champagne buckets full of tequila, the mounds of lamb chops and mountains of string beans, the trays of coffee éclairs, the bowls of pistachio ice cream, the movie stars, the fashionable and the grand.

"He'll never believe you now," he said. "He's going to sue you for the Monte Carlo apartment, and the boat."

It was the most magnificent party yet.

~

Nine months later, Corinne retrieved my mother from the Getz family plot in Cannes, and I buried my parents' ashes together in the Columbarium of the Père Lachaise cemetery.

I'd stayed in Santa Fe; now I lived with Kim, a painter, and he came with me.

We stood with Corinne by the Columbarium outside the Père Lachaise office. I held the box with Jules's ashes in my arms, Kim held Joyce's ashes in their metal canister. Corinne carried two Baccarat roses that I'd bought at the florist outside the gate. I looked up at the long wall above us where the names of the great were engraved over cubbyholes bearing their ashes, and wondered where, in that pantheon, my parents would go.

"*Non, non, non,*" said the Père Lachaise official. Jules and Joyce Buck weren't going in the wall at all, we were informed, but in the *sous-sol.* The basement? I felt the box begin to shake in my arms. My father did not want to be in any fucking basement, who the fuck did they think he was? White rage from the box, white rage through me.

"I'm not going in the basement!" shouted a voice through me.

"Shhh," said Kim.

"It's okay," said Corinne. "The *sous-sol* is very nice."

We followed the official to a wide staircase, went down a flight, turned a corner. The small room looked like a *boîte de nuit,* maybe the ground-floor bar at Castel's. Names engraved in gold on square white marble slabs; not far away, I read Modigliani. Arthur, however, not Amedeo. A halogen standing lamp, turned low, registered as a flicker. The cubbyhole waiting for my parents was at chest level. The box went in, the cocktail shaker went in next—Joyce always liked sleeping nearer to the door. I had a photograph of the two of them, young and smiling, taken in a train station at the beginning of their European adventures, perhaps Hamburg, perhaps Paris, definitely 1952; I slipped it into the hole, and then the two roses. It was April 12, 2002, a Friday.

Bury your dead, pay your taxes, and justice will be done. It took less than a week.

On Monday, April 15, in Santa Fe, I wrote checks to pay the taxes on my severance.

On April 16, the *New York Times* ran a full-page story on Carine Roitfeld, now officially editor in chief of Paris *Vogue.*

At six in the morning on April 17, Joyce's birthday, Susan Train's phone call woke me at six in the morning. She whooped, "The witch is dead!"

"What?"

"Gardner's been fired," she said. "Champagne corks are popping all over Condé Nast."

Anjelica sent me a battery-driven dancing doll of James Brown singing, "I Feel Good."

~

One month later, the cathedral of Our Lady of the Angels was completed, and the bronze doors, the tympanum, and the Virgin Mary that Bob Graham had worked on for five years were ready to be installed.

We left the Venice house after dinner and drove many miles to the foundry, where the massive bronzes were loaded onto flatbed trucks ringed with striped flags, and we followed the trucks in Bob's van at five miles an hour along surface streets to downtown Los Angeles. A spotlit crane slowly hoisted the doors as big as houses into place in the cathedral wall. Anjelica and I watched until we ran out of awe and wandered between saplings in the garden; then I went into the unfinished cathedral, made a nest of mover's blankets in the space where the altar would go, and took a nap.

When I came out, the sky was gray but not yet light. I ran my hands along the lowest bas-reliefs on the door. Bob had made cartouches of the animals once worshipped as gods. An eagle, a turtle, a flying serpent, an ibis, a dove rose from the cold bronze, warm to the touch. Up there in the center of the tympanum in the night was the Virgin.

We came back the next day to see her in the sun; as we arrived at the cathedral, my cell phone rang; I answered, annoyed at the distraction. It was Jonathan Newhouse.

"Joan, I owe you an apology," he said. "That Gardner Bellanger's a psycho. She tried to do the same thing to Carine that she'd done to you. But this time I saw it coming."

"Good," I said, "but I really can't talk right now."

I put my cell back in my bag, and looked up at the statue of the young woman with a strong nose and big lips standing above the bronze doors, two feet planted on the crescent moon. No veil, arms bare. I remembered Jules saying that Bob was making the arms too long, and I looked up to catch the fault, but from so far below, the long arms extended welcome in grace. And just as Bob had promised, the round hole behind her head transformed the sunlight into a halo.

He'd made the Virgin's arms the right length for the angle at which she would be seen; he'd aligned the sun by compass point to make a golden crown at noon. Everything is perspective. Where you stand changes what you see.

EPILOGUE

"Don't relapse," the jazzman had said as I left Cottonwood.

"Not a chance," I'd said, "not with what I've learned." *Vogue* was my poison. I was strong and wise from my forty days in the desert.

"The thing is," he'd added, "when you relapse, that's when it really kills you."

I'd never go back to *Vogue.*

In Santa Fe I floated in a haze of mourning, watched the hollyhocks grow too tall, invited friends to stay in what would have been my father's room. I wasn't his creature anymore. I'd have to learn how to live without Jules watching me.

"The veil is thinner here," said a friend who lived in a commune. Seven thousand feet above sea level, where the air is too thin to carry smells, we climbed steep beds of needles between Ponderosa pines and took hairpin turns up new trails through the woods. On a high ledge out at Bandelier, Pueblo boys with long black hair ran past us barefoot, training for a Native race. The sky over Santa Fe was full of promise and drama, the earth immobile, landlocked. I stretched time out so that I could feel it on my skin. I basked in being no one.

I went hiking with a man as pure as I hoped to be. The next day I watched the twin towers in flames on a big-screen television at a neighbor's house. The world upended, I decided to stay in Santa Fe and be safe from the alarming shape history was taking.

Before breakfast most days, we hiked up Atalaya Hill to a big rock from which we'd gaze down on the water tanks behind Saint John's College, the dull adobe scatter of Santa Fe. But I soon learned that the houses that looked like earth were built in a style called Mission Pueblo. The city fathers had chosen it at an architectural exhibition in San Diego to attract tourists with the romance of the Southwest after New Mexico became a state in 1912. I was chagrined to have chosen yet another fantasy as my new truth.

I was working on a play; I didn't want to write "he" or "she" or "I," I wanted everyone to have their own voice, just as they had at Cottonwood. It wasn't easy and I wasn't very good at it. My tactile descriptions were of no use in a play, where characters had to be motivated by needs. Straight prose was easier than the complicated architecture of characters in motion on a stage.

Anna Wintour called me after 9/11. "So many people are grieving now," she said. "Would you write about grief?" It seemed cogent enough to write about my parents, an opportunity, even, to present them to the world, even if it was through *Vogue.* I wrote the article, and went back to my play. *House & Garden* asked me to write a column called "The Slow Life" to document my new dropout existence in the high desert; with the slight feeling that I was selling off little pieces of myself, I agreed.

Your mind goes on two tracks; what you want to do, and what you do. I wanted to grow beyond my past; I missed the things that were my past.

For the first time in my life, I had money, not huge money, but more than I'd ever had before. I bought an ecologically sound house with solar panels on the roof, and filled it with everything I'd carted around the world. Jules, it turned out, had a little money that came in each year. Grateful, I took his precious Cubist still life to be cleaned. As I wrote a check to the restorer, I asked what an Alfréd Réth still life was worth these days. The restorer looked online; a larger one had sold that year for less than I'd just paid to clean mine. And so it goes with treasures.

My difficulties with the play gave me license to disobey my father. To write for actors, didn't I have to learn how to breathe and move like they did? I studied a form of improvisation called Action Theater with the former dancer who'd created it, Ruth Zaporah, and freed my mind from references, from trying to make sense of things. I learned to pay attention to every moment. The practice was repetitive and dull, but it provided the structure in which to play onstage, always with a partner. If I planned what I'd do before we stood up to perform, my plan obscured the moment, and nothing came to me; if I planned nothing, together we could build an infinite imaginary world.

If I can do this, I thought, I don't need my balms and my intoxicants: the famous names and the glamour.

But whenever American *Vogue* asked me to write a piece, I said yes. I liked the attention from my editor there; I liked the deadline adrenaline.

"Be careful," said Kim, the pure boyfriend.

I was perceived as living in the high desert, but in truth it was a condo near the center of Santa Fe. The people I performed with were dropouts, retirees, baggers at Whole Foods. I was an amateur at last, humble, unseen, an amateur among amateurs.

There were more assignments, interviews, profiles. I slipped back to the *Vogue* way of telling things, the praise of surface. Anna Wintour offered me a contract; I became American *Vogue*'s television critic, and piles of screeners arrived from the networks, for me to review. I watched the shows and imagined acting in them. I wanted to work with actors who weren't baggers at Whole Foods. Humility began to pall; I wanted response, applause, success. I wanted fame.

I inched back to New York. By 2006, I'd sold the solar house and bought a loft in Hell's Kitchen to be near the theaters. I left Kim behind in Santa Fe.

Your mind moves on two tracks; I was a humble, ageing acting student; I was, once again, *Vogue.* And because I lay on the crowded concrete floor of the basement of a church on West 100th Street once a week, cycling through a preparation for acting class, I believed I was a new person and that *Vogue* was only something I did to earn enough money to live in New York and be near my teachers.

Acting briefly took on the shimmer of a possible career. Nora Ephron knew I could pass for French and cast me in *Julie & Julia* as the head of the Cordon Bleu cooking school. Wearing dark red lipstick, tight suits, and a snarl, my job as Madame Brassart was to tell Julia Child, over the course of many scenes, that she had no talent. I channeled every dismissive French woman I'd ever met and curled my lip at Meryl Streep, who came back at me with Julia Child's cheery determination. For a few days of pure pleasure, Meryl Streep was my ally and my partner.

Irina Brook cast me in a play about Marguerite Duras, in which I finished off a bottle of fake wine and talked about love, men, and alcohol. My pay was $500 a week; acting was an indulgence that would not support me. I was grateful to have *Vogue*.

The Internet was slowly killing magazines, but Condé Nast seemed untouched. *Traveler* sent me to Istanbul, where I spent days in the archaeological museum; they sent me to Rome, where I spent weeks wandering in the ruins. If I could write about the ancient world, I was staying true to myself.

The world economy collapsed, and now I took all of American *Vogue*'s assignments, without judging their worth. I let *Vogue* decide what was interesting. It was my words they wanted, not my opinion. I interviewed actresses, a model who'd become First Lady of France. I did what I was asked to do. They flew me in business class. I stayed in nice hotels.

Relapse begins when you start to forget what you know is important. When you start grabbing at the little treats.

Anna Wintour wanted an interview with the wife of Syria's president Bashar al-Assad, so in December of 2010, I was asked to go to Damascus. It was a terrible idea, but I didn't call Anna to ask her what she was thinking.

My relapse was complete.

"I'm not a political reporter," I told the commissioning editor. I couldn't begin to comprehend the complexities of the Middle East or write in depth about a country that disturbed me.

"That's not what we want," said the editor. "It's museums. The First Lady's getting the Louvre to help excavate the ruins in Syria. You like ruins." There were over five thousand archaeological sites in Syria, and the prospect of seeing the legendary city of Palmyra in the company of a First Lady overrode my misgivings.

The assignment felt wrong, but I thought that was my fear speaking, my father's voice saying, "Big mistake." Assad's father had been a tyrant, but the son was said to be a reformer. John Kerry had visited, the United States had just resumed diplomatic relations and was sending a new ambassador. Syria had become oddly compelling among fashionable people. My old friend Christian Louboutin had bought himself a small palace in Aleppo and knew the Assads. "For dictators, they really care about their people," he told me. The line was flip; but I'd called a shoe designer, not a State Department official. Within the limits of the glossy view of life, it was a good enough endorsement. And I'd see Palmyra.

I caught the flu. The doctor asked if I wanted a note to excuse me from the assignment. "Not a chance," I said. "I'm a trouper."

I packed my felt-tip pens and went to Damascus for *Vogue*. The First Lady didn't take me to Palmyra, but instead to a youth center full of eager teenagers talking about democracy. I sat in my hotel room, afraid to go out into the ominous, dust gray city. It was the first place I'd ever been that I didn't want to explore. That wasn't what *Vogue* wanted to know. I had a minder; someone hacked my computer, I was watched. I focused on the First Lady's youth in London, her former career as a banker, her accessories, the silvery gold of the railings outside her office, the lighting fixture over her dining table. I saw the First Lady, her aides, the hotel, a shop full of silk, a souk; in a cold, underlit museum, I saw four-thousand-year-old statues of praying men with startled painted eyes.

On the last of my nine days in Damascus, a fruit seller set himself on fire in Tunisia and ignited the Arab Spring. Back in New York, I watched the events unfold on television as people across the Middle East demanded democracy. I didn't want to write the profile and told my editor that we should hold off on the story. "We need it for the

March Power issue," he said, "and no one's going to notice your piece anyway."

I couldn't disappoint. I wrote the profile in my *Vogue* voice. I described surfaces, didn't probe, and made tiny jokes. Assad, I wrote, had been elected with "a startling 97% of the vote." It wasn't *Vogue* to say that he'd been elected with "a clearly rigged 97%," not when his wife was the subject. *Vogue* made me rewrite it four times, to highlight the glamour of the First Lady, but it still ended with an incongruous scene that I found hilarious: Assad at a Catholic Christmas children's concert, singing "Jingle Bell Rock," waving a little bell, saying, "This is how you have peace in the Middle East."

Vogue titled the piece "A Rose in the Desert" and put it in the March issue. The photograph of the First Lady and the title belonged to a puff piece, and in truth, despite my mention of the secret police, Hamas, and the abandoned Jewish quarter, that's what it was. In February 2011, before the magazine came out, *Vogue* put the piece online.

The attacks were immediate, blistering, and universal. Every day I was shamed online, called a shill for the Syrians; I read the comments in disbelief. Assad had not yet shown he was a murderer like his father, and he struck me, if anything, as a little dim. But only three weeks later he revealed he was a monster.

His wife had talked about teaching children democracy. In mid-March, twelve schoolboys in Daar'a, a town south of Damascus, were caught writing graffiti that said, "The people want regime change." The children were arrested; upon their release, it was clear that some had been tortured. The families held public protests; Assad's forces shot the protesters, and then kept shooting. I watched the violence on television with horror, waiting every day for it to stop, but it escalated. The teenagers I'd met at the youth center were probably dead.

With every outrage Assad perpetrated on his people, I was attacked across the Internet, on sites for newspapers, magazines, political groups. I was called a stooge, an apologist for a tyrant. In the comments that I couldn't stop reading, I was everything I most despised.

For the rest of 2011, *Vogue* gave me no more assignments; in the fall, the managing editor said they could not renew me because I had not fulfilled my contract.

There was no severance to cushion the parting this time, and I fell to earth shamed and humiliated. No notion of a dream life being over; it was my reputation that was gone, and my income, and the *Vogue* aura that had shielded me from reality for forty years.

I didn't stretch out time to feel it on my skin as I had in Santa Fe; that was for the privileged. I had to survive. Nothing came in for me to review anymore; invitations stopped, there were fewer and fewer emails, friends dissolved. I was excoriated online for two years. I was a pariah.

In the days of the Bible, a scapegoat was an actual goat that villagers chose to blame for whatever tragedies occurred—drought, fire, famine, lightning strikes. The goat, heaped with the guilt for inexplicable events, was driven out of the village and into the wilderness. With the goat gone, surely peace and prosperity would return.

The thing was, they didn't kill the goat. It wandered off and climbed hills and chewed on stubby trees and drank from streams. It had a life after the exile, and possibly found another village where it could be the new goat, and maybe even find another goat to rut with and make more goats. And back at the first village, drought and famine went on as before.

I went to Tucson at the invitation of a curator friend and lived in a museum for three months, where I wrote and performed monologues to very small audiences. I wandered across the state of Georgia on a bus with other storytellers on The Unchained Tour, an offshoot of *The Moth*. We told stories in bookstores, to larger audiences than the ones in Tucson. I came back to New York. It was a dark and helpless time.

And that is when I came to myself.

I didn't have to pretend anything anymore. I didn't even have to pretend to be authentic. My humiliation made me cringe, made me weep, and then I was done with that and wanted to laugh again. I decided to do two things: to write this book, and to find joy.

I can no longer bring myself to write profiles, to ask questions, transcribe answers, collect flattering quotes to build dutiful portraits of strangers. I write about what I love, the people I have loved. As I assembled the improbable and conflicting events I've known, I found I had to describe the illusions I'd been brought up in, the illusions I lived in, because those illusions shaped everything that happened. That's when I began to feel real. As I endeavored to tell the truth about how I saw things, other people came to life. Love is possible only when you stop pretending.

New friends appeared, and with them new forms of friendship. My presence was no longer the promise of attention from *Vogue*; my presence was simply a person, being present. I don't have to practice long exercises to be in the moment; I know that the moment is all there is, and I'd better make it good. The new friends are often younger. I'm sometimes aware, when I see my hand as it reaches for a dish or when I catch my face reflected in a mirror, that I'm an older person. Because by now I am over sixty and have far more past than future, I am considered wise, which is other people's illusion, not mine. This makes it all the more joyful to insist on a game of charades, or any game. To insist on laughter.

New friends helped me, gave me places to work, and money. I sold the trophies from the *Vogue* years and was surprised that two Helmut Newton photographs brought in more money than my jewels. I got to know auctioneers and salerooms as well as my parents had. Many of the props and costumes from those days are gone; those that I didn't sell, I give away. But the more I give, the more there is to give, and the giving has no end.

Last year, Anjelica gave me Ricki's necklace. The necklace that hung in Ricki's closet shrine at St. Clerans, that Gladys Hill spirited away from Ricki's London bedroom after her death, the necklace that an aged lady in a wheelchair presented to Anjelica on her wedding day. The object that embodied my aspirations when I was eleven years old. It came to me after all. Later, it will go to Allegra.

Forty-eight faces carved into lava from Pompeii, set back to back, two by two, in a dull gold chain centered on a Maltese cross pendant made up of four rams' heads on the front, and four on the back. There's a tiny nick by one of the rams' heads. The little faces are

Roman nobles and actors, monsters and heroes, maybe there's a god or two in there.

It has the weight of constancy. I can run my fingers along the faces, and when I pick it up to put it on, the lavas knock together with a solid sepia sound. It's right here, right now, but it reaches back in time to golden afternoons when I sat between the pillars of the portico at St. Clerans, eyes shut tight, flying into my imagination with the girl who would always be three years younger, and who grew into my oldest friend. The necklace is the kind that was made in the eighteenth century for travelers on the Grand Tour, so they could imagine the world that existed before Vesuvius buried Pompeii under pumice and ash. It was created to evoke the past, and it comes from the place where reality and imagination meet, the only place where I truly feel at home.

ACKNOWLEDGMENTS

My first thanks go to my patient and sagacious editor Peter Borland, whose enduring forbearance in the face of a landslide of stories pushed me ever toward the true. And to Andy McNicol, agent and muse.

This book has been my home for the last five years; for a long time I worked in borrowed places. Mirella Haggiag loaned me her apartment in Rome and the desk of her late husband, Roberto; her housekeeper, Chiara, fed me three times a day. I continued on the top floor of a converted firehouse in Tucson, where Anne-Marie Russell, then the director of MOCA, gave me a three-month residency at the museum. The following autumn, Eugenia Melian loaned me her Paris apartment. In the winter, Jenni Muldaur loaned me her house in the woods, and Edwina von Gal loaned me her house on a marsh. The following summer, thanks to Miranda Dunne Parry, I found a place of my own near Rhinebeck, surrounded by trees.

Remarkable people carried me through the helplessness set off by this dive into the past, foremost Emily Contrastano, who appeared in the summer of 2012, dealt adroitly and sometimes fiercely with the material world, and ploughed just as fiercely through early drafts.

Aneeta Clark, who is now a private chef in New York City, helped me out financially, and more than once. The generosity of Carolyn Marks Blackwood allowed me to ford the last months as I finished the book. Tim McHenry, Glenn O'Brien, Isabel Coixet, and Catherine Milinaire came through with practical acts of friendship, as did Christopher Niquet, who also edited the thousands of photographs to tell a story. Just as the Paris wardrobe faded with age, Zac Posen gave me new clothes.

The initial encouragement to tell my stories came from George Dawes Green, the founder of The Moth, its director Catherine Burns, and Sarah Austin Jenness, who helped me tell "The Ghost of the Rue Jacob" at the Players Club. The story appears in the book in a fuller and more gruesome version. Joan Tewkesbury listened patiently from Santa Fe once a week as I read chapters aloud to her on the phone.

Anjelica Huston and Allegra Huston, my two semisisters, read the manuscript and shed light on their side of the stories. Charlotte Rampling filled in some blanks, as did Eugenia Melian; Janis Getz told me what she remembered about our family.

Because this is principally the story of the spell my father cast over me, some solid friends barely appear in the final draft: Valerie Wade, Peter Eyre, Dante Leonelli, Pat Birch, Kathy Rayner, Annie Ohayon, Michael Childers, Barbet Schroeder, Kim Moss, Terry McDonell, Tom Luddy, Mark Kidel, Phil Pavel, Jaclyn Bashoff, Marie Liz Unwin, Joel Kaye, and John Barrett. Departed friends, though part of my life, were not part of the story: Peter Buckley, Emi Califri, Barbara Epstein, and Kathleen Tynan, whom I miss to this day.

~

I'm indebted to those who taught me how to play with others: Ruth Zaporah, Elizabeth Kemp, Jean Claude van Itallie, Irina Brook, Yibin Li, Nicole Ansari, Sadie Jemmett, Winsome Brown, Mariana Hellmund.

To the magazine editors who like to laugh: Glenda Bailey, Stefano Tonchi, Armand Limnander, Alix Browne, Laura Brown, and Charlotte Cowles.

To the new friends who inspire me: Aimée, Rupert, Nicholas, Hogan, Michael, Ieva, Ian, Gideon, Pamela, Ruth C., Margaret, Ann, and Blythe.

At Atria Books and Simon & Schuster, I am grateful for the expert care provided by Judith Curr, Paul Olsewski, Suzanne Donahue, Felice Javit, Lisa Keim, Albert Tang, Jackie Jou, Kimberly Goldstein, Dana Sloan, Meryll Preposi, Bryden Spevak, Esther Paradelo, Jim Thiel, Isolde Sauer, David Chesanow, Anne Cherry, Anne Newgarden, and Nancy Wolff.

I want to thank Timothy Welles for information about the MMPI, Allen Mayer for steering me through fire, Carol Kaplan for advice, Prosper Keating for diving into the fray. Thanks to my photographer friends: Dominique Nabokov, Brigitte Lacombe, Jean-Luce Huré, Roxanne Lowitt, Serge Lutens, Coke O'Neal, Jean-Baptiste Mondino, Jean Pigozzi, Matthew Rolston, Richard Young, and June Newton aka Alice Springs, for permission to reproduce their work in these pages.

INDEX